Messages

Building Interpersonal Communication Skills

Fifth Canadian Edition

Joseph A. DeVito

Hunter College of the City/University of New York

Rena Shimoni

Bow Valley College

Dawne Clark

Mount Royal University

PEARSON

Toronto

Vice President, CMPS: Gary Bennett
Editorial Director: Claudine O'Donnell
Acquisitions Editor: David Le Gallais
Marketing Manager: Jennifer Sutton
Program Manager: Madhu Ranadive
Project Manager: Richard di Santo, Andrea Falkenberg
Developmental Editor: Cheryl Finch
Production Services: Jogender Taneja, iEnergizer Aptara®, Ltd.
Permission Project Manager: Erica Mojzes/Kathryn O'Handley
Photo Permissions Researcher: Kerri Wilson, Lumina Datamatics
Literary Permissions Researcher: Ganesh Krishnan, Lumina Datamatics
Cover Designer: Anthony Leung
Cover Image: Ffly/Fotolia

10 9 8 7 6 5 4 3 2 1 [V011]

Library and Archives Canada Cataloguing in Publication
DeVito, Joseph A., 1938-, author
  Messages: building interpersonal communication skills/Joseph A. DeVito, Rena Shimoni, Dawne Clark.—
Fifth Canadian edition.
  Includes bibliographical references and index.
  ISBN 978-0-13-308167-1 (pbk.)
  1. Interpersonal communication-Textbooks.   I. Shimoni, Rena, 1948-, author
II. Clark, Dawne, 1952-, author   III. Title.
BF637.C45D48 2015
158.2
                                        C2015-902118-9

ISBN: 978-0-13-308167-1

*To our students and colleagues from whom we continually learn, and to our families
who remind us every day of the joy (and challenges)
of interpersonal communication.*

BRIEF CONTENTS

CONTENTS

SPECIALIZED CONTENTS

TEST YOURSELF

These self-assessment tests help you analyze your own communication patterns and make plans for achieving greater interpersonal effectiveness.

ETHICAL MESSAGES

These discussions encourage you to consider the ethical implications of your interpersonal messages and will help you formulate your own code of the ethics of interpersonal communication.

SKILL-BUILDING EXERCISES

These exercises help you work actively with interpersonal communication concepts and practice the many and varied interpersonal skills discussed in the text.

WELCOME TO
MESSAGES: BUILDING INTERPERSONAL COMMUNICATION SKILLS,
FIFTH EDITION

It's a great pleasure to present this new edition of *Messages*. Although significantly revised, the book continues to emphasize its original two interrelated purposes: (1) to present you with an overview of interpersonal communication—what it is and what we know about it—and (2) to provide you with numerous ideas for improving your interpersonal communication and relationship skills. These two purposes influence everything included in the text—the topics discussed, the way each topic is presented, the specific skills highlighted, and the pedagogy incorporated.

This book was written in response to the need for a text that integrates **critical thinking** into all aspects of interpersonal communication, encourages the development of **interpersonal skills** (the practical skills for personal, social, and professional success), explains the influence of **culture** and **gender** on interpersonal communication, and stresses **listening** as an essential (but too often neglected) part of interpersonal communication. *Messages* answers these needs by providing thorough coverage of each of these major elements, which are introduced in Chapter 1 as integral components of interpersonal competence and then reinforced throughout the book through discussion, real-life examples, and exercises.

This fifth edition of *Messages* also responds to the specific needs of Canadian students. Although there are many similarities between Canadians and Americans, there are also clear cultural and demographic differences in our countries that affect communication. Therefore, we have included Canadian examples, told Canadian stories, and, where possible, quoted Canadian research. Because Canadians haven't been as prolific in communication research, we encourage our students to pursue graduate studies and add more original Canadian research to the existing knowledge bank!

WHAT'S NEW IN THE FIFTH EDITION?

This new edition of *Messages* is a major revision with new features and content that we hope will make your study of interpersonal communication more satisfying and rewarding.

- Each chapter begins with a profile of a Canadian who has made a significant contribution to Canadian society—and a discussion of the role of effective communication in the achievement of his or her contribution. The Canadian Profile Wrap-Up at the end of each chapter invites you to reconsider and perhaps think more deeply about this communication in light of what you learned in the chapter.
- **Learning objectives** focus on knowledge, application, and problem solving to highlight the major concepts and skills of the chapter. At the end of each major section a series of **questions** asks you to test yourself to see whether you can, in fact, accomplish the objectives.
- The concept that **choice** is central to all communication is integrated throughout the text; you're encouraged to consider your choices in many contexts throughout each chapter using Interpersonal Choice Points and Ethical Choice Points.
- Discussions throughout the book portray how **social media** is changing the way we communicate and relate interpersonally.
- **Developing Language and Communication Skills** boxes incorporate the latest brain research to examine how we learn vocabulary and the subtleties of interpersonal communication from birth through the teenage years. These serve as a reminder that communication abilities begin at birth, and continually develop and change over the life span.

- **Messages in the Media** boxes use brief examples and photos from popular television programs to introduce important concepts covered in each chapter.
- **Viewpoints** photos and captions ask you to consider a variety of communication issues, many of which are research based and/or focus on the themes of social media, the workplace, and culture.

CHAPTER-BY-CHAPTER UPDATES

Here, briefly, are some of the chapter-by-chapter changes. In addition to these changes, all chapters have been revised for greater clarity and less redundancy and include updated coverage of research and theory.

Part One: The Foundations of Communication

Chapter 1 offers new discussions of the choice nature of interpersonal communication and the nature and problems of information overload. Also new is an explanation of the Four Ways of Talking and Listening. The chapter has also been rearranged for greater clarity; the section on competence now concludes the chapter. *Chapter 2* on culture includes a new table on the metaphors of culture that presents an interesting way to view culture. New sections explore how culture connects us globally and how cultural behaviours and decisions in other parts of the world can cause confusion, concern, and discomfort here at home in Canada. *Chapter 3* has been significantly revised to explore perception of both the self and others. The chapter includes new sections on the ways in which social networks enable and encourage social comparisons and a new exercise on perception checking. *Chapter 4*, on listening, explains the process of listening, which is redefined to include social media message reading. A new section on Mindful Listening has been added, which provides insight into a new and growing field.

Part Two: The Building Blocks of Communication

Chapter 5, on verbal communication, covers verbal messages and contains new sections, including those on onymous and anonymous messages and immediacy. Also new are additional guidelines for appropriate use of cultural identifiers and a comparison table on confirmation and disconfirmation. *Chapter 6*, on nonverbal communication, has been reorganized around principles of nonverbal communication. The section on nonverbal competence has been reorganized around encoding and decoding skills. *Chapter 7*, on emotional messages, features a discussion of two new principles (that emotions can be used strategically and that emotions have consequences), along with a new visual of the model of emotions. Also new are tables on negative emotions at work, emotional happiness, verbal expressions of emotion, and a comparison table on ineffective and effective emotional expression. *Chapter 8*, on conversation messages, has been refocused to emphasize the skills involved in these interactions. Also new is a table on unsatisfying conversational partners, a new diagram explaining conversational turn taking, and a new self-test on small talk.

Part Three: Communication in Context

Chapter 9, on interpersonal relationships, has an expanded discussion of both positive and negative aspects of social media on relationships. Sections on cyberbullying and relationship violence have been updated. *Chapter 10*, on conflict, has been significantly revised to look at three commonly used strategies for mediating and resolving conflict drawn from cultural and spiritual orientations from around the world. The newest research on **conflict resolution** offers suggestions for mediating and resolving conflict. *Chapter 11*, on workplace communication, focuses on communication in the workplace, and provides and reviews effective communication strategies suitable for different workplace contexts and cultures.

MESSAGES FOCUS ON CONTEMPORARY TOPICS

Discussions of contemporary topics help you communicate effectively in today's increasingly complex world.

criticism is especially threatening and will surely be seen as a personal attack.

Active and Inactive Listening

Active listening is one of the most important communication skills you can learn (Gordon, 1975). Consider this brief statement from Julia, and the four possible responses that follow.

Julia: That creep gave me a C on the paper. I really worked on that project, and all I get is a lousy C.

Robert: That's not so bad; most people got around the same mark. I got a C, too.

Michael: So what? This is your last semester. Who cares about marks anyway?

Hana: You should be pleased with a C. Misha and Michael both failed, and John and Haruki both got a D.

Diana: You got a C on that paper you were working on for the last three weeks? You sound really angry and hurt.

All four listeners are probably eager to make Julia feel better, but they go about it in very different ways and—you can be sure—with very different outcomes. The first three listeners give fairly typical responses. Robert and Michael both try to minimize the significance of a C grade. Minimizing is a common response to someone who has expressed displeasure or disappointment; usually, it's also inappropriate. Although

VIEWPOINTS Politeness in Social Media

Much of the thinking and research on listening and politeness has focused on face-to-face communication skills. But how would you describe listening politeness on the phone or on social network sites? (See Table 4.4.) Do the same principles apply, or do we need an entirely different set to describe social networking listening politeness?

Social Media

Interpersonal communication via **social media** is now fully integrated throughout the book. Interpersonal communication, as viewed here, incorporates the varied forms of social media that are now an essential part of our communication lives. And so, to take just one example, the definition of listening—long defined as the reception of auditory signals—is redefined to include the reading of social media messages. The reasoning is simply that if posting on Facebook and Google+ are examples of interpersonal communication (which they surely are), then the reading of these messages must also be part of interpersonal communication and seems to fit most logically with listening.

The Aim of a Cultural Perspective

As illustrated throughout this text, culture influences interpersonal communications of all types (Moon, 1996). It influences what you say to yourself and how you talk with friends, partners, and family in everyday conversation. Adopting a cultural perspective will help you to understand how interpersonal communication works and to develop successful interpersonal skills.

And, of course, you need cultural understanding to communicate effectively in a wide variety of intercultural situations. Success in interpersonal communication—on your job, at school, and in your social life—will depend on your ability to communicate effectively with persons who are culturally different from yourself.

This emphasis on culture doesn't imply that you should accept all cultural practices or that all cultural practices are equal (Hatfield & Rapson, 1996). You've probably already encountered cultural practices that make you uncomfortable or that you simply can't support. Further, a cultural emphasis doesn't imply that you have to accept or follow the practices of your own culture. Often, personality factors (such as your degree of assertiveness, extroversion, or optimism) will prove more influential than culture (Hatfield & Rapson, 1996). Of course, going against your culture's traditions and values is often very difficult. But it's important to realize that culture influences; it does not determine.

As demonstrated throughout this text, cultural differences exist across the interpersonal communication spectrum—from the way you use eye contact to the way you develop or dissolve a relationship (Chang & Holt, 1996). But these differences shouldn't blind you to the great number of similarities existing among even the most widely separated cultures. Remember also that differences are usually matters

VIEWPOINTS Cultural Relativism

Part of Canada's multicultural approach is the belief in cultural relativism: that no culture is either superior or inferior to any other (Berry et al., 1992; Mosteller, 2008). So in 2013–2014 a controversy erupted when the Quebec government proposed a charter that it believed would increase social cohesion in the sec...

Culture

As in previous editions of *Messages*, the crucial role that culture plays in our communication experiences is a recurring theme. We live in a world defined by cultural diversity, where we interact with people differing in affectional orientation, socioeconomic position, ethnicity, religion, and nationality. Because of our growing global interdependence, we are impacted by the values, beliefs, and behaviours of others, even in countries seemingly far away. For this reason, this text not only focuses on culture in its own chapter but also integrates discussions of the impact and influence of culture throughout.

Conflict

Conflict is inevitable and, in some cases, can strengthen interpersonal relationships at school and work, at home, and socially. However, we are often not very good at knowing how to deal with conflict effectively and respectfully. How we relate to and communicate with others based on our culture, religion, or sense of self can determine whether conflict is positive or negative. The text offers some suggestions on how we might learn to mediate and resolve conflicts peacefully.

SKILL-BUILDING EXERCISE

Responding to Confrontations

Sometimes you'll be confronted with an argument that you can't ignore and that you must respond to in some way. Here are a few examples of confrontations. For each statement below, write a response in which you (a) let the person know that you're open to her or his point of view and that you view this perspective as useful information (listening openly), (b) show that you understand both the thoughts and the feelings that go with the confrontation (listening with empathy), and (c) ask the person what he or she would like you to do about it.

1. You're calling these meetings much too often and much too early to suit us. We'd like fewer meetings scheduled for later in the day.

2. There's a good reason why I don't say anything—you never listen to me anyway.

3. I'm tired of having all the responsibility for the kids—volunteering at their school, driving to soccer practice, checking homework, making lunch.

Confrontations can give you valuable feedback that will help you improve; if responded to appropriately, confrontations can actually improve your relationship.

MESSAGES EMPHASIZE CONTEMPORARY ISSUES

Discussions of important issues challenge students to ponder their communication decisions.

Choice

Throughout interpersonal interactions, we need to make choices: between saying one thing or another, between sending an email or calling on the phone, between being supportive or critical, and so on. Because of the central importance of choice, **Interpersonal Choice Points** (brief scenarios placed in the margins) invite an analysis of choices for communicating.

Politeness

Canadians are known around the world for being polite. Now interpersonal communication scholars, along with business professionals throughout the world, are coming to realize that politeness is more than simply being a nice person. While politeness can help us be better communicators, it can also cause challenges when we try to resolve conflicts. The role that politeness plays in interpersonal interactions and the skills for polite interpersonal communication are emphasized throughout the text.

Ethics

Because the messages we use have effects on others, they also have an ethical dimension. As such, ethics receives focused attention throughout the text. Chapter 1 introduces ethics as a foundational concept in all forms of interpersonal communication. In all remaining chapters, *Ethical Messages* boxes highlight a variety of ethical issues in interpersonal communication and ask us to apply ethical principles to various scenarios. We'll consider ethical issues that come into play in various communication situations; for example, with potentially conflicting cultural practices and ways to engage in interpersonal conflict ethically. These boxes will serve as frequent reminders that ethical considerations are an integral part of all the interpersonal communication choices/decisions you make.

Mindfulness

More and more educators, students, and employers are becoming aware of the benefits of mindfulness for general stress reduction and well-being. Introduced in chapter 2 and described in detail in chapter 4 in the context of effective listening, mindfulness can enhance both our relationships and our performance, whether in school or at the workplace. In our fast-paced world of multitasking, multiple electronic devices, and multiple demands on our time and attention, mindfulness training teaches us how to be truly in the present, how to focus, and how to be aware of our own feelings and perceptions. It helps us give undivided attention to the task at hand or to the person with whom we engage.

INTERPERSONAL CHOICE POINT

Reconsidering First Impressions

We all know that first impressions have a disproportionately high impact on our judgment of a person. Sometimes this leads to missing out on an opportunity to develop a wonderful friendship or to hire a person who would bring great value to a workplace. What are some of the things you can do to avoid the trap of making judgments based on first impressions? In what circumstances do you think you should trust your first impression?

Try to express surprise using only facial movements. Do this in front of a mirror, and try to describe in as much detail as possible the specific movements of the face that make up a look of surprise. If you signal surprise as most people do, you probably use raised and curved eyebrows, long horizontal forehead wrinkles, wide-open eyes, a dropped-open mouth, and lips parted with no tension. Even if there were differences from one person to another—and clearly there would be—you could probably recognize the movements listed here as indicative of surprise.

As you've probably experienced, you may interpret the same facial expression differently depending on the context in which it occurs. For example, in a classic study, when researchers showed participants a smiling face looking at a glum face, the participants judged the smiling face to be vicious and taunting. But when presented with the same smiling face looking at a fr___ ___ as pe___ful and ___ ___ 195__

Polite and Impolite Listening

Canadians are known throughout the world as a polite society. There are even jokes about the Canadian who apologizes when his foot is stepped on, even though it wasn't his fault. Politeness is often thought of as the exclusive function of the speaker, as solely an encoding or sending function. But politeness (or impoliteness) may also be signalled through listening (Fukushima, 2000).

INTERPERSONAL CHOICE POINT

Responding Politely

You're working as the manager at a restaurant, and a regular customer complains about the server: "I don't like the way she treated me, and I'm not coming back." What are some of the things you might say without losing the customer or your server (who's usually excellent)? Are there things you'd be sure not to say?

Of course, there are times when you wouldn't want to listen politely (for example, if someone is being verbally abusive or condescending or using racist or sexist language). In these cases, you might want to show your disapproval by conveying to the speaker that you're not even listening. But most often you'll want to listen politely, and you'll want to express this politeness through your listening behaviour. Here are a few suggestions for demonstrating that you are in fact listening politely. As you read these strategies, you'll notice that they're designed to be supportive of the speaker's needs for both positive face (the desire to be viewed positively) and negative face (the desire for autonomy).

ETHICAL MESSAGES

The Ethics of Impression Management

Impression management strategies may also be used unethically and for less-than-noble purposes. As you read these several examples, ask yourself at what point impression management strategies become unethical.

- People who use affinity-seeking strategies to get you to like them so that they can extract favours from you.
- People who present themselves as credible (as being competent, moral, and charismatic) when in fact they are not.
- People who use self-handicapping strategies to get you to see their behaviour from a perspective that benefits them rather than you.
- People who use self-deprecating strategies to get someone to do what they should be doing.
- People who use self-monitoring strategies to present a more polished image than one that might come out without this self-monitoring.
- People who use influence strategies to deceive and for self-gain.

- People who use image-confirming strategies to exaggerate their positive and minimize their negative qualities.

Ethical Choice Point

You're ready to join one (perhaps several) online dating services. You need to write your profile and are wondering whether, since everyone (or nearly everyone) exaggerates, you shouldn't also. Specifically, you're considering saying that you earn a very good salary (actually, it's not so great, but you're hoping for a promotion), are twenty pounds lighter (actually, you intend to lose weight), and own a condo (actually, that's a goal once you get the promotion and save enough for a down payment). If you don't exaggerate, you reason, you'll disadvantage yourself and not meet the people you want to meet. Also, you figure that people expect you to exaggerate and assume that you're probably a lot less ideal than your profile would indicate. Would this be ethical?

MINDFUL LISTENING

Debbi Cooper

Dr. Dina Wyshogrod is a practising clinical psychologist and an international trainer in Mindfulness-Based Stress Reduction (MBSR). This program teaches people how to listen to themselves, to become aware of the thoughts and feelings that are interfering with their being totally present in the moment. Knowing how to really listen to oneself may be very helpful in learning to really listen to others.

Q: You're a trained clinical psychologist and an author. What would you say is the most valuable skill you use in your work?

A: Being able to really listen.
Listening to someone, deeply, completely, is one of the most precious gifts you can ever give that p___

intention to focus fully on the person in front of you. Second, distractions don't arise only from outside, they arise from within: our roving minds scamper like monkeys, remembering things we have to do later, rehashing past events, scampering from association to association just as monkeys swing from branch to branch. This kind of internal agitation is perfectly normal; it's part of being human, so it's nothing we need to criticize ourselves for. At the same time, it requires that we train our minds to settle down, to become quieter, to become still, so that, sitting together, I can hear *you* talking to *me*, without all that internal noise. It's like getting a clear radio transmission with no static.

Q: What would you say is hardest about learning to genuinely listen?

The challenge in listening to someone else talk to you—about anything—is to stay focused and present and to bring your attention back when it wan___ We speak of this ___ giving ___ someone

PRACTICAL PEGADGOGY ENABLES US TO EXPLORE, UNDERSTAND, AND INTEGRATE CONCEPTS THAT WILL IMPROVE OUR INTERPERSONAL COMMUNICATION

Practical pedagogy helps students study and learn the concepts covered.

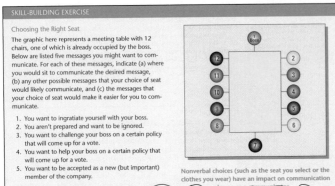

SKILL-BUILDING EXERCISE

Choosing the Right Seat

The graphic here represents a meeting table with 12 chairs, one of which is already occupied by the boss. Below are listed five messages you might want to communicate. For each of these messages, indicate (a) where you would sit to communicate the desired message, (b) any other possible messages that your choice of seat would likely communicate, and (c) the messages that your choice of seat would make it easier for you to communicate.

1. You want to ingratiate yourself with your boss.
2. You aren't prepared and want to be ignored.
3. You want to challenge your boss on a certain policy that will come up for a vote.
4. You want to help your boss on a certain policy that will come up for a vote.
5. You want to be accepted as a new (but important) member of the company.

Nonverbal choices (such as the seat you select or the clothes you wear) have an impact on communication and your image as a communicator.

Skills

Messages continues the focused approach to skill development that was established in the first edition. Improving interpersonal communication skills is integral to all the text discussions and appears in all chapters. **Skill-Building Exercises** appear throughout the text; completing these exercises will help us apply the material in the chapter to specific situations and thereby increase the effectiveness of our interpersonal skills.

Interactive Approach

This edition continues to provide numerous opportunities to interact with the material in the text in a number of ways. **Test Yourself** boxes appear throughout the text and invite us to analyze our patterns of communication and think about how we can alter our communication in the future. **Interpersonal Choice Points** appear throughout the text to encourage us to examine the choices we have available for communicating in actual real-life situations and to apply what we're learning to these situations. **Viewpoints** captions, accompanying all interior photos, pose questions (mostly based on interpersonal research) designed to elicit discussion of a variety of different viewpoints.

TEST YOURSELF

What's Your Time?

Indicate whether each of the following statements is true (*T*) or false (*F*) as it pertains to your general attitude and behaviour.

_____ 1. I work hard today basically because of tomorrow's expected rewards.
_____ 2. I enjoy life as it comes.
_____ 3. I enjoy planning for tomorrow and the future generally.
_____ 4. I avoid looking too far ahead.
_____ 5. I'm willing to endure difficulties if there's a pay-off/reward at the end.
_____ 6. I frequently put off work to enjoy the moment.
_____ 7. I prepare "to do" lists fairly regularly.
_____ 8. I'm late with assignments at least 25 percent of the time.
_____ 9. I get very disappointed with myself when I'm late with assignments.
_____ 10. I look for immediate payoffs/rewards.

How Did You Do? These questions were designed to raise the issue of present and future time orientation: whether you focus more on the present or more on the future. Future-oriented individuals would respond with *T* to odd-numbered statements (1, 3, 5, 7, and 9) and *F* to even-numbered questions (2, 4, 6, 8, and 10). Present-oriented individuals would respond in reverse: *F* for odd-numbered statements and *T* for even-numbered statements.

What Will You Do? As you read more about time and nonverbal communication generally, consider how these time orientations work for or against you. For example, will your time orientation help you achieve your social and professional goals? If not, what might you do about changing these attitudes and behaviours?

Learning Tools

An array of tools help you learn efficiently and study effectively. The **learning objectives** prefacing each chapter have been totally reworked to more accurately reflect current pedagogical thinking and emphasis. These objectives highlight the major concepts and skills of the chapter. The learning objectives

LEARNING OBJECTIVES *After reading this chapter, you should be able to:*

1. Understand the ranges of diversity within the workplace.
2. Describe the culture of a particular workplace.
3. Use different modes of workplace communication to become more effective in your place of employment.
4. Establish positive relationships with peers, supervisors, and people whom you supervise.
5. Use appropriate leadership skills.
6. Understand the principles of power in the workplace.
7. Use assertiveness when appropriate.

system used here identifies three major levels of thinking, each of which is included throughout the text (Bloom, 1956; Eggen & Kauchak, 2013; Teacher & Educational Development, 2005):

- **Knowledge** (recalling, remembering, and comprehending), introduced by such specific verbs as *define*, *paraphrase*, *describe*, and *differentiate*.
- **Application** (applying a concept to a new situation), introduced by such specific verbs as *diagram*, *illustrate*, *use*, and *give examples*.
- **Problem solving** (analyzing/breaking a concept into its parts, synthesizing/combining elements into a new whole, and evaluating/making value or appropriateness judgments), introduced by such specific verbs as *assess*, *construct*, *organize*, and *evaluate*.

INSTRUCTOR AND STUDENT RESOURCES

- **Test Item File.** This testbank, provided in Microsoft Word format, is a comprehensive test bank featuring 600 questions in multiple choice, true–false, short answer, and essay format.
- **Instructor's Manual.** The Instructor's Manual provides chapter overviews and learning and skill objectives for each chapter. It also offers ideas to activate class discussions and contains exercises to illustrate the concepts, principles, and skills of interpersonal communication.
- **PowerPoints.** Chapter-by-chapter PowerPoint presentations highlight the key concepts from the text. Several slides from each chapter have been reproduced and integrated within the text itself as In-Class Notes.
- **CourseSmart.** CourseSmart goes beyond traditional expectations—providing instant, online access to the textbooks and course materials you need at a lower cost for students. And even as students save money, you can save time and hassle with a digital eTextbook that allows you to search for the most relevant content at the very moment you need it. Whether it's evaluating textbooks or creating lecture notes to help students with difficult concepts, CourseSmart can make life a little easier. See how when you visit www.coursesmart.com/instructors.

Learning Solutions Managers

Pearson's Learning Solutions Managers work with faculty and campus course designers to ensure that Pearson technology products, assessment tools, and online course materials are tailored to meet your specific needs. This highly qualified team is dedicated to helping schools take full advantage of a wide range of educational resources by assisting in the integration of a variety of instructional materials and media formats. Your local Pearson Education sales representative can provide you with more details on this service program.

Pearson Custom Library

For enrolments of at least 25 students, you can create your own textbook by choosing the chapters that best suit your own course needs. To begin building your custom text, visit www.pearsoncustomlibrary.com. You may also work with a dedicated Pearson Custom editor to create your ideal text—publishing your own original content or mixing and matching Pearson content. Contact your local Pearson representative to get started.

All the instructor supplements are available for download from a password-protected section of Pearson Education Canada's online catalogue. Navigate to your book's catalogue page to view a list of supplements that are available. See your local sales representative for details and access.

Student Resources

CourseSmart CourseSmart goes beyond traditional expectations—providing instant, online access to the textbooks and course materials you need at a lower cost for students. And even as students save money, you can save time and hassle with a digital eTextbook that allows you to search for the most relevant content at the very moment you need it. Whether it's evaluating textbooks or creating lecture notes to help students with difficult concepts, CourseSmart can make life a little easier.

ACKNOWLEDGMENTS

The contribution of Karen Fiege from Bow Valley College is noted with gratitude. She reviewed some of the sections related to computer-based communication and provided invaluable insight. Thanks also to Michele Veldhoen, who helped explore new and sometimes controversial issues in global communication. The authors would like to express their appreciation to the staff at Pearson, who supported the development of this edition and who were open and responsive to our ideas for changes and additions to this text. Among them, Cheryl Finch needs to be commended for her patience and good humour that accompanied her competent professional involvement, ensuring that we attended to all the necessary details and gently reminding us of looming deadlines. Madhu Ranadive and David LeGallais are also thanked for their support. We would also like to express our gratitude to Pearson for giving us the opportunity to collaborate on the revision of this book. Many other professionals contributed to bringing this project to fruition. Thank you, Karen Alliston, for your sharp eye and problem-solving skills, and especially for your goodwill, good nature, and patience. Thank you as well for the kind support of Jogender Taneja who was responsible for managing the stages of production. As in the past, the exchange of ideas and the co-development of new ways of communicating with students about communication have been both enjoyable and enlightening.

Rena Shimoni and Dawne Clark

Dr. Rena Shimoni has an undergraduate degree in the humanities and a post-graduate certificate in Early Childhood Studies from the Hebrew University in Jerusalem; an M.Sc. in Applied Social Studies and Certification in Social Work from Oxford University, U.K.; and a Doctorate in Educational Policy and Administration from the University of Calgary. Her career has involved teaching in early childhood education and social work and served as Associate Dean of Health and Human Service Programs at Mount Royal College (now University), Dean of Health and Human Services, and Dean of Applied Research and Innovation at Bow Valley College in Calgary. She has co-authored three textbooks and several articles on children, families, communities, leadership, health workforce, online learning, and cross-cultural studies. She has directed a wide range of research projects in the field of health, education, and human service and has developed a number of new educational programs for health and human service professionals. Rena has spearheaded major projects engaging communities and post-secondary partners in collaborations resulting in enhanced learning opportunities for diverse populations. Currently Rena is serving as a Research Advisor to the VP Academic at Bow Valley College, and is a proud grandmother of two young boys.

Dr. Dawne Clark has been teaching children and those who work with children for over 40 years. She has a Ph.D. in Intercultural Education, Educational Policy and Administration from the University of Calgary. Currently, Dawne is a professor in the Department of Child Studies and Social Work and Director of the Centre for Child Well-Being (CCWB) at Mount Royal University in Calgary. Her research focuses on child well-being as broadly defined: early brain and child development, child and youth mental health, resilience, preschool physical literacy, and respectful practices with diverse and vulnerable children and families. The CCWB engages community partners, students, and faculty in a circle of learning with goals of mentorship, broad dissemination of knowledge, enhancing practice, and impacting policy development. Connected to the CCWB, the Child Development Lab is a unique facility that enables students, researchers, parents, and community partners to observe, learn, and enhance their skills in helping young children reach their potential. Dawne has three grown children and has recently become a grandmother.

AN INTRODUCTION TO LEARNING STYLES

It happens in nearly every college and university course: students attend classes, listen to lectures, and participate in class activities throughout the semester. Each student hears the same words at the same time and completes the same assignments. However, after finals, student experiences will range from fulfillment and high grades to complete disconnection and low grades or withdrawals.

Many causes may be involved in this scenario—different levels of interest and effort, for example, or outside stresses. Another major factor is learning style (any of many particular ways to receive and process information). Say, for example, that a group of students is taking a first-year composition class that is often broken up into study groups. Students who are comfortable working with words or happy when engaged in discussion may do well in the course. Students who are more mathematical than verbal, or who prefer to work alone, might not do as well. Learning styles play a role.

There are many different and equally valuable ways to learn. The way each person learns is a unique blend of styles resulting from abilities, challenges, experiences, and training. In addition, how one learns isn't set in stone; particular styles may develop or recede as responsibilities and experiences lead someone to work on different skills and tasks. The following assessment and study strategies will help you explore how you learn, understand how particular strategies may heighten your strengths and boost your weaknesses, and know when to use them.

MULTIPLE INTELLIGENCES THEORY

There is a saying, "It's not how smart you are, but how you're smart." In 1983, Howard Gardner, a Harvard University professor, changed the way people perceive intelligence and learning with his theory of multiple intelligences. This theory holds that there are at least eight distinct *intelligences* possessed by all people, and that every person has developed some intelligences more fully than others. Gardner defines an "intelligence" as an ability to solve problems or fashion products that are useful in a particular cultural setting or community. According to the multiple intelligences theory, when encountering an easy task or subject, you're probably using a more fully developed intelligence; when having more trouble, you may be using a less developed intelligence.

In the following table are descriptions of each of the intelligences, along with characteristic skills. The *Multiple Pathways to Learning* assessment, based on Gardner's work, will help you determine the levels to which your intelligences are developed.

INTELLIGENCES AND CHARACTERISTIC SKILLS

Intelligences	Description	Characteristic Skills
Verbal/Linguistic	Ability to communicate through language through listening, reading, writing, speaking	• Analyzing own use of language • Remembering terms easily • Explaining, teaching, learning, and using humour • Understanding syntax and meaning of words • Convincing someone to do something
Logical/Mathematical	Ability to understand logical reasoning and problem solving, particularly in math and science	• Recognizing abstract patterns and sequences • Reasoning inductively and deductively • Discerning relationships and connections • Performing complex calculations • Reasoning scientifically

---

*This material was originally created by Sarah Kravits.

Intelligences	Description	Characteristic Skills
Visual/Spatial	Ability to understand spatial relationships and to perceive and create images	• Perceiving and forming objects accurately • Manipulating images for visual art or graphic design • Finding one's way in space (using charts and maps) • Representing something graphically • Recognizing relationships between objects
Bodily/ Kinesthetic	Ability to use the physical body skilfully and to take in knowledge through bodily sensation	• Connecting mind and body • Controlling movement • Improving body functions • Working with hands • Expanding body awareness to all senses • Coordinating body movement
Intrapersonal	Ability to understand one's own behaviour and feelings	• Evaluating own thinking • Being aware of and expressing feelings • Taking independent action • Understanding self in relationship to others • Thinking and reasoning on higher levels
Interpersonal	Ability to relate to others, noticing their moods, motivations, and feelings	• Seeing things from others' perspectives • Cooperating within a group • Achieving goals with a team • Communicating verbally and nonverbally • Creating and maintaining relationships
Musical/ Rhythmic	Ability to comprehend and create meaningful sound and recognize patterns	• Sensing tonal qualities • Creating or enjoying melodies and rhythms • Being sensitive to sounds and rhythms • Using "schemas" to hear music • Understanding the structure of music and other patterns
Naturalistic	Ability to understand features of the environment	• Understanding nature, environmental balance, ecosystems • Appreciating the delicate balance in nature • Feeling most comfortable when in nature • Using nature to lower stress

PUTTING ASSESSMENTS IN PERSPECTIVE

Before you complete *Multiple Pathways to Learning*, remember: no assessment provides the final word on who you are and what you can and cannot do. An intriguing but imperfect tool, its results are affected by your ability to answer objectively, your mood that day, and other factors. Here's how to best use what this assessment, or any other, tells you:

Use assessments for reference. Approach any assessment as a tool with which you can expand your ideas of yourself. There are no "right" answers or "best" set of scores. Think of an assessment in the same way you would a pair of glasses or contacts. The glasses won't create new paths and possibilities, but they will help you see more clearly the ones that already exist.

Use assessments for understanding. Understanding which of your intelligences seem to be more fully developed will help prevent you from boxing yourself into limiting categories. Instead of saying "I'm no good in math," you might be able to make the subject easier by using appropriate strategies. For example, if you respond to visuals, you might draw diagrams of math problems; if you have language strengths, you might talk through the math problem with another. The more you know about your strengths, the more you'll be able to assess and adapt to any situation—in school, work, and life.

MULTIPLE PATHWAYS TO LEARNING

Rate each statement: rarely = 1,   sometimes = 2,   often = 3,   almost always = 4

Write the number of your response on the line next to the statement and total each set of 6 questions.

1. _____ I enjoy physical activities.
2. _____ I am uncomfortable sitting still.
3. _____ I prefer to learn through doing rather than listening.
4. _____ I tend to move my legs or hands when I'm sitting.
5. _____ I enjoy working with my hands.
6. _____ I like to pace when I'm thinking or studying.

_____ TOTAL for Bodily-Kinesthetic (B-K)

7. _____ I use maps easily.
8. _____ I draw pictures or diagrams when explaining ideas.
9. _____ I can assemble items easily from diagrams.
10. _____ I enjoy drawing or taking photographs.
11. _____ I do not like to read long paragraphs.
12. _____ I prefer a drawn map over written directions.

_____ TOTAL for Visual-Spatial (V-S)

13. _____ I enjoy telling stories.
14. _____ I like to write.
15. _____ I like to read.
16. _____ I express myself clearly.
17. _____ I am good at negotiating.
18. _____ I like to discuss topics that interest me.

_____ TOTAL for Verbal-Linguistic (V-L)

19. _____ I like math.
20. _____ I like science.
21. _____ I problem-solve well.
22. _____ I question why things happen or how things work.
23. _____ I enjoy planning or designing something new.
24. _____ I am able to fix things.

_____ TOTAL for Logical-Mathematical (L-M)

25. _____ I listen to music.
26. _____ I move my fingers or feet when I hear music.
27. _____ I have good rhythm.
28. _____ I like to sing along with music.
29. _____ People have said I have musical talent.
30. _____ I like to express my ideas through music.

_____ TOTAL for Musical (M)

31. _____ I like doing a project with other people.
32. _____ People come to me to help them settle conflicts.
33. _____ I like to spend time with friends.
34. _____ I am good at understanding people.
35. _____ I am good at making people feel comfortable.
36. _____ I enjoy helping others.

_____ TOTAL for Interpersonal (Inter)`

37. _____ I need quiet time to think.
38. _____ When I need to make a decision, I prefer to think about it before I talk about it.
39. _____ I am interested in self-improvement.
40. _____ I understand my thoughts, feelings, and behaviour.
41. _____ I know what I want out of life.
42. _____ I prefer to work on projects alone.

_____ TOTAL for Intrapersonal (Intra)

43. _____ I enjoy being in nature whenever possible.
44. _____ I would enjoy a career involving nature.
45. _____ I enjoy studying plants, animals, forests, or oceans.
46. _____ I prefer to be outside whenever possible.
47. _____ When I was a child I liked bugs, ants, and leaves.
48. _____ When I experience stress I want to be out in nature.

_____ TOTAL for Naturalist (N)

Face challenges realistically. Any assessment reveals areas of challenge as well as ability. Rather than dwelling on limitations (which can lead to a negative self-image) or ignoring them (which can lead to unproductive choices), use what you know from the assessment to look at where you are and set goals that will help you reach where you want to be. Following the assessment, you'll see information about the typical traits of each intelligence and more detailed study strategies geared toward the five intelligences most relevant for studying this text. During this course, make a point of exploring a large number of new study techniques; consider all the different strategies presented here, not just the ones that apply to your strengths.

Growth. Because you have abilities in all areas, though some are more developed than others, you may encounter useful suggestions under any of the headings. You will use different intelligences depending on the situation, and your abilities and learning styles will change as you learn.

Strategies help build strengths in all areas. Knowing your strongest learning styles isn't only about guiding your life toward your strongest abilities; it's also about choosing strategies to use when facing life's challenges. Using your strengths to boost your areas of challenge may help when you face tasks and academic areas that you find difficult. For example, if you're not strong in logical-mathematical intelligence and have to take a math course, the suggestions geared toward logical-mathematical learners may help you further develop that intelligence. As you complete the assessment, try to answer the questions objectively—in other words, answer the questions to best indicate who you are, not who you want to be (or who your parents or instructors want you to be). Remember, the assessment will show you where your strengths are; then it's up to you to use your strengths to support other areas.

SCORING THE ASSESSMENT

Find out what your scores are by completing the table below. A score of 20–24 indicates a high level of development in that particular type of intelligence, 14–19 a moderate level, and below 14 an underdeveloped intelligence.

	20–24 (Highly Developed)	14–19 (Moderately Developed)	Below 14 (Underdeveloped)
Bodily-Kinesthetic			
Visual-Spatial			
Verbal-Linguistic			
Logical-Mathematical			
Musical			
Interpersonal			
Intrapersonal			
Naturalist			

STRATEGIES FOR DIFFERENT LEARNING STYLES

Finding out what study strategies work best for you is almost always a long process of trial and error, often because there is no rhyme or reason to the search. If you explore strategies in the context of learning style, however, you'll give yourself a head start. The five intelligences that have the most relevance in this text are bodily-kinesthetic, interpersonal, logical-mathematical, verbal-linguistic, and visual-spatial. Now that you've completed the *Multiple Pathways to Learning* assessment, you'll be able to approach the text with a more informed view of what may help you most. We hope this self-assessment helps you become a more confident and effective learner.

CHAPTER

1

Introducing Interpersonal Communication

CANADIAN PROFILE: Justin Trudeau

Stephanie Gunther/Alamy

We rely on politicians to have highly developed interpersonal communications skills. In fact, voters are known to often choose politicians based not on their platforms but rather on their charisma and their ability to persuade voters that they're the best choice. Justin Trudeau, leader of the federal Liberal Party, is the son of Pierre Elliott Trudeau, who was prime minister from 1968 to 1979 and again from 1980 to 1984. While Trudeau may be following in his father's footsteps, he's adamant that he wants to be seen as his own person.

Trudeau appears to be willing to communicate openly about a number of topics (such as his use of marijuana), which often causes him trouble with the public and the media. He has said of himself, "I'm someone who stumbles my way through, leads with my chin in some cases, leads with my heart in all cases. . . . I was raised with pretty thick skin. And I think people are hungry for politicians who aren't afraid to say what they think and mean it" (Geddes, 2012).

What encourages people to enter politics? What determines the image they present to the nation and to voters? Trudeau explains his reason for entering politics this way: "Can I actually make a difference? Can I get people to believe in politics again? Can I get people to accept more complex answers to complex questions? I know I can. I know that's what I do very well. Why am I doing this? Because I can, not because I want to. Because I must" (Gatehouse, 2012).

As you work through this opening chapter, think about the types of conversational styles you're most familiar with and which ones you most value. What do you think, for example, about the ways in which politicians communicate?

LEARNING OBJECTIVES *After reading this chapter, you should be able to:*

1. Explain the personal and professional benefits to be derived from the study of interpersonal communication.

2. Define *interpersonal communication*.

3. Diagram a model of communication containing source–receiver, messages, channel, noise, and context, and define each of these elements.

4. Explain the principles of interpersonal communication, and give examples of each.

5. Define and illustrate the essential interpersonal communication competencies.

Lewis Jacobs/NBC/NBCU Photo Bank/Getty Images

The American television series *Community* features a group of community college students who interact in a wide variety of situations. Most of the time their communication patterns get them into trouble—not unlike people in real life. Clearly they could use a good course in interpersonal communication. This chapter introduces this most important form of communication.

WHY STUDY INTERPERSONAL COMMUNICATION?

Fair questions to ask at the beginning of this text are "What will I get out of this?" and "Why should I study interpersonal communication?" As with any worthwhile study, we can identify two major benefits: personal/social and professional.

Personal and Social Success

Your personal success and happiness depend largely on your effectiveness as an interpersonal communicator. Your close friendships and romantic relationships are made, maintained, and sometimes destroyed largely through your interpersonal interactions. In fact, the success of your family relationships depends heavily on the interpersonal communication among members. For example, in a survey of 1001 people over 18 years of age, 53 percent felt that a lack of effective communication was the major cause of marriage failure, a significantly greater percentage than those who cited money (38 percent) and in-law interference (14 percent) (Roper Starch, 1999).

Likewise, your social success in interacting with neighbours, acquaintances, and people you meet every day depends on your ability to engage in satisfying conversation—conversation that's comfortable and enjoyable.

Claudiu Paizan/Fotolia

VIEWPOINTS Good Communication

Women often report that an essential quality—perhaps the most significant quality—in a partner is the ability to communicate well. Compared with all the other factors you might consider in choosing a partner, how important is the ability to communicate well? What specific interpersonal communication skills would you consider "extremely important" in a life partner?

Professional Success

The ability to communicate well interpersonally is widely recognized as being crucial to professional success (Morreale & Pearson, 2008). From the initial interview at a job fair to interning, to participating in and then leading meetings, your skills at interpersonal communication will largely determine your success.

A 2013 survey conducted by the Bank of Montreal provided encouraging news for college and university graduates: half (51 percent) of the 500 Canadian businesses polled planned to hire students or recent grads (MarketWired, 2013). What were these businesses looking for in potential employees? Positive personality traits ranked highest (30 percent), followed by skill set (26 percent), work experience (15 percent), references and recommendations (8 percent), and finally, degree earned and school attended (only 3 percent). Another Canadian organization, Workopolis, surveyed top executives in a range of business and industries across Canada (Workopolis, 2013);

these executives said that they were finding it increasingly difficult to find potential employees with the desired characteristics. The executives ranked personality skills at 67 percent, even higher than did the BMO survey. The Workopolis survey determined that when employers speak of positive personality traits, they mean:

- A positive attitude
- Communication skills
- Strong work ethic
- Customer service skills
- Teamwork

Moreover, in a survey of employers who were asked what colleges or universities should place more emphasis on, 89 percent identified "the ability to effectively communicate orally and in writing," the highest of any skills listed (Hart Research Associates, 2010). Interpersonal skills also play an important role in preventing workplace violence (Parker, 2004) and in reducing medical mishaps and improving doctor–patient communication (Epstein & Hundert, 2002; Smith, 2004; Sutcliffe, Lewton, & Rosenthal, 2004). Indeed, the importance of interpersonal communication skills extends over the entire spectrum of professions.

Before you embark on an area of study that will be enlightening, exciting, and extremely practical, examine your assumptions about interpersonal communication by taking the accompanying self-test.

Can you explain why learning about interpersonal communication would be beneficial to your personal and professional life?

> ### INTERPERSONAL CHOICE POINT
>
> **Choices and Interpersonal Communication**
>
> Throughout this text, you'll find marginal items labelled *Interpersonal Choice Points*. These items are designed to encourage you to apply the material discussed to specific interpersonal situations by first analyzing your available choices and then making a communication decision.

TEST YOURSELF

What Do You Believe About Interpersonal Communication?

Respond to each of the following statements with *T* (true) if you believe the statement is usually true or *F* (false) if you believe the statement is usually false.

_____ 1. Good communicators are born, not made.

_____ 2. The more you communicate, the better you'll be at communicating.

_____ 3. In your interpersonal communications, a good guide to follow is to be as open, empathic, and supportive as you can be.

_____ 4. In intercultural communication, it's best to ignore differences and communicate just as you would with members of your own culture.

_____ 5. When there's conflict, your relationship is in trouble.

How Did You Do? As you've probably figured out, all five statements are generally false. As you read this text, you'll discover not only why these beliefs are false but also the trouble you can get into when you assume they're true.

For now and in brief, here are some of the reasons why each statement is (generally) false: (1) Effective communication is learned; all of us can improve our abilities and become more effective communicators. (2) It isn't the amount of communication that matters, it's the quality. If you practise bad habits, you're more likely to grow less effective than more effective. (3) Because each interpersonal situation is unique, the type of communication appropriate in one situation may not be appropriate in another. (4) Ignoring differences will often create problems; people from different cultures may, for example, follow different rules for what is and what is not appropriate in interpersonal communication. (5) All meaningful relationships experience conflict; the trick is to manage it effectively.

What Will You Do? This is a good place to start practising the critical-thinking skill of questioning commonly held assumptions—about communication and about you as a communicator. Do you hold beliefs that may limit your thinking about communication? For example, do you believe that certain kinds of communication are beyond your capabilities? Do you impose limits on how you see yourself as a communicator?

THE NATURE OF INTERPERSONAL COMMUNICATION

Although this entire text is in a sense a definition of interpersonal communication, a working definition will be useful at the start. **Interpersonal communication** is the verbal and nonverbal interaction between two or more interdependent people. This relatively simple definition implies a variety of characteristics.

DEVELOPING LANGUAGE AND COMMUNICATION SKILLS

Serve and Return

We're learning a great deal about the importance of the early years for children's healthy development. Babies' brains aren't just born; they're also built through the relationships, experiences, and environments around them. This building process begins with back-and-forth interactions with an adult, much like a game of tennis, ping pong, or volley-ball. Healthy development occurs when infants "serve" to adults using babbling, gestures, or cries, and adults "return" by responding with words, smiles, tickles, or songs. If the adult doesn't notice the serve or drops it, the game is disrupted. Serve and return, then, involves interactions with caring adults and builds healthy brains. If you'd like to learn more, go to http://developingchild.harvard.edu and look for the "Serve and Return" section.

Interpersonal Communication Involves Interdependent Individuals

Interpersonal communication is the communication that takes place between people who are in some way "connected." Interpersonal communication would thus include what takes place between a son and his father, an employer and an employee, two sisters, a teacher and a student, two lovers, two friends, and so on. Although largely dyadic in nature, interpersonal communication is often extended to include small, intimate groups such as the family. Even within a family, however, the communication that takes place is often dyadic—mother to child, sister to brother, and so on.

Not only are the individuals simply "connected," they are also *interdependent*: what one person does has an effect on the other person. The actions of one person have consequences for the other person. In a family, for example, a child's trouble with the police will affect the parents, other siblings, extended family members, and perhaps friends and neighbours. Even a stranger asking for directions from a local resident can lead to consequences for both—the stranger doesn't get lost, and the resident might realize that he or she doesn't know the street names and can provide only contextual directions (for example, "Turn at the mailbox").

Interpersonal Communication Is Inherently Relational

Because of this interdependency, interpersonal communication is inevitably and essentially relational in nature. Interpersonal communication takes place in a relationship, affects the relationship, and defines the relationship. The way you communicate is determined in large part by the kind of relationship that exists between you and the other person. You interact differently with your interpersonal communication instructor and with your best friend; you interact with a sibling in ways very different from the ways you interact with a neighbour, a work colleague, or a casual acquaintance.

But notice also that the way you communicate will influence the kind of relationship you have. If you interact in friendly ways, you're likely to develop a friendship. If you regularly exchange hateful and hurtful messages, you're likely to develop an antagonistic relationship. If you each regularly express respect and support for each other, a respectful and supportive relationship is likely to develop. This is surely one of the most

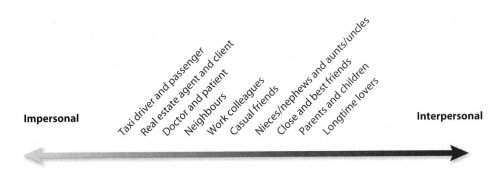

FIGURE 1.1

An Interpersonal Continuum

Here is one possible interpersonal continuum. Other people would position the relationships differently. You may want to try constructing an interpersonal continuum of your own relationships.

Source: An Interpersonal Continuum. Copyright © 2011, 2008 by Pearson Education, Inc.

obvious observations you can make about interpersonal communication. And yet so many people seem not to appreciate this very clear relationship between what you say and the relationship that develops (or deteriorates).

Interpersonal Communication Exists on a Continuum

Interpersonal communication exists along a continuum (see Figure 1.1), ranging from relatively impersonal at one end to highly personal at the other (Miller, 1978, 1990). At the impersonal end of the continuum is simple conversation between people who really don't know each other—the server and the customer, for example. At the highly personal end is the communication that takes place between people who are intimately interconnected—a father and son, two longtime partners, or best friends, for example. A few characteristics distinguish the impersonal from the personal forms of communication and are presented in Table 1.1 (Miller, 1978).

TABLE 1.1

IMPERSONAL AND INTERPERSONAL COMMUNICATION

Impersonal Communication	Interpersonal Communication
Social role information: You interact largely on the basis of the social roles you occupy; for example, server and customer, cab driver and passenger.	**Personal information:** You interact largely on the basis of personal roles; for example, friends, partners, parents and children, cousins.
Social rules: You interact according to the social rules defining your interaction; for example, as a server, you greet the customers, hand them menus, and ask if there's anything else you can do.	**Personal rules:** You interact according to the rules you've both established rather than to any societal rules; for example, a mother and daughter follow the rules they themselves have established over the years.
Social messages: You exchange messages in a narrow range of topics—you talk to the server about food and service, not about your parents' divorce—with little emotion and little self-disclosure.	**Personal messages:** You exchange messages on a broad range of topics—you talk about food and also about your parents' divorce—with much emotion and self-disclosure.

Interpersonal Communication Involves Verbal and Nonverbal Messages

The interpersonal interaction involves the exchange of verbal and nonverbal messages. The words you use as well as your facial expressions—your eye contact and your body posture, for example—send messages. Likewise, you receive messages through your sense of hearing as well as through your other senses, especially visual and touch. Even silence sends messages. These messages, as you'll see throughout this text, will vary greatly depending on the other factors involved in the interaction. You don't talk to a best friend in the same way you talk to your professor or your parents, for example.

One of the great myths in communication is that nonverbal communication accounts for more than 90 percent of the meaning of any message. Actually, it depends. In some situations, the nonverbal signals will carry more of your meaning than the words you use. In other situations, the verbal signals will communicate more information. Most often, of course, they work together. And so, rather than focusing on which channel communicates the greater percentage of meaning, it's more important to focus on the ways in which verbal and nonverbal messages occur together.

Interpersonal Communication Exists in Varied Forms

Often, interpersonal communication takes place face to face: talking with other students before class, interacting with family or friends over dinner, trading secrets with intimates. This is the type of interaction that probably comes to mind when you think of interpersonal communication. But, of course, much conversation takes place online. Online communication is a major part of people's interpersonal experience throughout the world. Such communications are important personally, socially, and professionally.

The major online types of conversation differ from one another and from face-to-face interaction in important ways. Let's take a look at a few of the main similarities and differences (also see Table 1.2).

Some computer-mediated communication (for example, email, tweets, or posts on Facebook) is **asynchronous**, meaning that it doesn't take place in real time. You may send your message today, but the receiver may not read it for a week and may take another week to respond. Consequently, much of the spontaneity created by real-time communication is lost here. You may, for example, be very enthusiastic about a topic when you send your email, but by the time someone responds you'll have practically forgotten it. Email is also virtually inerasable, a feature that has important consequences and that we discuss later in this chapter.

Through instant messaging (IM), you interact online in (essentially) real time; the communication messages are **synchronous**—they occur at the same time and are similar to phone communication except that IM is text-based rather than voice-based. Through IM you can also play games, share files, listen to music, send messages to cell phones, announce company meetings, and do a great deal else with short, abbreviated messages. Among post-secondary students, as you probably know, the major purpose of IM seems to be to maintain "social connectedness" (Kindred & Roper, 2004).

In chat rooms and social networking groups, you often communicate both synchronously (when you and a friend are online at the same time) and asynchronously (when you're sending a message or writing on the wall of a friend who isn't online while you're writing). Social networking sites give you the great advantage of being able to communicate with people you'd never meet or interact with otherwise. And because many of these groups are international, they provide excellent exposure to other cultures, other ideas, and other ways of communicating—making them a good introduction to intercultural communication.

TABLE 1.2

FACE-TO-FACE AND COMPUTER-MEDIATED COMMUNICATION

Throughout this text, face-to-face and computer-mediated communication are discussed, compared, and contrasted. Here is a brief summary of just some communication concepts and some of the ways in which these two forms of communication are similar and different.

Human Communication Element	Face-to-Face Communication	Computer-Mediated Communication
Source		
Presentation of self and impression management	Personal characteristics are open to visual inspection; disguise is difficult.	Personal characteristics are revealed when you want to reveal them; disguise is easy.
Speaking turn	You compete for speaker time with others; you can be interrupted.	It's always your turn; speaker time is unlimited; you can't be interrupted.
Receiver		
Number	One or a few who are in your visual field.	Virtually unlimited.
Opportunity for interaction	Limited to those who have the opportunity to meet.	Unlimited.
Third parties	Messages can be repeated to third parties but not with complete accuracy.	Messages can be retrieved by others or forwarded verbatim to anyone.
Impression formation	Impressions are based on the verbal and nonverbal cues the receiver perceives.	Impressions are based on text messages and posted photos and videos.
Context		
Physical	Essentially the same physical space.	Can be in the next cubicle or separated by miles.
Temporal	Communication is synchronous; messages are exchanged at the same (real) time.	Communication may be synchronous (as in chat rooms) or asynchronous (as in email).
Channel		
	All senses participate in sending and receiving messages.	Visual (for text, photos, and videos) and auditory.
Message		
Verbal and nonverbal	Words, gestures, eye contact, accent, vocal cues, spatial relationships, touching, clothing, hair, and so on.	Words, photos, videos, and audio messages.
Permanence	Temporary unless recorded; speech signals fade rapidly.	Messages are relatively permanent.

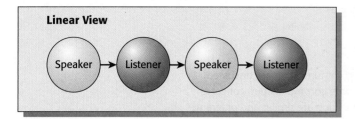

Linear View

Speaker → Listener → Speaker → Listener

FIGURE 1.2

The Linear View of Interpersonal Communication

This figure represents a linear view of communication, in which the speaker speaks and the listener listens.

Interpersonal Communication Is Transactional

Some early theories viewed the communication process as linear (see Figure 1.2). In this linear view of communication, the speaker spoke and the listener listened; after the speaker finished speaking, the listener would speak. Communication was seen as proceeding in a relatively straight line. Speaking and listening were also seen as taking place at different times—when you spoke, you didn't listen, and when you listened, you didn't speak. A more satisfying view (Figure 1.3), and the one currently held, sees communication as a transactional process in which each person serves simultaneously as speaker and listener. According to the transactional view, at the same time that you send messages, you're also receiving messages from your own communications and from the reactions of the other person. And at the same time that you're listening, you're also sending messages. In a transactional view, then, each person is seen as both speaker and listener, as simultaneously communicating and receiving messages.

Interpersonal Communication Involves Choices

Throughout your interpersonal life and in each interpersonal interaction, you're presented with *choice points*—moments when you have to make a choice as to whom you communicate with, what you say, what you don't say, how you phrase what you want to say, and so on. This text aims to give you reasons grounded in interpersonal communication theory and research for the varied choices you'll be called upon to make in your interpersonal interactions. The text also aims to give you the skills you'll need to execute these well-reasoned choices.

You can look at the process of choice in terms of John Dewey's (1910) steps in reflective thinking, a model used by contemporary

INTERPERSONAL CHOICE POINT

Communicating an Image

A new position is opening at work, and you want it. Your immediate supervisor is likely the one to make the final decision. What are some of your options for making yourself look especially good so that you can secure this new position?

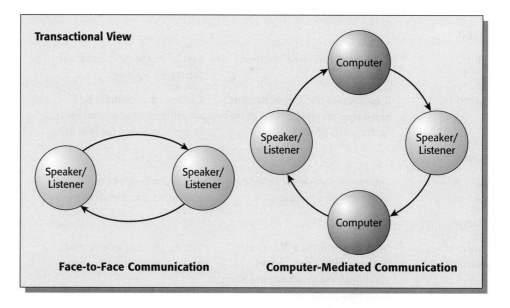

Transactional View

Speaker/Listener ⇄ Speaker/Listener

Computer · Speaker/Listener · Computer · Speaker/Listener

Face-to-Face Communication   **Computer-Mediated Communication**

FIGURE 1.3

The Transactional View of Interpersonal Communication

This figure represents a transactional view, in which each person serves simultaneously as speaker and listener; at the same time that you send messages, you also receive messages from your own communications as well as from the reactions of the other person(s).

theorists for explaining small-group problem solving and conflict resolution. It can also be used to explain the notion of choice in five steps.

- *Step 1: The problem.* View a communication interaction as a problem to be resolved, as a situation to be addressed. Here you try to understand the nature of the communication situation, what elements are involved, and, in the words of one communication model, who did what to whom with what effect. Let's say that you've said something you shouldn't have and it's created a problem between you and your friend, romantic partner, or family member. You need to resolve this problem.
- *Step 2: The criteria.* Here you ask yourself what your specific communication goal is. What do you want your message to accomplish? For example, you may want to admit your mistake, apologize, and be forgiven.
- *Step 3: The possible solutions.* Here you ask yourself what some of your communication choices are. What are some of the messages you might communicate?
- *Step 4: The analysis.* Here you identify the advantages and disadvantages of each communication choice.
- *Step 5: The selection and execution.* Here you communicate what you hope will resolve the problem and get you forgiveness.

As a student of interpersonal communication, you would later reflect on this communication situation and identify what you learned, what you did well, and what you could have done differently.

 Can you define interpersonal communication and explain its major characteristics?

THE ELEMENTS OF INTERPERSONAL COMMUNICATION

Given the basic definition of interpersonal communication, the transactional perspective, and an understanding that interpersonal communication occurs in many different forms, let's look at each of the essential elements in interpersonal communication: source–receiver, messages, feedback, feedforward, channel, noise, context, and competence (see Figure 1.4). Along with this discussion, you may wish to visit the websites of some of the major communication organizations to see how they discuss communication. See, for example, the websites of the Canadian Communication Association, the International Communication Association, and the Canadian Association for Journalism.

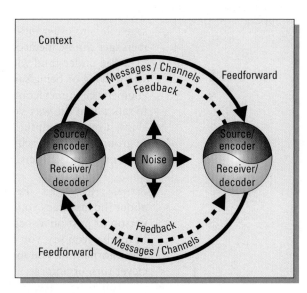

FIGURE 1.4

The Process of Interpersonal Communication

This model puts into visual form the various elements of the interpersonal communication process. How would you diagram this process?

Source: DeVito, Joseph, The Interpersonal Communication Book, 13e. Pearson. 2013.

Source–Receiver

Interpersonal communication involves at least two persons. Each functions as a **source** (formulates and sends messages) and operates as a **receiver** (receives and understands messages). The linked term *source–receiver* emphasizes that each person is both source and receiver.

By putting your meanings into sound waves and gestures, facial expressions, or body movements, you're putting your thoughts and feelings into a **code**, or a set of symbols—a process called *en*coding. When you translate those symbols into ideas, you're taking them out of the code they're in, a process called *de*coding. So we can call speakers (or, more generally, senders) encoders: those who put their meanings *into* a code. And we can call listeners (or, more generally, receivers) **decoders**: those who take meanings *out of* a code. Since encoding and decoding activities are combined in each person, the term *encoding–decoding* is used to emphasize this inevitable dual function.

Usually you encode an idea into a code that the other person understands; for example, you use words and gestures for which both you and the other person have similar meanings. At times, however, you may want to exclude others; so, for example, you might speak in a language that only one of your listeners knows or use jargon to prevent others from understanding. At other times, you may assume incorrectly that the other person knows your code and unknowingly use words or gestures that the other person simply doesn't understand. For interpersonal communication to occur, then, meanings must be both encoded and decoded. If Jamie has his eyes closed and is wearing headphones as his dad is speaking to him, interpersonal communication is not taking place—simply because the messages, both verbal and nonverbal, are not being received.

Messages

For interpersonal communication to occur, **messages** that express your thoughts and feelings must be sent and received. Interpersonal communication may be verbal or nonverbal, but it's usually a combination of both. You communicate interpersonally with words as well as with gestures, emoticons, varied fonts, touch, photos, videos, and audio, for example. Everything about you has the potential to send interpersonal messages, and every message has an **effect**, or outcome. In face-to-face communication, your messages are both verbal and nonverbal; you supplement your words with facial expressions, body movements, and variations in vocal volume and rate. When you communicate through a keyboard, your message is communicated with words as well as with photos and videos, for example.

Three important types of messages need to be mentioned here: metamessages, feedback, and feedforward.

METAMESSAGES   One very special type of message is the **metamessage**. This type of message refers to other messages; it's a message about a message. Both verbal and nonverbal messages can be metacommunicational. Verbally, you can convey metamessages such as "Do you understand what I'm saying?" Nonverbally, you can wink to communicate that you're lying or being sarcastic. Your interpersonal effectiveness will often hinge on your competence in metacommunication. For example, in conflict situations, it's often helpful to talk about the way you argue or what your raised voice means. In romantic relationships, it may be helpful to talk about what each of you means by "exclusive" or "love." In group projects at school, it's often necessary to talk about the ways people delegate tasks or express criticism.

FEEDBACK MESSAGES   **Feedback** is a special type of message that conveys information about the messages you send. When you send a spoken or written message to another person or post on a social media site, you get feedback from your own message: you hear what you say, you feel the way you move, you see what you write. On the basis of this information, you may correct yourself, rephrase something, or perhaps smile at a clever turn of phrase.

You also get feedback from others. The person with whom you're communicating is constantly sending you messages that indicate how he or she is receiving and responding to your messages. Nods of agreement, smiles, puzzled looks, paraphrasing, and questions asking for clarification are all examples of feedback. In fact, it wouldn't be much of an exaggeration to say that one of the main purposes of posting to social media sites is to get positive feedback from others—likes, +1s, thumbs up, blog comments, and retweets, for example.

Notice that in face-to-face communication you can monitor the feedback of the other person as you're speaking. Often, in online communication, that feedback will come much later and thus is likely to be more clearly thought out and perhaps more

closely monitored. Also, when you give feedback on social media sites such as Facebook by
hitting the "like" button, your feedback isn't
limited to the person whose post you like; your
feedback goes on your page and is visible to
everyone who looks at your site.

FEEDFORWARD MESSAGES   Much as feedback
contains information about messages already
sent, **feedforward** conveys information about
messages before you send them. For example,
you might use feedforward to express your
desire to chat a bit, saying something like, "Hey,
I haven't seen you all week; what's been going
on?" Or you might give a brief preview of your
main message and say something like, "You'd
better sit down for this; you're going to be
shocked." Or you might send someone a complimentary note before asking them to be your "friend." Or
you might ask others to hear you out before they judge
you. The subject heading on your email, the tag line after
your name on your social media site, and the phone numbers and names that come up on your cell phone are likewise clear examples of feedforward. These messages tell the listener something about the
messages to come or about the way you'd like the listener to respond.
Nonverbally, you give feedforward by your facial expressions, eye contact,
and physical posture; with these nonverbal messages, you tell the other
person something about the messages you'll be sending. A smile may signal a pleasant message; eye avoidance may signal that the message to
come is difficult and perhaps uncomfortable to express.

Tomas Del Amo/Alamy

VIEWPOINTS Feedback

What effect do you think feedback has in establishing and
maintaining satisfying friendships or romantic relationships?
How would you characterize ideal relationship feedback?

INTERPERSONAL CHOICE POINT

Giving Feedforward

The grades were just posted for a course, and
you got an A. Your dorm mate tells you that
she's failed and then asks you about your
grade. You feel that you want to preface your
remarks. What kind of feedforward might you
give in this case?

Channel

The communication **channel** is the medium through which message signals pass. The
channel works like a bridge connecting source and receiver. Normally, two, three, or four
channels are used simultaneously. For example, in face-to-face speech interactions, you
speak and listen, using the vocal–auditory channel. You also, however, make gestures and
receive these signals visually, using the visual channel. Similarly, you emit odours and
smell those of others (using the chemical channel). Often you touch one another, and this
too communicates (using the tactile channel).

Another way to classify channels is by the means of communication. Thus, face-
to-face contact, telephones, email, movies, television, smoke signals, and telegraph
would be types of channels. Of most relevance today, of course, is the difference
between face-to-face and computer-mediated interpersonal communication: interaction through email, social network sites, instant messaging, news postings, film, television, radio, or fax.

In many of today's organizations (and increasingly in many private lives), people are
experiencing **information overload,** which occurs when you have to deal
with an excessive amount of information and when much of that information is ambiguous or complex. As you can easily appreciate, advances
in information technology have led to increasingly greater information
overload. Today, for example, Canadians are exposed to more information in one year than their great-grandparents were in their entire lives!
Having hundreds of friends who post hundreds of messages, photos,
and videos creates information overload in even the youngest social
media users.

INTERPERSONAL CHOICE POINT

Channels

You want to ask someone out on a date and
are considering how you might go about it.
What are your choices among channels? Which
channel would be the most effective? Which
channel would provoke the least anxiety?

"I used to call people, then I got into e-mailing, then texting, and now I just ignore everyone."

Alex Gregory/The New Yorker Collection/www.cartoonbank.com

One of the problems with information overload is that it absorbs an enormous amount of time for people at all levels of an organization. The more messages you have to deal with, the less time you have for those messages or tasks that are central to your functions. Research finds that when you're overloaded, you're more likely to respond to simpler messages and to generate simpler messages, which may not always be appropriate (Jones, Ravid, & Rafaeli, 2004). Similarly, errors become more likely simply because you can't devote the needed time to any one item. Information overload has even been linked to health problems in more than one-third of managers (Lee, 2000). *Technostress* is a term that denotes the anxiety and stress resulting from a feeling of being controlled by the overwhelming amount of information and from the inability to manage that information in the time available.

Noise

Noise is anything that interferes with receiving a message. Just as messages may be auditory or visual, noise, too, comes in both auditory and visual forms. Four types of noise are especially relevant:

- *Physical noise* is interference that is external to both the speaker and listener; it hampers the physical transmission of the signal or message and includes impediments such as the noise of passing cars, the hum of a computer, extraneous messages, illegible handwriting, blurred type or fonts that are too small or difficult to read, misspellings and poor grammar, and pop-up ads.
- *Physiological noise* is created by barriers within the sender or receiver and includes impairments such as loss of vision, hearing loss, articulation problems, and memory loss.
- *Psychological noise* is mental interference in the speaker or listener and includes preconceived ideas, wandering thoughts, biases and prejudices, closed-mindedness, and extreme emotionalism.
- *Semantic noise* is interference created when the speaker and listener have different meaning systems; types of semantic noise include linguistic or dialectical differences, the use of jargon or overly complex terms, and ambiguous or overly abstract terms whose meanings can be easily misinterpreted.

INTERPERSONAL CHOICE POINT

Noise Reduction
Looking around the classroom or your room, what are some of the things you can do to reduce physical noise?

A useful concept in understanding noise and its importance in communication is **signal-to-noise ratio**. In this phrase, the term *signal* refers to information that you'd find useful; *noise* refers to information that is useless (to you). So, for example, mailing lists or blogs that contain lots of useful information would be high on signal and low on noise, and those that contain lots of useless information would be high on noise and low on signal.

All communications contain noise. Noise can't be totally eliminated, but its effects can be reduced. Making your language more precise, sharpening your skills for sending and receiving nonverbal messages, and improving your listening and feedback skills are some ways to combat the influence of noise.

Context

Communication always takes place within a context: an environment that influences the form and the content of communication. At times, this context is so natural that you ignore it, just as you do with street noise. At other times, the context stands out, and the ways in which it restricts or stimulates your communications are obvious. Think, for example, of the different ways you'd talk at a funeral, in a quiet restaurant, or at a rock concert. And consider how the same "How are you?" will have very different meanings depending on the context: said to a passing acquaintance, it means "Hello," whereas said to a sick friend in the hospital, it means "How are you feeling?"

The **context of communication** has at least four dimensions: physical, social–psychological, temporal, and cultural.

- *Physical dimension.* The room, workplace, or outdoor space in which communication takes place—the tangible or concrete environment—is the physical dimension. When you communicate with someone face to face, you're both in essentially the same physical environment. In computer-mediated communication, you may be in drastically different environments; one of you may be on a beach in San Juan and the other may be in a Bay Street office.
- *Social–psychological dimension.* This includes, for example, the status relationships among the participants: distinctions such as employer versus employee or salesperson versus store owner. The formality or informality, the friendliness or hostility, and the cooperativeness or competitiveness of the interaction are also part of the social–psychological dimension.
- *Temporal or time dimension.* This dimension has to do with where a particular message fits into a sequence of communication events. For example, if you tell a joke about sickness immediately after your friend tells you she's sick, the joke will be perceived differently from the same joke told as one of a series of similar jokes to your friends in the locker room of the gym.
- *Cultural dimension.* The cultural dimension consists of the rules, norms, beliefs, and attitudes of the people communicating that are passed from one generation to another. For example, in some cultures, it's considered polite to talk to strangers; in others, that's something to be avoided.

Can you draw/diagram a model of communication that contains source–receiver, messages, channel, noise, and context and illustrates the relationship among these elements? Can you define each of these elements?

PRINCIPLES OF INTERPERSONAL COMMUNICATION

Another way to define interpersonal communication is to consider its major principles. These principles are significant in terms of explaining theory; they also, as you'll see, have very practical applications.

Interpersonal Communication Is Purposeful

Interpersonal communication can be used to accomplish a variety of purposes. Understanding how interpersonal communication serves these varied purposes will help you more effectively achieve your own interpersonal goals.

- *To learn.* Interpersonal communication enables you to learn, to better understand the world of objects, events, and people—whether you do this face to face or online. In fact, your beliefs, attitudes, and values are probably influenced more by interpersonal encounters than by formal education. Through interpersonal communication, you also learn about yourself—your strengths and your weaknesses.
- *To relate.* Interpersonal communication helps you relate to others and to form meaningful relationships, whether it's face to face or online. Such relationships help to alleviate loneliness and depression, enable you to share and heighten your pleasures, and generally make you feel more positive about yourself.
- *To influence.* Very likely, you influence the attitudes and behaviours of others in your interpersonal encounters—to vote a particular way, to try a new diet, to see a movie, or to believe that something is true or false. The list is endless.

"I loved your E-mail, but I thought you'd be older."

VIEWPOINTS Interpersonal Metaphors

How would you explain interpersonal communication or
interpersonal relationships in terms of metaphors such
as a seesaw, a ball game, a flower, ice skates, a micro-
scope, a television sitcom, a work of art, a book, a
rubber band, or a software program?

- *To help*. Therapists serve a helping function professionally
  by offering guidance through interpersonal interaction.
  But everyone interacts to help in everyday life: online and
  offline, you console a friend who has broken off a love
  affair, counsel a fellow student about courses to take, or
  offer advice to a colleague at work.
- *To play*. Tweeting your weekend activities, discussing sports
  or dates, posting a clever joke or photo on some social
  media site, and in general just passing the time are play
  functions. Far from frivolous, this extremely important
  purpose gives your activities a necessary balance and your
  mind a needed break from all the seriousness around you.

In research on the motivations/purposes for using social networking sites, it's the relationship purpose that dominates. One
research study, for example, finds the following motivations/
purposes, in order of frequency mentioned (Smith, 2011):

- Staying in touch with friends
- Staying in touch with family
- Connecting with friends with whom you've lost contact
- Connecting with those who share your interests
- Making new friends
- Reading comments by celebrities
- Finding romantic partners

Popular belief and recent research agree that men and
women use communication for different purposes. Generally,
men seem to communicate more for information, whereas
women seem to communicate more for relationship purposes
(Colley et al., 2004; Shaw & Grant, 2002). Gender differences also occur in computer
communication. For example, women tend to chat more for relationship reasons while
men chat more to play and to relax (Leung, 2001).

Interpersonal Communication Is a Package of Signals

Communication behaviours, whether they involve verbal messages, gestures, or some
combination thereof, usually occur in "packages" (Pittenger, Hockett, & Danehy, 1960).
Usually, verbal and nonverbal behaviours reinforce or support each other. All parts of a
message system normally work together to communicate a particular meaning. You don't
express fear with words while the rest of your body is relaxed. You don't express anger
through your posture while your face smiles. Your entire body works together—verbally
and nonverbally—to express your thoughts and feelings.

You probably pay little attention to your body's "packaged" nature; it goes unnoticed. But when there's an incongruity—when the chilly handshake belies the friendly verbal greeting, when the nervous posture belies the focused stare, when the constant
preening belies the expressions of being comfortable and at ease—you take notice. Invariably you begin to question the credibility, the sincerity, and the honesty of the individual.

Interpersonal Communication Involves Content *and* Relationship Messages

Interpersonal messages combine content and relationship dimensions. **Content messages**
focus on the real world, on something external to both speaker and listener. **Relationship
messages**, on the other hand, focus on the relationship/connection between the individuals.
For example, a supervisor may say to a trainee, "See me after the meeting." This simple
message has a content message that tells the trainee to see the supervisor after the meeting.
It also contains a relationship message that says something about the connection between

the supervisor and the trainee. Even the use of the simple statement shows there is a status difference that allows the supervisor to require that the trainee appear. You can appreciate this most clearly if you visualize this statement being made by the trainee to the supervisor. It appears awkward and out of place because it violates the normal relationship between supervisor and trainee.

Deborah Tannen, in her book *You're Wearing That?* (2006), gives many examples of content and relationship communication and the problems that can result from different interpretations. For example, the mother who says, "Are you going to quarter those tomatoes?" thinks she's communicating solely a content message. To the daughter, however, the message is largely relational and may be perceived as a criticism of the way she intends to cut the tomatoes. Questions, especially, may appear to be objective and focused on content but are often perceived as attacks, as in the title of Tannen's book. For example, here are some questions that you may have been asked—or that you yourself may have asked. Try identifying the potential relationship messages that the listener might receive in each case.

"It's not about the story. It's about Daddy taking time out of his busy day to read you a story."
P. C. Vey/The New Yorker Collection/www.cartoonbank.com

- *You're* calling *me?*
- Did you say that you're applying to *medical* school?
- You're in *love?*
- You paid $100 for *that?*
- And that's *all* you did?

Many conflicts arise because people misunderstand relationship messages and can't clarify them. Other problems arise when people fail to see the difference between content messages and relationship messages. Arguments over the content dimension of a message—such as what happened in a movie—are relatively easy to resolve. You may, for example, simply ask a third person what took place or see the movie again. Arguments at the relationship level, however, are much more difficult to resolve, in part because people seldom recognize that the argument is about relationship messages.

Interpersonal Communication Is a Process of Adjustment

The principle of **adjustment** holds that interpersonal communication can take place only to the extent that the people talking share the same communication system. We can easily understand this when dealing with speakers of two different languages; miscommunication may occur. The principle, however, takes on particular relevance when you realize that no two people share identical communication systems. Parents and children, for example, not only have very different vocabularies but also, and more importantly, different meanings for some of the terms they have in common. (Consider, for example, the differences between parents' and children's understanding of such terms as *music*, *success*, and *family*.) Different cultures and social groups, even when they share a common language, also have different nonverbal communication systems. To the extent that these systems differ, communication will be hindered.

Part of the art of interpersonal communication is learning the other person's signals, how they're used, and what they mean. People in close relationships—either as close friends or as romantic partners—realize that learning the other person's signals takes a long time and, often, great patience. If you want to understand what another person means— by smiling, by saying "I love you," by arguing about trivial matters, by making self-deprecating comments—you have to learn that person's system of signals. Furthermore, you have to share your own system of

INTERPERSONAL CHOICE POINT

Corrective Messaging

In the heat of an argument, you said you never wanted to see your partner's family again. Your partner reciprocated, saying that the feeling was mutual. Now, weeks later, there remains great tension between you, especially when you find yourself with one or both families. What communication choices do you have for apologizing and putting this angry outburst behind you? What channel would you use?

Distinguishing Content and Relationship Messages

How would you communicate both the content and the relationship messages in the following situations?

1. After a date that you didn't enjoy and don't want to repeat, you want to express your sincere thanks, but you don't want to be misinterpreted as communicating any indication that you'd go on another date with this person.
2. You're ready to commit yourself to a long-term relationship but want your partner to sign a prenuptial agreement before moving any further. You need to communicate both your desire to keep your money and to move the relationship to the next level.

3. You're interested in dating a friend on Facebook who attends the same college or university as you do and with whom you've been chatting for a few weeks. But you don't know whether the feeling is mutual. You want to ask for the date but to do so in a way that, if you're turned down, you won't be embarrassed.

Content and relationship messages serve different communication functions. Being able to distinguish between them is a prerequisite to using and responding to them effectively.

signals with others so that they can better understand you. Although some people may know what you mean by your silence or by your avoidance of eye contact, others may not. You can't expect others to decode your behaviours accurately without help.

This principle is especially important in intercultural communication, largely because people from different cultures may use different signals or sometimes the same signals to signify quite different things. For example, in much of Canada, focused eye contact means honesty and openness. But in Japan and in many First Nations cultures, that same behaviour may signify arrogance or disrespect.

An interesting theory largely revolving around adjustment is **communication accommodation theory**. This theory holds that speakers will adjust or accommodate to the speaking style of their listeners in order to gain social approval and greater communication efficiency (Giles, 2009; Giles et al., 1987). For example, when two people have a similar speech rate, they seem to be attracted to each other more than to those with dissimilar rates (Buller et al., 1992). Another study even showed that people accommodate in their emails. For example, responses to messages that contain politeness cues were significantly more polite than responses to emails that didn't contain such cues (Bunz & Campbell, 2004). So, for example, if you say "thank you" and "please," others are more likely to use politeness cues as well.

Interpersonal Communication Involves Power

Power is a major component of interpersonal communication. You can't communicate without making some implicit comment on your power or lack of it. When in an interactional situation, therefore, recognize that on the basis of your verbal and nonverbal messages, people will assess your power and will interact accordingly.

No interpersonal relationship exists without a power dimension. Look at your own relationships and those of your friends and relatives. In each relationship, one person has more power than the other. In interpersonal relationships among some Canadians, the more powerful person is often the one who has a higher level job or the one who has more money. In other cultures, the factors that contribute to power may be different and may include a person's family background, age, education, or wisdom.

Although all relationships involve power, they differ in the types of power people use and to which they respond. Research has identified six types of power: legitimate, referent, reward, coercive, expert, and information or persuasion (French & Raven, 1968; Raven, Centers, & Rodrigues, 1975). As you listen to the messages of others (and your

INTERPERSONAL CHOICE POINT

Unwanted Talk
Your supervisor at work continually talks about sex. You fear your lack of reaction has been interpreted as a sign of approval. You need to change that but at the same time not alienate the person who can fire you. What are some of things you might do to stop this unwanted talk?

own) and as you observe the relationships of others (and your own), consider the role of power, how it's expressed, and how it's responded to. The more sensitive you become to the expression of power—in messages and in relationships—the more effective your interpersonal messages are likely to be.

Interpersonal Communication Is Ambiguous

All messages are ambiguous to some degree. **Ambiguity** is a condition in which a message can be interpreted as having more than one meaning. Sometimes ambiguity results when we use words that can be interpreted differently. Informal time terms offer good examples; different people may interpret terms such as *soon, right away, in a minute, early,* and *late* very differently. The terms themselves are ambiguous.

INTERPERSONAL CHOICE POINT

How to Disambiguate
You've gone out with someone for several months and want to reduce ambiguity about the future of the relationship and discover your partner's level of commitment. But you don't want to scare your partner. What are some things you can say or do to find answers to your very legitimate questions?

Some degree of ambiguity exists in all interpersonal communication. When you express an idea, you never communicate your meaning exactly and totally; rather, you communicate your meaning with some reasonable accuracy—enough to give the other person a reasonably clear idea of what you mean. Sometimes, of course, you're less accurate than you anticipated and your listener gets the wrong idea or becomes offended when you only meant to be humorous. Because of this inevitable uncertainty, you may qualify what you're saying, give an example, or ask, "Do you know what I mean?" These clarifying tactics help the other person understand your meaning and reduce uncertainty (to some degree).

Similarly, all relationships contain uncertainty. Consider a close interpersonal relationship of your own, and ask yourself the following questions. Answer each question according to a six-point scale in which 1 means "completely or almost completely uncertain" and 6 means "completely or almost completely certain." How certain are you about these questions?

1. Do you know what you can and can't say to each other? Are there certain topics that will cause problems?
2. Do you know how your partner feels about you, and does your partner know how you feel about him or her?
3. Do you know how you and your partner would characterize and describe the relationship? Would it be similar? Different? If different, in what ways?
4. How does your partner see the future of the relationship? Does your partner know how you feel about the relationship's future?

Very likely you were not able to respond with a 6 for all four questions. And it's equally likely that your relationship partner would be unable to respond to every question with a 6. These questions—paraphrased from a relationship uncertainty scale (Knobloch & Solomon, 1999) and other similar rankings—illustrate that you probably experience some degree of uncertainty about the norms that govern your relationship communication (question 1), the degree to which the two of you see the relationship in similar ways (question 2), the definition of the relationship (question 3), and/or the relationship's future (question 4).

The skills of interpersonal communication presented throughout this text can give you tools for appropriately reducing ambiguity and making your meanings as unambiguous as possible.

Artwork by Stephen Kroninger

Although Prime Minister Stephen Harper may try to build a (metaphorical) wall to keep reporters and others at a distance, his position of power makes that impossible. As prime minister, he is required to be regularly available to comment.

Interpersonal Communication Is Inevitable, Irreversible, and Unrepeatable

Three characteristics often considered together are interpersonal communication's *inevitability*, *irreversibility*, and *unrepeatability*.

COMMUNICATION IS INEVITABLE   Often communication is intentional, purposeful, and consciously motivated. Sometimes, however, you're communicating even though you may not think you are or may not even want to. Take, for example, the student sitting in the back of the room with an "expressionless" face, perhaps staring out the window. The student may think that she or he isn't communicating with the teacher or with the other students. On closer inspection, however, you can see that the student *is* communicating something—perhaps lack of interest or simply anxiety about a private problem. In any event, the student is communicating whether she or he wishes to or not—demonstrating the principle of **inevitability**. Similarly, the colour and type of your cell phone, the wallpaper in your room, and the type and power of your computer or cell phone communicate messages about you. You can't *not* communicate.

In the same way, you can't *not* influence the person with whom you interact (Watzlawick, 1978). Persuasion, like communication, is also inevitable. Research suggests that the influencing power of communication extends to electronic as well as face-to-face communication. For example, website content is manipulated to draw users to visit certain sites and to make specific choices (Knobloch et al., 2003). The issue, then, is not whether you will or will not persuade or influence another; rather, it's how you'll exert your influence.

> **INTERPERSONAL CHOICE POINT**
>
> **The Irreversibility of Interpersonal Communication**
>
> You refer to your best friend's current romantic partner with the name of the ex-partner. From both their expressions, you can tell that your friend has never mentioned the ex. What can you say to get your friend out of the trouble you've just created? To whom (primarily) would you address your explanation?

COMMUNICATION IS IRREVERSIBLE   Notice that only some processes can be reversed. For example, you can turn water into ice and then reverse the process by turning the ice back into water. Other processes, however, are irreversible. You can, for example, turn grapes into wine, but you can't reverse the process and turn wine into grapes. Interpersonal communication is an irreversible process. Although you may try to qualify, deny, or somehow reduce the effects of your message, you can't withdraw the message you've conveyed. Similarly, once you press the send key, your email is in cyberspace and impossible to take back. Because of **irreversibility**, be careful not to say things you may wish to withdraw later.

In online communication, the messages are written and may be saved, stored, and printed. Both face-to-face and online messages may be kept confidential or revealed publicly. But computer messages can be made public more easily and spread more quickly than face-to-face messages. Interestingly enough, only 55 percent of teens online say they don't post content that might reflect negatively on them in the future (Lenhart et al., 2011). And, increasingly, employers and even some colleges and universities are asking that candidates open their social networking accounts during the interview (Raby, 2012).

Because electronic communication is often permanent, you may wish to be cautious when you're emailing, posting your profile, or posting a message. Specifically:

> **INTERPERSONAL CHOICE POINT**
>
> **Getting Out of a Tight Spot**
>
> You write a gossipy email about Ellen (revealing things that you promised to keep secret) to your mutual friend Ella but inadvertently send it to Ellen herself. What are some of the things you can say that might help you get out of this awkward situation?

- Emessages are virtually impossible to destroy. Often emessages that you think you've deleted will remain on servers and workstations and may be retrieved by a clever hacker or simply copied and distributed.
- Emessages can easily be made public. Your words, photos, and videos on your blog or on a social networking site can be sent to anyone.
- Emessages are not privileged communication; they can be easily accessed by others and used against you. And you won't be able to deny saying something; it will be there in black and white.

Remember, too, that even when you restrict your information to one group or circle of friends, you can never be sure that a person you intended to receive the message won't pass it on to someone you'd prefer to exclude.

COMMUNICATION IS UNREPEATABLE   The reason why communication is unrepeatable is simple: everyone and everything is constantly changing. As a result, you can never recapture exactly the same situation, frame of mind, or relationship dynamics that defined a previous interpersonal act. For example, you can never repeat meeting someone for the first time, comforting a grieving friend, or resolving a specific conflict.

You can, of course, try to amend a communication; for example, you can say, "I'm sorry I came off as pushy; can we try again?" Notice, however, that even when you say this, you haven't erased the initial (and perhaps negative) impression. Instead, you try to counteract this impression by going through the motions again. In doing so, you hope to create a more positive impact that will lessen the original negative effect.

Can you explain and give examples of each of the principles governing interpersonal communication?

INTERPERSONAL COMPETENCE

Your ability to communicate effectively is your **interpersonal competence** (Spitzberg & Cupach, 1989; Wilson & Sabee, 2003). A major goal of this text is to expand and enlarge your competence so that you'll have a greater arsenal of communication options at your disposal. The greater your interpersonal competence, the more options you'll have for communicating with friends, partners, and family; with colleagues at school or on the job; and in just about any situation in which you communicate with another person. The greater your competence, the greater your own power to accomplish successfully what you want to accomplish—to ask for a raise or a date; to establish temporary work relationships, long-term friendships, or romantic relationships; to communicate empathy and support; or to gain compliance or resist the compliance tactics of others.

In short, interpersonal competence includes knowing how interpersonal communication works and how best to achieve your purposes by adjusting your messages according to the context of the interaction, the person with whom you're interacting, and a host of other factors discussed throughout this text. Let's spell out more clearly the traits of a competent interpersonal communicator.

The Competent Interpersonal Communicator Thinks Critically and Mindfully

Without critical thinking, there can be no competent exchange of ideas. Critical thinking is logical thinking; it's thinking that is well reasoned, unbiased, and clear. It involves thinking intelligently, carefully, and with as much clarity as possible. It's the opposite of what you'd call sloppy, illogical,

The Everett Collection

VIEWPOINTS Interpersonal Competence
What characters in television sitcoms or dramas do you think demonstrate superior interpersonal competence? What characters demonstrate obvious interpersonal incompetence?

or careless thinking. And, not surprisingly, according to one study of corporate executives, critical thinking is one of the stepping stones to effective management (Miller, 1997).

A special kind of critical thinking is mindfulness. **Mindfulness** is a state of awareness in which you're conscious of your reasons for thinking or behaving. In its opposite, **mindlessness**, you lack conscious awareness of what or how you're thinking (Langer, 1989). To apply interpersonal skills effectively in conversation, you need to be mindful of the unique communication situation you're in, of your available communication options, and of the reasons why one option is likely to be better than the others (Burgoon, Berger, & Waldron, 2000; Elmes & Gemmill, 1990).

To increase mindfulness, try the following suggestions (Langer, 1989).

■ *Create and re-create categories.* Group things in different ways; remember that people are constantly changing, so the categories into which you may group them should also change. Learn to see objects, events, and people as belonging to a wide variety of categories. Try to see, for example, your prospective romantic partner in a variety of roles—child, parent, employee, neighbour, friend, financial contributor, and so on.

■ *Be open to new information and points of view,* even when these contradict your most firmly held beliefs. New information forces you to reconsider what might be outmoded ways of thinking and can help you challenge long-held but now inappropriate beliefs and attitudes.

■ *Beware of relying too heavily on first impressions* (Chanowitz & Langer, 1981; Langer, 1989). Treat first impressions as tentative, as hypotheses that need further investigation. Be prepared to revise, reject, or accept these initial impressions.

■ *Think before you act.* Especially in delicate situations such as anger or commitment messages, it's wise to pause and think over the situation mindfully (DeVito, 2003). In this way, you'll stand a better chance of acting and reacting appropriately.

INTERPERSONAL CHOICE POINT

Questionable Posts

Your friend has been posting some rather extreme socio-political statements that you think might turn out to be detrimental when searching for a graduate school or job. You've always been honest with each other but careful because you're both very sensitive to criticism. What are some ways you can bring up this topic without seeming critical?

The Competent Interpersonal Communicator Is Skilful

This text explains the theory of and research in interpersonal communication in order to provide you with a solid understanding of how interpersonal communication works. With that understanding as a firm foundation, you'll be better able to develop and master the very practical skills of interpersonal communication, including those of empathy, power and influence, listening, politeness, using verbal and nonverbal messages, managing interpersonal conflict, and establishing and maintaining satisfying interpersonal relationships.

In learning the skills of interpersonal communication (or any set of skills), you'll probably at first sense an awkwardness and self-consciousness; the new behaviours may not seem to fit comfortably. As you develop more understanding and use the skills more, this awkwardness will gradually fade and the new behaviours will begin to feel comfortable and natural. You'll facilitate your progress toward mastery if you follow a logical system of steps. Here's one possible system, called STEP (Skill, Theory, Example, Practise):

1. Get a clear understanding of what the *skill* is.
2. Understand the *theory*; if you understand the reasons for the suggestions offered, it will help make the skill more logical and easier to remember.
3. Develop *examples,* especially your own; these will help to make the material covered here a more integral part of communication behaviour.
4. *Practise* with the Skill-Building Exercises included in this text. Practise alone at first, then with supportive friends, and then in general day-to-day interactions.

Assessing Your Social Network Profile

Examine your own social network profile (or that of a friend) in terms of the principles of interpersonal communication discussed in this chapter.

1. What purposes does your profile serve? In what ways might it serve the five purposes of interpersonal communication identified earlier (to learn, relate, influence, play, and help)?
2. In what way is your profile page a package of signals? In what ways do the varied words and pictures combine to communicate meaning?
3. Can you identify and distinguish between content and relational messages?
4. In what ways, if any, have you adjusted your profile as a response to the ways in which others have fashioned their profiles?

5. What messages on your profile are ambiguous? Bumper stickers and photos should provide a useful starting point.
6. What are the implications of inevitability, irreversibility, and unrepeatability for publishing a profile on and communicating via social network sites?
7. If you were to review your profile as a potential future employee, would you see yourself as a skilful communicator—as a critical and mindful thinker, culturally aware, ethical, and self-aware?

Heightened awareness of how messages help create meanings should increase your ability to make more reasoned and reasonable choices in your interpersonal interactions.

The Competent Interpersonal Communicator Is Culturally Aware and Sensitive

The term **culture** refers to the lifestyle of a group of people. A group's culture consists of its values, beliefs, artifacts, ways of behaving, and ways of communicating. Culture includes all that members of a social group have produced and developed—their language, ways of thinking, art, laws, and religion. Culture is transmitted from one generation to another not through genes but through communication and learning, especially through the teachings of parents, peer groups, schools, religious institutions, and government agencies. Because most cultures teach women and men different attitudes and ways of communicating, many of the gender differences we observe may be considered cultural. So, while not minimizing the biological differences between men and women, most people agree that gender differences are, in part, cultural.

Competence is sometimes culture specific; communications that prove effective in one culture will not necessarily prove effective in another. For example, giving a birthday gift to a close friend would be appreciated by members of many cultures and in some cases would be expected. But Jehovah's Witnesses frown on this practice because they don't celebrate birthdays (Dresser, 1999, 2005). Given the vast range of cultural differences that affect interpersonal communication, every chapter discusses the role of culture, and Chapter 2 focuses exclusively on culture and intercultural communication.

The Competent Interpersonal Communicator Is Ethical

Interpersonal communication also involves questions of **ethics**, the study of good and bad, of right and wrong, of moral and immoral. Ethics is concerned with actions and behaviours; it's concerned with distinguishing between behaviours that are moral (ethical, good, and right) and those that are immoral (unethical, bad, and wrong). Not surprisingly, there's an ethical dimension to any interpersonal communication act (Bok, 1978; Neher & Sandin, 2007).

It's useful to distinguish between an objective and a subjective view of ethics. If you take an *objective view*, you'd argue that the rightness or wrongness of an act is absolute and exists apart from the values or beliefs of any individual or culture. With this view, you'd hold that there are standards that apply to all people in all situations at all times. If lying, false advertising, using illegally obtained evidence, or revealing secrets you've promised to keep were considered unethical, then they would be unethical regardless of circumstances or of cultural values and beliefs. In an objective view, the end can never justify the means; an unethical act is never justified regardless of how good or beneficial its results (or ends) might be.

If you take a *subjective view*, you'd claim that the morality of an act depends on a specific culture's values and beliefs as well as on the particular circumstances. Thus, from a subjective position, you would claim that the end might justify the means—a good result can justify the use of unethical means to achieve that result. For example, you'd argue that lying is wrong to win votes or to sell cigarettes but that lying can be ethical if the end result is positive (such as trying to make someone feel better by telling them they look great or telling an ill person that they'll feel better soon).

Each field of study defines what is and what is not ethical to its concerns. It's important that you be very familiar with the code of ethics for your current profession or the one you're planning on entering. Check to see whether there's anything in those professional codes that refers specifically to communication. Here are some examples of communication organizations that provide codes of ethics:

- Canadian Public Relations Society
- Canadian Association of Broadcasters
- Radio and Television News Directors of Canada (whose code of ethics is called "The Standard for Canadian Excellence in Electronic Journalism")

In addition to this introductory discussion, ethical dimensions of interpersonal communication are presented in each of the remaining chapters in "Ethical Messages" boxes. Here, as a kind of preview, are just a few of the ethical issues raised in these boxes. As you read these questions, think about your own ethical beliefs and how these beliefs influence the way you'd answer the questions.

- What are your ethical obligations as a listener? See Ethics box, Chapter 4.
- When it is unethical to remain silent? See Ethics box, Chapter 6.
- When is gossiping ethical, and when is it unethical? See Ethics box, Chapter 8.
- At what point in a relationship do you have an obligation to reveal intimate details of your life? See Ethics box, Chapter 9.
- Are there ethical and unethical ways to engage in conflict and conflict resolution? See Ethics box, Chapter 10.

The Competent Interpersonal Communicator Demonstrates Self-Awareness, Empathy, Respect, Genuineness, and Humility

Harlow et al. (2005) identify five core dimensions of effective interpersonal communication: self-awareness, empathy, respect, genuineness, and humility. Chapter 3 is devoted to helping you gain *self-awareness*, an understanding of yourself. *Empathy*, the ability to put yourself in the position of the speaker, is reviewed in Chapter 4. *Respect* is something you feel both for yourself and the other person. *Genuineness* means not pretending or putting up a false front. *Humility* refers to not thinking that you're always right or that you have all the answers (remember that it can be quite tiresome to engage in conversation with someone who knows everything).

Can you define and illustrate the four interpersonal competencies (mindful and critical thinking, an arsenal of interpersonal skills, an awareness of cultural differences and sensitivity to them, and an ethical foundation)?

FOUR WAYS OF TALKING AND LISTENING

Effective communication requires skills in both effective talking and listening. Using a process called "Four Ways of Talking and Listening," developed by Adam Kahane (2007) and based on the work of Otto Scharmer, will help you gain more from this text.

As illustrated in Figure 1.5, the goal is to recognize the four modes—*downloading, debating, reflective dialogue,* and *generative dialogue*—in your own and others' discussions and to learn to navigate through each of them. Moving counterclockwise from *downloading* in the bottom left box to *generative dialogue* in the top left box will increase the meaning, quality, and effectiveness of your discussions.

Downloading occurs when we say what we usually say or what we think we're supposed to say. It's predictable and efficient; however, it doesn't leave room for discussion because it tends to be rigid and constrained.

Debating occurs when we move from what we think we should say to what we're really thinking. We say what we think and speak our minds openly. And yet, while debating encourages us to observe other people and perspectives, it can cause us to make judgments about them.

Reflective dialogue occurs when we step outside of ourselves and begin to listen with empathy. It also occurs when we begin to listen to ourselves (self-awareness) and how we're communicating.

Generative dialogue, the most powerful communication mode, occurs when we're fully present in the conversation. In this mode, we learn to trust the others in the conversation and to suspend judgment about what they're saying. There is a flow to the conversation that doesn't often occur in the other modalities. In a generative dialogue, meaning emerges not from each individual but from all those who are discussing as a group.

Each modality has legitimacy and a place in conversation depending on the time, purpose, and context of the conversation. If we need information about an assignment's due date or where to meet a friend, downloading will be just fine. However, if we want to reach a meaningful level of dialogue, such as when we're working to deepen a relationship or considering how to make meaningful changes in, say, student centre services, we need to be talking and listening in the reflective and generative dialogue modes.

Try this exercise to see what levels of talking and listening you can achieve. In pairs or triads, take about five minutes to tell the story of why each of you chose your current program of studies. Was this your own choice or were you influenced by others? How will this program help you accomplish your life goals?

After each person has taken a turn, debrief. What modes of conversation did you use as a group? How did each mode influence your understanding of the others in the conversation? How does this approach to talking and listening reflect other concepts discussed in this chapter (such as feedback, feedforward, empathy, self-awareness, and so on)?

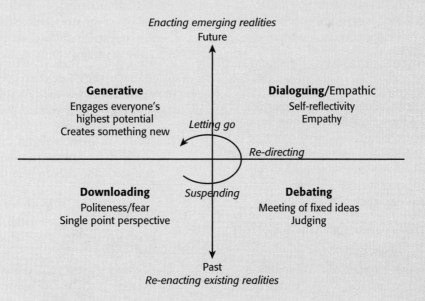

FIGURE 1.5
Four Ways of Talking and Listening

Source: Reprinted with the permission of the publisher. From 'Transformative Scenario Planning: Working Together to Change the Future' Copyright © (2012) by Kahane, Berrett-Koehler Publishers Inc. San Francisco, CA

Justin Trudeau appears to have a different political communication style than most politicians. What communication styles do you look for in politicians? How do you want them to talk—about what they plan to do if elected or about the deficiencies of the other candidates? What's important for you when you consider who might be the best candidate for your vote?

Stephanie Gunther/Alamy

SUMMARY OF CONCEPTS AND SKILLS

This chapter explored the reasons for studying interpersonal communication, its nature, its essential elements, several principles of interpersonal communication, and interpersonal competence.

Why Study Interpersonal Communication?

1. It's an essential and inevitable part of human experience as well as having numerous personal and professional benefits.

The Nature of Interpersonal Communication

2. Interpersonal communication refers to a type of communication that occurs between interdependent individuals, is inherently relational, exists on a continuum, involves both verbal and nonverbal messages, exists in varied forms, and is best viewed as a transactional process involving choices.

The Elements of Interpersonal Communication

3. Essential to an understanding of interpersonal communication are the following elements: source–receiver, encoding–decoding, messages (including metamessages, feedback, and feedforward), channel, noise (physical, physiological, psychological, and semantic), and context (physical, social–psychological, temporal, and cultural).

Principles of Interpersonal Communication

4. Interpersonal communication is
   - purposeful; through interpersonal communication we learn, relate, influence, play, and help.
   - a package of signals that usually reinforce but may also contradict one another.
   - a combination of content and relationship messages; we communicate about objects and events in the world but also about relationships between sources and receivers.
   - a process of adjustment in which each of us accommodates to the specialized communication system of the other.
   - integrally connected with power.
   - ambiguous to some extent.
   - inevitable (communication will occur whether we want it to or not), irreversible (once something is received, it remains communicated and cannot be erased from a listener's memory), and unrepeatable (no communication act can ever be repeated exactly).

Interpersonal Competence

5. Interpersonal competence is best viewed as consisting of both a knowledge of and a skill in interpersonal communication, an understanding and control of power strategies, effective listening, critical thinking and mindfulness, cultural understanding, politeness, and ethics.

   In addition to the above concepts, this chapter covered several interpersonal skills. As you read over the list, place a check beside those you feel you'd like to work on.

   _____1. *Feedback*. Listen to both verbal and nonverbal feedback—from yourself and from others—and use these cues to help you adjust your messages.
   _____2. *Feedforward*. Use feedforward when you feel your listener needs background or when you want to ease into a particular topic, such as bad news.
   _____3. *Channel*. Assess your channel options (for example, face-to-face conversation versus email or voicemail message) before communicating important messages.
   _____4. *Noise management*. Reduce physical, physiological, psychological, and semantic noise as best you can; use repetition and restatement, and when in doubt, ask whether you're being clear.

____5. *Mindfulness.* Create and re-create categories, be open to new information and points of view, avoid relying too heavily on first impressions, and think before you act.

____6. *Purposes.* Adjust your interpersonal communication strategies on the basis of your specific purpose.

____7. *Packaging.* Make your verbal and nonverbal messages consistent; inconsistencies often create uncertainty and misunderstanding.

____8. *Content and relationship.* Listen to both the content and the relationship aspects of messages, distinguish between them, and respond to both.

____9. *Context adjustment.* Adjust your messages to the physical, cultural, social-psychological, and temporal context.

____10. *Communication options.* Assess your communication options before communicating, in light of inevitability, irreversibility, and unrepeatability.

VOCABULARY QUIZ: The Language of Interpersonal Communication

Match the terms of interpersonal communication with their definitions. Record the number of the definition next to the appropriate term.

____ interpersonal communication (4)
____ interpersonal competence (19)
____ feedback (10)
____ ambiguity (17)
____ context of communication (13)
____ feedforward (11)
____ relationship messages (14)
____ source–receiver (9)
____ encoding (9)
____ communication as a transactional process (8)

1. Messages sent back to the source in response to the source's messages.
2. Each person in the interpersonal communication act.
3. Information about messages that are yet to be sent.
4. Presence of more than one potential meaning.
5. The rules and norms, beliefs and attitudes of the people communicating.
6. Communication as an ongoing process in which each part depends on each other part.
7. Communication that takes place between persons who have a relationship.
8. Messages referring to the connection between the two people communicating.
9. The understanding of and ability to use the skills of interpersonal communication.
10. The process of sending messages; for example, in speaking or writing.

These 10 terms and additional terms used in this chapter can be found in the glossary.

2

Culture and Interpersonal Communication

Jacques Boissinot/CP Images

Canada is a nation of distinguished immigrants. Many organizations, from local immigrant-serving agencies to national corporations, regularly honour those who are new to Canada and who have made considerable contributions to our country. One of these distinguished Canadians is former governor general Adrienne Clarkson.

Clarkson, who was born in Hong Kong in 1939, came to Canada as a refugee with her parents during the

Second World War. After graduating from university in Ottawa, she became involved in broadcasting, journalism, the arts, and public service. In 1999 she was sworn in as Canada's 26th governor general. As a representative of Her Majesty the Queen in Canada, the position is largely ceremonial; however, Clarkson worked to transform this role into one that would encourage all Canadians to be proud of who they are. To this end, she is a strong supporter of Canada's Armed Forces. In 2007, Clarkson was the first Canadian to be named colonel-in-chief of the Princess Patricia Canadian Light Infantry (PPCLI), which celebrated their 100th anniversary in 2014. She also has a passionate interest in Canada's north and First Nations and actively promotes acceptance, belonging, and civic responsibility for all peoples of Canada. The Blood tribe in Alberta has made Adrienne Clarkson an honorary chief, and has named her "Grandmother of Many Nations."

As you work through this chapter, think about the many ethnically diverse Canadians you know and have met. How are their conversational styles different from (or perhaps similar to) your own? How can we develop stronger communication styles because of our diversity?

LEARNING OBJECTIVES *After reading this chapter, you should be able to:*

1. Understand and explain the importance of culture in interpersonal communication; define *enculturation*, *ethnic identity*, and *acculturation*.

2. Explain and give examples of how cultural differences influence communication. Be aware of your own cultural orientations.

3. Apply the strategies for improving intercultural communication and acknowledge which areas require your focused attention to improve.

4. Recognize and understand the stages and impact of culture shock.

The Essence of Culture

1. In a group of three or four, discuss the following questions. Write your responses on a flip chart and be prepared to present your ideas to the full group.
   a. Given the definition of culture, what elements of culture are universal (shared by all human beings across the world)?
   b. What elements of culture do you think are shared by members of a group?
   c. What elements of culture do you think are unique to you as an individual?
2. As a large group, discuss the elements provided in each of the three categories:
   a. universal
   b. shared
   c. unique

Was it easy to determine what would go in each category? What were the criteria for choosing elements for each category?

3. Is there any overlap among categories? Why might that be? Are there any items that all groups agreed on? Again, why might that be?
4. As a large group, consider and discuss the following:
   a. If you were to move to another culture that is very different from your own, which of these cultural elements would be easiest to give up, should you need to?
   b. Which would be the most difficult? Why?
   c. What can this tell you about families who move to Canada from very different cultures? How much can we expect them to change? To keep?
   d. How might we support families in this process?

CULTURE

Central to all forms of interpersonal communication is culture. The more you understand about culture, the more effective you'll be in a wide variety of interpersonal interactions. Here we explore the relationship between culture and interpersonal communication, the major orientation differences among cultures, and the forms and skills of **intercultural communication**.

Culture (introduced briefly in Chapter 1) consists of the relatively specialized lifestyle of a group of people that is passed on from one generation to the next not through genes but rather through socialization.

Culture is not synonymous with race or nationality. The term *culture* does not refer to colour of skin or shape of eyes, as these are genetically inherited, not passed on through socialization.

Learning Culture

Culture includes all that members of a social group have produced and developed—their language, ways of thinking, art, laws, and religion—and that is transmitted from one generation to another through a process known as **enculturation**. You learn the values of your culture (that is, you become enculturated) through the teachings of your parents, peer groups, schools, religious institutions, government agencies, and media. When discussing the learned nature of culture, Hall (1976) explains that everything people do and are is modified by this cultural learning, which gradually sinks below the surface of the mind to appear as innate. Thus, one's own culture appears natural and right and as the only way to act.

Through enculturation, you develop an **ethnic identity**, a commitment to the beliefs and philosophies of your culture (Chung & Ting-Toomey, 1999). This can cause you to compare your culture with other cultures and to judge others on the basis of your own culture; in other words, to be ethnocentric.

Acculturation refers to the processes by which a person's culture is modified through direct contact with or exposure to another culture, through, say, the mass media (Kim, 1988). For example, when immigrants settle in a new country, their own culture becomes influenced by the host culture. Gradually, the values, ways of behaving, and beliefs of the host culture become more and more a part of the immigrants' culture. At the same time, of course, the host culture changes, as it adopts new foods, new words, and new world-views from the immigrants who have come. Generally, however, the culture of the immigrant changes more.

The acceptance of the new culture depends on several factors (Kim, 1988). Immigrants who come from cultures similar to the host culture will become acculturated more easily. Similarly, those who are younger and better educated become acculturated more quickly than do older and less educated persons. Considerations such as climate, rural/urban settings, and societal laws and norms play a major role in how easily immigrants are able to acculturate. Personality factors are also relevant. People who are risk-takers and open-minded, for example, have greater acculturation potential. As well, people who are familiar with the host culture before immigration—whether through interpersonal contact or mass media exposure—will be acculturated more readily.

Canada is unique in that it is guided by its focus on multiculturalism—an acceptance and understanding of all the different cultural groups in a community. Yet Canadians seem to have difficulty describing a Canadian culture or a Canadian identity. We often describe it in terms of what Canadians are not—we are not Americans, for example, and we are not aggressive. Bibby (1990) contends that Americans have created a creed that binds, a commitment to ties of church, family, school, community, and individualism with a pronounced group context. Canadians, on the other hand, don't seem to have an ideology of "Canadianism." While Americans have their own homegrown heroes, Canadians often ignore their historical record and almost exclusively adopt the heroes of other nations.

And yet Canadians are generally proud of their "mosaic" concept of society, as opposed to the American "melting pot" version. Bibby (1990) maintains that what is holding our country together is not loyalty to anything in particular but rather a tenuous agreement to co-exist. As a result, Canadians have become "champions of choice" (Bibby, 1990). We seem so interested in and willing to adopt the foods, clothing, books, music, and activities of other countries that we find it hard to remember what might be distinctly Canadian. And maybe this is exactly what is Canadian—the multicultural component of our society.

DEVELOPING LANGUAGE AND COMMUNICATION SKILLS

Learning Language

When infants are born, their brains contain trillions of neurons, as many as there are stars in the Milky Way. Through relationships and experiences, these neurons connect to form synapses—the structure of the brain. Infants are born with the ability to learn to speak any language; it all depends on what they hear around them. It's quite possible for young children to learn to speak two, three, or more languages in their first five years. As we age, however, we lose the ability to distinguish among specific linguistic sounds and find it difficult to create them (which is why we learn new languages with an accent). The best time to learn new languages is in the first few years of life—when our brains have virtually unlimited linguistic capacity.

Table 2.1 lists ways of looking at culture through metaphor; these metaphors may help make some important concepts about culture more memorable.

Which of these metaphors fits most closely with how you view culture in Canada? Which metaphor would be the ideal one, in your opinion? Do you think the idea of a Canadian mosaic needs to change given increasing immigration and globalization?

TABLE 2.1

Seven Metaphors of Culture

Here are seven metaphors for culture; each conveys a different way of understanding how culture functions. These insights are taken from a variety of sources, including Hall (1976) and Hofstede, Hofstede, and Minkov (2010).

Metaphor	Assumed Meaning
Salad/jelly beans	Like separate items in a salad or different jelly beans in a jar, cultures are individual, and yet they work together with other cultures to produce an even better combination.
Iceberg	Like the iceberg, only a small part of culture is visible; most of culture and its influences are hidden from easy inspection.
Tree	Like the tree, only the trunk, branches, and leaves are visible; the root system, which gives the tree its structure and function, is hidden from view.
Melting pot	Cultures blend into one amalgam and lose their individuality, but the blend is better than any one of the ingredients.
Software	Culture dictates what we do and don't do, much as a software program does. Without being aware of it, people are to some extent programmed by their culture to think and behave in certain ways.
Organism	Culture, like an organism, uses its environment (other cultures) to grow but maintains boundaries so that its uniqueness is not destroyed.
Mosaic	Just as a beautiful mosaic is made up of pieces of different shapes, sizes, and colours, so is culture; the whole, the combination, is more beautiful than any individual piece.

The Importance of Culture

Understanding the role of culture in effective interpersonal communication is important for a variety of reasons. Here are a few:

- *Demographic changes.* Whereas at one time Canada was a country largely populated by Europeans (primarily of British and French origins) and First Nations peoples, it is now greatly influenced by large numbers of new citizens from Latin and South America, Africa, and Asia. With these changes have come different customs and the need to understand and adapt to new ways of looking at communication.
- *Economic interdependence.* Today most countries are economically linked with one another. Our economic lives, then, depend on our ability to communicate effectively across cultures. Similarly, our political well-being depends in large part on that of other cultures. Political unrest or financial problems in any part of the world—Africa, Europe, or the Middle East, to take a few examples—affect our own security. Intercultural communication and understanding now seem more crucial than ever.
- *Communication technology.* Technology has made intercultural interaction easy, practical, and inevitable. It's common to have social-network friends from different cultures, and these relationships require a new way of looking at communication and culture.

International news reports are becoming more and more popular, in part because we live in a global environment where events thousands of miles away in countries we've only read about exert powerful influences on us all. Understanding the role of culture in interpersonal communication, then, is essential.

Paul Chiasson/The Canadian Press

VIEWPOINTS Cultural Relativism

Part of Canada's multicultural approach is the belief in cultural relativism: that no culture is either superior or inferior to any other (Berry et al., 1992; Mosteller, 2008). So in 2013–2014 a controversy erupted when the Quebec government proposed a charter that it believed would increase social cohesion in the secular province by banning the wearing of obvious religious symbols such as head scarves, turbans, crosses, and kipas. The bill died when the government lost the election, but if it had passed, do you think the charter would have created more social cohesion, or less? Is there such a thing as too much religious or cultural freedom? How do we determine what constitutes "too much freedom"?

■ *Culture-specific nature of interpersonal communication.* Still another reason why understanding the role of culture is so important is that interpersonal competence is culture specific. As we'll see throughout this chapter, what proves effective in one culture may prove ineffective (and even offensive) in another.

The Aim of a Cultural Perspective

As illustrated throughout this text, culture influences interpersonal communications of all types (Moon, 1996). It influences what you say to yourself and how you talk with friends, partners, and family in everyday conversation. Adopting a cultural perspective will help you to understand how interpersonal communication works and to develop successful interpersonal skills.

And, of course, you need cultural understanding to communicate effectively in a wide variety of intercultural situations. Success in interpersonal communication—on your job, at school, and in your social life—will depend on your ability to communicate effectively with persons who are culturally different from yourself.

This emphasis on culture doesn't imply that you should accept all cultural practices or that all cultural practices are equal (Hatfield & Rapson, 1996). You've probably already encountered cultural practices that make you uncomfortable or that you simply can't support. Further, a cultural emphasis doesn't imply that you have to accept or follow the practices of your own culture. Often, personality factors (such as your degree of assertiveness, extroversion, or optimism) will prove more influential than culture (Hatfield & Rapson, 1996). Of course, going against your culture's traditions and values is often very difficult. But it's important to realize that culture influences; it does not determine.

As demonstrated throughout this text, cultural differences exist across the interpersonal communication spectrum—from the way you use eye contact to the way you develop or dissolve a relationship (Chang & Holt, 1996). But these differences shouldn't blind you to the great number of similarities existing among even the most widely separated cultures. Remember also that differences are usually matters of degree. For example, most cultures value politeness, love, and honesty, but not all value these to the same degree. Moreover, advances in media and technology and the widespread use of social media are influencing cultures and cultural change and are perhaps homogenizing different cultures to some degree, lessening differences, and increasing similarities.

? Can you explain the role and importance of culture in interpersonal communication (the culture-specific nature of interpersonal communication, the economic and political interdependence of all people, the advances in communication technology, and the demographic changes that are so much a part of contemporary society)? Can you define *enculturation*, *ethnic identity*, and *acculturation*?

CULTURAL DIFFERENCES

For effective interpersonal communication to take place in a global world, goodwill and good intentions are helpful—but they are not enough. If you're going to be effective, you need to know how cultures differ and how these differences influence communication. Research supports several major cultural distinctions that are crucial for more effective interpersonal communication: (1) individualist or collectivist orientation, (2) emphasis on context(whether high or low), (3) power structure, (4) masculinity–femininity, (5) tolerance for ambiguity, (6) long- and short-term orientation, and (7) indulgence or restraint. Each of these dimensions of difference has significant impact on all forms of communication (Gudykunst, 1994; Hall & Hall, 1987; Hofstede, Hofstede, & Minkov, 2010).

Before reading about these dimensions, take the accompanying self-test. It will help you think about your own cultural orientations and will personalize the text discussion and make it more meaningful.

Individualist and Collectivist Cultures

The distinction between individualistic and collectivist cultures revolves around the extent to which the individual's or the group's goals are given greater importance (see Table 2.2). Individual and collective tendencies are not mutually exclusive; this is not an all-or-none orientation but rather one of emphasis. Thus, you may, for example, compete with other members of your basketball team for most baskets or the award for most valuable player. In a game, however, you act in a way that will benefit the team. In actual practice, both individualistic and collectivist tendencies will help you and your team each achieve your goals. Even so, these tendencies may conflict. For example, do you shoot for the basket and try to raise your own individual score or do you pass the ball to another player who is better positioned to score the basket and thus benefit your team?

In an **individualistic culture**, you are responsible for yourself and perhaps your immediate family; in a **collectivist culture** you are responsible for the entire group. Success in an individualistic culture is measured by the extent to which you surpass other members of your group; you would take pride in standing out from the crowd. And your heroes—in sports, for example—are likely to be those who are unique and who stand apart. In a collectivist culture, success is measured by your contribution to the achievements of the group as a whole; you would take pride in your similarity to other members of your group. Your heroes are more likely to be team players who perhaps work behind the scenes and don't stand out from the rest of the group's members.

INTERPERSONAL CHOICE POINT

Conflicting Cultural Beliefs

You've just begun a new job, and your new work colleagues are discussing a cultural practice that you feel is unethical. Your colleagues argue that each culture has a right to its own practices and beliefs. Given your own beliefs about this issue, and about cultural diversity and cultural sensitivity, what are some of the things you can say to be true to your beliefs and yet not jeopardize your new position?

INTERPERSONAL CHOICE POINT

Thinking About Cultural Communication

What role does intercultural communication currently play in your personal life? Your school life? Your professional life? Has this role changed in the last five years? Is it likely to change in the next five years? Why or why not?

Chuck Savage/CORBIS Canada

VIEWPOINTS Interethnic Friendships

How do you, your family, and your friends view interethnic friendships? Interethnic romantic relationships? Are there certain interethnic relationships that are approved of and others that are not approved?

TEST YOURSELF

What's Your Cultural Orientation?

For each of the items below, select either *a* or *b*. In some cases, you may feel that neither *a* nor *b* describes yourself accurately; in these cases, simply select the one that's closer to your feeling. As you'll see when you read the next section, these are not *either/or* preferences, but *more-or-less* preferences.

1. Success, to my way of thinking, is better measured by
   a. the extent to which I surpass others.
   b. my contribution to the group effort.
2. My heroes are generally
   a. people who stand out from the crowd.
   b. team players.
3. If I were a manager, I would likely
   a. reprimand a worker in public if the occasion warranted.
   b. always reprimand in private regardless of the situation.
4. In communicating, it's generally more important to be
   a. polite rather than accurate or direct.
   b. accurate and direct rather than polite.
5. As a student (and if I feel well informed), I feel
   a. comfortable challenging a professor.
   b. uncomfortable challenging a professor.
6. In choosing a life partner or even close friends, I feel more comfortable
   a. with someone not necessarily from my own culture and class.
   b. with those from my own culture and class.
7. In a conflict situation, I'd be more likely to
   a. confront conflicts directly and seek to win.
   b. confront conflicts with the aim of compromise.
8. If I were a manager of an organization, I would stress
   a. competition and aggressiveness.
   b. worker satisfaction.
9. As a student, I'm more comfortable with assignments in which
   a. there is freedom for interpretation.
   b. there are clearly defined instructions.
10. Generally, when approaching an undertaking with which I've had no experience, I feel
    a. comfortable.
    b. uncomfortable.
11. Generally,
    a. I save money for the future.
    b. I spend what I have.
12. My general belief about child-rearing is that
    a. children build strong relationships when cared for by mothers and others.
    b. children should be cared for only by their mothers.
13. For the most part,
    a. I believe I'm in control of my own life.
    b. I believe my life is largely determined by forces out of my control.
14. In general,
    a. I have leisure time to do what I find fun.
    b. I have little leisure time.

How Did You Do?

- Items 1–2 refer to the *individualist or collectivist orientation; a* responses indicate an individualist orientation, and *b* responses indicate a collectivist orientation.
- Items 3–4 refer to the *high- and low-context* characteristics; *a* responses indicate a high-context focus, and *b* responses indicate a low-context focus.
- Items 5–6 refer to the *power distance* dimension; *a* responses indicate greater comfort with a low power distance, and *b* responses indicate comfort with a high power distance.
- Items 7–8 refer to the *masculine–feminine* dimension; *a* responses indicate a masculine orientation; *b* responses, a feminine orientation.
- Items 9–10 refer to the *tolerance for ambiguity* or uncertainty; *a* responses indicate high tolerance, and *b* responses indicate a low tolerance.
- Items 11–12 refer to the *long- or short-term orientation; a* responses indicate long-term orientation, and *b* responses indicate short-term orientation.
- Items 13–14 refer to *indulgent or restraint orientation; a* responses indicate indulgent, and *b* responses indicate restraint cultures.

What Will You Do? Understanding your preferences in a wide variety of situations as being culturally influenced (at least in part) is a first step toward controlling them and toward changing them should you wish to do so. This understanding also helps you modify your behaviour for greater effectiveness in certain situations. The remaining discussion in this section further explains these orientations and their implications.

In an individualistic culture, you're responsible to your own conscience and responsibility is largely an individual matter. In a collectivist culture, you're responsible to the rules of the social group and responsibility for an accomplishment or a failure is shared by all members. Competition is promoted in individualistic cultures, while cooperation is promoted in collectivist cultures.

TABLE 2.2

SOME INDIVIDUALISTIC AND COLLECTIVIST CULTURE DIFFERENCES

This table is based on the work of Hofstede (1997) and Hall and Hall (1987), and on interpretations by Gudykunst (1991) and Victor (1992). As you read through the table, consider which statements you agree with, which you disagree with, and how these beliefs influence your communications. Can you identify additional differences between individualistic and collectivist cultures?

Individualistic (Low-Context) Cultures	Collectivist (High-Context) Cultures
Your own goals are most important.	The group's goals are most important.
You're responsible for yourself and to your own conscience.	You're responsible for the entire group and to the group's values and rules.
Success depends on your surpassing others; competition is emphasized.	Success depends on your contribution to the group; cooperation is emphasized.
Clear distinction is made between leaders and members.	Little distinction is made between leaders and members; leadership is normally shared.
Personal relationships are less important; hence, little time is spent getting to know each other in meetings.	Personal relationships are extremely important; hence, much time is spent getting to know each other in meetings.
Directness is valued; face-saving is seldom considered.	Indirectness is valued; face-saving is a major consideration.

High- and Low-Context Cultures

In a **high-context culture**, much of the information in communication is in the context or in the person—for example, information shared through previous communications, through assumptions about each other, and through shared experiences. The information is not explicitly stated in the verbal message. In a **low-context culture**, most information is explicitly stated in verbal messages or, in formal transactions, in written (contract) form.

To appreciate the distinction between high and low context, consider giving directions ("Where's the post office?") to someone who knows the neighbourhood and to a newcomer to your city. To someone who knows the neighbourhood (a high-context situation), you can assume the person knows the local landmarks, so you can give directions such as "next to the laundromat on Main Street" or "at the corner of Victoria and King." To the newcomer (a low-context situation), you can't assume the person shares any of the information you have, so you'd have to use only those directions that even a stranger would understand; for example, "Make a left at the next stop sign" or "Go two blocks and then turn right."

Generally, high-context cultures are also collectivist cultures. These cultures place great emphasis on personal relationships and oral agreements (Victor, 1992). Low-context cultures, on the other hand, are generally individualistic cultures. These cultures place less emphasis on personal relationships and more emphasis on the written, explicit explanation, and, for example, on the written contracts in business transactions.

Members of high-context cultures spend a lot of time getting to know each other before any important transactions take place. Because of this prior personal knowledge, a great deal of information is shared and therefore doesn't have to be explicitly stated. Members of low-context cultures spend less time getting to know each other and, therefore, don't have that shared knowledge. As a result, everything has to be stated explicitly. High-context societies, for example, rely more on nonverbal cues in reducing uncertainty (Sanders et al., 1991).

When this simple difference isn't taken into account, misunderstandings can easily result. For example, the directness and explicitness characteristic of the low-context culture may prove insulting, insensitive, or unnecessary to members of the high-context culture. Conversely, to members of a low-context culture, someone from a high-context culture may appear vague, underhanded, or dishonest in his or her reluctance to be explicit or engage in communication that a low-context member would consider open and direct.

Another frequent difference and source of misunderstanding between high- and low-context cultures is face-saving (Hall & Hall, 1987). People in high-context cultures place a great deal more emphasis on face-saving. For example, they're more likely to avoid argument for fear of causing others to lose face, whereas people in low-context cultures (with their individualistic orientation) will use argument to win a point. Similarly, in high-context cultures, criticism should take place only in private so that the person who is the object of criticism can save face. You'll see this in a classroom where some students are embarrassed to be singled out for public praise whereas others shine. Low-context cultures may not make this public–private distinction.

Members of high-context cultures are reluctant to say no for fear of offending and causing the person to lose face. So, it's necessary to understand when a high-context individual's yes means yes and when it means no. For example, in a classroom some students will say they understand class material even if they don't. The difference isn't in the words themselves but rather in the way they're used. It's easy to see how the low-context individual may interpret this reluctance to be direct—to say no—as a weakness or as a negative comment directed at the teacher.

> ## INTERPERSONAL CHOICE POINT
>
> ### Giving Directions in High- and Low-Context Situations
> To further appreciate the distinction between high and low context, consider giving directions to a specific place on campus to someone who knows the campus and who you can assume knows the local landmarks (which would resemble a high-context situation) and to a newcomer to your campus who you can't assume is familiar with campus landmarks (which would resemble a low-context situation). How would you give directions in the two different cases?

Masculine and Feminine Cultures

When denoting cultural orientations, the terms *masculine* and *feminine*, used by Geert Hofstede and his associates (2010) to describe this cultural difference, should be taken not as perpetuating stereotypes but rather as reflecting some of the commonly held assumptions of a sizable number of people throughout the world. Some intercultural theorists note that equivalent terms would be cultures based on *achievement* and *nurturance*, but, because research is conducted under the terms *masculine* and *feminine* and because these are the terms you'd use to search electronic databases, we use these terms here (Hofstede et al., 2010; Lustig & Koester, 2010).

Cultures differ in the extent to which gender roles are distinct or overlap (Hofstede, 1997). A highly **masculine culture** typically values men for their aggressiveness, material success, and strength, whereas women are valued for their modesty, focus on the quality of life, and tenderness. In a highly **feminine culture** both men and women are valued for their modesty, concern for relationships and the quality of life, and tenderness.

Masculine cultures socialize their children to be assertive, ambitious, and competitive. Students in such cultures are conditioned to strive to be the best, and school failure is considered shameful and extremely significant. Feminine cultures emphasize quality of life and close interpersonal relationships. Students in these cultures place less importance on individual grades and are content to be average in school (Hofstede, 1997). In Hofstede and colleagues' latest work (2010), of 76 countries ranked in terms of their masculinity, Canada ranked 33rd.

A masculine organization emphasizes the bottom line and rewards its workers on the basis of their contribution to the organization. A feminine organization is more likely to emphasize worker satisfaction and to

> ## INTERPERSONAL CHOICE POINT
>
> ### Feminine and Masculine Cultures
> You come from a highly feminine (or nurturing) culture and are working with colleagues who epitomize the highly masculine (or achievement oriented) culture. Assertiveness (even aggressiveness) is rewarded and paid attention to while your cooperativeness leads you to be ignored. You want to explain this cultural difference to your colleagues and at the same time ensure that your contributions will be listened to and evaluated fairly instead of being ignored. What are some of the things you might say to achieve your goal? To whom would you relay this message (to everyone, to one or two)?

reward its workers on the basis of need. An employee with a large family, for example, may get raises that a single person wouldn't get even if the single person contributed more to the organization.

Masculine cultures are more likely to confront conflicts directly and to competitively argue out any differences; they're more likely to emphasize win–lose conflict strategies. Feminine cultures are more likely to emphasize compromise and negotiation; they're more likely to emphasize win–win solutions to conflicts.

Conceptions of masculinity and femininity change over time and as circumstances change. For example, Haddad and Lam (1988) conducted interviews with over 100 new Canadian fathers from nine different national or ethnic backgrounds. Only a small proportion of these men (17 percent) upheld their traditional view of the role of the father after being in Canada for some time. The other participants in the study adapted their beliefs, either for pragmatic reasons or in order to maximize the well-being of their family.

"Because my genetic programming prevents me from stopping to ask directions—that's why!"

Donald Reilly/The New Yorker Collection/www.cartoonbank.com

High- and Low-Power-Distance Cultures

In some cultures, power is concentrated in the hands of a few; there's a great difference between the power held by these people and the power of the ordinary citizen. These are called **high-power-distance cultures** (Hofstede et al., 2010). In **low-power-distance cultures**, power is more evenly distributed throughout the citizenry.

These differences influence communication in numerous ways. For example, in high-power-distance cultures, there's a great power differential between students and teachers; students are expected to be modest, polite, and respectful. In contrast, in low-power-distance cultures (and you can see this clearly in Canadian classrooms), students are expected to demonstrate their knowledge and command of the subject matter, participate in discussions with the teacher, and even challenge the teacher—something that many members of high-power-distance cultures wouldn't even think of doing.

High- and low-power-distance orientations aren't black and white; rather, like many other cultural considerations, they exist on a continuum. Even in democracies in which everyone is equal under the law (or should be), there are still great power distances between those in authority—the employers, the police, the politicians—and ordinary citizens, just as there are between those who are rich and those who are poor, as we recently saw in the Occupy movements throughout Canada and the United States ("We are the 99 percent").

High- and Low-Ambiguity-Tolerant Cultures

In some cultures, people do little to avoid uncertainty and have little anxiety about not knowing what will happen next. In other cultures, however, there is much anxiety about uncertainty and it is strongly avoided.

Members of **high-ambiguity-tolerant cultures** don't feel threatened by unknown situations; uncertainty is a normal part of life and people accept it as it comes. Because high-ambiguity-tolerant cultures are comfortable with ambiguity and uncertainty, they minimize the importance of rules governing communication and relationships (Hofstede et al., 2010; Lustig & Koester, 2010). People in these cultures readily tolerate individuals who don't follow the same rules as the cultural majority, and they may even encourage different approaches and perspectives.

Students in high-ambiguity-tolerant cultures appreciate freedom in education and prefer vague assignments without specific timetables. These students want to be rewarded for creativity and readily accept when an instructor may not know something or needs to check some information.

Members of **low-ambiguity-tolerant cultures** do much to avoid uncertainty and have a great deal of anxiety about not knowing what will happen next; they see uncertainty as threatening and as something that must be counteracted (Hofstede et al., 2010).

Low-ambiguity-tolerant cultures create very clear-cut rules for communication that must not be broken. For example, students in these uncertainty-avoidant cultures prefer highly structured learning experiences with little ambiguity; they prefer specific objectives, detailed instructions, and definite timetables. These students expect to be judged on the basis of producing the right answers and expect the instructor to have all the answers all the time (Hofstede et al., 2010).

Long- and Short-Term Orientation Cultures

Some cultures teach a **long-term orientation**, an orientation that promotes the importance of future rewards, and so, for example, members of these cultures are more apt to save for the future and to prepare for the future academically (Hofstede et al., 2010). On the other hand, cultures fostering a **short-term orientation** look more to the past and the present. Instead of saving for the future, members of this culture spend their resources for the present and, not surprisingly, want quick results from their efforts. Students in long-term cultures will likely attribute their success or failure in school to their own efforts while students in short-term cultures will likely attribute their success or failure to luck or chance.

These cultures also differ in their view of the workplace. Organizations in long-term-oriented cultures look to profits in the future. Managers or owners and workers in such cultures share the same values and work together to achieve a common goal. Organizations in short-term-oriented cultures, on the other hand, look to more immediate rewards. Managers and workers are very different in their thinking and in their attitudes about work.

Indulgent and Restraint Cultures

Cultures also differ in their emphasis on indulgence or restraint (Hofstede et al., 2010). Cultures high in **indulgence** are those that emphasize the gratification of desires; they focus on living well and enjoying life. These cultures have more people who feel that they have

- *Life control:* the feeling of being able to do as they please (at least to a significant degree), that they have freedom of choice to do or not do what they want.
- *Leisure:* the feeling of having leisure time to do what they find fulfilling and fun.

Cultures high in **restraint**, on the other hand, are those that foster the curbing of such gratification and its regulation by social norms. Restraint cultures have more people who see themselves as lacking control of their own lives and who have little or no leisure time to engage in fun activities (Hofstede et al., 2010).

Indulgent cultures don't generally place great value on thrift; instead the value is on buying what is needed. Restrained cultures place considerably more value on thrift. Another finding is that indulgent cultures place high importance on friendship and having lots of friends whereas restrained cultures place less importance on friendships. Somewhat worrying, perhaps, is the finding that death rates from cardiovascular diseases are significantly higher in restrained than in indulgent cultures, and that significantly more members of indulgent cultures describe their health as "very good" (Hofstede et al., 2010).

INTERPERSONAL CHOICE POINT

Culture versus Culture

Your friend is pressed for time and asks you to do the statistical analyses for a term project. Your first impulse is to say yes because in your culture it would be extremely impolite to refuse to do a favour for someone you've known for so long. Yet you know that providing this kind of help is considered unethical at Canadian colleges and universities. You want to help your friend but also want to avoid doing anything that would be considered deceitful and might result in punishment. How might you respond to your friend's request while abiding by the standards of your institution and, at the same time, not insulting your friend or contradicting your own cultural beliefs?

Can you explain and give examples of the major cultural distinctions and the ways they affect communication (individualist or collectivist orientation, emphasis on context [either high or low], power structure, masculine [achievement] or feminine [nurturing] orientation, tolerance for ambiguity, long- and short-term orientation, and indulgent or restraint)?

IMPROVING INTERCULTURAL COMMUNICATION

Murphy's law ("If anything can go wrong, it will") is especially applicable to intercultural communication. Of course, intercultural communication is subject to all the same barriers and problems as are the other forms of communication discussed throughout this text. Above all, intercultural communication depends on both the social and the cultural sensitivity of those communicating. *Social sensitivity* refers to a person's ability to read the cues, verbal and nonverbal, sent by another. You've likely been in at least one situation where, despite all the cues you give that you want to end a conversation, the person you're talking to seems oblivious. You can start walking toward the door, get out your car keys, and give verbal cues such as "I really have to go now" or "I'm going to be late," and still the other keeps talking. Daniel Goleman (who invented the term *emotional intelligence*) suggests that people like this have a form of "social dyslexia" (2013). The opposite of this is what Goleman calls *social intuition*, an ability to accurately detect the verbal and nonverbal cues that the other is sending. Interestingly, Goleman suggests that nonverbal messages are often more powerfully read by those with social intuition than are verbal cues.

Similar to social sensitivity, *cultural sensitivity* is an attitude and way of behaving in which you're aware of and acknowledge cultural differences. Cultural sensitivity is crucial on a global scale in efforts toward world peace and economic growth; it's also essential for effective interpersonal communication and for general success in life (Franklin & Mizell, 1995). Without cultural sensitivity, there can be no effective interpersonal communication between people who differ in gender, ethnicity, nationality, or affectional orientation. So be mindful of the cultural differences between yourself and the other person. For example, the close physical distance that is normal in Arab cultures may prove too familiar or too intrusive in much of Canada, the United States, and northern Europe. The empathy that most Canadians welcome may be uncomfortable for most Koreans (Yun, 1976).

On the following pages we discuss eight suggestions designed to counteract the barriers that are unique to intercultural communication (Barna, 1997; Ruben, 1985; Spitzberg, 1991).

Recognize and Reduce Your Ethnocentrism

Ethnocentrism, one of the biggest obstacles to intercultural communication, is the tendency to see others and their behaviours through your own cultural filters, often as distortions of your own behaviours. It is the tendency to evaluate the values, beliefs, and behaviours of your own culture as more positive, superior, logical, and natural than those of other cultures. To achieve effective interpersonal communication, you need to see both yourself and others as different, but neither as inferior or superior—not a very easily accomplished task.

We are all ethnocentric to some degree; however, ethnocentrism exists on a continuum (see Table 2.3). People are neither completely ethnocentric nor not at all ethnocentric; rather, most are somewhere between these polar opposites. Most important for our purposes is that you become aware of where you might tend toward enthnocentricity (such as in child rearing or dating, for example). It's also important to acknowledge that your degree of ethnocentrism will influence your interpersonal (intercultural) communications.

TABLE 2.3

THE ETHNOCENTRISM CONTINUUM

Drawing from several researchers (Lukens, 1978; Gudykunst, 1994; Gudykunst & Kim, 1992), this table summarizes some interconnections between ethnocentrism and communication. The table identifies five levels of ethnocentrism; the general terms under "Communication Distances" characterize the major communication attitudes that dominate the various levels. Under "Communications" are some ways people might behave given their particular degree of ethnocentrism. How would you rate yourself on this scale?

Degree of Ethnocentrism	Communication Distances	Communications
Low	Equality	Treats others as equals; evaluates other ways of doing things as equal to own ways
	Sensitivity	Wants to decrease distance between self and others
	Indifference	Lacks concern for others but is not hostile
	Avoidance	Avoids and limits interpersonal interactions with others; prefers to be with own kind
High	Disparagement	Engages in hostile behaviour; belittles others; views own culture as superior to other cultures

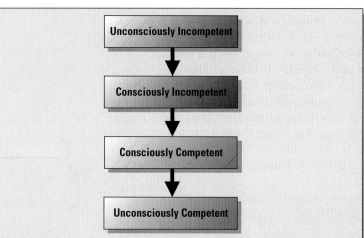

Unconsciously Incompetent: At this very basic stage, we're completely unaware that people from different cultures have different values and beliefs. This deeply affects our ability to communicate in meaningful ways.

Consciously Incompetent: At this second stage, we're aware of differences but struggle with how to communicate effectively across those differences.

Consciously Competent: This stage moves into a level of competent communication as we work hard to learn to communicate better and often worry that we'll offend or make mistakes.

Unconsciously Competent: Now we're comfortable with many forms of intercultural communication. We recognize cultural differences and have developed strategies to allow us to communicate freely. We know we're still learning about others, and we're open to continually revising our communication skills to become more effective.

FIGURE 2.1
Consciousness Continuum

Source: Based on Calgary Regional Association for Quality Child Care and Diversity Learning Institute. Clue into inclusion: A workshop toolkit (2001), Calgary, Alberta.

Be Mindful

Being mindful is generally helpful in intercultural communication situations (Hajek & Giles, 2003). In the consciousness continuum shown in Figure 2.1, the first stage is being *unconsciously incompetent*. This means that you behave with assumptions that are neither logical nor reasonable. For example, you know that cancer isn't contagious, and yet you may avoid touching cancer patients. You know that people who can't see don't have hearing problems, and yet you may use a louder voice when talking to people without sight. When the discrepancies between evidence and behaviours are pointed out, you realize that these behaviours aren't logical or realistic. You have now reached the stage of being *consciously incompetent*.

At this point, you question your knowledge and behaviour and are ready to make changes. However, it's still a conscious process for you to be more mindful. As your awareness and understanding improve, you find that you don't have to think as often about appropriate behaviour toward others. You are now *consciously competent*. The goal of being mindful is to finally reach the stage where positive behaviours toward others come naturally. You don't have to think or question whether you're offending others; you're simply mindful of what is appropriate and respectful. You are now *unconsciously competent*.

Face Fears

Another factor that stands in the way of effective intercultural communication is fear (Gudykunst, 1994; Stephan & Stephan, 1985). For example, you may become anxious about your ability to control the intercultural situation or you may worry about your own level of discomfort. You may worry that you'll be taken advantage of by a member of another culture. Depending on your own stereotypes, you may be concerned about being lied to, financially duped, or made fun of. You may fear that you'll offend members of another group. This could lead you to try hard to be politically correct or even to be unwilling to communicate at all. Conversely, you may worry about negative reactions from members of your own group if you try to communicate with others. These fears can easily create sufficient anxiety to make you avoid holding effective intercultural communications.

Some fears, of course, are reasonable. In many cases, however, fears are groundless. Either way, you need to assess your concerns logically and weigh their consequences carefully. Then you'll be able to make informed choices about your communications.

Giulio Andreini/MARKA/Alamy

VIEWPOINTS Cultural Imperialism

The theory of cultural imperialism argues, in part, that certain developed countries, such as those of North America and Western Europe, dominate the cultures of countries importing their products, especially their internet, movies, and television. What do you think of the influence that Western television and social media have on other cultures throughout the world? How do you evaluate this trend?

Avoid Overattribution and Stereotyping

You'll read in Chapter 3 that **overattribution** is the tendency to attribute too much of a person's behaviour or attitudes to one of that person's characteristics: "She thinks that way because she's a woman"; "He believes that because he was raised a Catholic." In intercultural communication situations, overattribution can occur in two ways: in the tendency to see too much of what a person believes or does as being caused by the person's cultural identification, and in the tendency to see a person as a spokesperson for a particular culture. Therefore, be careful not to assume that everyone from India is Hindu and vegetarian or that all students of Chinese origin are good in math. People's ways of thinking and behaving are influenced by a wide variety of factors; culture is just one of those factors.

Originally, the word *stereotype* was a printing term referring to a plate that printed the same image over and over. Likewise, a sociological or psychological **stereotype** is a fixed impression of a group of people. Everyone has attitudinal stereotypes—of national groups, religious groups, or perhaps of criminals, prostitutes, teachers, or plumbers.

Stereotyping can lead to two major barriers. First, you may have a tendency to characterize a person as part of a group and assign perceived qualities to both the person and the group (often negative). If that happens, you'll fail to appreciate the multifaceted nature of all people and all groups. For example, consider your stereotype of a high-frequency computer user. It may be that this image is quite different from the research findings, which show that such users are as often female as male and are as sociable, popular, and

Ryan McVay/Getty Images

Do you agree with the assumption that everyone is ethnocentric to some degree? If so, where would you place yourself on the ethnocentric continuum when the "other" is a person of the opposite sex? A member of a different affectional orientation? A different nationality? A member of a different religion?

Tom Cheney/The New Yorker Collection/www.cartoonbank.com

self-assured as their peers who aren't into heavy computer use (Schott & Selwyn, 2000). Second, because stereotyping can also lead you to ignore the unique characteristics of an individual, you may fail to benefit from the special contributions each person can bring to an encounter.

SKILL-BUILDING EXERCISE

Seven Paths to Effective Intercultural Communication

The characteristics of conversational effectiveness (discussed in detail in Chapter 8) are especially useful in intercultural communication. However, caution should be exercised, since there are likely to be important cultural differences in the way these characteristics are expected to be used.

1. Be open to differences among people. Be especially open to different values, beliefs, attitudes, and ways of behaving. Cultural differences may help explain differences in openness and in responsiveness to openness.

2. Empathize with the other person. Try to see the world from this different perspective. Use attentive, interested facial expressions and body posture, along with understanding and agreement responses, to communicate your empathy. Be aware, however, that some cultures may feel that such an approach is too personal or is indiscreet.

3. Communicate positiveness to others; it helps put the other person at ease. However, the appropriateness of positive statements about the self will vary greatly with the culture. For example, some cultures expect speakers to use self-denigrating comments and to minimize their own successes and abilities. Other cultures expect success and ability to be acknowledged openly and without embarrassment.

4. Be sensitive to the differences in turn-taking. Many North Americans, especially those from large urban centres, have the habit of interrupting or of completing the other person's sentences. Some cultures consider this especially rude.

5. Be aware of your comfort level with open "air time" in communication. Some cultures are uncomfortable with silence and like to ensure that all air time is full of talk, whereas others are more comfortable with silence and like to take time to think before responding.

6. Communicate expressiveness. When differences among people are great, some feel uneasy and unsure of themselves. Counteract this by communicating genuine involvement in the interaction. Recognize, however, that some cultures may frown upon too much expressiveness. So don't assume that the absence of expressiveness shows an unwillingness to participate in conversation; it may simply indicate a difference in the way members of different cultures reveal their feelings.

7. Be other-oriented by focusing your attention and the conversation on the other person. Use techniques to show other-orientation, such as active listening, asking questions, and maintaining eye contact (see Chapter 8). Some cultures, however, may find these techniques too intrusive. So, look carefully for feedback that comments on your own degree of other-orientation.

Recall a recent intercultural interaction that did not go as well as it might have. If you were having the same conversation today, what could you do to make it more effective?

ETHICAL MESSAGES

Culture and Ethics

Throughout history there have been cultural practices that today would be judged unethical, such as sacrificing virgins to the gods and burning people who held different religious beliefs. Even today there are practices woven deep into the fabric of different cultures that you might find unethical. As you read these few examples of current cultural practices, consider what Canadian cultural practices people in other cultures might judge as unethical.

- Only men can initiate divorce.
- Female genital mutilation (FMG) or female circumcision, where part or all of a young girl's genitals are surgically altered, is a practice rooted in gender inequality; related to this practice are ideas about

purity, modesty, aesthetics, and attempts to control women's sexuality.
- Women do not report spousal abuse because it reflects negatively on the family.
- Sexual activity between members of the same gender is punishable by imprisonment and even death.

Ethical Choice Point

Your neighbour is being abused by her husband—emotionally and physically. Although the two of you have often talked about this, she refuses to report her husband or to consider leaving him. It's not in her culture, she says; it will reflect badly on both families. What is your ethical obligation in this case?

Identify Uncertainty and Ambiguity

All communication interactions involve uncertainty and ambiguity. Not surprisingly, these are greater when there are wide cultural differences (Berger & Bradac, 1982; Gudykunst, 1989, 1993). Because of this, it takes more time and effort to reduce uncertainty during intercultural communications and to communicate meaningfully. Reducing your uncertainty about another person is worth the effort, however; it will not only make your communication more effective but may also increase your liking for the person (Douglas, 1994).

Techniques such as active listening (see Chapter 4) and perception checking (see Chapter 3) help you check on the accuracy of your perceptions and allow you to revise and amend any incorrect perceptions. As well, being specific in your own communications reduces ambiguity and the chances of misunderstandings; for example, misunderstanding is a lot more likely if you talk about "neglect" (a highly abstract concept) than if you refer to "forgetting my last birthday" (a specific event).

Keep in mind that words can mean different things to people depending on their age and gender (see Chapter 5). Think of how your own vocabulary and use of words may be quite different from some of the understandings your parents or grandparents have of these words. Consider how we use slang and how that may confuse those for whom English is a second language (see Table 2.4). Seeking feedback helps you correct any possible misconceptions almost immediately. Ask for feedback on whether you're making

TABLE 2.4

DO YOU MEAN WHAT YOU SAY?

What You Say	What You Mean
How are you?	Hello.
Let's have lunch sometime.	I'm just being polite.
I'll have to think about it.	I've thought about it and the answer is no.
You might want to consider doing X.	You must do X.
Sounds great.	It's fine.
It's not bad.	It's bad.
That's a great idea, but . . .	It's not a good idea.

yourself clear ("Does that make sense?" or "Do you see where to put the widget?"). Similarly, ask for feedback to make sure you understand what the other person is saying ("Do you mean you'll never speak with them again? Do you really mean that?").

Recognize Differences

To communicate interculturally, you need to recognize the differences between yourself and people who are culturally different, the differences within the culturally different group, and the numerous differences in meaning that arise from cultural differences.

DIFFERENCES BETWEEN YOURSELF AND CULTURALLY DIFFERENT PEOPLE   When you assume that all people are similar and ignore the differences between yourself and those who are culturally different from you, your intercultural efforts are likely to fail. This is especially true with values, attitudes, and beliefs. It's easy to see and accept different hairstyles, clothing, and foods, but when it comes to values and beliefs, it's easier to assume (mindlessly) that deep down we're all similar. We aren't. When you assume similarities and ignore differences, you may implicitly communicate to others that you feel your ways are the right ways and their ways are the wrong ways. The result is confusion and misunderstanding on both sides.

DIFFERENCES WITHIN THE CULTURALLY DIFFERENT GROUP   Be mindful of the differences within any cultural group. Just as we know that all Canadians are not alike, neither are all Sudanese, Koreans, or Mexicans. Within each culture there are many smaller cultures. These smaller cultures differ from each other and from the majority culture. As well, keep in mind the acculturation process, and the effects this will have on immigrants over time in a host country. Those who've been in Canada for many years may have very different cultural understandings than those who are newly arrived.

SIAL Montreal

Further, members of one smaller culture within a larger one may share a great deal with members of that same smaller culture in another part of the world. For example, farmers in Saskatchewan may have more in common with farmers in Borneo than with bankers in Toronto. The farmers will be concerned with, and knowledgeable about, weather conditions and their effects on crop growth, about crop rotation techniques, and about soil composition. Of course, farmers may also have drastically different views on such issues as government subsidies, trade regulations, and sales techniques from bankers as well as from each other.

DIFFERENCES IN MEANING   In Chapter 5 we note that meaning doesn't exist in the words we use; rather, it exists in the person using the words. This principle is especially important in intercultural communication. Consider, for example, the different meanings of the word *woman* to a Canadian and an Afghan, of *religion* to a born-again Christian and an atheist, or of *lunch* to a Chinese rice farmer and a Bay Street advertising executive. Even though different groups may use the same word, its meanings will vary greatly depending on the listeners' cultural definitions.

When it comes to nonverbal messages, the potential differences are even greater. For example, the over-the-head clasped hands that signify victory to a North American may signify friendship to a Russian. To someone from Britain, holding up two fingers to make a V signifies victory. To certain South Americans, however, it's an obscene gesture that corresponds to our extended middle finger. Tapping the side of your nose will signify that you and the other person are in on a secret if you're in England or Scotland, but that the other person is nosy if you're in Wales. A friendly wave of the hand is insulting in Greece, where the wave of friendship must show the back rather than the front of the hand.

Has anyone ever assumed something about you (because you were a member of a particular culture) that wasn't true? Have you ever been asked to speak on behalf of "your" group? Did you find this disturbing?

Adjust Your Communication

Intercultural communication (in fact, all interpersonal communication) takes place only to the extent that you and the person you're trying to communicate with share the same system of symbols. Your interaction will be hindered to the extent that your language and nonverbal systems differ. Therefore, it's important to adjust your communication to compensate for cultural differences.

This principle takes on particular relevance when you realize that even within a given culture, no two persons share identical symbol systems. Parents and children, for example, not only have different vocabularies but also, and more importantly, associate different meanings with some of the terms they both use. People in close relationships—either as best friends or as romantic partners—realize that learning the other person's signals takes a long time and, often, great patience. If you want to understand what another person means—by smiling, by saying "I love you," by arguing about trivial matters, by self-deprecating comments—you have to learn the person's system of signals.

In the same way, part of the art of intercultural communication is learning the other culture's signals, how they're used, and what they mean. Furthermore, you have to share your own system of signals with others so that they can better understand you. Although some people may know what you mean by your silence or by your avoidance of eye contact, others may not. You can't expect others to decode your behaviours accurately without help.

Adjusting your communication is especially important in intercultural situations, largely because people from different cultures use different signals—or sometimes use the same signals to signify quite different things. For example, focused eye contact means honesty and openness for most Canadians. But in Japan and in First Nations cultures, that same behaviour may signify arrogance or disrespect, particularly if engaged in by a youngster with someone significantly older.

Communication accommodation theory holds that speakers will adjust or accommodate to the communication style of their listeners in order to interact more pleasantly and efficiently (Giles et al., 1987). As you adjust your messages, recognize that each culture has its own rules and customs for communication (Barna, 1997; Ruben, 1985; Spitzberg, 1991). These rules identify what is appropriate and what is inappropriate. Thus, in Canadian culture, you might call a person you wish to date three or four days in advance. In certain Asian cultures, you might call the person's parents weeks or even months in advance. In Canadian culture, you may say, as a general friendly gesture (and not necessarily as a specific invitation), "Come over and pay us a visit sometime." In some cultures, such a comment is sufficient to prompt the listeners to actually visit at their convenience.

Recognize Culture Shock

Culture shock is the psychological reaction you experience when you encounter a culture very different from your own (Furnham & Bochner, 1986). Culture shock is normal; most people experience it when, at some time in their lives, they go away to university, travel, or move to a new city or country. The experience can be unpleasant and frustrating, and can sometimes lead to a permanently negative attitude toward the new culture. Understanding that culture shock is normal will help lessen any potential negative implications. One obvious way to prevent at least some culture shock is to learn as much as you can about the new culture before experiencing it.

At some stages, culture shock results from your feelings of alienation, conspicuousness, and difference from everyone else. When you lack knowledge of the rules and customs of the new society, you can't communicate effectively. You're apt to blunder frequently and seriously. In your culture shock, you may not know basic things:

- How to ask someone for a favour or pay someone a compliment
- How to extend or accept an invitation
- How early or how late to arrive for an appointment or how long to stay
- How to distinguish seriousness from playfulness and politeness from indifference
- How to dress for an informal, formal, or business function
- How to order a meal in a restaurant or how to summon a waiter

Culture shock occurs in four general stages, which apply to a wide variety of encounters with the new and the different (Oberg, 1960).

- *Stage one: The honeymoon.* At first you experience fascination, even enchantment, with the new culture and its people. In many ways, culture shock can be similar to moving away from home for the first time to go to school. You have your own apartment. You're your own boss—finally, on your own! Among people who are culturally different, the early (and superficial) relationships of this stage are characterized by cordiality and friendship. Many tourists remain at this stage because their stay in foreign countries is so brief.
- *Stage two: The crisis.* In the crisis stage, the differences between your own culture and the new one create problems. If you've just moved to your own apartment, for example, you no longer find dinner ready when you get home and you have to make it yourself. Your clothes aren't washed or ironed unless you do it yourself. Feelings of frustration and inadequacy come to the fore. This is the stage at which you experience the actual shock of the new culture. In a study of students from more than 100 countries who were studying in 11 foreign countries, 25 percent of the students experienced depression when they reached this stage of culture shock (Klineberg & Hull, 1979).
- *Stage three: The recovery.* During the recovery period, you gain the skills necessary to function effectively in the new culture. You learn how to plan a meal, shop, and cook. You find a local laundry and figure you'll learn to iron later. You feel more comfortable with the language and ways of the society. Your feelings of inadequacy subside.
- *Stage four: The adjustment.* At the final stage, you adjust to and come to enjoy both the new culture and the new experiences. You may still experience periodic difficulties and strains, but, on the whole, the experience is pleasant. Actually, you're now a pretty decent cook and have some new dishes in your repertoire. You're coming to enjoy shopping for new foods and cooking different dishes. You're becoming fluent and have developed some close friendships.

Time spent in a foreign country is not in itself sufficient for the development of positive attitudes; in fact, negative attitudes toward the new culture seem to develop over time. Rather, friendships with locals are crucial for satisfaction with the new culture. Maintaining contacts only with expatriates or sojourners isn't sufficient (Torbiorn, 1982). Unfortunately, many expats who live in compounds with other expats (a common overseas situation) never really become functioning participants in their new society.

People may also experience a kind of reverse culture shock when they return home after living in a foreign culture (Jandt, 2009). Consider, for example, members of the Canadian Armed Forces who serve overseas for extended periods of time or who serve extended tours of duty in war-torn countries. Upon returning to their bases in Cold Lake or Moose Jaw, they too may experience culture shock. If they've been in developing countries, they may struggle with our Canadian excesses (large meals, huge shopping malls, big cars, and so on) and how easily we waste and throw out food and other goods. They may also have a heightened awareness of the importance of family. Students who live and study abroad and then return home may also experience culture shock. In these cases, however, the recovery period is usually shorter and the sense of inadequacy and frustration is less.

John Nordell/The Image Works

A commonly encountered case of culture shock occurs with international students. If you're an international student, can you describe your culture shock experiences? If you're not an international student, can you visualize the culture shock you might experience if you were to study in another culture?

The suggestions outlined in the preceding sections will go a long way toward helping you communicate more effectively in all situations, and especially in intercultural interactions. These suggestions are, however, most effective when they're combined with the essential skills of all interpersonal communication as discussed throughout this text.

? Can you paraphrase the strategies of intercultural communication and apply the suggestions for increasing intercultural effectiveness (recognize and reduce your ethnocentrism, be mindful, face your fears, avoid overattribution and stereotyping, identify uncertainty and ambiguity, recognize differences, adjust your communication, and recognize culture shock)?

CANADIAN PROFILE: WRAP-UP

Jacques Boissinot/
CP Images

In her role as governor general and since, Adrienne Clarkson has worked to encourage pride among all Canadians, including those who were original peoples or who chose to make Canada their new home. What distinguished Canadians do you know? How have they contributed to Canada, in large or small ways? In what ways are you able to make contributions to your country? How can learning to communicate sensitively with the many cultures in Canada contribute to your own abilities to make Canada stronger?

SUMMARY OF CONCEPTS AND SKILLS

This chapter explored culture and intercultural communication, the ways in which cultures differ, and ways to improve intercultural communication.

Culture

1. Culture consists of the relatively specialized lifestyle of a group of people that is passed on from one generation to the next through communication rather than through genetic inheritance.
2. Culture is an essential ingredient in interpersonal communication because of demographic changes, economic and political interdependence of nations, advances in communication technology, and the culture-specific nature of interpersonal communication.
3. Each generation transmits its culture to the next generation through the process of enculturation and helps to develop a member's ethnic identity.
4. Through acculturation, one culture is modified through direct contact with or exposure to another culture.

Cultural Differences

5. Cultures differ in the degree to which they teach an individualist orientation (the individual is the most important consideration) or a collectivist orientation (the group is the most important consideration).

6. Cultures differ in the way information is communicated. In high-context cultures, much information is in the context or in the person's nonverbals; in low-context cultures, most of the information is explicitly stated in the message.
7. Cultures differ in the degree to which gender roles are distinct or overlap. Highly masculine (or achievement-oriented) cultures view men as assertive, oriented to material success, and strong, and view women as modest, focused on the quality of life, and tender. Highly feminine (or nurturing) cultures encourage both men and women to be modest, oriented to maintaining the quality of life, and tender, and they socialize people to emphasize close relationships.
8. Cultures differ in their power structures; in high-power-distance cultures, there is considerable difference in power between rulers and the ruled, whereas in low-power-distance cultures, power is, in theory, more evenly distributed.
9. Cultures differ in the degree to which they tolerate ambiguity and uncertainty. High-ambiguity-tolerant cultures are comfortable with uncertainty, whereas low-ambiguity-tolerant cultures are not.
10. Cultures differ in their being long-term oriented (a focus that promotes future rewards) or short-term

oriented (a focus that stresses more immediate rewards).

11. Cultures differ in their degree of indulgence (emphasizing the gratification of desires) or restraint (emphasizing moderation).

Improving Intercultural Communication

12. Intercultural communication encompasses a broad range of interactions, and includes interactions between cultures, ethnic groups, age groups, religions, and nations.

13. Many strategies can help make intercultural communication more effective. For example, recognize and reduce your ethnocentrism by learning about other cultures, communicating mindfully, facing your fears, confronting your tendencies to over-attribute and stereotype, reducing uncertainty and ambiguity, recognizing differences, adjusting your communication on the basis of cultural differences, and recognizing culture shock.

In addition, this chapter considered some important skills. Check those you wish to work on.

____ 1. *Cultural influences.* Communicate with an understanding that culture influences communication in all its forms.

____ 2. *Individualist and collectivist cultures.* Adjust your messages and your listening with an awareness of differences in individualist and collectivist cultures.

____ 3. *High- and low-context cultures.* Adjust your messages and your listening in light of the differences between high- and low-context cultures.

____ 4. *Masculine and feminine cultures.* Adjust your messages and your listening to differences in achievement and nurturing orientations.

____ 5. *High- and low-power-distance cultures.* Adjust your messages on the basis of the power structure that is written into the culture.

____ 6. *High and low tolerance for ambiguity.* Adjust your messages on the basis of the degree of the ambiguity tolerance of the other people.

____ 7. *Ethnocentric thinking.* Recognize your own ethnocentric thinking and how it influences your verbal and nonverbal messages.

____ 8. *Intercultural communication.* Become mindful of (1) differences between yourself and others, (2) differences within the cultural group, (3) differences in meanings, and (4) differences in cultural customs.

____ 9. *Appreciating cultural differences.* Look at cultural differences not as deviations or deficiencies but as the differences they are. Recognizing differences, however, doesn't necessarily mean that you must accept them.

VOCABULARY QUIZ: The Language of Intercultural Communication

Match the terms of intercultural communication with their definitions. Record the number of the definition next to the appropriate term.

____ high-context culture (33)
____ acculturation (27)
____ intercultural communication (27)
____ low-context culture (33)
____ ethnocentrism (37)
____ culture (27)
____ low-power-distance cultures (35)
____ enculturation (27)
____ individualistic cultures (31)
____ collectivist cultures (31)

1. A culture in which most information is explicitly encoded in the verbal message.
2. The values, beliefs, artifacts, and ways of communicating of a group of people.
3. The process by which culture is transmitted from one generation to another.
4. Communication that takes place between persons of different cultures or persons who have different cultural beliefs, values, or ways of behaving.
5. The process through which a person's culture is modified through contact with another culture.
6. The tendency to evaluate other cultures negatively and our own culture positively.
7. Cultures in which power is relatively evenly distributed.
8. Cultures that emphasize competition and individual success and in which your responsibility is largely to yourself.
9. A culture in which much information is in the context or the person and is not made explicit in the verbal message.
10. Cultures that emphasize the member's responsibility to the group.

These 10 terms and additional terms used in this chapter can be found in the glossary.

CHAPTER

3

Perception of Self and Others

LEARNING OBJECTIVES *After reading this chapter, you should be able to:*

1. Define *self-concept, self-awareness,* and *self-esteem,* and apply the suggestions for increasing self-awareness and self-esteem.

2. Explain the five stages of perception.

3. Define the factors that influence interpersonal perception and apply the suggestions for

increasing accuracy in your own interpersonal perception.

4. Explain and give examples of the strategies of impression management and use these when appropriate and ethical.

This chapter discusses two interrelated topics—the self and perception. After explaining the nature of the self (self-concept, self-awareness, and self-esteem) and the nature of perception, we look at the ways in which you form impressions of others and how you manage the impressions you convey to others.

THE SELF IN INTERPERSONAL COMMUNICATION

Let's begin this discussion by focusing on several fundamental aspects of the self: self-concept (the way you see yourself), self-awareness (your insight into and knowledge about yourself), and self-esteem (the value you place on yourself). In these discussions, you'll see how these dimensions influence and are influenced by the way you communicate.

Self-Concept

You no doubt have an image of who you are; this is your **self-concept**. It consists of your feelings and thoughts about your strengths and weaknesses, your abilities and limitations, and your aspirations and worldview (Black, 1999). Your self-concept develops from at least four sources: (1) the image of you that others have and that they reveal to you, (2) the comparisons you make between yourself and others, (3) the teachings of your culture, and (4) the way you interpret and evaluate your own thoughts and behaviours (see Figure 3.1).

OTHERS' IMAGES OF YOU   If you wanted to see the way your hair looked, you'd probably look in a mirror. But what would you do if you wanted to see how friendly or how assertive you are? According to the concept of the *looking-glass self* (Cooley, 1922), you'd look at the image of yourself that others reveal to you through their behaviours, and especially through the way they treat you and react to you.

Of course, you wouldn't look to just anyone. Rather, you'd look to those who are most significant in your life—to your *significant others*. As a child, for example, you'd look to your parents and then to your elementary schoolteachers. As an adult you might look to your friends and romantic partners. If these significant others think highly of you, you'll see a positive self-image reflected in their behaviours; if they think little of you, you'll see a more negative image.

FIGURE 3.1

The Sources of Self-Concept

This diagram depicts the four sources of self-concept, the four contributors to how you see yourself: others' images of you; social comparisons; cultural teachings; and your own observations, interpretations, and evaluations. As you read about self-concept, consider the influence of each factor throughout your life. Which factor influenced you most as a preteen? Which influences you the most now? Which will influence you the most 25 or 30 years from now?

Source: The Sources of Self-Concept FIGURE 3.1 [PU P. 54]. ISBN: 0205688640. Copyright © 2011, 2008 by Pearson Education, Inc.

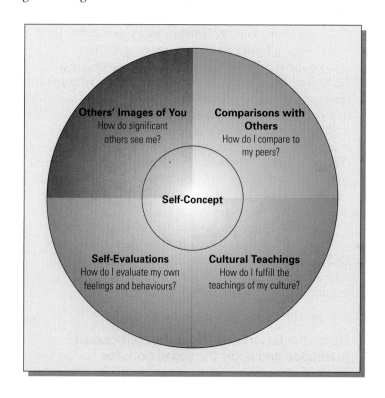

Others' Images of You — How do significant others see me?

Comparisons with Others — How do I compare to my peers?

Self-Concept

Self-Evaluations — How do I evaluate my own feelings and behaviours?

Cultural Teachings — How do I fulfill the teachings of my culture?

DEVELOPING LANGUAGE AND COMMUNICATION SKILLS

Relationships and Experiences

Research shows that significant brain development takes place in the first five years of life and sets the foundation for learning, success at work and in relationships, and health for the rest of our lives. Children's brains develop best when they're surrounded by nurturing, caring adults and have stimulating positive experiences. When children know that adults care for them, they learn that they're appreciated for who they are. When children have positive experiences, they learn that they're capable and develop confidence. How can you help young children develop positive perceptions of themselves and others? Sing, talk, and play together; read, cuddle, and care; ask for help when you're stressed; trust yourself. If you'd like to learn more, go to www.albertafamilywellness.org.

COMPARISONS WITH OTHERS   Another way in which you develop your self-concept is by comparing yourself with others. When you want to gain insight into who you are and how effective or competent you are, you probably look to your peers. For example, after an exam, you probably want to know how you performed relative to the other students in your class; and if you play on a baseball team, it's important to know how your batting average compares with that of others on the team.

Social networking sites, and social media generally, have provided us with the tools (all very easy to use) to perhaps estimate our individual worth or perhaps make us feel superior. Here are just a few ways in which social media enables you to find out how you stand.

- *Search engine reports.* Type in your name on Google, Bing, or Yahoo, for example, and you'll see the number of websites on which your name (and similarly named others) appears.
- *Network spread.* Your number of friends on Facebook or your contacts on LinkedIn or Plaxo is in some ways a measure of your potential influence. Not surprisingly, there are websites that will surf the net to help you contact more social network friends.
- *Online influence.* Network sites such as Klout and Peer-Index provide you with a score (from 0 to 100) of your online influence. Your Klout score, for example, is a combination of your "true reach"—the number of people you influence, "amplification"—the degree to which you influence them, and "network"—the influence of your network. Postrank Analytics provides you with a measure of engagement—the degree to which people interact with, pay attention to, read, or comment on what you write.
- *Twitter activities.* The number of times you tweet might be one point of comparison, but more important is the number of times you're tweeted about or your tweets are repeated (retweets). Twitalyzer will provide you with a three-part score—an impact score, a Klout score, and a Peer Index score—and will enable you to search the "Twitter elite" for the world as well as for any specific area (you can search by postal code). Assuming your Twitter score is what you'd like it to be, a single click will enable you to post this score on your own Twitter page.

Reuters/CORBIS Canada

What sense of self do members of the Royal Family project? How much of their self-concept do you think comes from the extensive grooming they've received for their role as royals? How might a person develop a positive sense of self without such a privileged background?

■ *Blog presence.* Your blog presence is readily available from your Stats tab, where you can see how many people have visited your blog since inception or over the past year, month, week, or day. And you'll also see a map of the world indicating where people who are visiting your blog come from.

CULTURAL TEACHINGS   Through your parents, teachers, and the media, your culture instills in you a variety of beliefs, values, and attitudes—about success (how you define it and how you should achieve it); about your religion, ethnicity, or nationality; and about the ethical principles you should follow in business and in your personal life. These teachings provide benchmarks against which you can measure yourself. Your success in, for example, achieving what your culture defines as success will contribute to a positive self-concept. A perceived failure to achieve what your culture promotes (for example, not being in a permanent relationship by the time you're 30) may contribute to a negative self-concept.

SELF-EVALUATIONS   Just as others form impressions of you based on what you do, you react to your own behaviour; you interpret and evaluate it. These interpretations and evaluations help to form your self-concept. For example, let's say you believe that lying is wrong. If you lie, you'll evaluate this behaviour in terms of your internalized beliefs about lying. You'll thus react negatively to your own actions. You may, for example, experience guilt if your behaviour contradicts your beliefs. In contrast, let's say you tutored another student and helped him or her pass a course. You would probably evaluate your involvement positively; you'd feel good about it and, as a result, about yourself.

Self-Awareness

Your **self-awareness** represents the extent to which you know yourself. Understanding how your self-concept develops is one way to increase your self-awareness: the more you understand about why you view yourself as you do, the better you'll understand who you are. Additional insight is gained by looking at self-awareness through the Johari model of the self, or your "four selves" (Luft, 1984).

YOUR FOUR SELVES   Self-awareness is neatly explained by the model of the four selves, the Johari window. This model, presented in Figure 3.2, has four basic areas,

FIGURE 3.2

The Johari Window

Visualize this model as representing your self. The entire model is of constant size, but each section can vary, from very small to very large. As one section becomes smaller, one or more of the others grows larger. Similarly, as one section grows, one or more of the others must get smaller. For example, if you reveal a secret and thereby enlarge your open self, this shrinks your hidden self. Further, this disclosure may in turn lead to a decrease in the size of your blind self (if your disclosure influences other people to reveal what they know about you but that you haven't known). How would you draw your Johari window to show yourself when interacting with your parents? With your friends? With your professors? (The name *Johari*, by the way, comes from the first names of the two people who developed the model, Joseph Luft and Harry Ingham.)

Source: Luft, J. (1984). *Group processes: An introduction to group dynamics* (p. 60). Reprinted by permission of Mayfield Publishing Company, Mountain View, CA.

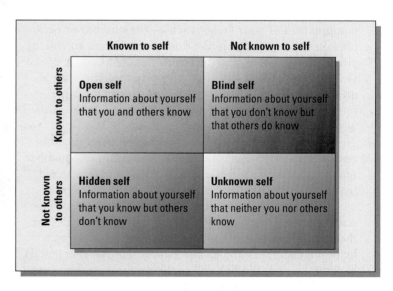

or quadrants, each of which represents a somewhat different self. The Johari model emphasizes that the several aspects of the self are not separate pieces but rather interactive parts of a whole. Each part is dependent on each other part. Like that of interpersonal communication, this model of the self is transactional.

Each person's Johari window will be different, and each individual's window will vary from one time to another and from one interpersonal situation to another.

- *The open self* represents all the information, behaviours, attitudes, feelings, desires, motivations, and ideas that you and others know. The type of information included here might range from your name, ethnicity, and gender to your age, political and religious affiliations, and financial situation. Your open self will vary in size depending on the situation you're in and the person with whom you're interacting.
- *The blind self* represents all the things about yourself that others know but of which you're ignorant. These may vary from the relatively insignificant habit of saying "You know" or rubbing your nose when you get angry to things as significant as defence mechanisms, conflict strategies, or repressed experiences. Where blind areas exist, communication will be more difficult. Yet blind areas always exist. You can shrink you blind area by asking questions, but you can never entirely eliminate it.
- *The hidden self* contains all that you know of yourself that you keep secret. In any interaction, this area includes everything you don't want to reveal, whether it's relevant or irrelevant to the conversation. At the extremes, the overdisclosers tell all—their relationship difficulties, their financial status, and just about everything else—while the underdisclosers tell nothing; they'll talk about you but not about themselves.
- *The unknown self* represents truths about yourself that neither you nor others know. Sometimes this unknown self is revealed through hypnosis, projective tests, or dreams. Mostly, however, it's revealed by the fact that you're constantly learning things about yourself that you didn't know before—for example, that you become defensive when someone asks you a question or voices disagreement or that you compliment others in the hope of being complimented back.

GROWING IN SELF-AWARENESS   Here are five ways you can increase your self-awareness:

- *Ask yourself about yourself.* One way to ask yourself about yourself is to take an informal "Who am I?" test (Bugental & Zelen, 1950; Grace & Cramer, 2003). Title a piece of paper "Who Am I?" and write 10, 15, or 20 times "I am . . ." Then complete each of the sentences. Try not to give only positive or socially acceptable responses; just respond with what comes to mind first. Take another piece of paper and divide it into two columns; label one column "Strengths" and the other column "Weaknesses." Fill in each column as quickly as possible. Using these first two tests as a base, take a third piece of paper, title it

Nigel Hicks/Dorling Kindersley

VIEWPOINTS Cultural Background

Your cultural background will significantly influence your responses to this simple "Who Am I?" test. In one study, for example, participants from Malaysia (a collectivist culture) and from Australia and Great Britain (individualist cultures) completed the test. Malaysians produced significantly more group self-descriptions and fewer idiocentric (meaning self-centred) self-descriptions than did the Australian or British respondents (Bochner, 1994). If you completed the "Who Am I?" test, can you identify responses that were influenced by your cultural orientation, particularly your collectivist–individualist orientation? Did other cultural factors influence your statements?

"Self-Improvement Goals," and complete the statement "I want to improve my . . ." as many times as you can in five minutes. Because you're constantly changing, these self-perceptions and goals also change, so update them frequently.

Remember the Johari Window as you complete this exercise. What is included in both your "blind" and your "unknown" windows will be impossible for you to list in any column at this point. Consider how the following activities may help you open these windows.

- *Listen to others.* You can learn a lot about yourself by seeing yourself as others do. In most interpersonal interactions, people comment on you in some way—on what you do, what you say, or how you look. Sometimes these comments are explicit; most often they're found in the way others look at you, in what they talk about, or in their interest in what you say. Pay close attention to this verbal and nonverbal information.
- *Actively seek information about yourself.* Actively seek out information to reduce your blind self. You need not be so obvious as to say, "Tell me about myself" or "What do you think of me?" But you can use everyday situations to gain self-information: "Do you think I was assertive enough when asking for the raise?" or "Would I be thought too forward if I invited myself for dinner?" Do not, of course, seek this information constantly; your friends would quickly find others with whom to interact.
- *See your different selves.* Each person with whom you have an interpersonal relationship views you differently; to each you're a somewhat different person. Yet you're really all of these selves, and your self-concept will be influenced by each of these views as they're reflected back to you in everyday interpersonal interactions. For starters, visualize how you're seen by your mother, your father, your teachers, your best friend, the stranger you sat next to on the bus, your employer, your neighbour's child. The experience will give you new and valuable perspectives on yourself.
- *Increase your open self.* When you reveal yourself to others and increase your open self, you also reveal yourself to yourself. At the very least, you bring into clearer focus what you may have buried within. As you discuss yourself, you may see connections that you'd previously missed and, with the aid of feedback from others, you may gain still more insight. Also, by increasing the open self, you increase the likelihood that a meaningful and intimate dialogue will develop that will enable you to get to know yourself better. This important process, called self-disclosure, is considered in Chapter 8, along with its advantages and disadvantages.

MESSAGES IN THE MEDIA

ABC/Courtesy Everett Collection/CP Images

In the Canadian cop show *Rookie Blue*, a decision is made to bring a therapist into the police division. This makes sense in light of the fact that by increasing our ability to understand ourselves and others, our accuracy in interpersonal perception and communication will be enhanced. What are your thoughts about this change in the division?

Self-Esteem

Self-esteem is a measure of how valuable you think you are. If you have high self-esteem, you think highly of yourself; if you have low self-esteem, you view yourself negatively. Before reading further about this topic, consider your own self-esteem by taking the accompanying self-test.

The basic idea behind self-esteem is that when you feel good about yourself—about who you are and what you're capable of doing—you will perform better. When you think like a success, you're more likely to act like a success. Conversely, when you think you're a failure, you're more likely to act like a failure. When you visualize yourself as being successful and effective during a job interview, for example, you're more likely to give a good impression. If, on the other hand, you think you're going to forget what you want to say or say something totally stupid, you are less likely to be successful.

Interestingly enough, your self-esteem seems to influence the method of communication you choose. For example, if you have low self-esteem, you're likely to prefer email, whereas if you have high self-esteem, you're more likely to prefer face-to-face interaction, at least in situations involving some degree of interpersonal risk (Joinson, 2001).

Here are five suggestions for increasing self-esteem that parallel the questions in the self-test.

ATTACK SELF-DESTRUCTIVE BELIEFS Challenge those beliefs you have about yourself that are unproductive or that make it more difficult for you to achieve your goals (Einhorn, 2006). Here, for example, are some beliefs that are likely to prove self-destructive (Butler, 1981).

- The belief that *you have to be perfect* causes you to try to perform at unrealistically high levels at work, school, and home.
- The belief that *you have to be strong* tells you that weakness and any of the more vulnerable emotions like sadness, compassion, or loneliness are wrong.
- The belief that *you have to please others* says that your worthiness depends on what others think of you.
- The belief that *you have to hurry up* compels you to do things quickly, to try to do more than can be reasonably expected in any given amount of time.
- The belief that *you have to take on more responsibilities* requires that you try to do more than any one person can be expected to handle.

TEST YOURSELF

How's Your Self-Esteem?

Respond to each of the following statements with *T* (for true) if the statement describes you at least a significant part of the time and *F* (for false) if the statement describes you rarely or never.

____ 1. Generally, I feel I have to be successful in all things.

____ 2. A number of my acquaintances are often critical or negative of what I do and how I think.

____ 3. I often tackle projects that I know are impossible to complete to my satisfaction.

____ 4. When I focus on the past, I more often focus on my failures than on my successes and on my negative rather than my positive qualities.

____ 5. I make little effort to improve my personal and social skills.

How Did You Do? "True" responses to the questions are generally seen as getting in the way of building positive self-esteem. "False" responses indicate that you think much as a self-esteem coach would want you to think.

What Will You Do? The following discussion elaborates on these five issues and illustrates why each of them creates problems for the development of healthy self-esteem. You might also want to visit the National Association for Self-Esteem's website. There you'll find a variety of materials for examining and for bolstering self-esteem.

dmitrieva/Shutterstock

VIEWPOINTS **Self-Esteem**

Despite its intuitive value, self-esteem has its critics (Epstein, 2005). For example, in many post-secondary institutions, there is concern about a perceived sense of student entitlement. Professors talk about how their students seem to feel that they "deserve" an A simply because they were one of the top students in their high school class. As a student, do you see examples of what might be entitlement among your classmates? Do you feel entitled to get good grades even though you may not have worked hard for them?

These beliefs set unrealistically high standards and therefore almost always end in failure. As a result, you may develop a negative self-image, seeing yourself as someone who constantly fails. So, replace these self-destructive beliefs with more productive ones, such as "I succeed in many things; I don't have to succeed in everything" and "It would be nice to be loved by everyone, but it isn't necessary to my happiness." In other words, try to protect yourself from perfection! See Table 3.1 for a summary and comparison of these destructive beliefs and constructive counterparts.

BEWARE THE IMPOSTOR PHENOMENON   The **impostor phenomenon** refers to the tendency to disregard outward signs of success and to consider yourself an "impostor": a fake, a fraud, one who doesn't really deserve to be considered successful (Clance, 1985; Harvey & Katz, 1985). Even though others may believe you're a success, you "know" they're wrong. As you might expect, this tendency is more likely in new situations—a new job, say. One of the dangers of this belief is that it may prevent you from seeking advancement in your profession, believing that you won't be up to the task. Interestingly, this phenomenon seems to be more prevalent among women, even those who are highly successful. Becoming aware that such beliefs are not uncommon and that they're not necessarily permanent should help relieve some of these misperceptions. Another useful aid is to develop a relationship with an honest and knowledgeable mentor who will not only teach you the ropes but will let you know that you're successful.

SEEK OUT NOURISHING PEOPLE   Psychologist Carl Rogers (1970) drew a distinction between noxious and nourishing people. Noxious people criticize and find fault with just about everything. Nourishing people, on the other hand, are positive and optimistic.

TABLE 3.1

DESTRUCTIVE AND CONSTRUCTIVE BELIEFS

Destructive Beliefs	Constructive Beliefs
I need to **be perfect**.	I'm not perfect, no one is; and I don't need to be perfect, but I'm not bad.
I need to **be strong**.	It's nice to be strong sometimes but also nice to be able to show vulnerability.
I need **to please** everyone.	It would be nice if I pleased everyone, but that's really impossible; besides, there's no need to please everyone.
I need **to hurry**; I can't waste time.	I can stop and pause and not always be in a hurry.
I need to **do more**.	There is a limit on what one person can do; I do what I can do and don't do the rest.

Most important, they reward us, stroke us, and make us feel good about ourselves. To enhance your self-esteem, seek out these people. Avoid noxious people, those who make you feel negatively about yourself. At the same time, seek to become more nourishing yourself so that you each build up the other's self-esteem.

Identification with people similar to you also seems to increase self-esteem. For example, deaf people who identify with the larger deaf community have been found to have greater self-esteem than those who don't so identify (Jambor & Elliott, 2005). Similarly, identification with your cultural group also seems helpful in developing positive self-esteem (McDonald et al., 2005).

WORK ON PROJECTS THAT WILL RESULT IN LEARNING   Some people want to fail (or so it seems). Often, they select projects that will result in failure simply because these projects are impossible to complete. Avoid this trap and select projects that are reasonable and have a chance of success. Each success will help build self-esteem. However, if a project does fail, learn from that failure. Increasingly, professionals are recognizing that they can learn from failure when it helps them to pinpoint what not to do again. The mantra "fail forward and fail fast" describes a process used by entrepreneurs and innovators.

REMIND YOURSELF OF YOUR SUCCESSES   Some people have a tendency to focus on and to exaggerate their failures, their missed opportunities, and their social mistakes. However, it's been found that those witnessing these failures give them much less importance (Savitsky, Epley, & Gilovich, 2001). If your objective is to correct what you did wrong or to identify the skills that you need to improve next time, then focusing on failures can have some positive value. However, if you focus solely on failure without any plans for correction, then you're probably just making life more difficult for yourself. We have a tendency to focus more on the negative comments than on the positive. For example, think about a professor's comments on a research paper. Even though the majority of comments are positive, we often become fixated on the one or two negative (hopefully constructive) comments.

SECURE AFFIRMATION   An affirmation is simply a statement asserting that something is true. In discussions of self-concept and self-awareness, affirmation is used to refer to positive statements about yourself, statements asserting that something good or positive is true of you. It's frequently recommended that you remind yourself of your successes with affirmations—that you focus on your good deeds; on your positive qualities, strengths, and virtues; and on your productive and meaningful relationships with friends, loved ones, and relatives (Aronson, Cohen, & Nail, 1998; Aronson, Wilson, & Akert, 2013). One useful way to look at self-affirmation is in terms of "I am," "I can," and "I will" statements (Van Praagh, 2010).

- *"I am" statements* focus on your self-image and how you see yourself; they might include "I am a worthy person," "I am responsible," "I am capable of loving," and "I am a good team player."
- *"I can" statements* focus on your abilities; they might include "I can accept my past but also let it go," "I can learn to be a more responsive partner," "I can assert myself when appropriate," and "I can control my anger."
- *"I will" statements* focus on useful and appropriate goals you want to achieve; they might include "I will get over my guilty feelings," "I will study more effectively," "I will act more supportively," and "I will not take on more responsibility than I can handle."

Another way to think about this is to consider the notion of "inner talk." Think about how you talk to yourself in different situations. Often, this inner talk is negative and destructive. How might you redirect this inner talk to be more affirming? The idea behind the advice about self-esteem is that the way you talk to yourself will influence

INTERPERSONAL CHOICE POINT

Lowering Self-Esteem
Your brother has entered a relationship with someone who constantly puts him down; this has lowered his self-esteem to the point where he has no self-confidence. If this continues, you fear your brother may again experience severe bouts of depression. What options do you have for dealing with this problem? What, if anything, would you do?

what you think of yourself. If you affirm yourself—if you tell yourself that you're a friendly person, that you can be a leader, that you will succeed on the next test—you will soon come to feel more positively about yourself.

Some research, however, argues that such affirmations—although extremely popular in self-help books—may not be very helpful. These critics contend that, if you have low self-esteem, you're not going to believe your self-affirmations simply because you don't have a high opinion of yourself to begin with (Paul, 2001). They propose that the alternative to self-affirmation is to secure affirmation from others. You do this largely by becoming more interpersonally competent. The more competent you become, the more positive affirmations you'll receive from others, and it is this affirmation from others that, these researchers argue, is more helpful than self-talk in raising self-esteem.

 Can you define *self-concept, self-awareness,* and *self-esteem* and apply the suggestions for increasing your own self-awareness and self-esteem?

PERCEPTION IN INTERPERSONAL COMMUNICATION

Perception is the process by which you become aware of objects, events, and especially people through your senses: sight, smell, taste, touch, and hearing. Perception is an active, not a passive, process. Your perceptions result from what exists in the outside world and from your own experiences, desires, needs and wants, loves and hatreds. Among the reasons perception is so important in interpersonal communication is that it influences your communication choices. The messages you send and listen to will depend on how you see the world, on how you size up specific situations, and on what you think of yourself and of the people with whom you interact.

Interpersonal perception is a continuous series of processes that blend into one another and can take place in a split second. For convenience of discussion, we can separate interpersonal perception into five stages: (1) your senses pick up some kind of stimulation; (2) you organize the stimuli in some way; (3) you interpret and evaluate what you perceive; (4) you store it in memory; and (5) you retrieve it when needed.

Stage One: Stimulation

At this first stage, your sense organs are stimulated—you hear a new song, see a friend, smell someone's perfume, taste an orange, receive an instant message, or feel another's sweaty palm. Naturally, you don't perceive everything; rather, you engage in **selective perception**, a general term that includes selective attention, selective exposure, and intensity:

■ In **selective attention**, you attend to those things that you anticipate will fulfill your needs or will prove enjoyable. For example, when daydreaming in class, you don't hear

Ariel Skelley/Glow Images

VIEWPOINTS **Selective Perception**
Consider your own selective perception, particularly as it occurs in the classroom or in the workplace. In what ways is your selective perception useful? In what ways might it prove disadvantageous?

what the instructor is saying until your name is called. Your selective attention mechanism then focuses your senses on your name.

- Through **selective exposure**, you expose yourself to messages that will confirm your existing beliefs, contribute to your objectives, or prove satisfying in some way. For example, after you buy a car, you're more apt to listen to ads for the car you just bought because these messages tell you that you made the right decision. At the same time, you'd likely avoid ads for the cars that you considered but eventually rejected because these messages would tell you that you made the wrong decision.

- You're also more likely to perceive stimuli that are greater in *intensity* than surrounding stimuli and those that have novelty value (Kagan, 2002). For example, television commercials normally play at a greater intensity than regular programming to ensure that you take special notice. You're also more likely to notice the co-worker who dresses in a novel way than you are to notice the one who dresses like everyone else (Sriram & Shyam, 2006).

Stage Two: Organization

At the second stage, you organize the information your senses pick up. One of the major ways you organize information is by rules. One frequently used rule of perception is that of **proximity**, or physical closeness: Things that are physically close to each other are perceived as a unit. Thus, using this rule, you would perceive people who are often together or messages spoken one immediately after the other as units, as belonging together. You also assume that verbal and nonverbal signals sent at the same time are related.

Another rule is **similarity**: things that are physically similar (they look alike) are perceived to belong together and to form a unit. This principle of similarity would lead you to see people who dress alike as belonging together. Similarly, you might assume that people who work at the same jobs, who are of the same religion, who live in the same building, or who talk with the same accent belong together.

The rule of **contrast** is the opposite of similarity: when items (people or messages, for example) are very different from each other, you conclude that they don't belong together; they're too different from each other to be part of the same unit. If you're the only one who shows up at an informal gathering in a tuxedo, you'd be seen as not belonging to the group because you contrast too much with other members.

Another way you organize material is by creating mental templates or structures that help you organize the millions of items of information you come into contact with every day as well as those you already have in memory. These are referred to as **schemata**. Schemata may thus be viewed as general ideas about people (Torontonians, children, Americans); yourself (your qualities, abilities, and even liabilities); or social roles (what a police officer, professor, or multibillionaire CEO is like).

A **script** is an organized body of information about some action, event, or procedure. It's a general idea of how some event should play out or unfold; it's the rules governing events and their sequence. For example, you probably have a script for eating in a restaurant, with the actions organized into a pattern. Similarly, you probably have scripts for how you do laundry, conduct an interview, introduce someone to someone else, or ask for a date.

Stage Three: Interpretation–Evaluation

The interpretation–evaluation step (a combined term because the two processes can't be separated) is greatly influenced by your experiences, needs, wants, values, beliefs about the way things are or should be, expectations, physical and emotional state, and so on. Imagine, then, the complex nature of dialogue when all these factors differ radically from person to person and even from moment to moment as people interact with one another. Your interpretation–evaluation will be influenced by your rules, schemata, and scripts as well as by your gender. For example, women have been found to view others more positively than men do (Winquist, Mohr, & Kenny, 1998).

Judgments about members of other cultures are often ethnocentric; because of your stereotypes, you can easily (but inappropriately) apply these to members of other cultures. And so it's easy to infer that when members of other cultures do things that conform to your ways of doing things, they're right, and when they do things that contradict your ways, they're wrong—a classic example of ethnocentric thinking. This tendency can easily contribute to intercultural misunderstandings.

Stage Four: Memory

Your perceptions and their interpretations–evaluations are put into memory; they're stored so that you may ultimately retrieve them at some later time. So, for example, you have in memory your stereotype for university athletes and the fact that Ben Williams is a hockey player. Ben Williams is then stored in memory with "cognitive tags" that tell you that he's strong, ambitious, academically weak, and egocentric. Despite the fact that you haven't witnessed Ben's strength or ambitions and have no idea of his academic record or his psychological profile, you still may store your memory of Ben along with the qualities that make up your stereotype for university athletes. Knowing that Ben earned a C in French fits with your stereotype, but learning that he got an A in chemistry and is transferring to Queen's as a theoretical physics major doesn't. These facts are so inconsistent that you may question your stereotype or decide that Ben is an exception to the rule.

Stage Five: Recall

At some later date, you may want to recall or access the information you've stored in memory. Let's say you want to retrieve your information about Ben because he's the topic of discussion among you and a few friends. As we'll see in our discussion of listening in Chapter 4, memory isn't reproductive; you don't simply reproduce what you've heard or seen. Rather, you reconstruct what you've heard or seen into a whole that is meaningful to you. It's this reconstruction that you store in memory. When you want to retrieve this information, you may recall it with a variety of inaccuracies:

- *Stereotypes.* You're likely to recall information that is consistent with your stereotype; in fact, you may not even be recalling the specific information (say, about Ben) but may actually just be recalling your stereotype (which contains information about university athletes and, because of this, also about Ben).
- *Inconsistencies.* You're apt to fail to recall information that is inconsistent with your stereotype (Ben's A in chemistry); you have no place to put that information, so you easily lose it or forget it.
- *Contradictions.* You're more likely to recall information that *drastically* contradicts your stereotype (Ben's transfer to Queen's), because it forces you to think about (and perhaps rethink) your stereotype and its accuracy; it may even force you to revise your stereotype for university athletes in general.

INTERPERSONAL CHOICE POINT

Responding to Stereotypes

What are some of your communication options for dealing with people who persist in talking (and thinking) in stereotypes, assuming you want to educate them rather than alienate them?

 Can you explain the five stages of perception (stimulation, organization, interpretation–evaluation, memory, and recall) and use the suggestions for increasing your own perceptual accuracy at each of the stages?

Reflections on the Model of Perception

Before moving on to the more specific processes involved in interpersonal perception, let's spell out some of the implications of the five-stage model discussed above for your own interpersonal perceptions.

1. Everyone relies heavily on shortcuts. Rules, schemata, and scripts, for example, are all useful shortcuts that simplify your understanding, remembering, and recalling of information about people and events. If you didn't have these shortcuts, you'd have to treat every person, role, or action differently from every other person, role, or action. This would make every experience a new one, totally unrelated to anything you already know.
2. Shortcuts, however, may mislead you; they may contribute to your remembering things that are consistent with your schemata, even if they didn't occur, and to your distorting or forgetting of information that is inconsistent. Harlow et al. (2005) call these shortcuts assumptions, and suggest that they're caused by the inability to see past our own frame of reference.
3. What you remember about a person or an event isn't an objective recollection but is likely heavily influenced by your preconceptions or your schemata about what belongs and what doesn't belong, what fits neatly into the templates in your brain and what doesn't fit. Your reconstruction of an event or person contains a lot of information that wasn't in the original sensory experience—and may omit a lot that was in the experience.
4. Memory is especially unreliable when the information is ambiguous—when it can be interpreted in different ways. For example, you remember the parts of Ben's story that fit who you believe Ben to be and forget the parts that don't fit. Conveniently, but unreliably, schemata reduce ambiguity.

IMPRESSION FORMATION

Impression formation (sometimes referred to as *person perception*) refers to the processes you go through in forming an impression of another person, whether it's a person you meet face to face or a person whose profile you're reading on Facebook. Here you would make use of a variety of perception processes, each of which has pitfalls and potential dangers. Before reading about these processes that you use in perceiving other people, examine your own perception strategies by taking the self-test on the next page.

Impression Formation Processes

The ways in which you perceive another person and ultimately come to some kind of evaluation or interpretation of this person are influenced by a variety of processes. Here we consider some of the more significant: the self-fulfilling prophecy, personality theory, primacy–recency, consistency, and attribution.

SELF-FULFILLING PROPHECY A **self-fulfilling prophecy** is a prediction that comes true because you act on it as if it were true. Self-fulfilling prophecies occur in such widely different situations as parent–child relationships, educational settings, and business (Madon, Guyll, & Spoth, 2004; Merton, 1957; Rosenthal, 2002; Tierney & Farmer, 2004). There are four basic steps in the self-fulfilling prophecy:

1. You make a prediction or formulate a belief about a person or a situation. For example, you predict that Pat is friendly in interpersonal encounters.
2. You act toward that person or situation as if that prediction or belief were true. For example, you act as if Pat were a friendly person.
3. Because you act as if the belief were true, it becomes true. For example, because of the way you act toward Pat, Pat becomes comfortable and friendly.

How Accurate Are You at People Perception?

Respond to each of the following statements with *T* if the statement is usually or generally true (accurate in describing your behaviour) or with *F* if the statement is usually or generally false (inaccurate in describing your behaviour).

_____ 1. I make predictions about people's behaviours that generally prove to be true.

_____ 2. When I know some things about another person, I can pretty easily fill in what I don't know.

_____ 3. Generally my expectations are borne out by what I actually see; that is, my later perceptions usually match my initial expectations.

_____ 4. I base most of my impressions of people on the first few minutes of our meeting.

_____ 5. I generally find that people I like possess positive characteristics and people I don't like possess negative characteristics.

_____ 6. I generally attribute people's attitudes and behaviours to their most obvious physical or psychological characteristic.

How Did You Do? This brief perception test was designed to raise questions to be considered in this chapter, not to provide you with a specific perception score. All statements refer to perceptual processes that many people use but that often get us into trouble, leading us to form inaccurate impressions. The questions refer to several processes to be discussed below: self-fulfilling prophecy (Statement 1), personality theory (2), perceptual accentuation (3), primacy–recency (4), and consistency (5). Statement 6 refers to overattribution, one of the problems we encounter as we try to identify the motives for other people's and even our own behaviours.

What Will You Do? As you read this section, think about these processes and consider how you might use them more accurately and not allow them to get in the way of accurate and reasonable people perception. At the same time, recognize that situations vary widely and that strategies for clearer perception will prove useful most of the time but not all of the time. In fact, you may want to identify situations in which you shouldn't follow the suggestions that this text will offer.

4. You observe your effect on the person or the resulting situation, and what you see strengthens your beliefs. For example, you observe Pat's friendliness, and this reinforces your belief that Pat is, in fact, friendly.

Jeff Greenberg/PhotoEdit

We make self-fulfilling prophecies about ourselves as well as about others. For example, you predict that you'll do poorly in an examination, so you don't read the questions carefully and don't make any great effort to organize your thoughts or support your statements. Or you predict that people won't like you, so you don't extend yourself to others. You can also make positive predictions about yourself, and these too will influence your behaviour. For example, you can assume that others will like you and so approach them with a positive attitude and demeanour. Generally, how do your predictions influence your achieving your personal and professional goals?

The self-fulfilling prophecy also can be seen when you make predictions about yourself and fulfill them. For example, suppose you enter a group situation convinced that the other members will dislike you. Almost invariably you'll be proved right; the other members will appear to you to dislike you. What you may be doing is acting in a way that encourages the group to respond to you negatively. In this way, you fulfill your prophecies about yourself.

An example of the self-fulfilling prophecy is called the **Pygmalion effect.** In a well-known study, teachers were told that certain pupils were expected to do exceptionally well, although they were late bloomers. The names of these students were actually selected at random by the experimenters. The results, however, were not random. The students whose names were given to the teachers actually performed at a higher level than others. In fact, these students' school scores even improved more than did the other students'. The teachers' expectations probably prompted them to give extra attention to the selected students, thereby positively affecting their performance (Insel & Jacobson, 1975; Rosenthal & Jacobson, 1968). Studies have found the same general effect in military training and business settings: trainees and workers performed better when their supervisors were given positive information about them (McNatt, 2001). Researchers have identified the Pygmalion effect in contexts as varied as leadership, athletic coaching, and effective stepfamilies (Eden, 1992; Einstein, 1995; McNatt, 2001; Solomon et al., 1996).

PERSONALITY THEORY   Each person has a personality theory (often unconscious or implicit) that tells you which characteristics of an individual go with which other characteristics. Consider, for example, the following brief statements. Note the word in parentheses that you think best completes each sentence.

- Carlo is energetic, eager, and (intelligent, stupid).
- Kim is bold, defiant, and (extroverted, introverted).
- Joe is bright, lively, and (thin, heavy).
- Ava is attractive, intelligent, and (likeable, unlikeable).
- Susan is cheerful, positive, and (outgoing, shy).
- Shafiq is handsome, tall, and (friendly, unfriendly).

What makes some of these choices seem right and others wrong is your implicit personality theory, the system of rules that tells you which characteristics go with which other characteristics. Your theory may, for example, have told you that a person who is energetic and eager is also intelligent, not stupid—although there is no logical reason why a stupid person could not be energetic and eager.

If you believe that a person has some positive qualities, you're likely to infer that she or he also possesses other positive qualities (known as the **halo effect**). There is also a **reverse halo** (or "horns") effect: if you know a person possesses several negative qualities, you're more likely to infer that the person also has other negative qualities. The halo effect will lead you to perceive attractive people as more generous, sensitive, trustworthy, and interesting than those who are less attractive. And the reverse halo effect will lead you to perceive those who are unattractive as mean, dishonest, antisocial, and sneaky (Katz, 2003).

When forming impressions of others, consider whether you're making judgments on the basis of your theory of personality, perceiving qualities in an individual that your theory tells you should be present but aren't, or seeing qualities that aren't there (Plaks, Grant, & Dweck, 2005).

PERCEPTUAL ACCENTUATION   When poor and rich children were shown pictures of coins and later asked to estimate their value, the poor children's value estimates were much greater than the rich children's. Similarly, hungry people need fewer visual cues to perceive food objects and food terms than do people who are not hungry. This process, called **perceptual accentuation**, leads you to see what you expect or want to see. You see people you like as better looking and smarter than those you don't like. You magnify or accentuate what will satisfy your needs and desires: the thirsty person sees a mirage of water; the sexually deprived person sees a mirage of sexual satisfaction.

Perceptual accentuation can lead you to perceive what you need or want to perceive rather than what's really there and to fail to perceive what you don't want to perceive. For example, you may not perceive signs of impending relationship problems because you're seeing only what you want to see. Another interesting distortion created by perceptual accentuation is that you may perceive certain behaviours as indicative that someone likes you simply because you want to be liked.

PRIMACY–RECENCY   Assume for a moment that you're enrolled in a course in which half the classes are extremely dull and half extremely exciting. At the end of the semester, you evaluate the course and the instructor. Would your evaluation be more favourable if the dull classes occurred in the first half of the semester and the exciting classes in the second? Or would it be more favourable if the order were reversed? If what comes first exerts the most influence, you have a **primacy effect**. If what comes last (or most recently) exerts the most influence, you have a **recency effect**.

In the classic study on the effects of primacy–recency in interpersonal perception, post-secondary students perceived a person who was described as "intelligent, industrious, impulsive, critical, stubborn, and envious" more positively than a person described as "envious, stubborn, critical, impulsive, industrious, and intelligent" (Asch, 1946). Notice that the descriptions are identical; only the order was changed. Clearly, there's a tendency to use early information to get a general idea about a person and to use later information to make this impression more specific.

INTERPERSONAL CHOICE POINT

Reversing a First Impression
You made a really bad first impression in your interpersonal communication class. You meant to be funny but came off as merely sarcastic. What are some of the things you might say (immediately as well as later) to lessen the impact of this first impression?

The tendency to give greater weight to early information and to interpret later information in light of early impressions can lead you to formulate a total picture of an individual on the basis of initial impressions that may not be typical or accurate. For example, if you judge a job applicant as generally nervous when he or she may simply be showing normal nervousness at being interviewed for a much-needed job, you will have misperceived this individual. Similarly, this tendency can lead you to discount or distort subsequent perceptions so as not to disrupt your initial impression. For example, you may fail to see signs of deceit in someone you like because of your early impressions that this person is a good and honest individual.

CONSISTENCY   The tendency to maintain balance among perceptions or attitudes is called **consistency** (McBroom & Reed, 1992). You expect certain things to go together and other things not to go together. On a purely intuitive basis, for example, respond to the following sentences by noting your expected response:

1. I expect a person I like to (like, dislike) me.
2. I expect a person I dislike to (like, dislike) me.
3. I expect my friend to (like, dislike) my friend.
4. I expect my friend to (like, dislike) my enemy.
5. I expect my enemy to (like, dislike) my friend.
6. I expect my enemy to (like, dislike) my enemy.

According to most consistency theories, your expectations would be as follows: You would expect a person you liked to like you (1) and a person you disliked to dislike you (2). You would expect a friend to like a friend (3) and to dislike an enemy (4). You would expect your enemy to dislike your friend (5) and to like your other enemy (6). All these expectations are intuitively satisfying.

Further, you would expect someone you liked to possess characteristics you like or admire and would expect your enemies not to possess characteristics you like or admire. Conversely, you would expect people you liked to lack unpleasant characteristics and those you disliked to possess unpleasant characteristics.

Uncritically assuming that an individual is consistent can lead you to ignore or distort perceptions that are inconsistent with your picture of the whole person. For example, you may misinterpret Karim's unhappiness because your image of Karim is "happy, controlled, and contented."

Explaining Motivations

The process by which we try to explain the motivation for a person's behaviour is called **attribution**. Perhaps the major way we do this is to ask ourselves whether the person is in control of the behaviour. If people are in control of their own behaviour, then we feel justified in praising them for positive behaviours and blaming them for negative behaviours. You probably make similar judgments based on controllability in many situations. Consider, for example, how you would respond to a situation in which an acquaintance failed her history exam or had her car repossessed.

Very likely you'd be sympathetic if you felt that she wasn't in control of what happened; for example, if the exam was unfair or if she couldn't make her car payments because she'd lost her job as a result of discrimination. On the other hand, you probably wouldn't be sympathetic or might blame her for her problems if you felt she was in control of what happened; for example, if she went to a party instead of studying, or if she gambled her car payment money away.

Generally, research shows that if we feel people are in control of negative behaviours, we'll come to dislike them. If we feel people are not in control of negative behaviours, we'll come to feel sorry for them and not blame them for their negative circumstances.

Three Ways to Avoid Attribution Errors

Three major attribution problems can interfere with the accuracy of your interpersonal perceptions, whether on or off the job.

1. After getting a poor performance evaluation, you're more likely to attribute it to the difficulty of the job or the unfairness of the supervisor—that is, to uncontrollable factors. After getting an extremely positive evaluation, however, you're more likely to attribute it to your ability or hard work—that is, to controllable factors. This tendency is called the **self-serving bias**, or the inclination to take credit for the positive and deny responsibility for the negative (Hogg, 2002). To prevent this bias from distorting your attributions, consider the potential influences of both internal and external factors on your positive and negative behaviours. Ask yourself to what extent your negative behaviours may be due to internal (controllable) factors and your positive behaviours to external (uncontrollable) factors. Just asking the question will prevent you from mindlessly falling into the self-serving bias trap.

2. If someone you work with had alcoholic parents or was born into great wealth, you might attribute everything that person does to such factors. For example, "Sally has difficulty working on a team because she grew up in a home of alcoholics" or "Lillian lacks ambition because she always got whatever she wanted without working for it." This is called **overattribution**, which is the tendency to single out one or two obvious characteristics and attribute everything a person does to these one or two characteristics. To prevent overattribution, recognize that most behaviours result from a lot of factors, and that you almost always make a mistake when you select one factor and attribute everything to it.

3. When Nila is late for a meeting, you're more likely to conclude that she's inconsiderate or irresponsible than to attribute her lateness to a bus breakdown or to a traffic accident. This tendency to conclude that people do what they do because that's the kind of people they are rather than because of the situation they're in is called the **fundamental attribution error**. To avoid making this error, ask yourself if you're giving too much emphasis to internal factors and too little emphasis to external factors.

Have you ever fallen into one of these three errors in perceiving another person? What happened? What would you do differently now?

Attribution of causality can lead to several major barriers. Three such barriers (the self-serving bias, overattribution, and the fundamental attribution error) are examined in the Skill-Building Exercise above.

Increasing Accuracy in Impression Formation

Successful interpersonal communication depends largely on the accuracy of the impressions you form of others. We've already identified the potential barriers that can arise with each of the perceptual processes; for example, the self-serving bias or overattribution. In addition to avoiding these barriers, here are some ways to increase your accuracy in impression formation.

ANALYZE YOUR IMPRESSIONS   Subject your perceptions to logical analysis and to critical thinking. Here are three suggestions:

■ *Recognize your own role in perception.* Your emotional and physiological state will influence the meaning you give to your perceptions. A movie may seem hysterically funny when you're in a good mood but just plain stupid when you're in a bad mood. Understand your own biases; for example, do you tend to perceive only the positive in people you like and only the negative in people you don't like?

■ *Avoid early conclusions.* On the basis of your observations of behaviours, formulate hypotheses to test against additional information and evidence; avoid drawing conclusions that you then look to confirm. Look for a variety of cues pointing in the

INTERPERSONAL CHOICE POINT

Overattribution

Your work colleagues attribute your behaviour, attitudes, values, and just about everything you do to your ethnic origins—a clear case of over-attribution. What are some of the things you can say to explain how this thinking isn't logical without alienating the people you're going to have to work with for a considerable time?

same direction. The more cues point to the same conclusion, the more likely it is that your conclusion will be correct. Be especially alert to contradictory cues that seem to refute your initial hypotheses. At the same time, seek validation from others. Do others see things in the same way you do? If not, ask yourself whether your perceptions may be distorted in some way.

■ *Avoid mind reading.* Don't try to read the thoughts and feelings of other people merely from observing their behaviours. Regardless of how many behaviours you observe and how carefully you examine them, you can only *guess* what is going on in someone's mind. A person's motives aren't open to outside inspection; you can only make assumptions based on overt behaviours.

■ *Beware the **just-world hypothesis**.* Many people believe that the world is just: good things happen to good people and bad things happen to bad people (Aronson, Wilson, & Akert, 2013; Hunt, 2000). Put differently, you get what you deserve! Even when you mindfully dismiss this assumption, you may use it mindlessly when perceiving and evaluating other people. Consider a particularly vivid example: if a woman is raped in certain cultures, she's considered by many in that culture (certainly not all) to have disgraced her family and to be deserving of severe punishment—in many cases, even death. And although you may claim that this is unfair, much research shows that even in Canada and the United States, many people do blame the victim for being raped, especially if the victim is male (Adams-Price, Dalton, & Sumrall, 2004; Andersen, 2004). The belief that the world is just creates perceptual distortions by leading you to overemphasize the influence of internal factors (this happened because this person is good or bad) and to de-emphasize the influence of situational factors (the external circumstances) in your attempts to explain the behaviours of other people or even your own behaviours.

REDUCE YOUR UNCERTAINTY   In every interpersonal situation, there is some degree of uncertainty. However, a variety of strategies can help reduce this uncertainty (Berger & Bradac, 1982; Brashers, 2007; Gudykunst, 1994).

■ Observing another person while he or she is engaged in an active task, preferably interacting with others in an informal social situation, will often reveal a great deal about the person, as people are less apt to monitor their behaviours and more likely to reveal their true selves in informal situations. When you log on to an internet chat group and read the exchanges between the other group members before saying anything yourself, you're learning about the people in the group and about the group itself, thus reducing uncertainty. When uncertainty is reduced, you're more likely to make contributions that will be appropriate and less likely to violate the group's norms.

■ You can sometimes manipulate situations so as to observe the person in more specific contexts. Employment interviews, theatrical auditions, and student teaching are good examples of situations arranged to get an accurate view of the person in action.

■ Learn about a person through asking others. You might inquire of a colleague if a third person finds you interesting and might like to have dinner with you.

■ Interact with the individual. For example, you can ask questions: "Do you enjoy sports?" "What did you think of that computer science course?" "What would you do if you got fired?"

CHECK YOUR PERCEPTIONS   **Perception checking** is another way to help you further reduce your uncertainty and to make your perceptions more accurate. The goal of perception checking is to further explore the thoughts and feelings of the other person, not to prove that your initial perception is correct. In its most basic form, perception checking consists of two steps:

■ Describe what you see or hear or, better, what you *think* is happening. Try to do this as descriptively (not evaluatively) as you can. Sometimes you may wish to offer several possibilities: "You've called me from work a lot this week. You seem concerned that everything is all right at home" or "You haven't wanted to talk with me all week. You say that my work is fine but you don't seem to want to give me the same responsibilities that other editorial assistants have."

■ Seek confirmation: ask the other person if your description is accurate. Don't try to read the thoughts and feelings of another person just from observing his or her behaviours. Regardless of how many behaviours you observe and how carefully you examine them, you can only guess what is going on in someone's mind. So be careful that your request for confirmation doesn't sound as though you already know the answer. Avoid phrasing your questions defensively, as in, "You really don't want to go out, do you? I knew you didn't when you turned on that lousy television." Instead, ask for confirmation in as supportive a way as possible: "Would you rather watch TV?" or "Are you worried about me or the kids?" or "Are you displeased with my work? Is there anything I can do to improve my job performance?"

INCREASE YOUR CULTURAL SENSITIVITY Becoming aware of and being sensitive to cultural differences will help increase your accuracy in perception. For example, Russian or Chinese artists such as ballet dancers will often applaud their audience by clapping. Canadian audiences seeing this may interpret this as egotistical. Similarly, a German man will enter a restaurant before the woman in order to see whether the place is respectable enough for the woman to enter. This simple custom can easily be interpreted as rude when viewed by people from cultures in which it's considered courteous for the woman to enter first (Axtell, 1994, 2007).

Cultural sensitivity will help you exercise caution in decoding the nonverbal behaviours of others, especially important perhaps in deciphering facial expressions. For example, it's easier to interpret the facial expressions of members of your own culture than those of members of other cultures (Weathers, Frank, & Spell, 2002). This "in-group advantage" will assist your perceptional accuracy for members of your own culture but will often hinder your accuracy for members of other cultures, especially if you assume that all people express themselves similarly (Elfenbein & Ambady, 2002). The suggestions for improving intercultural communication offered in Chapter 2 are applicable to increasing your cultural sensitivity in perception.

SKILL-BUILDING EXERCISE

Explaining Your Perceptions

Complete the following table by providing a description of how you perceive each incident and how you'd go about seeking confirmation. If you have several possible explanations for the incident, describe each of these in the second column. In the third column, indicate the choices you have for seeking clarification of your initial impressions—what are your choices for asking for clarification?

Incident	Your Perceptions and Possible Interpretations or Meanings	Choices for Seeking Clarification
You've extended an invitation to a classmate to be a Facebook friend but have heard nothing back.		
Your manager at work seems to spend a lot of time with your peers but very little time with you. You're concerned about the impression you're making.		
The person you've been dating for the past several months has stopped calling for a date. The messages have become fewer and less personal.		

Can you define the factors that influence interpersonal perception (self-fulfilling prophecy, personality theory, perceptual accentuation, primacy–recency, consistency, and the attribution of control)? Can you apply the skills for increasing your accuracy in impression formation?

IMPRESSION MANAGEMENT: GOALS AND STRATEGIES

Impression management (some writers use the term *self-presentation* or *identity management*) refers to the processes you go through to create the impression you want the other person to have of you.

Impression management is largely the result of the messages you communicate. In the same way that you form impressions of others largely on the basis of how they communicate (verbally and nonverbally), you also communicate an impression of yourself through what you say (your verbal messages), how you act and dress, and even how you decorate your office or apartment (your nonverbal messages). Communication messages, however, aren't the only means for impression formation and management. For example, you also judge others by the people with whom they associate, the number of friends they have on their social media site, their Twitter score, their financial status, or their ethnicity or gender. Or you might rely on what others have said or posted about the person and form impressions that are consistent with these comments.

Part of the art of interpersonal communication is to be able to manage the impressions you give to others. Mastering the art of impression management will enable you to present yourself as you want others to see you, at least to some extent.

The strategies you use to achieve this desired impression will naturally depend on your specific goal. Here are seven major interpersonal communication goals and their corresponding strategies.

To Be Liked: Affinity-Seeking and Politeness Strategies

If you want to be liked—say you're new at school or on the job and you want to be well liked, included in the activities of other students or work associates, and thought of highly by these other people—you will likely use affinity-seeking strategies and politeness strategies.

AFFINITY-SEEKING STRATEGIES   As you can see from the list of **affinity-seeking strategies** that follows, their use is likely to increase your chances of being liked (Bell & Daly, 1984). Such strategies are especially important in initial interactions, and their use has even been found to increase student motivation when used by teachers (Martin & Rubin, 1994; Myers & Zhong, 2004; Wrench, McCroskey, & Richmond, 2008).

- Be of help to the Other (the other person).
- Present yourself as comfortable and relaxed when with the Other.
- Follow the cultural rules for polite, cooperative conversation with the Other.
- Appear active, enthusiastic, and dynamic.
- Stimulate and encourage the Other to talk about himself or herself; reinforce disclosures and contributions of the Other.
- Include the Other in your social activities and groupings.
- Listen to the Other attentively and actively.
- Communicate interest in the Other.
- Appear optimistic and positive rather than pessimistic and negative.
- Show respect for the Other.
- Communicate warmth and empathy to the Other.
- Demonstrate that you share significant attitudes and values with the Other.
- Communicate supportiveness of the Other's interpersonal interactions.

Although this research was conducted before social media became important ways to communicate, you can easily see how the same strategies could be used in online communication. For example, you can post photos to show that you're active and enthusiastic;

you can follow the rules for polite interaction by giving "likes" and "+1s" to others; and you can communicate interest in the other person by inviting him or her to hang out or join a group, by commenting on a post, or by retweeting. Not surprisingly, plain old flattery goes a long way toward making you liked. Flattery has been found to increase your chances for success in a job interview, increase the tip a customer is likely to leave, and even increase the credibility you're likely to be seen as having (Sieter, 2007; Varma, Toh, & Pichler, 2006; Vonk, 2002).

There is also, however, a negative effect that can result from the use of affinity-seeking strategies—as there is for all of these impression-management strategies. Using affinity-seeking strategies too often or in ways that appear insincere may lead people to see you as trying to ingratiate yourself for your own advantage and not really meaning "to be nice."

POLITENESS STRATEGIES We can view politeness strategies, which are often used to make ourselves appear likeable, in terms of negative and positive types (Brown & Levinson, 1987; Goffman, 1967; Goldsmith, 2007; Holmes, 1995). Both of these types of politeness are responsive to two needs we each have:

- **positive face**—the desire to be viewed positively by others, to be thought of favourably
- **negative face**—the desire to be autonomous, to have the right to do as we wish

In the context of this text, politeness in interpersonal communication refers to behaviour that allows others to maintain both positive and negative face, and impoliteness refers to behaviours that attack either positive face (for example, you criticize someone) or negative face (for example, you make demands on someone).

To help another person maintain a *positive face*, you speak respectfully to and about the person, you give the person your full attention, and you say "Excuse me" when appropriate. In short, you treat the person as you would want to be treated. In this way, you allow the person to maintain a positive face through what is called *positive politeness*. You *attack* the person's positive face when you speak disrespectfully about the

Face to Face

You've been communicating with Pat over the internet for the past seven months, and you've finally decided to meet for coffee. You really want Pat to like you. What are some impression-management strategies you might use to get Pat to like you? What messages would you be sure not to communicate?

ETHICAL MESSAGES

The Ethics of Impression Management

Impression management strategies may also be used unethically and for less-than-noble purposes. As you read these several examples, ask yourself at what point impression management strategies become unethical.

- People who use affinity-seeking strategies to get you to like them so that they can extract favours from you.
- People who present themselves as credible (as being competent, moral, and charismatic) when in fact they are not.
- People who use self-handicapping strategies to get you to see their behaviour from a perspective that benefits them rather than you.
- People who use self-deprecating strategies to get someone to do what they should be doing.
- People who use self-monitoring strategies to present a more polished image than one that might come out without this self-monitoring.
- People who use influence strategies to deceive and for self-gain.

- People who use image-confirming strategies to exaggerate their positive and minimize their negative qualities.

Ethical Choice Point

You're ready to join one (perhaps several) online dating services. You need to write your profile and are wondering whether, since everyone (or nearly everyone) exaggerates, you shouldn't also. Specifically, you're considering saying that you earn a very good salary (actually, it's not so great, but you're hoping for a promotion), are twenty pounds lighter (actually, you intend to lose weight), and own a condo (actually, that's a goal once you get the promotion and save enough for a down payment). If you don't exaggerate, you reason, you'll disadvantage yourself and not meet the people you want to meet. Also, you figure that people expect you to exaggerate and assume that you're probably a lot less ideal than your profile would indicate. Would this be ethical?

INTERPERSONAL CHOICE POINT

Like and Unlike

Social media sites generally emphasize positiveness, and so there's a "like" on Facebook and a "+1" on Google+ but no "unlike" and no "–1," though there is a "thumbs up" and a "thumbs down" on StumbleUpon and YouTube and "+1" and a "–1" on Reddit. What are some other things you might do to signal online positiveness? How might you signal negative reactions?

person, ignore the person or the person's comments, and fail to use the appropriate expressions of politeness such as "thank you" and "please."

To help another person maintain a *negative face*, you respect the person's right to be autonomous and so you request rather than demand that he or she do something. You might also give the person an "out" when making a request, allowing the person to reject your request if that is what the person wants. And so you say, "If this is a bad time, please tell me, but I'm really strapped and could use a loan of $100" rather than "Lend me $100" or "You have to lend me $100." In this way, you enable the person to maintain negative face through what is called *negative politeness*.

Of course, we do this almost automatically; asking for a favour without any consideration for the person's negative face needs would seem totally insensitive. In most situations, however, this type of attack on negative face often appears in more subtle forms. To use Deborah Tannen's (2006) example, your mother's saying "Are you going to wear *that*?" attacks negative face by criticizing or challenging your autonomy. This comment also attacks positive face by questioning your ability to dress properly.

To Be Believed: Credibility Strategies

If you were a politician and wanted people to vote for you, at least part of your strategy would involve attempts to establish your **credibility** (which consists of your competence, character, and charisma). For example, to establish your competence, you might mention your great educational background or the courses you took that qualify you as an expert. Or you can post a photo with a Dalhousie parchment on the wall. To establish that you're of good character, you might mention how fair and honest you are, the causes you support, or your concern for those less fortunate. And to establish your charisma—your take-charge, positive personality—you might demonstrate enthusiasm in your face-to-face interactions as well as in your posts and in your photos, be emphatic, or focus on the positive while minimizing the negative.

Of course, if you stress your competence, character, and charisma too much, you risk being perceived as someone who's afraid of being seen as lacking these very qualities that you seem too eager to present to others. Generally, people who are truly competent need to say little directly about their own competence; their knowledgeable, insightful, and appropriate messages will reveal that competence.

To Hide Faults: Self-Monitoring Strategies

Much impression management is devoted not merely to presenting a positive image but to suppressing the negative, or using **self-monitoring strategies**. Here you carefully monitor (self-censor) what you say or do. You avoid your normal slang so as to make your colleagues think more highly of you; you avoid chewing gum so that you don't look juvenile or unprofessional; you avoid posting the photos from the last party you attended. While you readily disclose favourable parts of your experience, you actively hide the unfavourable parts.

However, if you self-monitor too often or too obviously, you risk being seen as someone unwilling to reveal himself or herself and perhaps not sufficiently trusting of others to feel comfortable disclosing your weaknesses as well as your strengths. In more extreme cases, you may be seen as dishonest, as hiding your true self, or as trying to fool other people.

To Be Followed: Influencing Strategies

In many instances, you'll want to get people to see you as a leader, as one to be followed in thought and perhaps in behaviour. Here you can use a variety of **influencing strategies**. One set of such strategies are those normally grouped under power and identified in Chapter 1. And so, for example, you'd stress your knowledge (information power), your expertise (expert power), or your right to lead by virtue of your position as, say, a doctor or judge or accountant (legitimate power).

SKILL-BUILDING EXERCISE

Applying Impression Management Strategies

Here are a few interpersonal situations in which you might want to use impression-management strategies. Identify at least two impression-management strategies you could use to achieve your goals in each of these situations.

1. You're interviewing for a job; you want to be seen as credible and as a good team player.
2. Your term paper isn't up to par; you don't want your instructor to think this is the level at which you normally function.
3. You've just started at a new school and you want to be careful not to make a fool of yourself—as you had at your previous school.
4. You're a police officer assigned to a neighbourhood patrol; you want to be seen as firm but approachable.

Everyone uses impression-management strategies; using them effectively and ethically isn't always easy, but it's almost always an available choice.

Influencing strategies can also easily backfire. If your influence attempts fail—for whatever reason—you will lose general influence. If you're seen as someone who's influencing others for self-gain, your persuasive attempts are likely to be rejected and perhaps seen as self-serving and resented.

To Confirm Self-Image: Image-Confirming Strategies

At times, you communicate to confirm your self-image, and so you'll use **image-confirming strategies**. If you see yourself as the life of the party, you'll tell jokes, post photos in which you are in fact the life of the party, and try to amuse people. At the same time that you confirm your own self-image, you also let others know that this is who you are, this is how you want to be seen. And, while you reveal aspects of yourself that confirm your desired image, you actively suppress revealing aspects of yourself that would disconfirm this image. Unfavourable wall postings, for example, are quickly removed.

If you use image-confirming strategies too frequently, you risk being seen as "too perfect to be for real." If you try to project this all-positive image, it's likely to turn people off—people want to see their friends and associates as being human, as having some faults, some imperfections. Moreover, image-confirming strategies invariably involve your talking about yourself, and with that comes the risk of being seen as self-absorbed.

Knowledge of these impression-management strategies and the ways in which they're effective and ineffective will give you a greater number of choices for achieving such widely diverse goals as being liked, being believed, hiding faults, being followed, and confirming your self-image.

Can you explain and give examples of the strategies of impression management for being liked, being believed, hiding faults, influencing others, and confirming your image? Can you apply the skills for effective (and ethical) impression management?

Managing Apprehension

Although most of us suffer from some communication apprehension, we can successfully manage it and control it—at least to some degree. Here are some suggestions (Beatty, 1988; McCroskey, 1997; McCroskey & Richmond, 1996).

Acquire Communication Skills and Experience If we lack typing skills, we can hardly expect to type very well. Yet we rarely assume that a lack of interpersonal skills and experience can cause difficulty with communication and create apprehension. It can. After all, if you've never had a job interview and have no idea how to proceed, it's natural to feel apprehensive about your first interview. In your communication course, you're gaining the skills of effective interpersonal interaction. Engage in experiences—even if they prove difficult at first—to help you acquire the skills you need most. The more preparation and practice you put into something, the more comfortable you'll feel with it.

Focus on Success The more you perceive a situation as one in which others will evaluate you, the greater your apprehension will be (Beatty, 1988). Employment interviews and asking for a date, for example, are anxiety provoking, largely because they're highly evaluative. Your prior history in similar situations also influences the way you respond to new ones. Prior success generally (though not always) reduces apprehension. Prior failure generally (though not always) increases apprehension. If you see yourself succeeding, you'll stand a good chance of doing just that. So think positively. Visualize others giving you positive evaluations. Concentrate your energies on doing the best job you can in any situation you find yourself in. Practise your new skills and seek new experiences; these will increase your chances for success (Saboonchi, Lundh, & Ost, 1999). Remember to "protect yourself from perfection."

Reduce Unpredictability The more unpredictable the situation, the greater your apprehension is likely to be. Since new and ambiguous situations are unpredictable, you naturally become anxious. In managing apprehension, therefore, try to reduce any unpredictability. When you're familiar with the situation and with what is expected of you, you're better able to predict what will happen. This will reduce the ambiguity and perceived newness of the situation. So, for example, if you're going to ask the boss for a raise, become familiar with the situation to the greatest extent you can. If possible, sit in the chair you will sit in, then rehearse your statement of the reasons you deserve the raise and the way in which you'll present them.

Put Apprehension in Perspective Whenever you engage in a communication experience, remember that the world won't end if you don't succeed. Keep in mind entrepreneurs' advice to "fail forward and fail fast" and to learn from your failures in a positive way. Also remember that other people aren't able to perceive your apprehension as sharply as you do. You may feel dryness in your throat and a rapid heartbeat; however, no one will know this but you.

CANADIAN PROFILE: WRAP-UP

Craig and Marc Kielburger have devoted their lives to encouraging young people to think of the needs of others and to build their own sense of competence, confidence, and power so that they may make a difference. How is an understanding of self and others important for Craig and Marc so that they can have this life focus and do the work they do? How can concepts like Me to We and We Days help young people better develop their own sense of self and others? How does your own sense of self and of others support your personal goals and ambitions?

SUMMARY OF CONCEPTS AND SKILLS

This chapter looked at the self and perception in inter-personal communication, as well as at impression formation and impression management.

The Self in Interpersonal Communication

1. Self-concept is the image you have of who you are. Sources of self-concept include others' images of you, social comparisons, cultural teachings, and your own interpretations and evaluations.

2. Self-awareness is your knowledge of yourself, the extent to which you know who you are. A useful way of looking at self-awareness is with the Johari window, which consists of four parts. The open self holds information known to self and others; the blind self holds information known only to others; the hidden self holds information known only to self; and the unknown self holds information known to neither self nor others.

3. Self-esteem is the value you place on yourself, your perceived self-worth.

Perception in Interpersonal Communication

4. Perception is the process by which you become aware of objects and events in the external world.

5. Perception occurs in five stages: (1) stimulation, (2) organization, (3) interpretation–evaluation, (4) memory, and (5) recall.

Impression Formation

6. Six important processes influence the way you form impressions: self-fulfilling prophecies may influence the behaviours of others; personality theory allows you to conclude that certain characteristics go with certain other characteristics; primacy–recency may influence you to give extra importance to what occurs first (a primacy effect) or to what occurs last (a recency effect); the tendency to seek and expect consistency may influence you to see what is consistent and not to see what is inconsistent; and attributions of control, the process through which you try to understand the behaviours of others, are made in part on the basis of your judgment of controllability.

Impression Management: Goals and Strategies

7. Among the goals and strategies of impression management are to be liked (affinity-seeking and politeness strategies); to be believed (credibility strategies that establish your competence, character, and charisma); to hide faults (self-monitoring strategies); to be followed (influencing strategies); and to confirm one's self-image (image-confirming strategies).

8. Each of these impression-management strategies can backfire and give others negative impressions. And each of these strategies may be used to reveal your true self or to present a false self and deceive others in the process.

This chapter also considered some useful skills. As you review these skills, check those you wish to work on.

_____ 1. *Self-awareness.* To increase self-awareness, ask yourself about yourself, listen to others, actively seek information about yourself, see your different selves, and increase your open self.

_____ 2. *Self-esteem.* To increase self-esteem, try attacking your self-destructive beliefs, using affirmative self-talk, seeking out nourishing people, and working on projects that will result in success or in which you can learn from failure. Most importantly, develop interpersonal competence.

_____ 3. *Selective perception.* Recognize the influence that your own selective attention and selective exposure have on your perceptual accuracy.

_____ 4. *Impression formation.* In forming impressions, take into consideration the possible influence of your own self-fulfilling prophecies, personality theories, tendencies to favour primacy or recency, expectations of consistency, and the attribution errors (self-serving bias, overattribution, and the fundamental attribution error) and adjust your perceptions accordingly.

_____ 5. *Perceptual accuracy.* To increase your accuracy in impression formation, analyze your impressions (recognize your role in perception, avoid early conclusions and mind-reading, and beware of the just-world assumptions), reduce uncertainty, check your perceptions, and become culturally sensitive by recognizing the differences between you and others as well as the differences among people from other cultures.

_____ 6. *Impression management.* Use the strategies of impression management ethically and with a clear understanding of their potential to backfire.

VOCABULARY QUIZ: The Language of the Self and Perception

Match the terms of self and perception with their definitions. Record the number of the definition next to the appropriate term.

_____ open self (51)
_____ self-esteem (53)
_____ the hidden self (51)
_____ self-monitoring strategies (68)
_____ affinity-seeking strategies (66)
_____ perception checking (64)
_____ just-world hypothesis (64)
_____ fundamental attribution error (63)
_____ halo effect (61)
_____ impression management (66)

1. Overvaluing internal factors and undervaluing external factors in impression formation.
2. Techniques designed to hide certain information from others.
3. The belief that good things happen to good people and bad things to bad people.
4. A process of gaining confirmation for your impressions.
5. The value you place on yourself.
6. The part of you that you and others know about yourself.
7. Seeing good things in people we have already evaluated positively.
8. Techniques to make you appear more likeable.
9. The processes by which one controls his or her desired impression.
10. That part of yourself that you normally do not reveal to others.

These 10 terms and additional terms used in this chapter can be found in the glossary.

CHAPTER

4

Listening in Interpersonal Communication

CANADIAN PROFILE: Mayor Naheed Nenshi

Todd Korol/Reuters/Landov

In 2010, Naheed Nenshi was elected mayor of Calgary on a wave of social media campaigning and support. Two years later, disaster struck the city when its downtown, located between two rivers, experienced massive flooding—the most costly natural disaster in Canadian history. But the city banded together in support of communities and individuals, and in only 10 days, the "Come Hell or High Water" campaign rallied thousands of volunteers to repair the heavily flood-damaged Stampede Grounds and host the "World's Largest Outdoor Show" on schedule. And throughout the emergency, Nenshi demonstrated the power of listening. As the *Globe and Mail* (Bennett, 2014) reported,

He worked for 43 straight hours without sleep: tweeting, imploring, directing, assisting, cheering on and cheering up residents who saw homes ruined and possessions literally float away. He was cheerleader, director, benevolent scolder. "Help your neighbours," he exhorted, "be it with a shovel or a ride. Hug your emergency providers." His new "home" became the back seat of helicopters or in front of news cameras. He provided updates several times a day—one in the middle of the night. He used Twitter to get the word out. Wellwishers finally started a social media movement to get him to go home and take a nap.

Mayor Nenshi is indeed a master of social media; he uses it to communicate with Calgarians, building relationships one person and one tweet at a time. In an era where politicians often find themselves distanced from those they represent, Naheed Nenshi seems to have found a way to engage with citizens both in person and on social media—he won his second term by a landslide.

As you work through this chapter, consider what elements of powerful listening Naheed Nenshi appears to understand and use. How does social media fit into listening? What techniques would you like to learn and use?

LEARNING OBJECTIVES *After reading this chapter, you should be able to:*

1. Listen more effectively at each of the five stages of listening.

2. Describe the four major barriers to effective listening, and apply the suggestions for reducing those barriers as you practise listening.

3. Identify the five styles of listening, and select and use the appropriate style for specific situations.

4. Explain the major cultural and gender differences found in listening, and apply your understanding of these differences as you listen.

5. Use appropriate paraphrasing, questioning, and expressions of empathy as you listen.

Television talk shows often demonstrate the principles of effective listening, and when they do, they're enjoyable to watch. But it's even more impressive to see a Canadian celebrity using his listening skills for an important social cause, as when George Stroumboulopoulos takes part in a campaign to fight world hunger. What makes you think he's listening carefully to the person he's with?

In light of Facebook, Twitter, wikis, blogs, and other social media, we need to expand the traditional definition of listening as the receiving and processing of auditory signals. If posting messages on social media sites is part of interpersonal communication (which it surely is), then reading and responding to these messages must also be part of communication and most logically a part of listening. **Listening**, then, may be defined as *the process of receiving, understanding, remembering, evaluating, and responding to verbal and/or nonverbal messages.*

Regardless of what you do, listening will prove a crucial communication component and will serve both work-related and relationship functions. At work, whether you're a temporary intern or a high-level executive, you need to listen if you're going to function effectively. If you're not convinced of this, take a look at the many websites (for example, the Conference Board of Canada's) that talk about the skills needed for success in today's workplace.

Listening also is crucial to developing and maintaining relationships of all kinds. You expect a friends or romantic partners to listen to you, and you're expected to listen to them in turn. Listening also plays a significant role in the management of interpersonal conflict; listening effectively to the other person, even during a heated argument, will go a long way toward helping you manage the conflict and preventing it from escalating into a major blowup.

Effective listening will result in an increase in your ability to learn, and to relate to and influence others. You will hear more, empathize more, and come to understand others more deeply. In turn, you will profit from the insights of others, acquire more useful information on the basis of which to make decisions, and find that people who know how to listen gain respect and esteem from others. To truly listen to a person is perhaps the most precious gift one can give, whether to a loved one, a friend, or simply another human being (Wyshogrod, 2014).

Here we look at the stages of the listening process, the major barriers to listening effectiveness, the varied styles of listening for different situations, and some cultural and gender differences in listening.

THE STAGES OF LISTENING

Listening is a five-stage process of (1) receiving, (2) understanding, (3) remembering, (4) evaluating, and (5) responding to verbal and/or nonverbal messages, as represented in Figure 4.1. All five stages overlap. When you listen, you're performing all five processes at essentially the same time. For example, when listening in conversation, you're not only processing what you hear for understanding, but you're also putting it into memory storage, critically evaluating what was said, and responding (nonverbally and perhaps with verbal messages as well).

As you'll see from the following discussion, listening involves a collection of skills that work together at each of these five stages. Listening can go wrong at any stage; by the same token, you can enhance your listening ability by strengthening the skills needed for each step of the process.

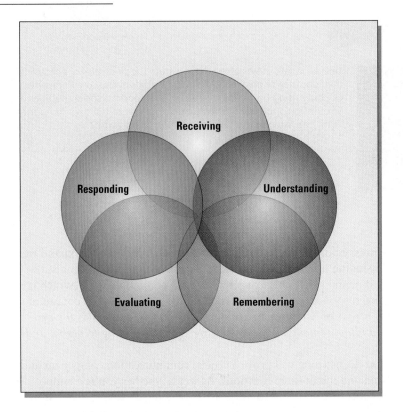

FIGURE 4.1

The Five Stages of Listening

Both this model and the suggestions for listening improvement throughout this chapter draw on theories and models that listening researchers have developed (for example, Barker & Gaut, 2002; Brownell, 2010; Nichols, 1995; Nichols & Stevens, 1957; Steil, Barker, & Watson, 1983).

Source: The Five Stages of Listening. ISBN: 0205688640. Copyright © 2011, 2008 by Pearson Education, Inc.

Receiving

Listening begins, but doesn't end, with receiving messages the speaker sends. In listening, you receive both the verbal and the nonverbal messages—not only the words but also the gestures, facial expressions, variations in volume and rate, accompanying photos, and lots more.

The following suggestions should help you receive messages more effectively:

- *Focus attention* on the speaker's verbal and nonverbal messages, on both what is said and what is not said, rather than on how you'll respond.
- *Maintain your role* as listener, and avoid interrupting the speaker until he or she is finished.
- *Avoid assuming that you understand* what the speaker is going to say before he or she actually says it.
- *Practise techniques* that minimize "internal and external" noise and distractions.

Understanding

Understanding occurs when you learn what the speaker means or when the meaning you get is essentially the same as what the speaker sent. Understanding includes both the thoughts that are expressed and the emotional tone that accompanies them; for example, the urgency or the joy or the sorrow expressed in the message.

GUIDELINES FOR ACCESSIBLE COMMUNICATION

There is a range of conditions that can interfere with a person's ability to communicate effectively, and gaining an understanding of these conditions can be helpful. One useful handbook (Accessibility Directorate of Ontario, 2009) features a number of tips and guidelines for ensuring access to communication for those with communication disabilities. For example, if you're communicating with a person who is deaf or has a hearing loss, consider the following suggestions:

- Make sure the person is looking at you before you start talking and that he or she can see your mouth.
- Find out what the person wants to use when communicating with you. He or she may want to use his or her own amplifier or communication device or may request that you write down what you're saying.
- Speak clearly and at a moderate pace; don't shout.
- Upon request, arrange to have a sign language interpreter present.

TABLE 4.1

LISTENING IN THE CLASSROOM

In addition to the general guidelines for listening noted throughout this chapter, here are a few suggestions for making your listening for understanding in the classroom more effective.

General Suggestions	Specific Suggestions
Prepare yourself to listen.	Sit up front where you can see your instructor and any visual aids clearly and comfortably. Remember that you listen with your eyes as well as your ears.
Avoid distractions.	Avoid mental daydreaming, and put away physical distractions like your laptop, smartphone, or newspaper.
Pay special attention to the introduction.	Listen for orienting remarks and for key words and phrases such as "major reasons," "three main causes," and "first." These cues will help you outline the lecture.
Take notes in outline form.	Listen for headings, and then use these as major topics in your outline. When the instructor says, "There are four kinds of noise," you have your heading and can record a numbered list of four kinds of noise.
Assume relevance.	A piece of information may eventually prove irrelevant (unfortunately), but if you listen with the assumption of irrelevancy, you'll never hear anything relevant.
Listen for understanding.	Avoid taking issue with what is said until you understand fully and then, of course, take issue if you wish. But, generally, don't waste listening time rehearsing your responses; you risk missing additional explanation or qualification.

Currently, of course, a large part of your listening will take place in the classroom—listening to the instructor and to other students, essentially for understanding. (See Table 4.1.)

In understanding, try to

- *see the speaker's messages from the speaker's point of view.* Avoid judging the message until you've fully understood it—as the speaker intended it.
- *rephrase/paraphrase* the speaker's ideas in your own words.
- *ask questions* to clarify or to secure additional details or examples if necessary.

Remembering

Effective listening depends on remembering. For example, when Kaya says she's planning to buy a new car, the effective listener remembers this and at a later meeting asks about the car. When Joe says his mother is ill, the effective listener remembers this and inquires about her health later in the week.

DEVELOPING LANGUAGE AND COMMUNICATION SKILLS

Developing Vocabulary

Babies begin communicating at birth by crying. They start to coo between six and eight weeks of age and, at 16 weeks, start to laugh and experiment with vocal play. Between six and nine months old, children are babbling and will generally speak their first word around their first birthday. By the time they're 18 months old or so, they can say about 50 words but are likely to understand three times as many. As they move toward school age, they will generally add 10 to 20 new words to their vocabulary each week; elementary schoolchildren learn an average of 20 new words a day. Sadly, as we get older, we lose the ability to learn words as quickly as children do—imagine how well you'd do in college or university if you were able to learn that many new terms each week. If you'd like to learn more, go to YouTube and search for "The Postal Code Lottery."

In some small-group and public speaking situations, you can augment your memory by taking notes or by taping the messages. And in many work situations, taking notes is common and may even be expected. In most interpersonal communication situations, however, note taking is inappropriate—although you often do write down a telephone number, an appointment, or directions.

Perhaps the most important point to understand about memory is that what you remember isn't what was said but what you *remember* was said. Memory for speech isn't reproductive; that is, you don't simply reproduce in your memory what the speaker said. Rather, memory is reconstructive: you actually reconstruct the messages you hear into a system that makes sense to you.

If you want to remember what someone says or the names of various people, this information needs to pass from your **short-term memory** (the memory you use to, say, remember a phone number just long enough to write it down) into long-term memory. Short-term memory is very limited in capacity—you can hold only a small amount of information there. **Long-term memory** is unlimited. To facilitate the passage of information from short- to long-term memory, here are four suggestions:

- *Focus* your attention on the central ideas. Even in the most casual conversation, there are central ideas. Fix these in your mind. Avoid focusing on minor details, which often lead to detours in listening and in conversation.
- *Organize* what you hear; summarize the message in a more easily retained form. Chunk the message into categories; for example, if you want to remember 15 or 20 items to buy in the supermarket, you'll remember more if you group them into chunks—say, produce, canned goods, and meats.
- *Unite* the new with the old; relate new information to what you already know. Avoid treating new information as totally apart from all else you know. There's probably some relationship, and if you identify it, you're more likely to remember the new material.
- *Repeat* names and key concepts to yourself or, if appropriate, aloud. By repeating the names or key concepts, you rehearse them and, as a result, learn and remember them. If you're introduced to Alice, you'll stand a better chance of remembering her name if you say, "Hi, Alice" than if you say just "Hi."

Evaluating

Evaluating consists of judging messages in some way. At times you may try to evaluate the speaker's underlying intent, often without conscious awareness. For example, Elaine tells you that she's up for a promotion and is really excited about it. You may then try to judge her intention. Does she want you to use your influence with the company president? Is she preoccupied with her accomplishment and thus telling everyone about it? Is she looking for a pat on the back? Generally, if you know the person well, you'll be able to identify the intention and therefore be able to respond appropriately.

In evaluating,

- *resist evaluation* until you fully understand the speaker's point of view.
- *assume that the speaker is a person of goodwill.* Give the speaker the benefit of any doubt by asking for clarification on issues that you feel you must object to.
- *distinguish facts from opinions* and personal interpretations and identify any biases, self-interests, or prejudices that may lead the speaker to slant unfairly what is presented.

So while many people might think of listening as sitting quietly and attending while another person is talking, listening is in fact a very active process. Note that Figure 4.2 includes the same outer circles representing the five stages of listening that appeared in

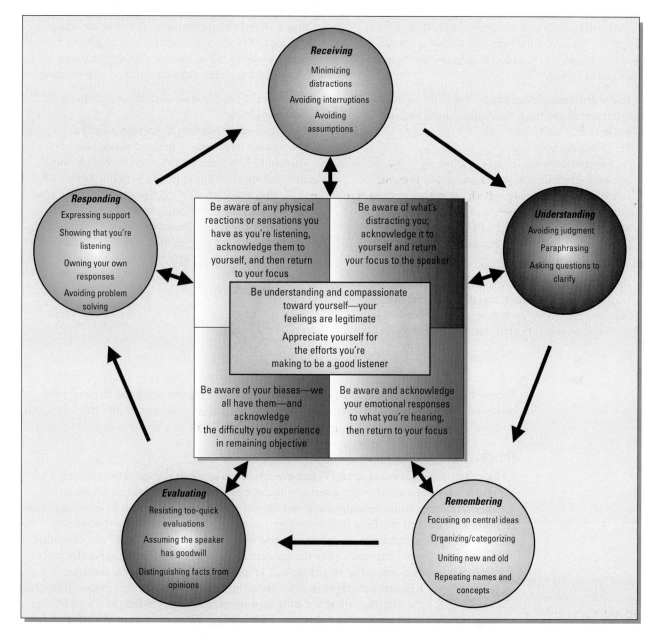

FIGURE 4.2

The Dynamic Process of Listening: Incorporating Mindfulness into the Stages of Listening

Within the five circles representing the stages of listening, the squares depict the physical, emotional, and cognitive processes of active, mindful listening in which the thoughts and feelings of both listener and speaker are respected (Wyshogrod, 2014).

Source: Adapted by Shimoni and Wyshogrod (2014).

MINDFUL LISTENING

Debbi Cooper

Dr. Dina Wyshogrod is a practising clinical psychologist and an international trainer in Mindfulness-Based Stress Reduction (MBSR). This program teaches people how to listen to themselves, to become aware of the thoughts and feelings that are interfering with their being totally present in the moment. Knowing how to really listen to oneself may be very helpful in learning to really listen to others.

Q: You're a trained clinical psychologist and an author. What would you say is the most valuable skill you use in your work?

A: Being able to really listen.
Listening to someone, deeply, completely, is one of the most precious gifts you can ever give that person. It's not the special province of psychologists or other healing professionals; many people have the ability to listen deeply and fully to others. It is a skill that can be developed with training and practice.

Q: So what does "listening deeply" mean?
First, the most obvious: eliminating all external distractions. Not multitasking. Letting the answering machine field your calls. Turning off your mobile phone (not just putting it on vibrate) or the iPod. Make a conscious intention to focus fully on the person in front of you. Second, distractions don't arise only from outside, they arise from within: our roving minds scamper like monkeys, remembering things we have to do later, rehashing past events, scampering from association to association just as monkeys swing from branch to branch. This kind of internal agitation is perfectly normal; it's part of being human, so it's nothing we need to criticize ourselves for. At the same time, it requires that we train our minds to settle down, to become quieter, to become still, so that, sitting together, I can hear *you* talking to *me*, without all that internal noise. It's like getting a clear radio transmission with no static.

Q: What would you say is hardest about learning to genuinely listen?
The challenge in listening to someone else talk to you—about anything—is to stay focused and present and to bring your attention back when it wanders. We speak of this as giving someone our undivided attention. Our minds can wander because we're preoccupied with something in our own lives, or because the subject being described is painful for us to listen to and triggers our own emotional reactions. It's important to acknowledge these reactions, make a mental note of them, and then bring your attention back to the speaker.

Source: Dr. Dina Wyshogrod

Figure 4.1; these are now accompanied by inner squares representing the internal processes related to self-awareness and self-acceptance that enhance our ability to truly listen.

Responding

Responding occurs in two forms: (1) responses you make while the speaker is talking and (2) responses you make after the speaker has stopped talking. Responses made while the speaker is talking should be supportive and should acknowledge that you're listening. These responses are **backchannelling cues:** messages (words and gestures) that let the speaker know you're paying attention, as when you nod in agreement or say, "I see" or "Uh-huh."

Responses after the speaker has stopped talking are generally more elaborate, and might include empathy ("I know how you must feel"); requests for clarification ("Do you mean this new health plan will replace the old plan, or will it only be a supplement?"); challenges ("I think you may need to provide more evidence"); and/or agreement ("You're absolutely right, and I'll support your proposal when it comes up for a vote"). You can improve this responding phase of listening if you

- *express support* and understanding for the speaker throughout the conversation.
- *use varied cues that say "I'm listening"* (for example, nodding, using appropriate facial expressions, or saying "I see").

INTERPERSONAL CHOICE POINT

Giving Anti-Listening Cues

One of your friends is a storyteller; instead of talking about the world and about people, he tells endless stories—about things that happened a long time ago that he finds funny (though no one else does). You just can't deal with this any longer. What are some options you have for ending this kind of "conversation"?

TABLE 4.2

INEFFECTIVE AND EFFECTIVE LISTENING

Listening Stage	Ineffective Listening	Effective Listening
At the **receiving** stage, you note not only what is said (verbally and nonverbally) but also what is omitted.	Attention wanders, distractions are attended to	1. **Focus your attention** on the speaker's verbal and nonverbal messages. 2. **Avoid distractions** in the environment. 3. **Maintain your role as listener** and avoid interrupting.
Understanding is the stage at which you learn what the speaker means, the stage at which you grasp both the thoughts and the emotions expressed.	Assume you understand what the speaker is going to say; interpret the speaker's message from your own point of view; make no attempt to seek clarification	1. **Avoid assuming you understand** what the speaker is going to say before he or she actually says it. 2. **See the speaker's messages from the speaker's point of view.** 3. **Ask questions** for clarification. 4. **Rephrase (paraphrase)** the speaker's ideas in your own words.
Effective listening depends on **remembering**.	Fail to distinguish between central and peripheral ideas	1. **Focus** your attention on the central ideas. 2. **Organize** what you hear. 3. **Unite** the new with the old. 4. **Rehearse;** repeat names and key concepts to yourself or, if appropriate, aloud.
Evaluating consists of judging the messages in some way.	Evaluate immediately; group facts and opinions together; fail to notice biases; influenced by fallacious reasoning	1. **Resist evaluation** until you fully understand the speaker's point of view. 2. **Distinguish facts from opinions** and personal interpretations by the speaker. 3. **Identify any biases,** self-interests, or prejudices in the speaker. 4. **Recognize some of the popular but fallacious forms of "reasoning"** speakers may employ, such as **name-calling, testimonial, and bandwagon.**
Responding occurs in two phases: responses you make while the speaker is talking and responses you make after the speaker has stopped talking.	Fail to give the speaker appropriate feedback	1. **Support the speaker.** 2. **Own your responses.** 3. **Resist "responding to another's feelings" with "solving the person's problems."** 4. **Focus on the other person.** 5. **Avoid being a thought-completing listener.**

- *own your own responses;* that is, state your thoughts and feelings as your own, using "I-messages"—for example, saying, "I don't agree" rather than "No one will agree with that."
- *avoid the common problem-causing listening responses* such as being static or overly expressive, giving feedback that is monotonous and not responsive to the messages, avoiding eye contact, or appearing preoccupied with, say, a cell phone.

Table 4.2 provides a comparison of effective and ineffective listening at each of these five stages.

Can you define *listening* and its five stages (receiving, understanding, remembering, evaluating, and responding)? Can you apply the skills for more effective listening that were recommended for each of these stages?

Some people, when they get older, lose some memory ability. But this happens far less than most people's stereotypes would suggest. What are your stereotypes of older people's listening abilities and habits?

auremar/Shutterstock

INTERPERSONAL CHOICE POINT

Ageist Language

At the organization where you work, ageist language is rampant in small groups but totally absent in formal meetings. You want to point out this hypocrisy but don't want to make enemies or have people think you're going to cause legal problems for them. What options do you have for accomplishing what you want but without incurring negative reactions?

LISTENING BARRIERS

In addition to practising the various skills for each stage of listening, consider some of the common general barriers to listening. Here are just four such barriers, along with suggestions for dealing with them as both listener and speaker, since both speaker and listener are responsible for effective listening.

Distractions: Physical and Mental

Physical barriers might include, for example, hearing impairment, a noisy environment, or loud music. Multitasking (say, watching TV, texting, and listening to someone) with the aim of being supportive simply doesn't work. As both listener and speaker, try to remove whatever physical barriers can be removed; for those that you can't remove, adjust your listening and speaking to lessen the effects as much as possible. As a listener, focus on the speaker; you can attend to the room and the other people later.

Mental distractions are in many ways similar to physical distractions; they get in the way of focused listening. These barriers often occur when you're thinking about your upcoming Saturday night date or becoming too emotional to think (and listen) clearly. In listening, recognize that you can think about your date later. In speaking, make what you say compelling and relevant to the listener.

Biases and Prejudices

In biased and prejudiced listening, you hear what the speaker is saying through stereotypes. This type of listening occurs when you listen differently to a person because of his or her race, affectional orientation, age, or gender when these characteristics are irrelevant to the message.

Such listening can occur in a wide variety of situations. For example, when you dismiss a valid argument or attribute validity to an invalid argument because the speaker is of a particular race, affectional orientation, age, or gender, you're listening with prejudice.

However, there are many instances in which these characteristics are pertinent to your evaluation of the message. For example, the sex of a speaker talking about pregnancy, fathering a child, birth control, or surrogate motherhood probably is, most would agree, relevant to the message. So in these cases, taking the gender of the speaker into consideration is not sexist listening. It is, however, sexist listening to assume that only one gender can be an authority on a particular topic or that one gender's opinions are without value. The same is true when listening through the filter of a person's race, affectional orientation, or age.

Lack of Appropriate Focus

Focusing on what a person is saying is obviously necessary for effective listening. And yet there are many influences that can lead you

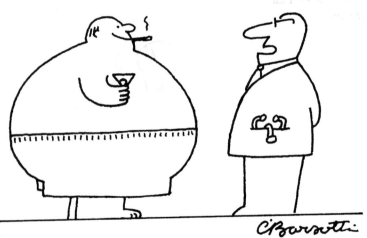

"All these years, and you haven't listened to a damn thing I've said, have you?"

Charles Barsotti/The New Yorker Collection/www.cartoonbank.com

ETHICAL MESSAGES

Ethical Listening

As a listener, you generally have at least three ethical obligations:

First, you generally owe the other person an honest hearing, without prejudgment, putting aside prejudices and preconceptions as best you can. At the same time, you owe the person your best effort at understanding emotionally as well as intellectually what he or she means. This doesn't mean, however, that there aren't situations when you don't owe the speaker a fair hearing.

Second, you generally owe the other person honest responses. Just as you should be honest with the listener when speaking, you should be honest with the speaker when listening. This means giving open and honest feedback and also reflecting honestly on the questions that the speaker raises. Again, this doesn't mean that there aren't situations in which you don't owe the speaker an honest response.

Third, you owe yourself the right to accept your responses to what you hear as normal, natural, and understandable. You won't always like what you hear—what you hear may bring up associations that are difficult, or that simply bore you. By recognizing and accepting your responses with empathy toward yourself, you'll be able to make space between what you hear (the stimulus) and how you choose to respond to the speaker.

These obligations, as you might have guessed, vary with the interpersonal relationship between yourself and the other person. If this other person is a life partner, then your obligations are considerable. If this other person is a stranger, your obligations are less. Generally, as the intimacy of a relationship increases, so do your obligations to serve as a supportive and honest listener.

Ethical Choice Point

Shawna and her partner, Driss, have lived together for two years. Whereas Shawna was raised in Canada, Driss arrived two years ago, a refugee from a part of the world that has undergone major conflict and much suffering. As they began to plan their future together, Driss feels that he should finally share the details of his past with Shawna. But Shawna hesitates, wondering if it may change her perception of him. Is there an ethical obligation here both to share and to listen?

---

astray. For example, listeners often get lost because they focus on irrelevancies—on, say, an especially vivid example that conjures up old memories. Try not to get detoured from the main idea; don't get hung up on unimportant details. Try to repeat the idea to yourself and see the details in relation to this main concept. As a speaker, try to avoid language or examples that may divert attention away from your main idea.

At times people will listen only for information that has an obvious relevance to them. But this type of listening only prevents you from expanding your horizons. And it's quite possible that information that you originally thought irrelevant will eventually prove helpful.

Avoid interpreting everything in terms of what it means to you; see other perspectives. As a speaker, be sure to make what you say relevant to your specific listener.

Another misplaced focus is often on the responses a listener is going to make while the speaker is still speaking. Anticipating how you're going to respond or what you're going to say (and even interrupting the speaker) just prevents you from hearing the message in full. Instead, make a mental note of something and then get back to listening. As a speaker, when you feel someone is preparing to argue with you, ask the person to hear you out: "I know you disagree with this, but let me finish and we'll get back to that."

Premature Judgment

Perhaps the most obvious form of premature judgment is assuming you know what the speaker is going to say—and so there's no need to really listen. Instead, let the speaker say what he or she is going to say before you decide that you already know it. As a speaker, of course, it's

Larry Williams/Corbis

VIEWPOINTS Listening Barriers

The four barriers discussed here are certainly not the only ones that get in the way of effective listening. What other types of barriers can you identify? Put differently, in what types of interpersonal situations do you have difficulty listening?

SKILL-BUILDING EXERCISE

Explaining the Barriers to Listening

Taking into consideration your own attitudes, beliefs, values, and opinions, what obstacles to listening would you identify for each of the following interpersonal situations?

1. Colleagues at work are discussing how they can persuade management to restrict the company gym to men only.
2. Students in your computer science class are talking about planting a virus in the college computer as a way of protesting recent decisions by the administration.
3. A campus religious group is conferring about its plan to prevent same-sex couples from attending the prom.

4. A group of faculty and students is discussing a campaign to prevent the military from recruiting on campus.

No one can listen apart from his or her own attitudes, beliefs, values, and opinions; these always get in the way of accurate listening. Your objective should be to become aware of them, acknowledge them to yourself, and then make a conscious effort to to minimize their interference with your listening.

often wise to assume that listeners will do exactly this, so it may be helpful to make clear that what you're saying will be unexpected.

A common listener reaction is to draw conclusions or judgments based on incomplete evidence. Sometimes listeners will stop listening after hearing, for example, an argument they disagree with or a sexist or culturally insensitive remark. Instead, this is a situation that calls for especially concentrated listening so that you don't rush to judgment. Wait for the evidence or argument; avoid making judgments before you gather all the information. Listen first, judge second. As a speaker, be aware of this tendency, and when you feel this is happening, ask for a suspension of judgment. A simple "Hear me out" is often sufficient to prevent a listener's too early judgment.

 Can you describe the four major barriers to effective listening (physical and mental distractions, biases and prejudices, lack of appropriate focus, and premature judgment)? Can you apply the suggestions for effectiveness in your own listening?

STYLES OF LISTENING EFFECTIVELY

Listening is situational (Brownell, 2010). As we've seen, the way you listen should depend on the situation you're in. You don't listen to a speech by the prime minister in the same way you listen to your friend telling you about the party you missed. At the least, you need to adjust your listening on the basis of (1) your purposes (are you listening to learn? to give comfort?) and (2) your knowledge of and relationship to the other person (does this person exaggerate or lie? or need support or perhaps a reality check?). The following discussion will provide specific suggestions for how to adjust your listening style and how to avoid the pitfalls of and barriers to ineffective listening. We'll look at five dimensions of listening: the empathic–objective, nonjudgmental–critical, surface–deep, polite–impolite, and active–inactive dimensions. Before doing so, take the accompanying self-test.

Empathic and Objective Listening

If you're going to understand what a person means and what a person is feeling, you need to listen with some degree of **empathy** (Rogers, 1970; Rogers & Farson, 1981). To empathize with others is to feel with them, to see the world as they see it, to feel what they feel. When you listen empathically as a neighbour tells of having her apartment burgled and all her prized possessions taken, you can share on some level the loss and

TEST YOURSELF

How Do You Listen?

Respond to each statement using the following scale:
1 = always, **2** = frequently, **3** = sometimes, **4** = seldom, and **5** = never.

_____ 1. I listen actively, communicate acceptance of the speaker, and prompt the speaker to further explore his or her thoughts.

_____ 2. I listen to what the speaker is saying and feeling; I try to feel what the speaker feels.

_____ 3. I listen without judging the speaker.

_____ 4. I listen to the literal meanings that a speaker communicates; I don't look too deeply into hidden meanings.

_____ 5. I listen without active involvement; I generally remain silent and take in what the other person is saying.

_____ 6. I listen objectively; I focus on the logic of the ideas rather than on the emotional meaning of the message.

_____ 7. I listen politely even to messages that contradict my attitudes and beliefs.

_____ 8. I'll interrupt a speaker when I have something really relevant to say.

_____ 9. I listen critically, evaluating the speaker and what the speaker is saying.

_____10. I look for the hidden meanings, the meanings that are revealed by subtle verbal or nonverbal cues.

How Did You Do? These statements focus on the ways of listening discussed in this chapter. All of these ways are appropriate at some times but not at other times. It depends. So the only responses that are really inappropriate are "always" and "never." Effective listening is listening that is tailored to the specific communication situation.

What Will You Do? Consider how you might use these statements to begin to improve your listening effectiveness. A good way to do this is to review these statements and identify situations in which each statement would be appropriate and situations in which each statement would be inappropriate.

---

emptiness she feels. Only when you achieve empathy can you fully understand another person's meaning. Empathic listening will also help you enhance your relationships (Barrett & Godfrey, 1988; Snyder, 1992).

Although empathic listening is the preferred mode of responding in most communication situations, there are times when you need to go beyond it and measure the speaker's meanings and feelings against some objective reality. For example, while it's important to listen to Peter tell you how the entire world hates him and to understand how he feels and why he feels this way, you need to then look a bit more objectively at the situation and perhaps see Peter's paranoia or self-hatred. Sometimes you have to put your empathic responses aside and listen with objectivity and detachment.

In adjusting your empathic and objective listening focus, keep the following recommendations in mind.

- *See from the speaker's point of view.* See the sequence of events as the speaker does, and try to figure out how this perspective can influence what the speaker says and does.
- *Engage in equal, two-way conversation.* To encourage openness and empathy, try to eliminate any physical or psychological barriers to equality. For example, step from behind the large desk separating you from your employees. Avoid interrupting the speaker—a sign that you think what you have to say is more important.

Trappe/Caro/Alamy

VIEWPOINTS Empathy

Sometimes we expect people to have more empathy for those who've faced challenges similar to ones they've faced themselves. In fact, this isn't always the case. People who have struggled hard to improve their economic status and move away from poverty sometimes find it difficult to empathize with poor people who aren't able to overcome these challenges.

INTERPERSONAL CHOICE POINT

Listening Empathically

Your mother has been having a difficult time at work. She was recently passed up for a promotion and received one of the lowest merit raises given in the company. "I'm not sure what I did wrong," she tells you. "I do my work, mind my own business, don't take my sick days like everyone else. How could they give that promotion to Helen, who's only been with the company for two years? Maybe I should just quit." What can you do and say that will demonstrate empathic listening?

INTERPERSONAL CHOICE POINT

Relationship Listening

A young nephew tells you that he can't talk with his parents. No matter how hard he tries, they don't listen. "I tried to tell them that I can't play baseball and I don't want to play baseball," he confides. "But they ignore me and tell me that all I need is practice." What are some of the things you can say or do that will show your nephew that you're listening?

- *Seek to understand both thoughts and feelings.* Don't consider your listening task finished until you've understood what the speaker is feeling as well as what he or she is thinking.
- *Avoid offensive listening*—the tendency to listen to bits and pieces of information that will enable you to attack the speaker or find fault with something the speaker has said (Floyd, 1985).
- *Strive to be objective* when listening to friends or foes alike. Your attitudes may lead you to distort messages—to block out positive messages about a foe or negative messages about a friend. Guard against "expectancy hearing," in which you fail to hear what the speaker is really saying and instead hear what you expect.

Nonjudgmental and Critical Listening

Effective listening includes both *nonjudgmental* and *critical* responses. You need to listen *nonjudgmentally*—with an open mind and with a view toward understanding. But you also need to listen *critically*—with a view toward making some kind of evaluation or judgment. Clearly, it's important to listen first for understanding while suspending judgment. Only after you've fully understood the relevant messages should you evaluate or judge.

Supplement nonjudgmental listening with critical listening. When you listen critically, you think logically and dispassionately about, for example, the stories your friends tell you or the sales pitch of the car dealer. Listening with an open mind will help you understand the messages better; listening with a critical mind will help you analyze and evaluate the messages. In adjusting your nonjudgmental and critical listening, focus on the following guidelines.

- *Keep an open mind.* Avoid prejudging. Delay your judgments until you fully understand both the content and the intention the speaker is communicating. Avoid either positive or negative evaluation until you have a reasonably complete understanding. Even when a friend tells you that he or she did something you disapprove of, nonjudgmental listening requires that you withhold making value judgments (in your mind as well as in your responses) that can get in the way of your understanding of your friend.
- *Avoid filtering out or oversimplifying complex messages.* Similarly, avoid filtering out undesirable messages. Clearly, you don't want to hear that something you believe is untrue, that people you care for are unkind, or that ideals you hold are self-destructive. Yet it's important that you re-examine your beliefs by listening to these messages.
- *Recognize your own biases.* These may interfere with accurate listening and cause you to distort message reception through a process of assimilation—the tendency to integrate and interpret what you hear or think you hear in keeping with your own biases, prejudices, and expectations. For example, are your ethnic, national, gender, or religious biases preventing you from appreciating a speaker's point of view?
- *Combat the tendency to sharpen*—to highlight, emphasize, and perhaps embellish one or two aspects of a message. Often the concepts that we tend to *sharpen* are incidental remarks that somehow stand out from the rest of the message. Be careful, therefore, about sharpening your blind date's "Thank you, I had a nice time" and assuming that the date was a big success—while ignoring the signs that it was just so-so, such as the lack of eye contact, the awkward silences, and the cell phone interruptions.
- *Avoid uncritical listening* when you need to make evaluations and judgments. Especially watch out for what are called "fallacies of language," language used to serve less than noble purposes, to convince or persuade you without giving you any reasons, and sometimes to fool you. Several of these are presented in Table 4.3.

INTERPERSONAL CHOICE POINT

Listening Without Judging

A classmate says to you: "I got a C on that paper. That's the worst grade I've ever received. I just can't believe I got a C. This is my major. What am I going to do?" What options do you have in this case for communicating without judging?

TABLE 4.3

Here are four language fallacies that often get in the way of meaningful communication and need to be identified in critical listening. After reviewing the list, take a look at some of the commercial websites for clothing, books, music, or any such product you're interested in and try to find examples of these fallacies.

Fallacy	Examples	Critical Notes
Weasel words are those whose meanings are slippery and difficult to pin down; for example, "help," "virtually," "as much as," "like" (as in "it will make you feel like new"), and "more economical."	A commercial claiming that Medicine M works "better than Brand X" but without specifying how much better or in what respect Medicine M performs better. It's quite possible that it performs better in one respect but less effectively according to nine other measures.	Ask yourself, "Exactly what is being claimed?" For example, "What does 'may reduce cholesterol' mean? What exactly is being asserted?"
Euphemisms make the negative and unpleasant appear positive and appealing.	An executive calls the firing of 200 workers "downsizing" or "reallocation of resources."	Euphemisms can make the mundane seem extraordinary or lies seem like the truth. Don't let words get in the way of accurate first-hand perception.
Jargon is the specialized language of a professional class, which may be used to intimidate or impress people who aren't members of that profession.	The language of the computer hacker, the psychologist, and the advertiser.	Don't be intimidated by jargon; ask questions when you don't understand.
Gobbledygook is overly complex language that overwhelms the listener instead of communicating meaning.	Extra-long sentences, complex grammatical constructions, and rare or unfamiliar words.	Some people just normally speak in complex language, but others use complexity to confuse and mislead. Ask for simplification when appropriate.

Surface and Depth Listening

In most messages, there's an obvious meaning that you can derive from a literal reading of the words and sentences. But in reality, most messages have more than one level of meaning. Sometimes the other level is the opposite of the literal meaning; at other times, it seems totally unrelated. Consider some frequently heard types of messages. Carol asks you how you like her new haircut. On one level, the meaning is clear: Do you like the haircut? But there's also another and perhaps more important level: Carol is asking you to say something positive about her appearance. In the same way, the parent who complains about working hard at the office or in the home may, on a deeper level, be asking for an expression of appreciation. The child who talks about the unfairness of the other children on the playground may be asking for comfort and love, for some expression of caring.

To appreciate these other meanings, you need to engage in *depth* listening. If you respond only to the *surface-level* communication (the literal meaning), you miss the opportunity to make meaningful contact with the other person's feelings and needs. If you say to the parent, "You're always complaining. I bet you really love working so hard," you fail to respond to the person's call for understanding and appreciation. In regulating your surface and depth listening, consider the following guidelines.

■ *Focus on both verbal and nonverbal messages.* Recognize both consistent and inconsistent "packages" of messages, and use these as guides for drawing inferences about the speaker's meaning. Ask questions when in doubt. Listen also to what is omitted. Remember that speakers communicate by what they leave out as well as by what they include. When Harry says things will be okay now that his relationship is finally over but says it with downcast eyes, deep breathing, and clenched hands, consider the possibility that Harry is really hurting and that things are not okay.

INTERPERSONAL CHOICE POINT

Content and Relational Messages

. Almost all verbal messages have both a content and a relational or emotional component. Sometimes it's difficult to know which component should be responded to, and it's often best to try to respond to both. "I failed my exams, and now I'll have to change my career goal" would likely be reported to you with some expression of anger, disappointment, or sadness. What response would address both the content and the emotional/relationship aspect of that statement?

- *Listen for both content and relational messages.* The student who constantly challenges the instructor is on one level communicating disagreement over content. However, on another level—the relationship level—the student may be voicing objections to the instructor's authority or authoritarianism. The instructor needs to listen and respond to both types of messages.
- *Make special note of statements that refer back to the speaker.* Remember that people inevitably talk about themselves. Whatever a person says is, in part, a function of who that person is. Attend carefully to those personal, self-referential messages. Realize that, when Sara tells you she fears the economy isn't going well, she may be voicing her own financial worries but phrasing them in the abstract.
- *Don't, however, disregard the literal meaning of interpersonal messages* in trying to uncover the more hidden meanings. Balance your listening between surface and underlying meanings. Respond to the different levels of meaning in the messages of others as you would like others to respond to yours—sensitively but not obsessively, readily but not overambitiously. When Tommy tells you he's not feeling well, don't ignore this literal meaning and assume that Tommy is just looking for attention.

Polite and Impolite Listening

Canadians are known throughout the world as a polite society. There are even jokes about the Canadian who apologizes when his foot is stepped on, even though it wasn't his fault. Politeness is often thought of as the exclusive function of the speaker, as solely an encoding or sending function. But politeness (or impoliteness) may also be signalled through listening (Fukushima, 2000).

Of course, there are times when you wouldn't want to listen politely (for example, if someone is being verbally abusive or condescending or using racist or sexist language). In these cases, you might want to show your disapproval by conveying to the speaker that you're not even listening. But most often you'll want to listen politely, and you'll want to express this politeness through your listening behaviour. Here are a few suggestions for demonstrating that you are in fact listening politely. As you read these strategies, you'll notice that they're designed to be supportive of the speaker's needs for both positive face (the desire to be viewed positively) and negative face (the desire for autonomy).

INTERPERSONAL CHOICE POINT

Responding Politely

You're working as the manager at a restaurant, and a regular customer complains about the server: "I don't like the way she treated me, and I'm not coming back." What are some of the things you might say without losing the customer or your server (who's usually excellent)? Are there things you'd be sure not to say?

- *Avoid interrupting the speaker.* Avoid trying to take over the speaker's turn. Avoid changing the topic. If you must say something in response to something the speaker said and can't wait until he or she finishes, then say it as briefly as possible and pass the speaker's turn back to the speaker.
- *Give **supportive listening** cues.* These might include nodding your head, giving minimal verbal responses such as "I see" or "Yes, it's true," or moving closer to the speaker. Listen in a way that demonstrates that what the speaker is saying is important. In some cultures, polite listening cues must be cues of agreement (Japanese culture is often used as an example); in other cultures, polite listening cues are attentiveness and support rather than cues of agreement (much of North American culture is an example).
- *Show empathy with the speaker.* Demonstrate that you understand and feel the speaker's thoughts and feelings by giving responses that show this level of understanding—smiling or cringing or otherwise echoing the feelings of the speaker. If you echo the speaker's nonverbal expressions, your behaviour is likely to be seen as empathic.
- *Maintain eye contact.* In much of Canada and the United States, this is perhaps the single most important rule. If you don't maintain eye contact when someone is talking to you, then you'll appear to be not listening and definitely not listening politely. This rule does not, however, hold true in all cultures. In some Aboriginal, Latin, and Asian

cultures, polite listening consists of looking down and avoiding direct eye contact, particularlywhen listening to a superior or a much older person.

■ *Give positive feedback.* Throughout the listening encounter and perhaps especially after the speaker's turn (when you continue the conversation as you respond to what the speaker has said), positive feedback is seen as polite and negative feedback as impolite. If you must give negative feedback, then do so in a way that doesn't attack the person's negative face; for example, first mention areas of agreement or what you liked about what the person said and stress your good intentions. And, most important, do it in private. Public criticism is especially threatening and will surely be seen as a personal attack.

Active and Inactive Listening

Active listening is one of the most important communication skills you can learn (Gordon, 1975). Consider this brief statement from Julia, and the four possible responses that follow.

Julia: That creep gave me a C on the paper. I really worked on that project, and all I get is a lousy C.
Robert: That's not so bad; most people got around the same mark. I got a C, too.
Michael: So what? This is your last semester. Who cares about marks anyway?
Hana: You should be pleased with a C. Misha and Michael both failed, and John and Haruki both got a D.
Diana: You got a C on that paper you were working on for the last three weeks? You sound really angry and hurt.

All four listeners are probably eager to make Julia feel better, but they go about it in very different ways and—you can be sure—with very different outcomes. The first three listeners give fairly typical responses. Robert and Michael both try to minimize the significance of a C grade. Minimizing is a common response to someone who has expressed displeasure or disappointment; usually, it's also inappropriate. Although well-intentioned, this response does little to promote meaningful communication and understanding. Hana tries to give the C grade a more positive meaning. Note, however, that all three listeners also say a great deal more: that Julia shouldn't be feeling unhappy, that her feelings aren't legitimate. These responses deny the validity of Julia's feelings and put her in the position of having to defend them.

Diana, however, is different. Diana uses **active listening**, a process of sending back to the speaker what the listener thinks the speaker meant, both literally and emotionally. Active listening, or paraphrasing, doesn't mean simply repeating the speaker's exact words. Rather, it's a process of putting into some meaningful whole your understanding of the speaker's total message—the verbal and the nonverbal, the content and the feelings.

In Canada, there are cultural differences in the process of active listening. French Canadians, for example, tend to be very expressive, whereas Aboriginal people would likely attend

AlbertoRuggieri/Images.com/Corbis

VIEWPOINTS Politeness in Social Media

Much of the thinking and research on listening and politeness has focused on face-to-face communication skills. But how would you describe listening politeness on the phone or on social network sites? (See Table 4.4.) Do the same principles apply, or do we need an entirely different set to describe social networking listening politeness?

TABLE 4.4

POLITENESS AND THE MOBILE DEVICE

The ubiquity of the cell phone and texting has led to enormous increases in communication, but it has also created problems, many of which are problems of politeness. Because much use occurs in public spaces, people often are forced to listen to conversations that don't involve them or to lose your attention when you send or respond to a text message.

General Rule	Specifics	Adjustments
Avoid using cell phones where inappropriate.	Especially avoid calling in restaurants, hospitals, theatres, museums, commuter buses or trains, and the classroom.	If you must make or take a call when in these various situations, try to move to a less public area.
Avoid texting when in a group.	Unless the text message concerns everyone and will be shared, avoid making everyone wait until you're finished.	If the text is especially important, excuse yourself and apologize for the inconvenience.
Silence your cell.	Put your phone on vibrate mode, or let your voicemail answer and take a message when your call might interfere with others.	When you can't avoid taking a call, speak as quietly as possible and as briefly as possible.
Avoid unwanted photo taking.	Don't take pictures of people who aren't posing for you, and delete photos if the person you photographed requests it.	Of course, if there's an accident or a robbery, you may want to photograph the events.
Avoid extended talking when your reception is weak.	Talking on your cell on a crowded street will probably result in poor reception, which is annoying to the other person.	In an emergency, caution trumps politeness.
Consider the other person.	It's easy to assume that when you have nothing better to do, the person you're calling also has nothing better to do.	As with any phone call, it's wise to ask if this is a good time to call—a strategy that helps maintain the autonomy (negative face) of the person you're calling.

to the conversation in a more subdued fashion. It's important to pay attention to the different forms active listening can take.

FUNCTIONS OF ACTIVE LISTENING   Active listening serves several important functions.

First, and perhaps most obvious, is that active listening enables you to *check understanding*. It helps you as a listener to confirm your understanding of what the speaker said and, more importantly, what he or she meant. Reflecting back perceived meanings to the speaker gives the speaker an opportunity to offer clarification and correct any misunderstandings.

Second, through active listening you let the speaker know that you *acknowledge and accept his or her feelings*. In the sample responses on the previous page, the first three listeners challenged Julia's feelings. But Diana, the active listener, who reflected back to Julia what she thought she meant, accepted what Julia was feeling. Diana also explicitly identified Julia's emotions ("You sound really angry and hurt"), allowing Julia an opportunity to correct her interpretation if necessary. Do be careful, however, to avoid sending what Gordon (1975) calls "solution messages." Solution messages tell the person how he or she *should* feel or what he or she *should* do. The four types of messages that send solutions and that you'll want to avoid in your active listening are (1) ordering messages—"Do this . . .," "Don't touch that . . ."; (2) warning and threatening messages—"If you don't do this, you'll . . .," "If you do this, you'll . . ."; (3) preaching and moralizing messages—"People should all . . .," "We all have responsibilities . . ."; and (4) advising messages—"Why don't you . . .," "What I think you should do is . . ."

Third, active listening *stimulates the speaker to explore his or her feelings and thoughts*. For example, Diana's response encourages Julia to elaborate on her feelings. This opportunity to elaborate will also help Julia deal with her feelings by talking them through.

INTERPERSONAL CHOICE POINT

Listening Actively

Your life partner comes home from work and is visibly upset. Your partner clearly has a need to talk about what happened but simply says, "Work sucks!" You're determined to use active listening techniques. What are some of the things you can say?

TECHNIQUES OF ACTIVE LISTENING   Three simple techniques may help you succeed in active listening:

- *Paraphrase the speaker's meaning.* Stating in your own words what you think the speaker means and feels can help ensure understanding and also shows interest in the speaker. Paraphrasing gives the speaker a chance to extend what was originally said.

    But in paraphrasing, be objective; be especially careful not to lead the speaker in the direction you think he or she should go. Also, be careful that you don't overdo it; only a very small percentage of statements need paraphrasing. Paraphrase when you feel there's a chance for misunderstanding or when you want to express support for the other person and keep the conversation going.
- *Express understanding of the speaker's feelings.* In addition to paraphrasing the content, echo the feelings the speaker expressed or implied ("You must have felt horrible"). This expression of feelings will help you further check your perception of the speaker's feelings. It also will allow the speaker to see his or her feelings more objectively—especially helpful when they're feelings of anger, hurt, or depression—and to elaborate on these feelings.
- *Ask questions.* Asking questions strengthens your own understanding of the speaker's thoughts and feelings and elicits additional information ("How did you feel when you read your job appraisal report?"). Ask questions to provide just enough stimulation and support so that the speaker feels that he or she can elaborate on these thoughts and feelings. These questions should further confirm your interest and concern for the speaker but not pry into unrelated areas or challenge the speaker in any way. Also, be careful that the tone of voice you use doesn't put the speaker on the defensive, as if she is being challenged.

Consider this dialogue and note the active listening techniques used throughout:

Pat: That jerk demoted me. He told me I wasn't an effective manager. I can't believe he did that, after all I've done for this place.
Chris: I'm with you. You've been manager for three or four months now, haven't you?
Pat: A little over three months. I know it was probationary, but I thought I was doing a good job.
Chris: Can you get another chance?
Pat: Yes, he said I could try again in a few months. But I feel like a failure.
Chris: I know what you mean. It sucks. What else did he say?
Pat: He said I had trouble getting the paperwork done on time.
Chris: You've been late filing the reports?
Pat: A few times.

SKILL-BUILDING EXERCISE

Identifying Examples of Listening Styles

Go to YouTube or another online video site and select interpersonal interactions from any of a variety of talk shows (for example, *George Stroumboulopoulos Tonight*, the CBC's *Morning* show, or *The Four*, an all-female indigenous talk show in Regina that shares a unique perspective from four First Nation and Métis women). Identify one or two of the following:

1. An example of empathic or objective listening. How does the person communicate this?
2. An example of nonjudgmental or critical listening. What does the person say or do that indicates he or she is listening in this way?
3. An example of surface or deep listening. What verbal and nonverbal behaviours enable you to distinguish between the two styles of listening?
4. An example of polite or impolite listening. What cues are used to communicate this?
5. An example of active or inactive listening. What does the person say that indicates he or she is listening actively or inactively?

Being able to identify the varied styles of listening is a first step in controlling and adjusting our own style of listening for greatest effectiveness.

Chris: Is there a way to delegate the paperwork?
Pat: No, but I think I know now what needs to be done.
Chris: You sound as though you're ready to give that manager's position another try.
Pat: Yes, I think I am, and I'm going to let him know that I intend to apply in the next few months.

Even in this brief interaction, Pat has moved from unproductive anger and feelings of failure to a determination to correct an unpleasant situation. Note, too, that Chris didn't offer solutions but "simply" listened actively.

As stressed throughout this discussion, listening is situational; the type of listening that is appropriate varies with the situation. You can visualize a listening situation as one in which you have to make choices among at least the five styles of effective listening just discussed. Each listening situation should call for a somewhat different configuration of listening responses; the art of effective listening is largely one of making appropriate choices along these five dimensions.

 Can you explain the five styles of listening (empathic and objective, nonjudgmental and critical, surface and deep, polite and impolite, and active and inactive listening)? Can you regulate your listening along these dimensions as appropriate for the situation you're in?

LISTENING, CULTURE, AND GENDER

Listening is difficult in part because of the inevitable differences in communication systems between speakers and listeners. Because each person has had a unique set of experiences, his or her communication and meaning system will differ from every other person's. And when speaker and listener come from different cultures or are of different genders, the differences and their effects are naturally that much greater. Let's look first at culture.

Culture and Listening

The culture in which you were raised will influence your listening in a variety of ways, including language and speech, direct and indirect styles, nonverbal differences, and feedback.

Even when speaker and listener speak the same language, they speak it with different meanings and different accents. No two speakers speak exactly the same language. Every speaker speaks an *idiolect*: a unique variation of the language (King & DiMichael, 1992). Speakers of the same language will, at the very least, have different meanings for the same terms because they've had different experiences.

Significant differences in expressions and idioms may be found regionally; for example, a Prince Edward Islander will talk about having a "strunt on today," referring to being sulky or in ill humour.

"Anything you say with an accent may be used against you."

Differences in meaning also occur between countries: in Canada, an invitation to "Come to tea" may mean dipping a teabag in a cup of hot water, but in Britain it can refer to enjoying a full meal.

Speakers and listeners who have different native languages and who may have learned English as a second language will have even greater differences in meaning. Translations are never precise and never fully capture the meaning in the other language. If you learned your meaning for *house* in a culture in which everyone lived in their own house with lots of land around it, then communicating with someone whose meaning was learned in a neighbourhood of high-rise tenements could be confusing. Although each of you will hear the word *house*, the meanings you'll develop will be drastically different. In adjusting your listening—especially in an intercultural setting—understand that the speaker's meanings may be very different from yours, even though you're speaking the same language.

Some cultures—those of Western Europe and North America, for example—favour **direct speech** in communication; they advise you to "say what you mean and mean what you say." Many Asian cultures, on the other hand, favour **indirect speech**; they emphasize politeness and

Ryan McVay/Getty Images

VIEWPOINTS Gender Differences

A popular belief is that men listen in the way they do to prove themselves superior and that women listen as they do to ingratiate themselves (differences substantiated by research are described below). Although there is no evidence to show that these beliefs are valid, they persist in the assumptions people make. What do you believe accounts for the differences in the way men and women listen?

maintaining a positive public image rather than literal truth. Listen carefully to persons with different styles of directness. Consider the possibility that the meanings the speaker wishes to communicate with, say, indirectness, may be very different from the meanings you would communicate with indirectness.

Variations in directness are often especially clear when people give feedback. Members of some cultures tend to give direct and honest feedback. Speakers from these cultures—Canada is a good example—expect feedback to be an honest reflection of what their listeners are feeling. In other cultures—Japan and Korea are good examples—it's more important to be positive than to be truthful; listeners may respond with positive feedback (say, in commenting on a business colleague's proposal) even though they don't feel positive. Listen to feedback, as you would all messages, with a full recognition that various cultures view feedback very differently.

Another area of difference is that of accents. In many classrooms throughout Canada there are a wide range of accents. Those whose native language is a tonal one, such as in Chinese languages (in which differences in pitch signal important meaning differences), may speak English with variations in pitch that may be puzzling to others. Those whose native language is Japanese may have trouble distinguishing *l* from *r*, because Japanese doesn't include this distinction. The native language acts as a filter and influences the accent given to the second language.

Responses to accents are often associated with stereotypes. In Canada, for example, some people associate a British accent with upper class, We often see T.V. commercials using actors with a British accent to advertise Finance Companies or expensive jewelry or cosmetics.

Speakers from different cultures also have different *display rules*: cultural rules that govern which nonverbal behaviours are appropriate and which are inappropriate in a public setting. As you listen to other people, you also "listen" to their nonverbals. If these are drastically different from what you expect on the basis of the verbal message, you may perceive a kind of noise or interference or even contradictory messages. Also, of

INTERPERSONAL CHOICE POINT

Support, Not Solutions
You need to make some major decisions in your life, and you need to bounce these off someone, just to help clarify them in your own mind. Your romantic partner almost always tries to solve your problems rather than just be a supportive listener. What can you say in preface (in feedforward) to get your partner to listen supportively and not try to solve your problem? What would you be sure not to say?

course, different cultures may give very different meaning to a particular nonverbal gesture than you do, creating another potential listening obstacle.

Gender and Listening

Men and women learn different styles of listening, just as they learn different styles for using verbal and nonverbal messages. Not surprisingly, these different styles can create difficulties in opposite-sex interpersonal communication.

RAPPORT AND REPORT TALK   According to Deborah Tannen (1990) in her bestselling book *You Just Don't Understand: Women and Men in Conversation*, women seek to build rapport and establish closer relationships and use listening to achieve these ends. Men, on the other hand, will play up their expertise, emphasize it, and use it in dominating the interaction. They will talk about things; they report. Women play down their expertise and are more interested in talking about feelings and relationships and in communicating supportiveness (rapport talk). Tannen argues that the goal of a man in conversation is to be given respect, so he seeks to show his knowledge and expertise. A woman's goal, on the other hand, is to be liked, so she expresses agreement.

LISTENING CUES   Men and women display different types of listening cues and consequently show that they're listening in different ways. In conversation, a woman is more apt to give lots of listening cues—interjecting "Yeah" or "Uh-huh," nodding in agreement, and smiling. A man is more likely to listen quietly, without giving lots of listening cues as feedback. Women also make more eye contact when listening than do men, who are more apt to look around and often away from the speaker (Brownell, 2006). As a result of these differences, women seem to be more engaged in listening than do men.

AMOUNT AND PURPOSES OF LISTENING   Tannen argues that men listen less to women than women listen to men. The reason, says Tannen, is that listening places the person in an inferior position, whereas speaking places the person in a superior position. Men may seem to assume a more argumentative posture while listening, as if getting ready to disagree. They may also appear to ask questions that are more argumentative or that seek to puncture holes in the speaker's position as a way to play up their own expertise. Women, on the other hand, are more likely to ask supportive questions and perhaps offer evaluations that are more positive than those of men. Men and women act this wavy toward both men and women; their customary ways of talking don't seem to change depending on whether the listener is male or female.

Gender differences are changing drastically and quickly; it's best to take generalizations about gender as starting points for investigation and not as airtight conclusions (Gamble & Gamble, 2003). Further, as you've no doubt observed, the gender differences—although significant—are far outnumbered by the similarities. It's important to be mindful of both similarities and differences.

 Can you explain the major cultural and gender differences in listening and assess their influence on your own interpersonal interactions?

Todd Korol/Reuters/Landov

Calgary mayor Naheed Nenshi has shown himself to be a good listener, whether in person or through social media. Are you a good listener? What techniques in this chapter will help you increase how well you listen? How can you use social media to build connections with others by listening in meaningful ways?

SUMMARY OF CONCEPTS AND SKILLS

This chapter defined listening and some of its benefits; identified the five stages of listening; explained some of the barriers to listening, the styles of effective listening, and how best to adjust your listening to achieve maximum effectiveness; and looked at the wide cultural and gender differences in listening.

1. Listening has both work-related and relationship benefits and serves the same purposes as communication: to learn, to relate, to influence, to play, and to help.

The Stages of Listening

2. Listening may be viewed as a five-step process: receiving, understanding, remembering, evaluating, and responding. Listening difficulties and obstacles exist at each of these stages. Internal processes that accompany these include becoming aware of how internal and external stimuli are influencing you, acknowledging these, and making a conscious intention to return focus to the speaker.

Listening Barriers

3. Among the obstacles to effective listening are physical and mental distractions, biases and prejudices, lack of appropriate focus, and premature judgment.

Styles of Listening Effectively

4. Effective listening depends on finding appropriate balances among empathic and objective, nonjudgmental and critical, surface and depth, polite and impolite, and active and inactive listening.
5. Both listener and speaker share in the responsibility for effective listening.

Listening, Culture, and Gender

6. Members of different cultures differ in a number of communication dimensions that influence listening: speech and language, approaches to feedback, and nonverbal behavioural differences.

7. Men and women appear to listen differently; generally, women give more specific listening cues to show they're listening than do men.

This chapter also covered a wide variety of listening skills. Check those that you wish to work on.

_____ 1. *Receiving.* Focus attention on both the verbal and the nonverbal messages; both communicate essential parts of the total meaning.

_____ 2. *Understanding.* Relate new information to what you already know, ask questions, and paraphrase what you think the speaker said to make sure you understand.

_____ 3. *Remembering.* Identify the central ideas of a message, summarize the message in an easier-to-retain form, and repeat ideas (aloud or to yourself) to help you remember.

_____ 4. *Evaluating.* Try first to understand fully what the speaker means, then look to identify any biases or self-interests that might lead the speaker to give an unfair presentation.

_____ 5. *Responding.* Express support for the speaker by using I-messages instead of you-messages.

_____ 6. *Empathic and objective listening.* Punctuate the interaction from the speaker's point of view, engage in dialogue, and seek to understand the speaker's thoughts and feelings.

_____ 7. *Nonjudgmental and critical listening.* Keep an open mind, avoid filtering out difficult messages, and recognize your own biases. When listening to make judgments, listen extra carefully, ask questions when in doubt, and check your perceptions before criticizing.

_____ 8. *Surface and depth listening.* Focus on both verbal and nonverbal messages, on both content and relationship messages, and on statements that refer back to the speaker. At the same time, don't avoid the surface or literal meaning.

_____ 9. *Active and inactive listening.* Be an active listener: Paraphrase the speaker's meaning, express understanding of the speaker's feelings, and ask questions when necessary.

_____ 10. *Cultural differences in listening.* Be especially flexible when listening in a multicultural setting, realizing that people from other cultures give different listening cues and may operate with different rules for listening.

_____ 11. *Gender differences in listening.* Understand that women give more cues that they're listening and appear more supportive in their listening than men.

VOCABULARY QUIZ: The Language of Listening

Match the terms of listening with their definitions. Record the number of the definition next to the appropriate term.

_____ listening (73)
_____ direct speech (91)
_____ long-term memory(76)
_____ empathy (82)
_____ supportive listening (86)
_____ backchannelling cues (78)
_____ active listening (87)
_____ indirect speech (91)
_____ short-term memory(76)
_____ evaluating (76)

1. Speech in which the speaker's intentions are stated clearly and directly.
2. A process of sending back to the speaker what the listener thinks the speaker means.
3. The memory you use to remember information you need immediately or temporarily.
4. A stage in the listening process in which you make judgments about a message.
5. The memory that holds an unlimited amount of information indefinitely.
6. Speech that hides the speaker's true intentions; speech in which requests and observations are made indirectly.
7. A process of receiving, understanding, remembering, evaluating, and responding to messages.
8. Placing yourself in the position of the speaker so that you feel as the speaker feels.
9. Responses that listeners send back to the speaker as a kind of feedback.
10. Listening without judgment or evaluation; listening for understanding.

These 10 terms can also be found in the glossary.

CHAPTER

5

Verbal Messages

CANADIAN PROFILE: Tegan and Sara

Dominic Chan/CP Images

Tegan and Sara, the rock duo, are identical twins born in Calgary in 1980. They began writing their own music at age 15, formed a duo, and started performing. After making their first demo in their high school's recording studio, they won Calgary's Garage Warz competition in 1997 and used their prize of professional studio time to record more songs. They soon attracted national and international attention, and have since gone on to record seven albums and tour internationally.

While their music is not in itself political, the sisters are politically and socially engaged, actively campaigning on behalf of LGBTQ (lesbian, gay, bisexual, transgendered, and queer) equality, music education, youth organizations, literacy, and cancer research. Both sisters are now openly gay; however, they didn't initially want to be identified with a specific group of fans, hoping instead to achieve a wider popularity. With that fan base now secured, Sara and Tegan are supporters of several LGBTQ projects, including the WorldPride 2014 celebration in Toronto and the nonprofit organization Revel and Riot.

Tegan and Sara are only one example of how musicians have used their music to advocate for causes about which they're passionate. In another example, Neil Young's 2014 Honour the Treaties tour protested oil sands development in Canada's north and the resulting treatment of First Nations people. However, verbal communication rarely exists by itself, even in music. Neil Young's tour was criticized, for example, when semi-trailers carrying his equipment were left idling throughout the concerts—in seemingly direct contradiction of his musical message.

As you work through this chapter, think about the many forms of verbal communication we use, more or less effectively. Think also about how musical communication is often only one-directional—from the musicians to the audience—meaning that it's less of a conversation than a communication. Do you think music should be considered verbal communication?

LEARNING OBJECTIVES *After reading this chapter, you should be able to:*

1. Paraphrase the eight principles of verbal messages.

2. Distinguish between disconfirmation and confirmation, and use appropriate cultural identifiers without sexism, heterosexism, racism, and ageism.

3. Explain the ways in which language can distort thinking and apply the guidelines for communicating more logically.

When you communicate, you use two major signal systems—the verbal and the nonverbal. Verbal messages are those sent with words. (The word *verbal* refers to words, not to orality; verbal messages consist of both oral and written words.) Verbal messages don't include laughter, for example, nor the vocalized pauses you make when you speak (such as *er*, *hmm*, and *uh-uh*), nor the responses you make to others that are oral but don't involve words (such as *ha-ha*, *aha*, and *ugh*). These would be considered nonverbal—as are, of course, facial expressions, eye movements, gestures, and so on. This chapter focuses on verbal messages; Chapter 6 focuses on nonverbal messages.

PRINCIPLES OF VERBAL MESSAGES

A useful way to study verbal messages is to examine the principles that govern the way these messages work. Here we look at eight such principles: (1) meanings are in people, (2) messages are both denotative and connotative and communicate objective meanings as well as attitudes and values, (3) messages can be onymous (that is, the sender is known) or anonymous, (4) messages vary in abstraction, (5) messages vary in politeness, (6) messages vary in immediacy, (7) messages can deceive, and (8) messages vary in assertiveness.

Message Meanings Are in People

If you wanted to know the meaning of the word *love*, you might even turn to the internet. A Google search of the "definition of love" will provide several definitions; among them is "an intense feeling of deep affection." This is one of the word's denotative meanings. But where would you turn if you wanted to know what Pedro means when he says "I'm in love"? Of course, you'd turn to Pedro to discover his meaning. It's in this sense that meanings are not in words but in people. Consequently, to uncover meaning, you need to look into people and not merely into words.

Moreover, as you change, you also change the meanings you created out of past messages. Thus, although the message sent may not change, the meanings you created from it yesterday and the meanings you create today may be quite different. Yesterday, when a special someone said "I love you," you created certain meanings. But today, when you learn that the same "I love you" was said to three other people or when you fall in love with someone else, you drastically change the meanings you draw from those three words.

Corinna Goodman

VIEWPOINTS Intergenerational Messages

Corinna Goodman (third family member from left) is one of Canada's top female athletes in triathalon. Being part of a large, intergenerational family, she has lots of opportunities to notice how slang messages change over the years. *Swell, cool, awesome,* and *groovy* are examples of words that may have very different meanings to different generations. Sensitivity to how verbal messages can vary among age groups is only one of the many factors discussed in this chapter that influence effective verbal communication.

Meanings Are Denotative and Connotative

Two general types of meaning are essential to identify: denotation and connotation. **Denotation** refers to the meaning you'd find in a dictionary; it's the meaning that members of the culture assign to a word. **Connotation** is the emotional meaning that specific speakers/listeners give to a word. Take as an example the word *death*. To a doctor, this word might mean (denote) the time when the heart stops. This is an objective description of a particular event. On the other hand, to a mother who is informed of her son's death, the word means (connotes) much more. It recalls her son's youth, ambitions, family, illness, and so on. To her, *death* is a highly emotional, subjective, and personal word. These emotional, subjective, or personal associations make up the word's **connotative meaning**. In short, the denotation of a word is its objective definition, and the connotation of a word is its subjective or emotional meaning.

It's often the connotative meaning of words that is misunderstood by people who have come from other cultures. Many people who have learned English abroad, and may have an outstanding vocabulary, would find it difficult to understand the connotations of certain words as they're understood in North America. For example, compare the term *migrants* (used to designate Mexicans coming into the United States to better their economic condition) with the term *pioneers* (used to designate Europeans who came to Canada for the same reason) (Koppelman, 2005). Although both terms describe people engaged in essentially the same activity (and are essentially the same denotatively), one label is often negatively evaluated, and the other is more often positively valued (so that the terms differ widely in their connotations).

Messages Can Be Onymous or Anonymous

Onymous messages are "signed"; that is, the author of the message is clearly identified, as they are in books or articles and, of course, when you communicate face to face or (usually) by phone or chat. In many cases, you have the opportunity to respond directly to the speaker/writer and voice your opinions. **Anonymous messages** are those for which the author is not identified. For example, on faculty evaluation questionnaires and on RateMyProfessor.com, the ratings and the comments are published anonymously.

The internet has made anonymity extremely easy, and there are currently a variety of websites that offer to send your emails to your boss, your ex-partner, your secret crush, your noisy neighbours, or your inadequate lawyer—all anonymously. Thus, your message gets sent but you're not identified with it. For good or ill, you don't have to deal with the consequences of your message.

One obvious advantage of anonymity is that it allows people to express opinions that may be unpopular and may thus encourage greater honesty. In the case of RateMyProfessor.com, for example, anonymity ensures that the student writing negative comments about an instructor will not be penalized. The presumption is that anonymity encourages honesty and openness.

Anonymity also enables people to disclose their inner thoughts, fears, hopes, and dreams with a depth of feeling that they may be otherwise reluctant to do. A variety of websites that enable you to maintain anonymity are available for these purposes. And in these cases, not only are you anonymous, but the people who read your messages are also anonymous, a situation that is likely to encourage a greater willingness to disclose and to make disclosures at a deeper level than otherwise.

An obvious disadvantage is that, because there are no consequences to the message, anonymity can encourage people to go to extremes—to voice opinions that are outrageous. This in turn can easily spark conflicts that are likely to prove largely unproductive. With anonymous messages, you can't evaluate the credibility of the source. Advice on depres-

Digital Vision/Getty Images

VIEWPOINTS Communication Changes

Some people find it easier to pay attention to a speaker when they have a chance to paraphrase the speaker's words or ask a question for clarification. Some speakers find these interruptions annoying, while others see them as evidence that their audience is fully engaged. How do you respond when someone interrupts when you're talking in a meeting? Do you think there are gender differences in the frequency and nature of interruptions?

sion, for example, may come from someone who knows nothing about depression and may make useless recommendations.

Messages Vary in Directness

Think about how you might respond to the following verbal messages:

Indirect Messages	Direct Messages
I'm so bored; I have nothing to do tonight.	I'd like to go to the movies. Would you like to come?
Do you feel like hamburgers tonight?	I'd like hamburgers tonight. How about you?

Indirect messages attempt to get the listener to say or do something without committing the speaker. Direct messages state more clearly the speaker's preferences and then ask if the listener agrees. For the most part, the advantages of indirect messages are the disadvantages of direct messages, and the disadvantages of indirect messages are the advantages of direct messages.

ADVANTAGES OF INDIRECT MESSAGES   Indirect messages allow you to express a thought without insulting or offending anyone; they allow you to observe the rules of polite interaction. So instead of saying "I'm bored with this group," you say "It's getting late, and I have to get up early tomorrow." Instead of saying "This food tastes like cardboard," you say "I just started my diet" or "I just ate." In each instance you're stating a preference indirectly so as to avoid offending someone.

Sometimes indirect messages allow us to ask for compliments in a socially acceptable manner. A person who says, "I was thinking of getting a nose job" may hope to get the response "A nose job? You? Your nose is perfect."

DISADVANTAGES OF INDIRECT MESSAGES   Indirect messages, however, can also create problems. Consider the following dialogue:

> *Alexis:* You wouldn't like to have my parents over for dinner this weekend, would you?
> *Sam:* I really wanted to go to the beach and just relax.
> *Alexis:* Well, if you feel you have to go, I'll make the dinner myself. You go to the beach. I really hate having them over and doing all the work myself. It's such a drag shopping, cooking, and cleaning all by myself.

Given this situation, Sam has two basic alternatives. One is to stick with the plan to go to the beach and relax. In this case Alexis is going to be upset and Sam is going to feel guilty for not helping with the dinner. A second alternative is to give in to Alexis, help with the dinner, and not go to the beach. In that case, Sam is going to have to give up a much desired plan and is likely to resent Alexis's "manipulative" tactics. Regardless of which decision is made, this "win–lose" strategy creates resentment, competition, and often an "I'll get even" attitude. With direct requests, this type of situation is much less likely to develop. Consider:

> *Alexis:* I'd like to have my parents over for dinner this weekend. What do you think?
> *Sam:* Well, I really wanted to go to the beach and just relax.

Regardless of what develops next, both individuals are starting out on relatively equal footing. Each has clearly and directly stated a preference. Although at first these preferences seem mutually exclusive, it may be possible to meet both people's needs. For example, Sam might say, "How about going to the beach this weekend and having your parents over next weekend? I'm really exhausted; I could use the rest."

Scott J. Ferrell/Congressional Quarterly/Alamy

The characters on *Sesame Street*, the most successful children's show ever, have entertained and educated children for over three decades. Perhaps one ingredient of the show's success is that each character has a very distinctive verbal communication style, making him or her easily identifiable. In much the same way, we each have a distinctive verbal style that, as this chapter will demonstrate, has the potential to be made more effective.

Here is a direct response to a direct request. Unless there is some pressing need to have Alexis's parents over for dinner on the weekend, this response may enable each to meet the other's needs.

POLITENESS AND DIRECTNESS Directness is usually less polite—"Write me a recommendation"; "Lend me $100"—and may infringe on a person's need to maintain negative face, or autonomy. Indirectness is often more polite—"Do you think you could write a recommendation for me?"; "Would it be possible to lend me $100?"—because it allows the person to maintain autonomy and provides an acceptable way to refuse the request.

"Eh" isn't the only Canadian expression that derives its meaning from its cultural context. If you're unemployed you might be on the pogey; if you're going 10 clicks an hour you're probably driving too slowly; and if you're cold you might need to put on your toque. And depending on where you are in the country and how old you are, you'll be sitting on either a chesterfield or a couch. Can you think of other expressions that are particular to Canada or to your region?

Message Meanings Vary in Abstraction

Abstract terms refer to concepts and ideas that have no physical dimensions (for example, *freedom, love, happiness, equality, democracy*). **Concrete terms**, on the other hand, refer to objects, people, and happenings that you perceive with your senses of sight, smell, touch, hearing, or taste. But between these extremes are degrees of abstraction. Consider the following list of terms:

- entertainment
- TV show
- Canadian TV show
- recent Canadian TV show
- *Little Mosque on the Prairie*

At the top is the general or abstract word *entertainment*. Note that *entertainment* includes all the other items on the list, plus various other items—films, novels, drama, comics, and so on. *TV show* is more specific and concrete. It includes all the items below it as well as various other items, such as Indian TV shows or Russian TV shows. It excludes, however, all entertainment that is not TV. *Canadian TV show* is again more specific than TV show and excludes all shows that are not Canadian. *Recent Canadian TV show* further limits Canadian TV shows to a time period. *Little Mosque on the Prairie* specifies concretely the one item to which reference is made.

Effective verbal messages include words that range widely in abstractness. At times, a general term may suit your needs best; at other times, a more specific term may serve better. The general suggestion for effective communication is to use abstractions sparingly and to express your meanings specifically with words that are low in abstraction.

However, there are situations when terms high in abstraction would be more effective than specific terms. For example, in group situations where one wants to encourage creativity and the active participation of group members, beginning with an abstract statement may help create an atmosphere conducive to open discussion.

Message Meanings Vary in Politeness

It will come as no surprise that messages vary greatly in politeness. Polite messages reflect positively on the other person (for example, compliments or pats on the back) and respect the other person's right to be independent and autonomous (for example, asking permission or acknowledging the person's right to refuse). Impolite messages attack our needs to be seen positively (for example, criticism or negative facial expressions) and to be autonomous (making demands or forcing another to do something). A special case of politeness concerns the ever popular social networking sites (see Table 5.1).

The differences between direct and indirect messages may easily create misunderstandings. For example, a person who uses an indirect style of speech may be doing so to be polite and may have been taught this style by his or her culture. But if you assume instead that the person is using indirectness to be manipulative because your culture regards it as such, then miscommunication is inevitable.

POLITENESS AND GENDER   There are considerable gender differences in politeness (Dindia & Canary, 2006; Holmes, 1995; Kapoor et al., 2003; Tannen, 1994b). Research has found, for example, that women are more polite and more indirect in giving orders than are men; women would be

TABLE 5.1

SOCIAL NETWORKING POLITENESS

Social networking sites such as Facebook and Google+ have developed their own rules of politeness. Here are just five rules.

Rule of Politeness	Rule in Operation
Engage in networking feedforward before requesting friendship.	Sending a message complimenting the person's latest post provides some background and eases the way for a friendship request.
Avoid negativity.	Avoid writing negative or embarrassing messages or posting unflattering photos that may generate conflict.
Keep networking information confidential.	It's considered inappropriate and impolite to relay information on Facebook to those, for example, who are not themselves friends.
Be gentle in refusals.	Refuse any request for friendship gently or, if you wish, ignore it. If you're refused, don't ask for reasons; it's considered impolite.
Avoid making potentially embarrassing requests.	Avoid asking to be friends with someone who you suspect may have reasons for not wanting to admit you. For example, your work associate may not want you to see her or his profile.

more likely to say "It would be great if these letters could go out today" than "Have these letters out by three p.m." Generally, men speak indirectly when expressing meanings that violate the masculine stereotype (for example, messages of weakness, doubt, or incompetence). Women have also been found to express empathy, sympathy, and supportiveness more than men do. As well, they apologize more than men do, and make more apologies to other women (whereas men make more apologies to women than to other men). Some would argue that such differences are much less noticeable today among young adults; it would be interesting, then, to revisit these questions in new research.

 Facebook recently announced that it now has more than 50 terms to choose from for gender identity (Robinson, 2014). Does such a number of words tell us anything about the importance of gender identity in our culture?

Messages Vary in Immediacy

Immediacy is the sense of closeness—of togetherness, of oneness—between speaker and listener. When you communicate immediacy you convey a sense of interest and attention, a liking for and an attraction to the other person. You communicate immediacy with both verbal and nonverbal messages.

And, not surprisingly, people like people who communicate immediacy. You increase your interpersonal attractiveness—the degree to which others like you and respond positively to you—when you use immediacy behaviours. In addition, there is considerable evidence showing that immediacy behaviours are effective in workplace communication, especially between supervisors and subordinates (Richmond, McCroskey, & Hickson, 2012). For example, when a supervisor uses immediacy behaviours, he or she is seen by subordinates as interested and concerned; subordinates are therefore likely to communicate more freely and honestly about issues that can benefit both the supervisor and the organization. Workers with supervisors who communicate immediacy behaviours also have higher job satisfaction and motivation. It's important to remember, however, that there are large differences, both individual and cultural, in the degree of immediacy that is comfortable for different people.

Here are a few suggestions for communicating immediacy (Mottet & Richmond, 1998; Richmond, McCroskey, & Hickson, 2012):

- Self-disclose; reveal something significant about yourself.
- Refer to the other person's good qualities of, say, dependability, intelligence, or character—"You're always so reliable."
- Talk about commonalities, things you and the other person have done together or share.
- Demonstrate your responsiveness by giving feedback cues that indicate you want to listen more and that you're interested—"And what else happened?"
- Maintain appropriate eye contact, smile, and express your interest in the other person.
- Focus on the other person's remarks. Let the speaker know that you've heard and understood what was said, and give the speaker appropriate verbal and nonverbal feedback.

Messages Vary in Inclusion

Some messages are inclusive; they include all people present and they acknowledge the relevance of others. Other messages exclude specific people and, in some cases, entire cultural groups.

Messages of exclusion occur when in-group language is used in the presence of an out-group member. When doctors get together and discuss medicine, there's no problem. But when they get together with someone who isn't a doctor, they often fail to adjust to this new person. Instead, they simply continue with discussions of anatomy, symptoms, medication, and other topics that exclude others present. When those others are patients, serious communication problems can result.

Another form of excluding talk is using the terms of one's own cultural group as universal, as applying to everyone. For example, *church* refers to a place of worship for specific religions but not for all religions. Similarly, *Bible* refers to Christian religious scriptures and is not a general term for "religious scriptures." Nor does *Judeo-Christian tradition* include the religious traditions of everyone. Similarly, the terms *marriage*, *husband*, and *wife* refer to some heterosexual relationships and exclude others; they may also exclude gay and lesbian relationships.

When you're in a group, instead of using language that excludes one or more members, consider the principle of **inclusion**. Regardless of the type of communication situation you're in, try to find ways to include everyone in the interaction. Even if job-related issues have to be discussed in the presence of someone who isn't a fellow employee, you can include that person by, for example, seeking his or her perspective or drawing an analogy from his or her field.

Another way to practise inclusion in a group discussion is to fill in relevant details for those who may be unaware of them. When people, places, or events are mentioned, briefly identify them, as in "Margo—she's Jeff's daughter—worked for Simon Fraser."

Also consider the vast array of alternative terms that are inclusive rather than exclusive. For example, one could use *place of worship* instead of *church*, *temple*, or *mosque* when talking about religious houses of worship in general. Similarly, *committed relationship* is more inclusive than *marriage*; *couples therapy* is more inclusive than *marriage counselling*; and *life partner* is more inclusive than *husband* or *wife*. Referring to *religious scriptures* is more inclusive than *Bible*. Of course, if you're referring to a specific Baptist church or specific married heterosexual couples, then the terms *church* and *marriage* are appropriate.

Messages Can Deceive

Although we operate on the assumption that people tell the truth, it should come as no surprise to learn that some people do lie. Lying also begets more lying; when one person lies, the likelihood of the other person lying increases (Tyler, Feldman, & Reichert, 2006). **Lying** refers to the act of (1) sending messages (2) with the intention of giving another person information you believe to be false.

Large cultural differences exist in the way lying is defined and in the way lying is treated. For example, as children get older, Chinese and Taiwanese (but not Canadians) see lying about the good deeds that they do as positive (as you'd expect for cultures that emphasize modesty), and taking credit for these same good deeds is seen negatively (Lee et al., 2002). Some cultures consider lying to be more important than others do—in one study, for example, European Americans viewed lies less negatively than did Ecuadorians. Both, however, felt that lying to an out-group member was more acceptable than lying to an in-group member (Mealy, Stephan, & Urrutia, 2007).

 Either from memory or using an internet search engine, identify a situation in which a public figure claimed that his or her words were taken out of context. Research the original context. How has the meaning of the message changed as a result of being taken out of context?

TYPES OF LIES   Lies vary greatly in type; each lie seems a bit different from every other lie. Here is one useful system that classifies lies into four types (McGinley, 2000).

- *Pro-social deception: To achieve some good* These are lies that are designed to benefit the person lied to or lied about; for example, praising a person's effort in order to give him or her more confidence.

- *Self-enhancement deception: To make yourself look good* Presenting yourself as younger or as having a better job in your social networking profile is a common example.
- *Selfish deception: To protect yourself* These lies protect you; for example, not answering the phone because you want to do something else.
- *Antisocial deception: To harm someone* These lies are designed to hurt another person; for example, spreading false rumours about someone or falsely accusing an opposing candidate of some wrongdoing.

THE BEHAVIOUR OF LIARS   One of the more interesting questions about lying is how liars act. Do they act differently from those telling the truth? And, if they do act differently, how can we tell when someone is lying? These questions aren't easy to answer, and we're far from having complete answers. But we have learned a great deal.

For example, after an examination of 120 research studies, the following behaviours were found to most often accompany lying (DePaulo et al., 2003; Knapp, 2008):

- *Liars hold back.* They speak more slowly (perhaps to monitor what they're saying), take longer to respond to questions (again, perhaps monitoring their messages), and generally give less information and elaboration.
- *Liars make less sense.* Liars' messages contain more discrepancies, more inconsistencies.
- *Liars give a more negative impression.* Generally, liars are seen as less willing to be cooperative, smile less than truth-tellers, and are more defensive.
- *Liars are tense.* The tension may be revealed by their higher-pitched voices and their excessive body movements.

It is very difficult to detect when a person is lying and when a person is telling the truth. The hundreds of research studies conducted on this topic find that in most instances people judge lying accurately in less than 60 percent of the cases, only slightly better than chance (Knapp, 2008).

Lie detection is even more difficult (that is, less accurate) in long-standing romantic relationships—the very relationships in which the most significant lying occurs (Guerrero, Andersen, & Afifi, 2007). One important reason for this is the **truth bias**: we assume that the

---

INTERPERSONAL CHOICE POINT

White Lies
We often think of "white lies" as a socially preferable response in order to avoid hurting the other person. Is this always the case? Under what circumstances would you not be willing to tell a white lie to a friend and under what circumstances would you think a white lie preferable to the truth?

ETHICAL MESSAGES

Lying

Not surprisingly, lies have ethical implications. Some lies (pro-social, self-enhancement, and selfish deception lies) are considered ethical (for example, publicly agreeing with someone you really disagree with in order to enable the person to save face, saying that someone will get well despite medical evidence to the contrary, or simply bragging about your accomplishments). Other lies are considered not only ethical but required (for example, lying to protect someone from harm or telling the proud parents that their child is beautiful). Still other lies (largely those in the antisocial category) are considered unethical (for example, lying to defraud investors or to falsely accuse someone).

Ethical Choice Point

Of course, not all lies are easy to classify as ethical or unethical. For example, what would you do in each of these situations?

- *Would it be ethical for you to lie to get what you deserve but couldn't get any other way? For example, would it be ethical to lie to get a well-earned promotion or a raise?*
- *Would it be ethical for you to lie to your relationship partner to avoid a conflict and, perhaps, splitting up? Would it make a difference if the issue was a minor one (for example, you were late for an appointment because you wanted to see the end of the football game) or a major one (for example, continued infidelity)?*
- *Would it be ethical for you to lie to get yourself out of an unpleasant situation; for example, an unpleasant date, an extra office chore, or a boring conversation?*

person is telling the truth. This truth bias is especially strong in long-term relationships where it's simply expected that each person tells the truth (Knapp, 2008).

Message Meanings Vary in Assertiveness

Assertive messages express your real thoughts—even if they involve disagreeing or arguing with others—but are nevertheless respectful of the other person. Consider your own message behaviour. If you disagree with other people in a group, do you speak your mind? Do you allow others to take advantage of you because you're reluctant to say what you want? Do you feel uncomfortable when you have to state your opinion in a group? Questions such as these revolve around your degree of assertiveness. Increasing your level of assertiveness will enable you to deal with these experiences positively and productively. Before reading further about this type of communication, take the accompanying self-test.

NONASSERTIVE, AGGRESSIVE, AND ASSERTIVE MESSAGES   In addition to identifying some specific assertive behaviours (as in the assertiveness self-test), we can further understand the nature of assertive communication by distinguishing it from nonassertiveness and aggressiveness (Alberti, 1977).

Nonassertive Messages.   The term *nonassertiveness* refers to a lack of assertiveness in certain types of (or even in all) communication situations. People who are nonassertive fail to stand up for their rights. They operate with a "You win, I lose" philosophy; they give others what they want without concern for themselves (Lloyd, 2001). Nonassertive people often ask permission from others to do what is their perfect right.

Aggressive Messages.   Aggressiveness is the other extreme. Aggressive people operate with an "I win, you lose" philosophy; they care little for what the other person wants and focus only on their own needs. Aggressive communicators think little of the opinions, values, or beliefs of others and yet are extremely sensitive to others' criticisms of their own behaviour. Consequently, they frequently get into arguments with others.

Assertive Messages.   Assertive behaviour—behaviour that enables you to act in your own best interests without denying or infringing on the rights of others—is the generally desired alternative to nonassertiveness (which prevents you from expressing yourself) or

TEST YOURSELF

How Assertive Are Your Messages?

Indicate how true each of the following statements is about your own communication. Respond instinctively rather than in the way you feel you should respond.
Use a scale in which **5** = always or almost always true; **4** = usually true; **3** = sometimes true, sometimes false; **2** = usually false; and **1** = always or almost always false.

_____ 1. I would express my opinion in a group even if it contradicted the opinions of others.

_____ 2. When asked to do something that I really don't want to do, I can say no without feeling guilty.

_____ 3. I can express my opinion to my superiors on the job.

_____ 4. I can start up a conversation with a stranger on a bus or at a business gathering without fear.

_____ 5. I voice objection to people's behaviour if I feel that it infringes on my rights.

How Did You Do? All five items in this test identify characteristics of assertive communication. High scores (about 20 and above) would indicate a high level of assertiveness. Low scores (about 10 and below) would indicate a low level of assertiveness.

What Will You Do? The remaining discussion in this section clarifies the nature of assertive communication and offers guidelines for increasing your own assertiveness. These suggestions can help you not only to increase your assertiveness but also, when appropriate, to reduce your aggressive tendencies.

aggressiveness (which creates resentment and conflict). Assertive people operate with an "I win, you win" philosophy; they assume that both people can gain something from an interpersonal interaction, even from a confrontation. People who are assertive in interpersonal communication display four major behaviour patterns (Norton & Warnick, 1976):

- They express their feelings frankly and openly to people in general as well as to those in whom they may have a romantic interest.
- They volunteer opinions and beliefs, deal directly with interpersonal communication situations that may be stressful, and question others without fear.
- They stand up and argue for their rights, even if this may entail a certain degree of disagreement or conflict with relatives or close friends.
- They make up their own minds on the basis of evidence and argument instead of just accepting what others say.

In short, assertive people are more open, less anxious, more contentious, and less likely to be intimidated or easily persuaded than nonassertive people.

GUIDELINES FOR INCREASING ASSERTIVENESS   Most people are nonassertive in certain situations. If you're one of these people and if you wish to modify your behaviour in some situations, there are steps you can take to increase your assertiveness. (If you're nonassertive always and everywhere and are unhappy about this, then you may need to work with a therapist to change your behaviour.)

Analyze Assertive Messages.   The first step in increasing your assertiveness skills is to understand the nature of these communications. Observe and analyze the messages of others. Learn to distinguish the differences among assertive, aggressive, and nonassertive messages. Focus on what makes one behaviour assertive and another behaviour nonassertive or aggressive.

After you've gained some skills in observing the behaviours of others, turn your analysis to yourself. Analyze situations in which you're normally assertive and situations in which you're more likely to act nonassertively or aggressively. What circumstances characterize these situations? What do the situations in which you're normally assertive have in common? How do you speak? How do you communicate nonverbally?

Rehearse Assertive Messages.   To rehearse assertiveness, select a situation in which you're normally nonassertive. Build a ladder (or hierarchy) whose first step is a relatively nonthreatening message and whose second step would be a bit more risky but still safe and so on, until the final step, the desired communication. For example, let's say that you have difficulty voicing your opinion to your supervisor at work. The desired behaviour, then, is to tell your supervisor your opinions. A ladder or hierarchy of situations leading up to this desired behaviour might begin with visualizing yourself talking with your boss. Visualize this scenario until you can do it without any anxiety or discomfort. Once you've mastered this visualization, visualize a step closer to your goal: say, walking into your boss's office. Again, do this until your visualization creates no discomfort. Continue with these successive visualizations until you can visualize yourself telling your boss your opinion. As with the other visualizations, practise this until you can do it while totally relaxed. This is the mental rehearsal.

Role playing, using both voice and gesture, in front of a trusted friend or in supportive classroom setting, can be extremely helpful.

Communicate Assertively.   Communicating assertively is naturally the most difficult step, but obviously the most important. Here's a generally effective pattern to follow:

INTERPERSONAL CHOICE POINT

Acting Assertively

One of your colleagues or classmates uses terminology that is disrespectful of your ethnic, cultural, or religious group. You politely inform her that although you're certain there was no insult intended, you'd prefer that she not use this term. She doesn't respond in the way you'd hoped, and instead tells you that you shouldn't take everything so seriously. You need to be more assertive. What options do you have for communicating more assertively?

Evaluating Assertiveness

For any one of the following situations, discuss in a group or write individually (a) an aggressive, (b) a nonassertive, and (c) an assertive response. Then, in one sentence of 15 words or less, explain why your assertiveness message will prove more effective than the aggressive or nonassertive message.

1. You've just redecorated your apartment, expending considerable time and money in making it look exactly as you want it. A good friend of yours brings you a house gift—the ugliest poster you've ever seen—and insists that you hang it over your fireplace, the focal point of your living room.
2. Your friend borrows $150 and promises to pay you back tomorrow. But tomorrow passes, as do 20 subsequent tomorrows, and there is still no sign of the money. You know that your friend hasn't forgotten about the debt, and you also know that your friend has more than enough money to pay you back.
3. Your next-door neighbour repeatedly asks you to take care of her four-year-old while she runs some errand or another. You don't mind helping out in an emergency, but this occurs almost every day. You feel you're being taken advantage of and simply don't want to do this anymore.

Assertiveness is the most direct and honest response in situations such as these. Usually it's also the most effective.

1. *Describe the problem; don't evaluate or judge it.* "We're all working on this advertising project together. You're missing half our meetings, and you still haven't produced your first report."
2. *State how this problem affects you.* Be sure to use I-messages and to avoid messages that accuse or blame the other person. "My job depends on the success of this project, and I don't think it's fair that I have to do extra work to make up for what you're not doing."
3. *Propose solutions that are workable and that allow the person to save face.* "If you can get your report to the group by Tuesday, we'll still be able to meet our deadline. And I could give you a call an hour before the meeting to remind you."
4. *Confirm understanding.* "Is it clear that we just can't produce this project if you're not going to pull your own weight? Will you have the report to us by Tuesday?"
5. *Reflect on your own assertiveness.* Think about what you did. How did you express yourself verbally and nonverbally? What would you do differently next time?

Be cautious, however. It's easy to visualize a situation in which, for example, people are talking behind you in a movie and, with your newfound enthusiasm for assertiveness, you tell them to be quiet. It's also easy to see yourself getting smashed in the teeth as a result. In applying the principles of assertive communication, be careful that you don't go beyond what you can handle effectively.

Can you explain in your own words the eight principles of verbal messages? Can you apply the skills that are a part of these principles in your own verbal message sending and receiving?

CONFIRMATION AND DISCONFIRMATION

The terms *confirmation* and *disconfirmation* refer to the extent to which you acknowledge another person. **Disconfirmation** is a communication pattern in which you ignore someone's presence as well as his or her communications. You say, in effect, that this person, and what this person has to say, are not worth serious attention or effort, that this person, and this person's contributions, are so unimportant or insignificant that there is no reason to concern yourself with them.

Note that disconfirmation isn't the same as **rejection**. In rejection, you acknowledge but disagree with the person; you indicate your unwillingness to accept something the other person says or does. In disconfirming someone, however, you deny that person's significance; you claim that what this person says or does simply doesn't count.

Confirmation is the opposite communication pattern. In **confirmation**, you not only acknowledge the presence of the other person but also indicate your acceptance of this person, of this person's self-definition, and of your relationship as defined or viewed by this other person.

Consider this situation. You've been living with your partner, Pat, for the past six months, and you arrive home late one night. Pat is angry and complains about your being so late. Which of the following is most likely to be your response?

- Stop screaming. I'm not interested in what you're babbling about. I'll do what I want, when I want. I'm going to bed.
- What are you so angry about? Didn't you get in three hours late last Thursday when you went to that office party? So knock it off.
- You have a right to be angry. I should have called to tell you I was going to be late, but I got involved in an argument at work, and I couldn't leave until it was resolved.

In the first response, you dismiss Pat's anger and even indicate dismissal of Pat as a person. In the second response, you reject the validity of Pat's reasons for being angry but do not dismiss either Pat's feelings of anger or Pat as a person. In the third response, you acknowledge Pat's anger and the reasons for it. In addition, you provide some kind of explanation and, in doing so, show that both Pat's feelings and Pat as a person are important and that Pat has the right to know what happened. The first response is an example of disconfirmation, the second of rejection, and the third of confirmation. You can communicate both confirmation and disconfirmation in a wide variety of ways; Table 5.2 lists just a few.

We'll now consider four additional disconfirming practices—racism, heterosexism, ageism, and sexism. We'll then look at preferred "cultural identifiers," or confirming language practices, that are recommended for use with many groups.

Racism

Racism—like all the "isms" discussed in this section—exists on both an individual and an institutional level, as pointed out by educational researchers Kent Koppelman and R. Lee Goodhart (2005) and others. *Individual* racism consists of negative attitudes and beliefs that people hold about specific races or ethnic groups. The assumption that certain groups are intellectually inferior to others or are incapable of certain achievements is a clear example of individual racism. Prejudices against Aboriginal peoples, African Canadians, Arabs, and others have existed throughout history and are still a part of many people's lives today.

Institutionalized racism is seen in organizational behaviours such as de facto school segregation, corporations' reluctance to hire

<table>
<tr><td>

INTERPERSONAL CHOICE POINT

Discouraging Disconfirmation

For the past several months, you've noticed how disconfirming your neighbours are toward their preteen children; it seems the children can never do anything to the parents' satisfaction. What are some of the things you might say (if you do decide to get involved) to make your neighbours more aware of their communication patterns and the possible negative effects these might have? Through what channel would you send these messages?

</td></tr>
</table>

ImagesBazaar/Alamy

VIEWPOINTS Negative Terms

Many people feel that it's permissible for members of a particular culture to refer to themselves in terms that if said by outsiders would be considered racist, sexist, or heterosexist. Some researchers suggest that these terms may actually reinforce negative stereotypes that the larger society has already assigned to the group (Guerin, 2003). Yet others argue that, by using such labels, groups weaken the terms' negative impact. Do you refer to yourself using terms that would be considered offensive or politically incorrect if said by "outsiders"? What effects, if any, do you think such self-talk has?

TABLE 5.2

CONFIRMATION AND DISCONFIRMATION

This table identifies some specific confirming and disconfirming messages. As you review this table, try to imagine a specific illustration for each of the ways of communicating disconfirmation and confirmation (Galvin, Bylund, & Brommel, 2012; Pearson, 1993).

Disconfirmation	Confirmation
Ignores the presence or contributions of the other person; expresses indifference to what the other person says.	**Acknowledges** the presence and the contributions of the other person by either supporting or taking issue with what he or she says.
Makes no nonverbal contact; avoids direct eye contact; avoids touching and general nonverbal closeness.	**Makes nonverbal contact** by maintaining direct eye contact and otherwise demonstrating acknowledgment of the other.
Monologues; engages in communication in which one person speaks and one person listens; there is no real interaction.	**Dialogues;** engages in communication in which both persons are speakers and listeners; both are involved.
Jumps to interpretation or evaluation rather than working at understanding what the other person means.	**Demonstrates understanding** of what the other says or, when in doubt, asks questions.
Discourages, interrupts, or otherwise makes it difficult for the other person to express himself or herself.	**Encourages** the other person to express his or her thoughts and feelings by showing interest and asking questions.
Avoids responding or responds tangentially by shifting the focus of the message in another direction.	**Responds directly** and exclusively to what the other person says.

members of minority groups, and banks' unwillingness to extend mortgages and business loans to members of some groups or residents of some neighbourhoods. Racial profiling, in which people become crime suspects solely because of their apparent race, is another form of institutionalized racism.

Racist language is used by members of one culture to disparage members of other cultures, their customs, or their accomplishments. Racist language emphasizes differences rather than similarities and separates rather than unites members of different cultures. Generally, the dominant group uses racist language to establish and maintain power over other groups.

According to Andrea Rich (1974), "Any language that, through a conscious or unconscious attempt by the user, places a particular racial or ethnic group in an inferior position is racist." Racist language expresses racist attitudes. It also, however, contributes to the development of racist attitudes in those who use or hear the language. Even when racism is subtle, unintentional, or even unconscious, its effects are systematically damaging (Dovidio et al., 2002).

Examine your own language racism, and avoid

- using derogatory terms for members of a particular race or group of people.
- interacting with members of other races through stereotypes perpetuated by the media.
- including reference to race when it's irrelevant, as in referring to "an African Canadian surgeon" or "an Asian athlete."
- attributing economic or social problems to the race of individuals rather than to institutionalized racism or to general economic problems that affect everyone.

INTERPERSONAL CHOICE POINT

Insults
Your colleague frequently tells jokes that insult various nationalities. With the idea that meanings are in people, not in words, what are some of your options for responding to these "jokes"? What would you say?

Heterosexism

Heterosexism also exists on both individual and institutional levels. On an individual level, the term **heterosexism** refers to attitudes, behaviours, and language that disparage people who are lesbian, gay, bisexual, transgendered, or queer (LGBTQ) in the belief that all sexual behaviour that is not heterosexual is unnatural and deserving of criticism and condemnation. Beliefs such as these are at the heart of anti-gay violence and "gay bashing." Individual heterosexism also includes beliefs that homosexuals are more likely to commit crimes (there's actually no difference) and to molest children than are heterosexuals (actually, child molesters are overwhelmingly heterosexual married men) (Abel & Harlow, 2001; Koppelman, 2005), and that homosexuals cannot maintain stable relationships or effectively raise children, beliefs that contradict research evidence (Fitzpatrick et al., 1994; Johnson & O'Connor, 2002).

Institutional heterosexism is easy to identify. Examples include the ban on gay marriage in many American states, the Catholic Church's ban on homosexual priests, the U.S. military's former "Don't ask, don't tell" policy, and the many laws prohibiting adoption of children by gay people. In some cultures, homosexual relations are illegal (for example, in Pakistan, Yemen, and Iran, with sentences that can range from years in prison to death). And, interestingly enough, in some cultures homosexual relationships are illegal for men but legal for women (for example, in Palau, Cook Islands, Tonga, and Guyana).

Heterosexist language includes derogatory terms used for lesbians and gay men. For example, surveys in the U.S. military showed that 80 percent of those surveyed had heard "offensive speech, derogatory names, jokes or remarks" about gay people and that 85 percent believed that such derogatory speech was "tolerated" (*New York Times*, March 25, 2000, p. A12). Heterosexism also occurs in more subtle forms of language usage; for example, when you qualify a professional designation—as in "gay athlete" or "lesbian doctor"—you're saying, in effect, that athletes and doctors are not normally gay or lesbian.

Still another instance of heterosexism is the presumption of heterosexuality. People usually assume that the person they're talking to or about is heterosexual. And usually they're correct because most people are heterosexual. At the same time, however, this presumption denies the lesbian or gay identity legitimacy. The practice is very similar to the presumptions of whiteness and maleness that we've made significant inroads in eliminating.

Here are a few additional suggestions for avoiding heterosexist (or what some call homophobic) language:

- Avoid offensive nonverbal mannerisms that parody stereotypes when talking about gay men and lesbians. Avoid the "startled eye blink" with which some people react to gay couples (Mahaffey, Bryan, & Hutchison, 2005).
- Avoid "complimenting" gay men and lesbians by saying that they "don't look it." To gay men and lesbians, this is not a compliment. Similarly, expressing disappointment that a person is gay—often intended to be complimentary, as in comments such as "What a waste!"—is not really flattering.
- Avoid making the assumption that every gay or lesbian knows what every other gay or lesbian is thinking. It's very similar, as one comic put it, to asking an African American, "What do you think Jesse Jackson meant by that last speech?"
- Avoid overattribution, the tendency to attribute just about everything a person does, says, and believes to the fact that the person is gay or lesbian. This tendency helps to activate and perpetuate stereotypes.
- Remember that relationship milestones are important to all people. Ignoring anniversaries or birthdays of, say, a relative's partner is likely to cause hurt and resentment.

INTERPERSONAL CHOICE POINT

Homophobia

You're bringing your roommate home for the holidays; he's an outspoken gay activist, whereas your family is extremely homophobic, though you suspect it's largely because of a lack of knowledge. What are some of the things you can say to help prepare your family and your roommate for their holiday get-together? What channels might you use?

Ageism

Ageism is discrimination based on age; like other forms of discrimination, it occurs in both individual and institutionalized forms. On an individual level, ageism is seen in the general disrespect many have for older people. More specifically, it's seen in negative stereotypes that many people have about those who are older. It's instructive to remember that in some cultures—some Asian and some African cultures, for example—the old are revered and respected. Younger people seek them out for advice on economic, ethical, and relationship issues.

Although used mainly to refer to prejudice against older people, the word *ageism* can also refer to prejudice against younger age groups. For example, if you describe all teenagers as selfish and undependable, you're discriminating against a group purely because of their age and thus are being ageist in your statements.

Institutional ageism is seen in mandatory retirement laws and in age restrictions in certain occupations, such as those of pilot or air traffic controller (which impose age cutoffs rather than basing requirements on demonstrated competence). In some countries, people in their 70s and older aren't able to rent cars. In less obvious forms, institutional ageism is seen in the media's portrayal of old people as incompetent, complaining, and—perhaps most clearly evidenced in television and films—without romantic feelings. Rarely, for example, do TV shows or films show older people working productively, being cooperative and pleasant, and engaging in romantic and sexual relationships.

Popular language is replete with ageist phrases; as with racist and heterosexist language, we can all provide plenty of examples. Similarly, qualifying a description of someone in terms of his or her age—especially when it's irrelevant to the discussion—demonstrates ageism. You also communicate ageism when you speak to older people in overly simple words or explain things that don't need explaining.

Furthermore, it's a mistake to speak to an older person at an overly high volume; this suggests that all older people have hearing difficulties, and it tends to draw attention to the fact that you're talking down to the older person.

One useful way to avoid ageism is to recognize and avoid the illogical stereotypes that ageist language is based on, as in the following examples:

- Avoid talking down to a person because he or she is older. Older people are not mentally slow; most people remain mentally alert well into old age.
- Refrain from refreshing an older person's memory each time you see the person. Older people can and do remember things.
- Avoid implying that relationships are no longer important. Older people continue to be interested in relationships.
- Speak at a normal volume, and maintain a normal physical distance. Being older doesn't necessarily mean being hard of hearing or being unable to see; most older people hear and see quite well, sometimes with hearing aids or glasses.
- Engage older people in conversation as you would wish to be engaged. Most older people are interested in the world around them.

INTERPERSONAL CHOICE POINT

Ageism

One of your instructors is extremely sensitive when talking about women, different races, and different affectional orientations, but consistently speaks of old people using stereotypical and insulting language. What are some of the things you can say (you're in your early 20s and your instructor is at least 65) to voice your objection to this type of talk?

Chris Wattie/Reuters/Landov

What specialized verbal skills do politicians such as federal minister Rona Ambrose need to have? Given that so few Canadian women occupy high-level political positions, do you think Ambrose has changed her verbal communication style to increase her likelihood of success? In what ways?

Sexism

Sexism refers to the prejudicial attitudes toward men or women based on rigid beliefs about gender roles. Individual sexism may take the form of beliefs that women should be caretakers, should be sensitive at all times, and should acquiesce to men's decisions concerning political or financial matters. It also includes beliefs that men are insensitive, are interested only in sex, and are incapable of communicating feelings.

Institutional sexism, on the other hand, consists of customs and practices that discriminate against people because of their gender. Two clear examples are the widespread practice of paying women less than men for the same job and the discrimination against women in the upper levels of management. Another clear example of institutionalized sexism is the practice of automatically or near-automatically granting child custody to the mother rather than to the father in divorce cases.

Of particular interest here is **sexist language**: language that puts people (usually women) down because of their gender or that uses generic male terms to refer to both men and women. UNESCO's guidelines for gender-neutral language (Desprez-Bouanchaud et al., 1987), for example, concern such generic use of the words *man*, *he*, and *his*; the publication's cover page features a cartoon depicting a character touting the phrase "the brotherhood of man." And some well-known Canadian women, including writer Margaret Atwood and former prime minister Kim Campbell, have been campaigning to change the Canadian anthem's "in all thy sons command" to "in all of us command."

The following points will help ensure that you use gender-neutral language.

- Avoid using the word *man* generically. The word *man* refers most clearly to an adult male. To use the term to refer to both men and women emphasizes maleness at the expense of femaleness. Gender-neutral terms can easily be substituted. Instead of *mankind*, you can say *humanity*, *people*, or *human beings*. Instead of the *common man*, you can say *the average person* or *ordinary people*. Similarly, the use of terms such as *policeman* or *fireman* and other terms that presume maleness as the norm—and femaleness as a deviation from this norm—are clear and common examples of sexist language.

- Avoid using the words *he* and *his* as generic. There seems no legitimate reason why the feminine pronoun cannot alternate with the masculine pronoun to refer to hypothetical individuals, or why phrases such as *he or she* or *her or him* cannot be used instead of just *he* or *him*. Alternatively, you can restructure your sentences to eliminate any reference to gender. For example, the NCTE Guidelines (Penfield, 1987) suggest that instead of saying "The average student is worried about his grades," you can say "The average student is worried about grades." Instead of saying "Ask that each student hand in his work as soon as he's finished," you can say "Ask students to hand in their work as soon as they're finished."

- Avoid sex-role stereotyping. The words you use often reflect a sex-role bias—the assumption that certain roles or professions belong to men and others belong to women. When you make the hypothetical elementary schoolteacher female and the university professor male, or when you refer to doctors as male and nurses as female, you're sex-role stereotyping. This is also true when you include the sex of a professional, as in referring to a "female doctor" or a "male nurse."

Rostislav Glinsky/Shutterstock

VIEWPOINTS Language and Concept

A widely held assumption in anthropology, linguistics, and communication is that the importance of a concept to a culture can be measured by the number of words the language has for talking about the concept. So, for example, in English, there are lots of words for money, transportation, and communication—all crucial to the English-speaking world. With this principle in mind, consider these findings (Thorne, Kramarae, & Henley, 1983): in a search of English-language terms indicating sexual promiscuity, there were 220 terms referring to a sexually promiscuous woman but only 22 terms for a sexually promiscuous man. What does this finding suggest about our culture's attitudes and beliefs about promiscuity in men and women? In what ways is this changing?

"It doesn't have a damn thing to do with political correctness, pal. I'm a sausage, and that guy's a wienie."

Charles Barsotti/The New Yorker Collection/www.cartoonbank.com

Cultural Identifiers

Perhaps the best way to develop nonracist, nonheterosexist, nonageist, and nonsexist language is to examine the preferred cultural identifiers to use in talking to and about members of different groups. Keep in mind, however, that preferred terms frequently change over time and that there are often differences of opinion, so keep in touch with the most current preferences and be aware of the preference of the group to which you're referring. For example, note the way the terminology for referring to children with special needs has changed over time, or the terms used to describe people who have challenges related to mental health.

RACE AND NATIONALITY   In the United States, some research finds that the term *African American* is preferred over *black* in referring to Americans of African descent (Hecht, Jackson, & Ribeau, 2003). Other research, however, concludes that "a majority of blacks in America today do not have a preference" (Newport, 2007). *Black* is often used with *white*, as well as in a variety of other contexts (for example, in the United States, the Department of Black and Puerto Rican Studies, the *Journal of Black Studies*, and Black History Month). The terms *Negro* and *coloured*, although used in the names of some organizations in the United States (for example, the United Negro College Fund and the National Association for the Advancement of Colored People), are not appropriately used outside these contexts.

White is generally used to refer to those whose roots are in European cultures; analogous to *African Canadian* (which itself is based on terms such as *Irish Canadian* and *Italian Canadian*) is the phrase *European Canadian*. Few European Canadians, however, call themselves that; most prefer their national origins emphasized, as in, for example, *German Canadian* or *Greek Canadian*. *People of colour*—a more literary-sounding term appropriate perhaps to public speaking but awkward in most conversations—is preferred to *nonwhite*, which implies that whiteness is the norm and nonwhiteness is a deviation from that norm. The same is true of the term *non-Christian*: it implies that people who have other beliefs deviate from the norm.

Inuk (plural, *Inuit*) is preferred to *Eskimo*, which was applied to the indigenous peoples of Alaska and Canada by Europeans and literally means "raw meat eaters."

The word *Indian* technically refers only to someone from India, and is incorrectly used when applied to indigenous or native peoples of North America. *Aboriginal* or the name of the specific tribe or band is preferred; *First Nations* is the most commonly accepted term for non-Inuits and non-Métis peoples (Métis are a distinct group descended from both Natives and Europeans). Note that many native people self-identify as Indians, and in Canada, *Indian* is a legal term for native peoples in regard to government status and treaties.

Muslim (rather than the older *Moslem*) is the preferred form to refer to a person who adheres to the religious teachings of Islam. *Quran* (rather than *Koran*) is the preferred term for the scriptures of Islam. *Jewish people* is often preferred to *Jews*, and *Jewess* (a Jewish female) is considered derogatory.

When history was being written from a European perspective, Europe was taken as the focal point, and the rest of the world was defined in terms of its location relative to that continent. Thus, Asia became *the East* or *the Orient*, and Asians became *Orientals*—a term

INTERPERSONAL CHOICE POINT

Cultural Identifiers

You're at an international students open house, and all students are asked to talk about the cultural identifiers they prefer to have used in reference to themselves as well as the cultural identifiers they don't like. How might you explain the cultural identifiers you like and don't like?

INTERPERSONAL CHOICE POINT

Cultural Insensitivity

You inadvertently say something that you thought would be funny, but it turns out that you offended a friend with some culturally insensitive remark. What might you say to make it clear that you don't normally talk this way?

that is today considered "Eurocentric." People from Asia are *Asians*, just as people from Africa are *Africans* and people from Europe are *Europeans*.

AFFECTIONAL ORIENTATION   Generally, *gay* is the preferred term to refer to a man who has an affectional preference for other men, and *lesbian* is the preferred term for a woman who has an affectional preference for other women (Lever, 1995). (*Lesbian* means "homosexual woman," so the term *lesbian woman* is redundant.) *Homosexual* refers to both gay men and lesbians but more often to a sexual orientation to members of one's own sex and is often considered derogatory when used instead of *gay*. *Gay* and *lesbian* refer to a lifestyle and not just to sexual orientation. *Gay* as a noun, although widely used, may prove offensive in some contexts, as in "We have two gays on the team." Because most scientific thinking holds that sexuality is not a matter of choice, the terms *sexual orientation* and *affectional orientation* are preferred to *sexual preference* or *sexual status* (which is also vague).

In the case of same-sex marriages, there are two husbands or two wives. In a male–male marriage, each person is referred to as *husband*, and in the case of female–female marriage, each person is referred to as *wife*. Some same-sex couples—especially those who are not married—prefer the term *partner* or *lover*.

AGE AND SEX   *Older person* is preferred to *elder*, *elderly*, *senior*, or *senior citizen* (which technically refers to someone older than 65). Usually, however, terms designating age are unnecessary. There are times, of course, when you'll need to refer to a person's age group, but most of the time it isn't necessary—in much the same way that racial or affectional orientation terms are usually irrelevant.

Generally, the term *girl* should be used only to refer to very young females and is equivalent to *boy*. Neither term should be used for people older than 17 or 18. *Girl* is never used to refer to a grown woman, nor is *boy* used to refer to people in blue-collar positions, as it once was. *Lady* is negatively evaluated by many because it connotes the stereotype of the prim and proper woman. *Woman* or *young woman* is preferred. Although there are regional variations, the term *ma'am*, originally an honorific used to show respect, is probably best avoided because today it's often used as a verbal tag to comment (indirectly) on the woman's age or marital status (Angier, 1999).

Transgendered people (people who identify themselves as members of the sex opposite to the one they were assigned at birth and who may be gay or straight, male or female) are addressed according to their self-identified sex. Thus, if the person identifies herself as a woman, then the feminine name and pronouns are used—regardless of the person's biological sex. If the person identifies himself as a man, then the masculine name and pronouns are used.

Transvestites (people who prefer at times to dress in the clothing of the sex other than the one they were assigned at birth and who may be gay or straight, male or female) are addressed on the basis of their clothing. If the person is dressed as a woman—regardless of the birth-assigned sex—she is referred to and addressed with feminine pronouns and feminine name. If the person is dressed as a man—regardless of the birth-assigned sex—he is referred to and addressed with masculine pronouns and masculine name.

Can you distinguish between confirmation and disconfirmation? Can you use appropriate cultural identifiers without language that might be considered racist, heterosexist, ageist, or sexist?

GUIDELINES FOR USING VERBAL MESSAGES EFFECTIVELY

The principles governing the verbal messages system suggest a wide variety of ways for using language more effectively. Here are six additional guidelines for making your own verbal messages more effective and a more accurate reflection of the world in which we live: (1) focus on the actual: avoid labelling, (2) recognize complexity: avoid gross generalizations, (3) distinguish between facts and inferences: avoid fact–inference confusion, (4) discriminate among: avoid indiscrimination, (5) talk about the middle: avoid polarization, and (6) update messages: avoid static evaluation.

Focus on the Actual: Avoid Labelling

While labels provide us with a relatively easy way to extract the essence of a person or thing and communicate it succinctly, they're often unhelpful and even harmful. Think about the adjectives that are used to describe a person, and that sometimes come to represent the person totally. Labels sometimes prevent you from being guided by what you actually see, or by what is actually happening, and instead relate to the way someone is talked about or labelled.

Recognize Complexity: Don't Overgeneralize

Generalizations help us deal with complexity, but they're often misleading. They're also often related to stereotypes about particular groups or countries. So when you make generalizations, it's important to qualify them to ensure that you're not making a definitive statement. Phrases such as "in my experience" or "what struck my attention was" indicate that even if you're generalizing, you're not claiming to be the expert on the subject, and that there may be other, equally valid points of view.

Distinguish Between Facts and Inferences: Avoid Fact–Inference Confusion

Before reading this section, test your ability to distinguish facts from inferences by taking the accompanying self-test.

Eric Audras/Onoky/Age Fotostock

VIEWPOINTS **Labels**

One of the problems with the tendency to respond to labels is that these labels set up a kind of template through which you then see the thing or person. Having been told someone is deceitful, for example, you may then interpret future behaviours of this person through this *deceitful* label. What are some of the implications of this for writing your profile on social networking sites such as Facebook and LinkedIn? On dating sites such as Match.com and eHarmony?

Language enables you to form statements of facts and inferences without making any linguistic distinction between the two. For example, you can make statements about things you observe, and you can make statements about things you haven't observed. In form or structure, these statements are similar; they cannot be distinguished from each other by any grammatical analysis. For example, you can say, "She's wearing a blue jacket" as well as "She's harbouring an illogical hatred." In the first sentence, you can observe the jacket and the blue colour; the sentence constitutes a factual statement. But how do you observe "illogical hatred"? Obviously, this is an inferential statement, a statement that you make not solely on what you observe but on what you observe plus your own conclusions.

Distinguishing between these two types of statements doesn't imply that one type is better than the other. Both types of statements are useful; both are important. The problem arises when you treat an inferential statement as if it were fact; this is what's known as **fact–inference confusion**. Phrase your inferential statements as tentative. Recognize that such statements may be wrong. Leave open the possibility of other alternatives.

TEST YOURSELF

Can You Distinguish Facts from Inferences?

Carefully read the following report and the observations based on it. Indicate whether you think, on the basis of the information presented in the report, that the observations are true, false, or doubtful. Write *T* if the observation is definitely true, *F* if the observation is definitely false, and *?* if the observation may be either true or false. Judge the observations in order. Don't reread the observations after you've indicated your judgment, and don't change any of your answers.

A well-liked college teacher had just completed making up the final examinations and had turned off the lights in the office. Just then a tall, broad figure with dark glasses appeared and demanded the examination. The professor opened the drawer. Everything in the drawer was picked up, and the individual ran down the corridor. The dean was notified immediately.

_____ 1. The thief was tall and broad and wore dark glasses.

_____ 2. The professor turned off the lights.

_____ 3. A tall figure demanded the examination.

_____ 4. The examination was picked up by someone.

_____ 5. The examination was picked up by the professor.

_____ 6. A tall, broad figure appeared after the professor turned off the lights in the office.

_____ 7. The man who opened the drawer was the professor.

_____ 8. The professor ran down the corridor.

_____ 9. The drawer was never actually opened.

_____10. Three persons are referred to in this report.

How Did You Do? After you answer all 10 questions, form small groups of five or six and discuss the answers. Look at each statement from each member's point of view. For each statement, ask yourself, "How can you be absolutely certain that the statement is true or false?" You should find that only one statement can be clearly identified as true and only one as false; eight should be marked *?*

What Will You Do? Try to formulate specific guidelines that will help you distinguish facts from inferences.

Discriminate Among: Avoid Indiscrimination

Nature seems to abhor sameness at least as much as vacuums, for nowhere in the universe can you find identical entities. Everything is unique. Language, however, provides common nouns, such as *teacher*, *student*, *friend*, *war*, *politician*, and the like, that may lead you to focus on similarities. Such nouns can lead you to group together all teachers, all students, and all friends and perhaps divert attention from the uniqueness of each individual, object, and event.

The misevaluation known as **indiscrimination**—a form of stereotyping (see Chapter 2)—occurs when you focus on classes of individuals, objects, or events and fail to see that each is unique and needs to be looked at individually. Indiscrimination can be seen in such statements as "He's just like the rest of them: lazy, stupid, a real slob" or "Read a romance novel? I read one when I was 16. That was enough to convince me."

One useful antidote to indiscrimination is a device called the **index**, a spoken or mental subscript that identifies each individual in a group as an individual even though all members of the group may be covered by the same label. For example, when you think and talk of an individual politician as just a "politician," you may fail to see the uniqueness in this politician and the differences between this particular politician and other politicians. However, when you think with the index—when you

"Are you the angry young artist or the angry young bloodsucking dealer?"

Michael Crawford/The New Yorker Collection/www.cartoonbank.com

think not of politician but of politician1 or politician2 or politician3—you're less likely to fall into the trap of indiscrimination and more likely to focus on the differences among politicians. The more you discriminate among individuals covered by the same label, the less likely you are to discriminate against any group.

Talk About the Middle: Avoid Polarization

Polarization, often referred to as the fallacy of "either/or," is the tendency to look at the world and describe it in terms of extremes—good or bad, positive or negative, healthy or sick, brilliant or stupid, rich or poor, and so on. Polarized statements come in many forms; here are three examples: "After listening to the evidence, I'm still not clear who the good guys are and who the bad guys are" or "Well, are you for us or against us?" or "College had better get me a good job. Otherwise, this has been a big waste of time."

Most people exist somewhere between the extremes of good and bad, healthy and sick, brilliant and stupid, rich and poor. Yet there seems to be a strong tendency to view only the extremes and to categorize people, objects, and events in terms of these polar opposites.

You can easily demonstrate this tendency by filling in the opposites for each of the following words:

Opposite

tall:	_____	: _____	: _____	: _____	: _____	: _____	: _____	: _____
heavy:	_____	: _____	: _____	: _____	: _____	: _____	: _____	: _____
strong:	_____	: _____	: _____	: _____	: _____	: _____	: _____	: _____
happy:	_____	: _____	: _____	: _____	: _____	: _____	: _____	: _____
legal:	_____	: _____	: _____	: _____	: _____	: _____	: _____	: _____

Filling in the opposites should have been relatively easy and quick. The words should also have been fairly short. Further, if different people supplied the opposites, there would be a high degree of agreement among them. Now try to fill in the middle positions with words meaning, for example, "midway between tall and short," "midway between heavy and light," and so on. Do this before reading any further.

These midway responses (compared with the opposites) were probably more difficult to think of and took you more time. The responses should also have been long words or phrases of several words. Further, different people would probably agree less on these midway responses than on the opposites.

This exercise illustrates the ease with which you can think and talk in opposites and the difficulty you can have in thinking and talking about the middle. But recognize that the vast majority of cases exist between extremes. Don't allow the ready availability of extreme terms to obscure the reality of what lies in between (Read, 2004).

Update Messages: Avoid Static Evaluation

Language changes very slowly, especially when compared with the rapid pace at which people and things change. When you retain an evaluation of a person, despite the inevitable changes in that person, you're engaging in **static evaluation**.

To guard against static evaluation, use a device called **dating statements**: mentally date your statements and especially your evaluations. Remember that Gerry Smith 2010 is not Gerry Smith 2014; academic abilities 2010 are not academic abilities 2014. As a character in T. S. Eliot's play *The Cocktail Party* remarks, "What we know of other people is only our memory of the moments during which we knew them. And they have changed since then. . . . . [A]t every meeting, we are meeting a stranger."

These six guidelines won't solve all problems in verbal communication, but they will help you to more accurately align your language with the real world in its infinite complexity, facts and inferences, sameness and difference, extremes and middle ground, and constant change.

Review the guidelines for using verbal messages effectively and list the ways in which you can improve your verbal communication by following these guidelines.

CANADIAN PROFILE: WRAP-UP

Dominic Chan/CP Images

Music can stir an emotion or inspire us to think in different ways. Sometimes the music itself isn't the vehicle for this (meaning that the lyrics aren't necessarily targeted politically or socially) but rather the musicians' personalities or advocacy causes. How successful do you think music and musicians such as Tegan and Sara (with their LGBTQ message) or Neil Young (with his anti–oil sands message) are in causing audiences to think, respond, or react in new ways? Do you know of other examples of music being used to influence an audience? Have you ever been impacted by a musical message?

SUMMARY OF CONCEPTS AND SKILLS

This chapter looked at verbal messages: the nature of language and the ways in which language works; the concept of disconfirmation and how it relates to racism, heterosexism, ageism, and sexist language; and the ways in which you can use language more effectively.

Principles of Verbal Messages

1. Message meanings are in people, not in things.
2. Verbal messages are both denotative (objective and generally easily agreed upon) and connotative (subjective and generally highly individual in meaning).
3. Verbal messages can be onymous or anonymous.
4. Verbal messages vary in abstraction; they can range from extremely general to extremely specific.
5. Verbal messages vary in politeness, which can be viewed as strategies that enable a person to maintain a positive public image and autonomy.
6. Verbal messages can deceive, sometimes for acceptable reasons and sometimes for unethical and unacceptable reasons.
7. Messages vary in assertiveness and need to be clearly distinguished from nonassertive and aggressive messages.

Confirmation and Disconfirmation

8. Disconfirmation is the process of ignoring the presence and the communications of others. Confirmation means accepting, supporting, and acknowledging the importance of the other person.
9. Racist, heterosexist, ageist, and sexist messages unfairly put down and negatively evaluate groups and are seen in both individual and institutionalized forms.

Guidelines for Using Verbal Messages Effectively

10. Using verbal messages effectively involves substituting more accurate assumptions about language for conceptual distortions, the most important of which are

- labels, giving primary attention to the way something is talked about instead of to the actual thing
- generalizations, assuming that all can be known or said about something
- fact–inference confusion, treating inferences with the same certainty as facts
- indiscrimination, failing to see differences
- polarization, assuming that the extremes define the world
- static evaluation, assuming non-change

In addition, this chapter discussed a variety of verbal messages skills. Check those you wish to work on:

____ 1. *Meanings*. Look for meanings in people, not just in words.
____ 2. *Connotative meanings*. Clarify your connotative meanings if you have any concern that your listeners might misunderstand you; as a listener, ask questions if you have doubts about the speaker's connotations.
____ 3. *Abstractions*. Use both abstract and concrete language when describing or explaining.
____ 4. *Politeness*. Be careful of messages that will be perceived as impolite, messages that undermine a person's positive face (the need to be viewed

positively) or negative face (the need for autonomy).

____ 5. *Deception.* Be alert to messages that seek to deceive but be wary of reading signs of deception where there may be no deception involved.

____ 6. *Confirmation.* When you wish to be confirming, acknowledge (verbally and/or nonverbally) others in your group and their contributions.

____ 7. *Disconfirming language.* Avoid racist, heterosexist, ageist, and sexist language, which is disconfirming and insulting and invariably creates communication barriers.

____ 8. *Cultural identifiers.* Use cultural identifiers that are sensitive to the desires of others; when appropriate, make clear the cultural identifiers you prefer.

____ 9. *Labels.* Avoid labelling. Look to people and things first and to labels second.

____10. *Generalizations.* Avoid generalizing statements; they invariably misstate the reality and will often offend the other person.

____11. *Facts and inferences.* Distinguish facts (verifiably true past events) from inferences (guesses or hypotheses), and act on inferences with tentativeness.

____12. *Indiscrimination.* Treat each situation and each person as unique (when possible), even when they're covered by the same label. Index key concepts.

____13. *Polarization.* Avoid thinking and talking in extremes by using middle terms and qualifiers. But remember that too many qualifiers may make you appear unsure of yourself.

____14. *Dating statements.* Date your statements to avoid thinking of the world as static and unchanging. Reflect the inevitability of change in your messages.

VOCABULARY QUIZ: The Language of Verbal Messages

Match the terms of verbal messages with their definitions. Record the number of the definition next to the appropriate term.

____ polarization (116)
____ disconfirmation (106)
____ connotative meaning (97)
____ fact–inference confusion (114)
____ confirmation (107)
____ static evaluation (116)
____ indiscrimination (115)
____ ageism (110)
____ heterosexism (109)

1. Treating inferences as if they were facts.
2. The denial of change in language and in thinking.
3. The emotional, subjective aspect of meaning.
4. A communication pattern of acknowledgment and acceptance.
5. Disparagement of those who are LGBTQ as being unnatural.
6. The degree of generality or specificity of a term.
7. Discrimination based on age.
8. The failure to see the differences among people or things covered by the same label.
9. A communication pattern of ignoring a person's presence and his or her own communication.
10. A focus on extremes to the neglect of the middle.

These 10 terms and additional key terms from this chapter can be found in the glossary.

6

Nonverbal Messages

CANADIAN PROFILE: Samantha Nutt

War Child Canada/Dustin Rabin

What spurs a young recent medical-school graduate to a "lifetime of passionate advocacy for children and families in war-torn areas around the world" (www.warchild.ca)? In 1995, Samantha Nutt was volunteering with UNICEF in Baidoa, Somalia, known as the City of Death. Imagine being 25 years old and seeing a woman standing in a long line at the medical clinic desperately seeking help for her baby who has already died. Imagine being a volunteer and needing protection from gangs armed by rocket launchers by escorts who are high on drugs.

When Samantha Nutt returned to Canada after her time with UNICEF, she founded War Child, an organization dedicated to helping children, mothers, and families find ways to live safe, peaceful lives. War Child's core programming areas are education, opportunity, and justice. War disrupts a country not only during the conflict itself but for

years afterward. When children don't have the opportunity for education, they can't become productive members of their society as adults. And when children are traumatized during war, they suffer mentally and physically in ways that impact them for the rest of their lives. Societies suffer for generations as a result of the impact of war on children.

Dr. Nutt is a staff physician at Women's College Hospital in Toronto and an assistant professor of medicine at the University of Toronto. She works with children and families on the front line of major crises around the world. She is a respected authority on humanitarian issues, impacts of war, international aid, and foreign policy and current affairs. As such, Samantha Nutt is a frequent contributor to media and a highly sought-after public speaker. Her work has been acknowledged through many high-profile awards. She was named one of Canada's 25 Transformational Canadians by *The Globe and Mail* and has been recognized as a Young Global Leader by the World Economic Forum. In 2011 she was appointed to the Order of Canada for her contributions to improving the plight of young people in the world's worst conflict zones.

As you work through this chapter, think about how Samantha Nutt might use the nonverbal techniques described to advocate for peace and safety for children in war-torn areas. How might these techniques differ when she's working on the front line and when she's advocating in person and through various forms of media? Consider what lessons you can learn from this chapter, and from people who are well known, about the use of nonverbal communication in effectively (and ethically) advocating for something about which you are passionate.

LEARNING OBJECTIVES *After reading this chapter, you should be able to:*

1. Explain the six principles that identify the ways in which nonverbal communication functions.

2. Define the 10 channels of nonverbal messages, and give examples of messages in each channel.

3. Apply the encoding and decoding suggestions in your own nonverbal interactions.

A good way to begin the study of **nonverbal communication** (communication without words) is to consider your own beliefs about it. Which of the following statements do you believe are true?

____ **1.** Nonverbal communication conveys more meaning than verbal communication.

____ **2.** Understanding nonverbal communication will help enable you to tell what people are thinking, "to read a person like a book."

____ **3.** Studying nonverbal communication will enable you to detect lying.

____ **4.** Unlike verbal communication, the meanings of nonverbal signals are universal throughout the world.

____ **5.** When verbal and nonverbal messages contradict each other, it's wise to believe the nonverbal.

Actually, all of these statements are popular myths about nonverbal communication. Briefly, (1) in some instances, nonverbal messages may communicate more meaning than verbal messages, but, in most cases, it depends on the situation. You won't get very far discussing science and mathematics nonverbally, for example. (2) This is an impossible task; you may get ideas about what someone is thinking, but you really can't be certain on the basis of nonverbal behaviours alone. (3) Lie detection is a far more difficult process than any chapter or even series of courses could accomplish. (4) Although some nonverbal behaviours may be universal in meaning, many signals communicate very different meanings in different cultures. (5) People can be deceptive verbally as well as nonverbally; it's best to look at the entire group of signals before making a judgment, but even then it won't be an easy or sure thing.

Studying nonverbal communication and developing your nonverbal competence can yield two principal benefits (Burgoon & Hoobler, 2002; Burgoon, Guerrero, & Floyd, 2010). First, the greater your ability to encode and decode nonverbal signals, the higher your popularity and psychosocial well-being are likely to be. Not surprisingly, encoding and decoding abilities are highly correlated; if you're good at expressing yourself nonverbally, then you're likely to also be good at reading the nonverbal cues of others. This relationship is likely part of a more general relationship: people who are high in interpersonal skills are perceived to be high in such positive qualities as expressiveness, self-esteem, outgoingness, social comfort, sociability, and gregariousness. Interpersonal skills really do matter.

Second, the greater your nonverbal skills, the more successful you're likely to be in a wide variety of interpersonal situations, including close relationships, workplace relationships, teacher–student relationships, intercultural communication, courtroom communication, politics, and health care (Knapp, 2008; Richmond, McCroskey, & Hickson, 2008; Riggio & Feldman, 2005).

PRINCIPLES OF NONVERBAL COMMUNICATION

In this section we look at several principles of nonverbal communication, which also identify the varied functions that nonverbal messages serve (Afifi, 2007; Burgoon & Bacue, 2003; Burgoon, Guerrero, & Floyd, 2010). These principles, as you'll see, are applicable in both personal and workplace situations.

Nonverbal Messages Interact with Verbal Messages

Verbal and nonverbal messages interact with each other in six major ways: to accent, to complement, to contradict, to control, to repeat, and to substitute for each other.

■ *Accent.* Nonverbal communication is often used to accent or emphasize some part of the verbal message. You might, for example, raise your voice to underscore a particular word or phrase or look longingly into someone's eyes when saying "I love you."

■ *Complement.* Nonverbal communication may be used to complement, to add nuances of meaning not communicated by your verbal message. Thus, you might smile when telling a story (to suggest that you find it humorous) or frown and shake your head when recounting someone's deceit (to suggest your disapproval).

■ *Contradict.* You may deliberately contradict your verbal messages with nonverbal movements; for example, by crossing your fingers or winking to indicate that you're lying.

■ *Control.* Nonverbal movements may be used to control, or to indicate your desire to control, the flow of verbal messages, as when you purse your lips, lean forward, or make hand movements to indicate that you want to speak.

■ *Repeat.* You can repeat or restate the verbal message nonverbally. You can, for example, follow your verbal "Is that all right?" with raised eyebrows and a questioning look, or you can motion with your head or hand to repeat your verbal "Let's go."

■ *Substitute.* You may also use nonverbal communication to substitute for verbal messages. You can, for example, signal "okay" with a hand gesture. You can nod your head to indicate yes or shake your head to indicate no.

When you communicate electronically, of course, your message is conveyed by means of typed letters without the facial expressions or gestures that normally accompany face-to-face communication and without the changes in rate and volume that are a part of normal telephone communication. To compensate for this lack of nonverbal behaviour, you may, for example, post and refer to photos and videos that convey some of your message's meaning. This lack of nonverbal behaviour was the reason the emoticon was created (see Table 6.1). Sometimes called a "smiley" after the ever-present :), the emoticon is a typed symbol that communicates through a keyboard the nuances of the message normally conveyed by nonverbal expression. The absence of the nonverbal channel through which you can clarify your message— for example, smiling or winking to communicate sarcasm or humour—makes such typed symbols extremely helpful. As you'll also see from the table, emoticons are specific to a given culture.

TABLE 6.1

SOME POPULAR EMOTICONS

These are some of the emoticons used in computer communication. The first six are widely used in North America; the last three are popular in Japan and illustrate how culture influences such symbols. Because Japanese culture considers it impolite for women to show their teeth when smiling, the emoticon for a woman's smile shows a dot signifying a closed mouth. Depending on your computer, these typed symbols often auto-correct (as in the first two examples) into their graphic equivalents. Additional emoticons, acronyms, and abbreviations—in varied cultures—are plentiful on the internet.

Emoticon	Meaning	Emoticon	Meaning
:-) ☺	Smile: I'm kidding	{*****}	Hugs and kisses
:-(☹	Frown: I'm feeling down	^ . ^	Woman's smile
;-)	Wink	^ _ ^	Man's smile
*	Kiss	^0^	Happy
{}	Hug		

"Well, just look at you—that's why I'm king."

Charles Barsotti/The New Yorker Collection/www.cartoonbank.com

Nonverbal Messages Help Manage Impressions

It is largely through the nonverbal communications of others that you form impressions of them. Based on a person's body size, skin colour, and dress (which you may see face to face or online in photos and videos), as well as on the way the person smiles, maintains eye contact, and expresses himself or herself facially, you form impressions—you judge who the person is and what the person is like.

And, at the same time that you form impressions of others, you're also managing the impressions they form of you. As explained in the discussion of impression management in Chapter 3, you use different strategies to achieve different impressions. And of course many of these strategies involve nonverbal messages. For example:

- *To be liked*, you might smile, pat another on the back, and shake hands warmly. See Table 6.2 for some additional ways in which nonverbal communication may make you seem more attractive and more likeable.
- *To be believed*, you might use focused eye contact, a firm stance, and open gestures.
- *To excuse failure*, you might look sad, cover your face with your hands, and shake your head.
- *To secure help* by indicating helplessness, you might use open hand gestures, a puzzled look, and inept movements.
- *To hide faults*, you might avoid self-adaptors (self-touching movements, as described later in the chapter).
- *To be followed*, you might dress the part of a leader or display your diploma or awards where others can see them.
- *To confirm self-image and to communicate it to others*, you might dress in certain ways or decorate your apartment with things that reflect your personality.

Nonverbal Messages Help Form Relationships

Much of your relationship life is lived nonverbally. You communicate affection, support, and love, in part at least, nonverbally (Floyd & Mikkelson, 2005). At the same time, you also communicate displeasure, anger, and animosity through nonverbal signals.

You also use nonverbal signals to communicate the nature of your relationship with another person; you and that person communicate nonverbally with each other. These **tie signs** are signals that communicate your relationship status: they indicate the ways in which your relationship is tied together (Goffman, 1967; Knapp & Hall, 2010). Tie signs are also used to confirm the level of the relationship; for example,

TABLE 6.2

Ten Nonverbal Ways to Increase Your Attractiveness

Here are 10 nonverbal messages that help communicate your attractiveness and 10 that will likely create the opposite effect (Andersen, 1991; Riggio & Feldman, 2005).

Do	But Don't
Gesture to show liveliness and animation in ways that are appropriate to the situation and to the message.	Gesture for the sake of gesturing or gesture in ways that may prove offensive to members of other cultures.
Nod and lean forward to signal that you're listening and are interested.	Go on automatic pilot, nodding without any coordination with what's being said, or lean forward so much that you intrude on the other's space.
Smile and otherwise show your interest, attention, and positiveness facially.	Overdo it; inappropriate smiling is likely to be perceived negatively.
Make eye contact in moderation.	Stare, ogle, glare, or otherwise make the person feel that he or she is under scrutiny.
Touch in moderation when appropriate.	Touch excessively or too intimately. When in doubt, avoid touching another.
Use vocal variation in rate, rhythm, pitch, and volume to communicate your animation and involvement in what you're saying.	Fall into the pattern where, for example, your voice goes up and down, up and down, up and down without any relationship to what you're saying.
Use silence to listen the same amount of time as you speak. Show that you're listening with appropriate facial reactions, posture, and backchannelling cues, for example.	Listen motionlessly or in ways that suggest you're listening only half-heartedly.
Stand reasonably close to show a connectedness.	Exceed the other person's comfort zone.
Present a pleasant smell and be careful to camouflage the onion, garlic, or smoke that you're so used to you can't smell it.	Overdo the cologne or perfume or wear your body sweat as a sign of a heavy workout.
Dress appropriately to the situation.	Wear clothing that proves uncomfortable or that calls attention to itself and hence away from your message.

you might hold hands to see if this is responded to positively. And of course tie signs are often used to let others know that the two of you are tied together.

Tie signs vary in intimacy and may extend from the relatively informal handshake through more intimate forms such as hand holding and arm linking to very intimate contact such as full mouth kissing (Andersen, 1991).

Nonverbal Messages Structure Conversation

When you're in conversation, you give and receive cues—signals that you're ready to speak, to listen, to comment on what the speaker just said. These cues regulate and structure the interaction. These **turn-taking cues** may be verbal (as when you say

Dominic Chan/ CP Images

"Former Sports Illustrated Swimsuit Carol Alt" visits The Marilyn Denis Show on October 13, 2011 to promote her beauty and health food product line "Raw Essentials."

A number of talk shows today focus on such areas as beauty, health, and home design; guests on these shows have the opportunity to market products with which they are associated, using both verbal and nonverbal approaches. Subtle nonverbal cues suggest to us how to make a better impression—we're all familiar with watching people whose appearance reinforces the message that you can look and feel healthier with the help of their products. In fact, some talk shows have been criticized for disguising the advertising of particular products. They may never even talk about these products—but marketing researchers know all too well the powerful impact that nonverbal cues can have on our purchasing choices. Watch some of these shows with a view to noticing such cues in order to sensitize yourself to them as they occur in your everyday personal interactions. This chapter will help you recognize the power of nonverbal communication so that you may become a more effective nonverbal communicator and increase your awareness of the nonverbal messages you receive.

"What do you think?" and thereby give the speaking turn over to the listener). Most often, however, they're nonverbal; a nod of the head in the direction of someone else, for example, signals that you're ready to give up your speaking turn and want this other person to say something. You also show that you're listening and that you want the conversation to continue (or that you're not listening and want the conversation to end) largely through nonverbal signals of posture and eye contact (or the lack thereof).

Nonverbal Messages Can Influence and Deceive

You can influence others not only through what you say but also through your nonverbal signals. A focused glance that says you're committed; gestures that further explain what you're saying; and appropriate dress that says, "I'll easily fit in with this organization" are just a few examples of ways in which you can exert nonverbal influence.

Nonverbal Messages Are Crucial for Expressing Emotions

Nonverbal signals communicate a great part of your emotional experience. For example, you reveal your level of happiness or sadness or confusion largely through facial expressions. You also reveal your feelings by posture (for example, whether tense or relaxed), gestures, eye movements, and even the dilation of your pupils. As well, you use nonverbal messages to communicate unpleasant messages that you might feel uncomfortable putting into words (Infante, Rancer, & Avtgis, 2010). For example, you might avoid eye contact and maintain a distance between yourself and someone with whom you don't want to interact or with whom you want to decrease the intensity of your relationship.

At the same time, you also use nonverbal messages to hide your emotions. You might, for example, smile even though you feel sad so as not to dampen the party spirit. Or you might laugh at someone's joke even though you think it silly.

CP Photo/Frank Gunn

VIEWPOINTS Politicians and Babies

Have you ever known of a politician who didn't have a press photo with a baby? What do you think politicians are trying to convey with such images? What's important about the body language and message portrayed in these types of photos? After all, with the politician's ability to influence comes the ability to deceive—to mislead others into thinking that something is true when it's false, or that something is false when it's true. One common example of nonverbal deception is using your eyes and facial expressions to communicate a liking for other people when you're really only interested in gaining their support in some endeavour. Not surprisingly, you also use nonverbal signals to detect deception in others. For example, you may suspect a person of lying if he or she avoids eye contact, fidgets, and conveys inconsistent verbal and nonverbal messages.

Can you explain the basic principles of nonverbal communication (that nonverbal messages work together with verbal messages, help form impressions, define relationships, structure conversation, can influence and deceive, and are crucial to emotional expression)? Can you identify instances in which your own nonverbal messages illustrate each of these principles?

THE CHANNELS OF NONVERBAL MESSAGES

Nonverbal communication messages may use a variety of channels. Here we'll survey 11 channels: body gestures, body appearance, face, eye, space, artifactual, touch, paralanguage, silence, time, and smell.

Body Gestures

An especially useful classification in **kinesics**, or the study of communication through body movement, identifies five types of gestures: emblems, illustrators, affect displays, regulators, and adaptors (Ekman & Friesen, 1969).

Emblems are body gestures that directly translate into words or phrases—for example, the okay sign, the thumbs-up for "good job," and the V for victory. You use these consciously and purposely to communicate the same meaning as the words. But emblems are culture specific, so be careful when using your culture's emblems in other cultures (Axtell, 2007). For example, in North America, to say "hello" you wave with your whole hand moving from side to side, but in a large part of Europe, that same signal means "no." And in Greece, such a gesture would be considered insulting to the person to whom you're waving.

Illustrators enhance (literally "illustrate") the verbal messages they accompany. Most often you illustrate with your hands, but you can also illustrate with head and general body movements. For example, when referring to something on the left, you might gesture toward the left or nod in that direction. You also use illustrators to communicate the shape or size of objects you're talking about.

Affect displays include movements of the face (smiling or frowning, for example), as well as of the hands and general body (body tension or relaxation, for example), that communicate emotional meaning. You use affect displays to accompany and reinforce your verbal messages but also as substitutes for words; for example, you might smile while saying how happy you are to see your friend, or you might simply smile. Affect displays are often unconscious; frequently, for example, you smile or frown without awareness. At other times, however, you may smile with awareness, consciously trying to convey pleasure or friendliness.

Regulators are behaviours that monitor, control, coordinate, or maintain the speaking of another individual. When you nod your head, for example, you tell the speaker to keep on speaking; when you lean forward and open your mouth, you tell the speaker that you'd like to say something.

Adaptors are gestures that satisfy some personal need. **Self-adaptors** are self-touching movements; for example, rubbing your nose, scratching to relieve an itch, or moving your hair out of your eyes. **Alter-adaptors** are movements directed at the person with whom you're speaking, such as removing lint from a person's jacket, straightening a person's tie, or folding your arms in front of you to keep others at a comfortable distance. **Object-adaptors** are gestures focused on objects; for example, doodling on or shredding a Styrofoam coffee cup.

Body Appearance

Your general body appearance also communicates. Height, for example, has been shown to be significant in a wide variety of situations. Tall presidential candidates have a much better record of winning elections than do their shorter opponents. Tall people seem to be paid more and are favoured by personnel interviewers over shorter job applicants (Guerrero & Hecht, 2008; Jackson & Ervin, 1992; Keyes, 1980; Knapp & Hall, 1996). Taller people also have higher self-esteem and greater career success than do shorter people (Judge & Cable, 2004).

QxQ IMAGES/Datacraft/Getty Images

Your body also reveals your race (through skin colour and tone) and may even give clues as to your specific nationality. Your weight in proportion to your height will also communicate messages to others, as will the length, colour, and style of your hair.

Your general attractiveness, which includes both visual appeal and pleasantness of personality, is also a part of body communication. Attractive people have the advantage in just about every activity you can name. They get better grades in school, are more valued as friends and lovers, and are preferred as co-workers (Burgoon, Guerrero, & Floyd, 2010). Not surprisingly, positive facial expressions contribute to the perception of attractiveness for both men and women (Koscriski, 2007).

VIEWPOINTS Body Appearance

On a 10-point scale, with 1 indicating "not at all important" and 10 indicating "extremely important," how important is body appearance to your interest in another person? What are the features that you find most attractive? Are there particular physical features that would make you hesitate to engage with a person?

Facial Messages

Throughout your interpersonal interactions, your face communicates many things, especially your emotions. Facial movements alone seem to communicate messages about pleasantness, agreement, and sympathy; the rest of the body doesn't provide any additional information in those realms. But you'll need both facial and bodily cues to express the intensity with which an emotion is felt (Graham & Argyle, 1975; Graham, Bitti, & Argyle, 1975).

Try to express surprise using only facial movements. Do this in front of a mirror, and try to describe in as much detail as possible the specific movements of the face that make up a look of surprise. If you signal surprise as most people do, you probably use raised and curved eyebrows, long horizontal forehead wrinkles, wide-open eyes, a dropped-open mouth, and lips parted with no tension. Even if there were differences from one person to another—and clearly there would be—you could probably recognize the movements listed here as indicative of surprise.

As you've probably experienced, you may interpret the same facial expression differently depending on the context in which it occurs. For example, in a classic study, when researchers showed participants a smiling face looking at a glum face, the participants judged the smiling face to be vicious and taunting. But when presented with the same smiling face looking at a frowning face, they saw it as peaceful and friendly (Cline, 1956).

Not surprisingly, people who smile are judged to be more likeable and more approachable than people who don't smile or people who pretend to smile (Gladstone & Parker, 2002; Kluger, 2005).

FACIAL MANAGEMENT   As you learn your culture's nonverbal system of communication, you also learn certain facial management techniques that enable you to communicate your feelings in order to achieve the effect you want—for example, to hide certain emotions and to emphasize others. Consider your own use of such facial management techniques. Which of the following techniques do you use or see used by others (Richmond et al., 2012)?

- *To intensify*; for example, to exaggerate surprise to make your friends feel better when friends throw you a party
- *To deintensify*; for example, to cover up your own joy in the presence of a friend who didn't receive such good news

INTERPERSONAL CHOICE POINT

Reconsidering First Impressions

We all know that first impressions have a disproportionately high impact on our judgment of a person. Sometimes this leads to missing out on an opportunity to develop a wonderful friendship or to hire a person who would bring great value to a workplace. What are some of the things you can do to avoid the trap of making judgments based on first impressions? In what circumstances do you think you should trust your first impression?

- *To neutralize*; for example, to cover up your sadness to keep from depressing others
- *To mask*; for example, to express happiness to cover up your disappointment at not receiving the gift you expected

These facial management techniques help you display emotions in socially acceptable ways. For example, when someone gets bad news in which you may secretly take pleasure, the display rule dictates that you frown and otherwise nonverbally signal your displeasure. If you place first in a race and your best friend barely finishes, the display rule requires that you minimize your expression of pleasure in winning and avoid any signs of gloating. If you violate these display rules, you'll be judged as insensitive. So, although these techniques may be deceptive, they're also expected—and, in fact, required—by the rules of polite interaction.

FACIAL FEEDBACK   The **facial feedback hypothesis** holds that your facial expressions influence physiological arousal. In one study, for example, participants held a pen in their teeth to simulate a sad expression and then rated a series of photographs. Results showed that mimicking sad expressions actually increased the degree of sadness the participants reported feeling when viewing the photographs (Larsen, Kasimatis, & Frey, 1992). Generally, research finds that facial expressions can produce or heighten feelings of sadness, fear, disgust, and anger. But this effect does not occur with all emotions; smiling, for example, doesn't seem to make us feel happier (Burgoon, Guerrero, & Floyd, 2010). Further, it has not been demonstrated that facial expressions can eliminate one feeling and replace it with another. So if you're feeling sad, smiling won't eliminate the sadness and replace it with gladness. A reasonable conclusion seems to be that your facial expressions can influence some feelings but not all (Burgoon, Guerrero, & Floyd, 2010; Cappella, 1993).

CULTURE AND FACIAL EXPRESSION   A collaborative study conducted by a University of Alberta researcher and a Japanese and an American colleague confirmed that culture plays a vitally important role in how people interpret facial emotions. The study suggests that in cultures where emotional control is the standard, such as in Japan, the eyes are the main focus when interpreting emotions. In contrast, in cultures where emotion is openly expressed, such as in the United States, the focus is on the mouth to interpret emotion. This tells us that we may be mistaken if we think that expression of emotion is a universal language (Yuki, Maddux, & Masuda, 2007).

Eye Messages

Research on communication via the eyes (a study known technically as **oculesics**) shows that the duration, direction, and quality of eye movements communicate different messages. For example, in every culture there are strict, though unstated, rules for the proper duration for eye contact. In our culture, the average length of gaze is 2.95 seconds. The average

"Damn it, when things were going well there was nothing but eye contact."

Charles Barsotti/The New Yorker Collection/www.cartoonbank.com

TABLE 6.3

TIPS FOR INTERPERSONAL COMMUNICATION BETWEEN PEOPLE WITH AND PEOPLE WITHOUT VISUAL IMPAIRMENTS

People vary greatly in their visual abilities; some are totally blind, some are partially sighted, and some have unimpaired vision. Ninety percent of people who are "legally blind" have some vision. All people, however, have the same need for communication and information. Here are some tips for making communication better between those who have visual impairments and those without such difficulties.

If you're the person without visual impairment and are talking with a visually impaired person:

Generally	Specifically
Identify yourself.	Don't assume that the visually impaired person will recognize your voice.
Face your listener; you'll be easier to hear.	Don't shout. Most people who are visually impaired are not hearing impaired. Speak at your normal volume.
Encode into speech all the meanings you wish to communicate.	Remember that your gestures, eye movements, and facial expressions can't be seen by the visually impaired.
Use audible turn-taking cues.	When you pass the role of speaker to a person who is visually impaired, don't rely on nonverbal cues; instead, say something like "Do you agree with that, Joe?"
Use normal vocabulary and discuss topics that you would discuss with sighted people.	Don't avoid terms like *see* or *look* or even *blind*. Don't avoid discussing a television show or the way your new car looks; these are normal topics for all people.

If you're the person with visual impairment and are talking with a person without visual impairment:

Help the sighted person meet your special communication needs.	If you want your surroundings described, ask. If you want the person to read the road signs, ask.
Be patient with the sighted person.	Many people are nervous talking with people who are visually impaired for fear of offending. Put them at ease in a way that also makes you more comfortable.
Demonstrate your comfort.	When appropriate, let the other person know that you're comfortable with the interaction, verbally or nonverbally.

Sources: These suggestions were drawn from a variety of sources, including the websites of the Cincinnati Association for the Blind and Visually Impaired, the Association for the Blind of WA, the National Federation of the Blind, and the American Foundation for the Blind, all accessed May 9, 2012.

length of a mutual gaze (two persons gazing at each other) is 1.18 seconds (Argyle, 1988; Argyle & Ingham, 1972). When eye contact falls short of this amount, you may think the person is uninterested, shy, or preoccupied. When the appropriate amount of time is exceeded, you may perceive the person as showing unusually high interest. Table 6.3 lists suggestions for communicating between people with and without visual impairment.

EYE CONTACT　With eye contact, you send a variety of messages. One such message is a request for feedback. In talking with someone, we look at her or him intently, as if to say, "Well, what do you think?" As you might expect, listeners gaze at speakers more than speakers gaze at listeners.

Another function of eye contact is to inform the other person that the channel of communication is open and that he or she should now speak. This occurs regularly in conversation, when one person asks a question or finishes a thought and then looks to the other person for a response.

Eye contact may also send messages about the nature of the relationship. For example, if you engage in prolonged eye contact coupled with a smile, you'll signal a positive relationship. If you stare or glare at the person while frowning, you'll signal a negative relationship. If you roll your eyes, you'll signal disappointment or disgust or disagreement. Research indicates that this is one of the most hurtful of nonverbal aggressive behaviours (Rancer et al., 2010).

EYE AVOIDANCE The eyes are "great intruders," observed the famous sociologist Erving Goffman (1967). When you avoid eye contact or avert your glance, you help others maintain their privacy. You may do this when you see a couple arguing in public: you turn your eyes away (though your eyes may be wide open) as if to say, "I don't mean to intrude; I respect your privacy," a behaviour called **civil inattention**.

Eye avoidance can also signal lack of interest—in a person, a conversation, or some visual stimulus. At times you may hide your eyes to block off unpleasant stimuli (a particularly gory or violent scene in a movie, for example) or close your eyes to block out visual stimuli and thus heighten other senses. For example, you may listen to music with your eyes closed. Lovers close their eyes while kissing, and many prefer to make love in a dark or dimly lit room.

CULTURE, GENDER, AND EYE MESSAGES Not surprisingly, eye messages vary with both culture and gender. North Americans, for example, consider direct eye contact an expression of honesty and forthrightness, but the Japanese often view this as a lack of respect. A Japanese person will glance at the other person's face rarely, and then only for very short periods (Axtell, 1990). Interpreting another's eye contact messages with your own cultural rules is a risky undertaking; eye movements that you may interpret as insulting may have been intended to show respect.

Women make eye contact more and maintain it longer (both in speaking and in listening) than men. This holds true whether women are interacting with other women or with men, and may result from women's greater tendency to display their emotions (Wood, 1994). When women interact with other women, they display affiliative and supportive eye contact, whereas when men interact with other men, they avert their gaze (Gamble & Gamble, 2003).

Spatial Messages

Proxemics is the study of the ways in which people use space to communicate varied meanings (Hall, 1963, 1966). We can examine this broad area by looking at the messages communicated by proxemic distances and territory.

PROXEMIC DISTANCES Not surprisingly, the major proxemic distances correspond closely to the major types of relationships: intimate, personal, social, and public.

In **intimate distance**, ranging from actual touching to 46 centimetres, the presence of the other individual is unmistakable. Each person experiences the sound, smell, and feel of the other's breath. You use intimate distance for lovemaking, comforting, and protecting. This distance is so short that most people don't consider it to be proper in public.

Personal distance refers to the protective "bubble" that defines your personal space, ranging from 46 centimetres to 1.2 metres. This imaginary bubble keeps you protected and untouched by others. You can still hold or grasp another person at this distance but only by extending your arms; this allows you to take certain individuals such as loved ones into your protective bubble. At the outer limit of personal distance, you can touch another person only if both of you extend your arms. At this distance you conduct much of your interpersonal interactions—for example, talking with friends and family.

At **social distance**, ranging from 1.2 to 3.6 metres, you lose the visual detail you have at personal distance. You conduct impersonal business and interact at a social

David Mager/Pearson

VIEWPOINTS **The Speaker–Listener Gaze**

Listeners gaze at speakers more than speakers gaze at listeners (Knapp & Hall, 2010). The percentage of interaction time spent gazing while listening, for example, ranges from 62 to 75 percent; the percentage of time spent gazing while talking, however, ranges from 38 to 41 percent. When these percentages are reversed—when a speaker gazes at the listener for longer than "normal" periods or when a listener gazes at the speaker for shorter than "normal" periods—the conversational interaction becomes awkward. Try this out with a friend and see what happens. Even with mutual awareness, you'll notice the discomfort caused by this seemingly minor communication change.

TABLE 6.4

RELATIONSHIPS AND PROXEMIC DISTANCES

These four distances can be further divided into close and far phases; the far phase of one level (personal) blends into the close phase of the next level (social). Do your relationships also blend into one another? Or are your personal relationships totally separated from your social relationships? Do you think these differences would be applicable across all cultures? If so, in what ways would they differ?

Relationship	Distance
Intimate Relationship	**Intimate Distance** 0 —————— 46 centimetres close phase — far phase
Personal Relationship	**Personal Distance** 46 centimetres —————— 1.2 metres close phase — far phase
Social Relationship	**Social Distance** 1.2 —————— 3.6 metres close phase — far phase
Public Relationship	**Public Distance** 3.6 —————— 7.6+ metres close phase — far phase

Source: Relationship and Proxemic Distances. ISBN: 0205688640. Copyright © 2011, 2008 by Pearson Education, Inc.

gathering at this social distance. The more distance you maintain in your interactions, the more formal they appear. In offices of high officials, the desks are positioned so that the official is assured of at least this distance from clients.

Public distance, from 3.6 to 7.6 metres or more, protects you. At this distance, you could take defensive action if threatened. On a public bus or train, for example, you might try to keep at least this distance from a drunken passenger. Although at this distance you lose fine details of the face and eyes, you're still close enough to see what's happening.

The specific distances you maintain between yourself and other individuals depend on a wide variety of factors (Burgoon, Guerrero, & Floyd, 2010). Among the most significant factors are gender (women in same-sex dyads sit and stand closer to each other than do men and people approach women more closely than they approach men); age (people maintain closer distances with similarly aged others than they do with those much older or much younger); and personality (introverts and highly anxious people maintain greater distances than do extroverts). You'll also tend to maintain shorter distances with people you're familiar with than with strangers and with people you like than with those you don't like. Status plays a role in spatial distancing between people as well—people of equal status maintain shorter distances between themselves, whereas a higher-status person may approach the lower-status person more closely than vice versa. And like most aspects of interpersonal communication, culture is a significant factor. For example, people from northern European cultures and many North Americans stand farther apart from each other in conversation than do people from southern European and Middle Eastern cultures.

INTERPERSONAL CHOICE POINT

Inappropriate Spacing
Your friend is a "close talker," standing much too close to others when talking and making them feel uncomfortable. What (if anything) can you say or do to help your friend use space to communicate more effectively?

TERRITORIALITY   Another type of communication having to do with space is **territoriality,** which refers to how people use space to communicate ownership, possession, or occupancy (Beebe, Beebe, & Redmond, 2008) You interact basically in three types of territories (Altman & Taylor, 1973):

■ **Primary territories** are areas that you might call your own; these areas are your exclusive preserve. Primary territories might include your room, your desk, or your office.

- **Secondary territories** are areas that don't belong to you but which you have occupied and with which you're associated. They might include your usual table in the cafeteria, your regular seat in the classroom, or your neighbourhood turf.
- **Public territories** are areas that are open to all people; they may be owned by some person or organization, but they're used by everyone. These include places such as movie theatres, restaurants, and shopping malls.

When you're in your primary territory, you have an interpersonal advantage, often called the home field advantage. In their own home or office, people take on a kind of leadership role: they initiate conversations, fill in silences, assume relaxed and comfortable postures, and maintain their positions with greater conviction. In your own territory (your office, your home), you're dominant, and therefore you stand a better chance of getting your raise approved, your point accepted, or a contract resolved in your favour than if you were in someone else's territory (Marsh, 1988).

Like animals, humans mark both their primary and secondary territories to signal ownership. Humans use three types of markers: central markers, boundary markers, and earmarkers (Goffman, 1971). **Central markers** are items you place in a territory to reserve it for you—for example, a drink at the bar, books on your desk, or a sweater over a library chair.

Boundary markers serve to divide your territory from that of others. In the supermarket checkout line, the bar placed between your groceries and those of the person behind you is a boundary marker, as are fences, armrests that separate your chair from those on either side, and the contours of the moulded plastic seats on a bus.

Earmarkers—a term taken from the practice of branding animals on their ears—are identifying marks that indicate your possession of a territory or object. Trademarks, nameplates, and initials on a shirt or attaché case are all examples of earmarkers.

Markers are also important in giving you a feeling of belonging. For example, one study found that students who marked their college dorm rooms by displaying personal items stayed in school longer than did those who didn't personalize their spaces (Marsh, 1988).

INTERPERSONAL CHOICE POINT

Inviting and Discouraging Conversation
Sometimes you want to encourage people to come into your office and chat, and at other times you want to be left alone. What are some of the things you might do nonverbally to achieve each goal?

SKILL-BUILDING EXERCISE

Choosing the Right Seat

The graphic here represents a meeting table with 12 chairs, one of which is already occupied by the boss. Below are listed five messages you might want to communicate. For each of these messages, indicate (a) where you would sit to communicate the desired message, (b) any other possible messages that your choice of seat would likely communicate, and (c) the messages that your choice of seat would make it easier for you to communicate.

1. You want to ingratiate yourself with your boss.
2. You aren't prepared and want to be ignored.
3. You want to challenge your boss on a certain policy that will come up for a vote.
4. You want to help your boss on a certain policy that will come up for a vote.
5. You want to be accepted as a new (but important) member of the company.

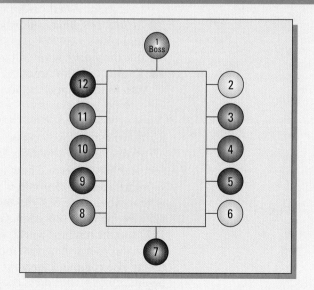

Nonverbal choices (such as the seat you select or the clothes you wear) have an impact on communication and on your image as a communicator.

Artifactual Messages

Artifactual messages are messages conveyed through objects or arrangements made by human hands. The colours you prefer, the clothing or jewellery you wear, the way you decorate your space, and even bodily scents communicate a wide variety of meanings.

COLOUR   Colour is a strong communicator; retailers and marketers, for example, have known for a long time that it plays a major role in sales. In a review of several studies related to colour psychology, a University of Winnipeg researcher found that people make up their minds about purchasing a service or product within 90 seconds of their first exposure, and that as much as 62 to 90 percent of their decision is based on colour alone. The researcher concluded that colours can influence not only moods and feelings, but also attitudes toward products (Singh, 2006). No wonder companies pay attention to packaging, as the appropriate use of colours can contribute to "brand image and charm" and inappropriate use of colours can be detrimental (Chang & Lin, 2010). A study that examined the impact of colour on adult students' mood and performance (Stone, 2001) suggested that colour can indeed exert a significant influence; for example, performance on a reading task in white, blue, and red environments, respectively, was found to be significantly lower in the red environment.

The meaning of colours also varies from one culture to another. To illustrate this cultural variation, here are just some of the many meanings that popular colours communicate in a variety of different cultures (Dresser, 1999, 2005; Dreyfuss, 1971; Hoft, 1995; Singh & Pereira, 2005). As you read this section, you may want to consider your own meanings for these colours and where your meanings came from.

- *Red*. In China, red signifies prosperity and rebirth and is used for festive and joyous occasions; in France and the United Kingdom, it indicates masculinity; in many African countries, blasphemy or death; and in Japan, anger and danger.
- *Green*. In North America, green signifies capitalism, go ahead, and envy; in Ireland, patriotism; among some Native Americans, femininity; to the Egyptians, fertility and strength; and to the Japanese, youth and energy.
- *Black*. In Thailand, black signifies old age; in parts of Malaysia, courage; and in much of Europe, death.
- *White*. In Thailand, white signifies purity; in many Muslim and Hindu cultures, purity and peace; and in Japan and other Asian countries, death and mourning.
- *Blue*. In Iran, blue signifies something negative; in Ghana, joy; among the Cherokee, it signifies defeat; for the Egyptians, virtue and truth; and for the Greeks, national pride.
- *Yellow*. In China, yellow signifies wealth and authority; in North America, caution and cowardice; in Egypt, happiness and prosperity; and in many countries throughout the world, femininity.
- *Purple*. In Latin America, purple signifies death; in Europe, royalty; in Egypt, virtue and faith; in Japan, grace and nobility; in China, barbarism; and in North America, nobility and bravery.

CLOTHING AND BODY ADORNMENT   People make inferences about who you are, at least in part, from the way you dress. Whether accurate or not, these inferences will affect what people think of you and how they react to you. Your socioeconomic class, your seriousness, your attitudes (for example, whether you're conservative or liberal), your concern for convention, your sense of style, and perhaps even your creativity will all be judged in part by the way you dress (Burgoon, Guerrero, & Floyd, 2010; Knapp & Hall, 1996; Molloy, 1977). In the business world, your clothing may communicate your position within the hierarchy and your willingness and desire to conform to the clothing norms of the organization. It may also communicate your professionalism, which seems to be the reason why some organizations favour dress codes (Smith, 2003). On the other hand, many of the technology companies like Google, Yahoo, and Apple encourage a more informal, casual style of dress.

In the classroom, research indicates, college and university students tend to perceive an instructor dressed informally as friendly, fair, enthusiastic, and flexible, and the same instructor dressed formally as prepared, knowledgeable, and organized (Malandro et al., 1989).

Body adornment also communicates who you are—from a concern about being up to date, to a desire to shock, to perhaps a lack of interest in appearances. Your jewellery, too, sends messages about you. Some jewellery is a form of **cultural display**, indicating a particular cultural or religious affiliation. Wedding and engagement rings are obvious examples that communicate specific messages. Visible brand names on shoes or clothing likewise convey messages. If you wear a Rolex watch or large precious stones, others are likely to infer that you're rich. Men who wear earrings will be judged differently from men who don't. What judgments people make will depend, of course, on who the receiver is, on the communication context, and on all the other factors identified throughout this text.

Body piercings have become increasingly popular, especially among the young. Nose and nipple rings and tongue and belly-button jewellery send a variety of messages. Although people wearing such jewellery may wish to communicate different meanings, those interpreting the messages of body piercings seem to infer that the wearers are communicating an unwillingness to conform to social norms and a willingness to take greater risks than those without such piercings (Forbes, 2001). Further, health care providers sometimes see tattoos and piercings as signs of such undesirable traits as impulsiveness, unpredictability, and a tendency toward being reckless or violent (Rapsa & Cusack, 1990; Smith, 2003). Tattoos— whether temporary or permanent—likewise communicate a variety of messages, often the name of a loved one or some symbol of allegiance or affiliation.

Although body piercings and tattoos are becoming more accepted generally, business experts continue to note the negative effects in terms of getting a job and suggest hiding them during job interviews (Ingegneri, 2008; Varenik, 2010).

SPACE DECORATION   The way you decorate your private spaces speaks about you. The office with a mahogany desk, bookcases, and oriental rugs communicates your importance and status within the organization, just as a metal desk and bare floor indicate a worker much further down in the hierarchy.

Likewise, people will make inferences about you based on the way you decorate your home. The expensiveness of the furnishings may communicate your status and wealth; their coordination may express your sense of style. The books and magazines reflect your interests, and the arrangement of chairs around a television set may reveal how important watching

Corbis Premium RF/Alamy

VIEWPOINTS **Defence Tactic**

A popular defence tactic in sex crimes against women, gay men, and lesbians is to blame the victim by referring to the way the victim was dressed and implying that the victim, by wearing certain clothing, provoked the attack. What do you think of this tactic? Is it likely to be effective? Is it ethical?

Gorin/Shutterstock

VIEWPOINTS **What Does Your Office Say About You?**

Businesses and professional offices take great pains to design their environment in order to present the image they wish to convey. What inferences would you make about the occupant of this office based solely on what appears in this photo?

television is to you. In fact, there's probably little in your home that wouldn't send messages from which others would draw inferences about you.

In a similar way, the absence of certain items will communicate something about you. Consider what messages you would get from a home where no television, phone, or books could be seen.

SMELL   Smell communication, or **olfactory communication**, is extremely important in a wide variety of situations, and is now big business. In the past few years a number of studies have provided scientific evidence of the power of scent to evoke emotional responses, to impact mood, to increase visual attention, to enhance concentration, and to influence our autonomic, endocrine, and immune functions (Bulsing et al., 2010; Kiecolt-Glaser et al., 2008; Seo et al., 2010; Weber & Heuberger, 2008; Willander & Larsson, 2007). Not surprisingly, scent is often used to sell products. Real estate agents, for example, often advise their clients to bake bread or boil vanilla and water in a pot to fill the house with the scent of home baking, which suggests an image of a happy family home to the potential buyers. On the other hand, people do respond differently to scent: what is pleasant to some may be less so to others. And today many employers request that employees refrain from using scent, as some people have strong allergic reactions to it.

Two particularly important messages that scent communicates are those of attraction and identification.

> **INTERPERSONAL CHOICE POINT**
>
> **Smelling**
> Your colleague in the next cubicle wears extremely strong cologne that you find horrendous. You can't continue smelling this horrible scent any longer. What choices do you have to correct this situation but not alienate your colleague?

- *Attraction messages.* People use perfumes, colognes, aftershave lotions, powders, and the like in an effort to enhance attractiveness. They also use scents to make themselves feel better. After all, when you smell pleasant, you feel better about yourself; when you smell unpleasant, you feel less good about yourself—and probably shower and perhaps put on some cologne.

- *Identification messages.* Smell is often used to create an image or an identity for a product (Spence, 2008). Advertisers and manufacturers spend millions of dollars each year creating scents for cleaning products and toothpastes, for example, which have nothing to do with products' cleaning power; instead, they function solely to create an image for the products. There is also evidence that we can identify specific significant others by smell. For example, young children were able to identify the T-shirts of their brothers and sisters solely by smell (Porter & Moore, 1981).

Touch Messages

Touch communication, or **tactile communication**, develops before the other senses; even in the womb, fetuses are stimulated by touch (Roizen & Oz, 2009). Soon after birth, the child is fondled, caressed, patted, and stroked. In turn, the child explores its world through touch and quickly learns to communicate a variety of meanings through touch. The nature of touch communication also varies with relationship stages. In the early stages of a relationship, you touch little; in intermediate stages (involvement and intimacy), you touch a great deal; and at stable or deteriorating stages, you again touch little (Guerrero & Andersen, 1991).

THE MEANINGS OF TOUCH   Researchers in the field of **haptics**—the study of touch—have identified the major meanings of touch (Jones & Yarbrough, 1985):

- *Positive feelings.* Touch may communicate such positive feelings as support, appreciation, inclusion, sexual interest or intent, or affection.
- *Playfulness.* Touch often communicates the desire to play, sometimes affectionately, sometimes aggressively.
- *Control.* Touch may control or direct the behaviours, attitudes, or feelings of the other person. To get attention, for example, you may touch a person as if to say "Look at me" or "Look over here."

- *Ritual.* Touching may also serve a ritual function; for example, shaking hands to say hello or putting your arm around another's shoulder when saying farewell.
- *Task-related.* Touching often occurs while you're performing some function, such as removing a speck of dust from another person's face or helping someone out of a car.

Different cultures view these types of touching differently. For example, some task-related touching, viewed as acceptable in much of North America, would be viewed negatively in some cultures. Among Koreans, for example, it's considered disrespectful for a storekeeper to touch a customer in, say, handing back change; it's considered too intimate a gesture. But members of other cultures, expecting some touching, may consider the Koreans' behaviour cold and insulting.

TOUCH AVOIDANCE   Much as we touch and are touched, we also avoid touch from certain people and in certain circumstances. Researchers in nonverbal communication have found some interesting relationships between **touch avoidance** and other significant communication variables (Andersen & Leibowitz, 1978; Hall, 1996). Among research findings, for example, is the fact that touch avoidance is positively related to communication apprehension; those who fear oral communication also score high on touch avoidance. Touch avoidance is also high with those who self-disclose little. Both touch and self-disclosure are intimate forms of communication; thus, people who are reluctant to get close to another person by self-disclosing also seem reluctant to get close by touching.

Older people have higher touch-avoidance scores for opposite-sex persons than do younger people. As we get older, we're touched less by members of the opposite sex, and this decreased frequency may lead us to avoid touching.

Males score higher on same-sex touch avoidance than do females, a finding that confirms popular stereotypes. Men avoid touching other men, but women may and do touch other women. On the other hand, women have higher touch-avoidance scores for opposite-sex touching than do men.

CULTURE AND TOUCH   Cultures vary greatly in their touching behaviour. For example, Muslim children are socialized not to touch members of the opposite sex, a practice that can easily be interpreted as unfriendly by North American children who are used to touching each other (Dresser, 2005).

One study on touch surveyed college students in Japan and in the United States (Barnlund, 1975) and found that students from the United States reported being touched twice as much as did the Japanese students. In Japan, there is a strong taboo against strangers touching, and the Japanese are therefore especially careful to maintain sufficient distance.

Some cultures—including many in southern Europe and the Middle East—are considered *contact cultures*, and others—such as those of northern Europe and Japan—are *noncontact cultures*. Members of contact cultures maintain close distances, touch one another in conversation, face each other more directly, and maintain longer and more focused eye contact. Members

Pavel L Photo and Video/Shutterstock

VIEWPOINTS To Touch or Not to Touch
How would you describe the rules of touch avoidance for passengers on a commuter train? For students at a football stadium? For members of your family at dinner? For a place of worship?

of noncontact cultures maintain greater distances in their interactions, touch each other rarely (if at all), avoid facing each other directly, and maintain much less direct eye contact.

As you can imagine, touching may also get you into trouble in another way. For example, touching that is too positive (or too intimate) too early in a relationship may send the wrong signals. Similarly, playing too rough or holding someone's arm to control their movements may be resented. Using ritualistic touching incorrectly or in ways that may be culturally insensitive may likewise get you into difficulty. In North America today there is growing recognition that touching can be highly disrespectful. Employers, for example, are much more careful not to touch their employees, as are college and university instructors with their students.

Paralanguage Messages

The term **paralanguage** refers to the vocal but nonverbal dimensions of speech. It refers to how you say something, not what you say. A traditional exercise students use to increase their ability to express different emotions, feelings, and attitudes is to repeat a sentence while accenting or stressing different words. One popular sentence is "Is this the face that launched a thousand ships?" Examine your own sensitivity to paralanguage variations by seeing if you get different meanings for each of the following questions based on where the emphasis or **stress** lies.

- *Is* this the face that launched a thousand ships?
- Is *this* the face that launched a thousand ships?
- Is this *the face* that launched a thousand ships?
- Is this the face that *launched* a thousand ships?
- Is this the face that launched *a thousand ships*?

In addition to stress and **pitch** (highness or lowness), paralanguage includes such voice qualities or vocal characteristics as **rate** (speed), **volume** (loudness), and **rhythm** as well as the vocalizations you make in crying, whispering, moaning, belching, yawning, and yelling (Argyle, 1988; Trager, 1958, 1961). A variation in any of these features communicates. When you speak quickly, for example, you communicate something different from when you speak slowly. Even though the words may be the same, if the speed (or volume, rhythm, or pitch) differs, the meanings people receive will also differ.

JUDGMENTS ABOUT PEOPLE   We often use paralanguage cues as a basis for judgments about people—for example, evaluations of their emotional state or even their personality. When the speaker and listener speak the same language, the listener can accurately judge the emotional state of a speaker from vocal expression alone. Paralanguage cues aren't as accurate, however, when used to communicate emotions to those who speak a different language (Albas, McCluskey, & Albas, 1976). Some emotions, of course, are easier to identify than others; it's easy to distinguish between hate and sympathy but more difficult to distinguish between fear and anxiety. And, of course, listeners vary in their ability to decode, and speakers in their ability to encode, emotions (Scherer, 1986).

Less reliable are judgments made about personality. Some people, for example, may conclude that those who speak softly feel inferior, believing that no one wants to listen to them, or that people who speak loudly have over-inflated egos. Such conclusions may be mistaken, however. There are lots of reasons why people might speak softly or loudly.

JUDGMENTS ABOUT COMMUNICATION EFFECTIVENESS   The rate or speed at which people speak is the aspect of paralanguage that has received the most attention (MacLachlan, 1979; Swanbrow, 2011). Rates of speech are of interest to the advertiser, the politician, and, in fact anyone who tries to convey information or influence others. They are especially important when time is limited or expensive.

In one-way communication (when one person is doing all or most of the speaking and the other person is doing all or most of the listening), those who talk fast (about 50 percent faster than normal) are more persuasive. People agree more with a fast speaker than with a slow speaker and

INTERPERSONAL CHOICE POINT

Criticizing with Kindness

A close friend is going to an important job interview dressed totally inappropriately and asks, "How do I look?" What are some of the things you can say that will boost your friend's confidence but at the same time get your friend to dress differently?

find the fast speaker more intelligent and objective. Generally, research finds that a 50 percent faster-than-normal speech rate lowers comprehension by only about 5 percent (Jones, Berry, & Stevens, 2007; MacLachlan, 1979). When the rate is doubled, the comprehension level drops only 10 percent. These 5 and 10 percent losses are more than offset by the increased speed; thus, the faster rates are much more efficient in communicating information. If speeds are more than twice the rate of normal speech, however, comprehension begins to fall dramatically.

Rate seems also to influence persuasion. For example, interviewers who called to ask people to participate in a survey were more successful when they spoke moderately fast, at a rate of about 3.5 words per second. Interviewers who spoke overly fast or very slowly were much less successful in gaining compliance (Swanbrow, 2011).

Not all cultures view speech rate in the same way. In one study, for example, Korean male speakers who spoke rapidly were given unfavourable credibility ratings, as opposed to the results obtained by Americans who spoke rapidly. Researchers have suggested that in individualistic societies, a rapid-rate speaker is seen as more competent than a slow-rate speaker, whereas in collectivist cultures, a speaker who uses a slower rate is judged more competent (Lee & Boster, 1992).

Silence Messages

Like words and gestures, **silence**, too, communicates impor-

BAVARIA/Taxi/Getty Images

VIEWPOINTS Spiral of Silence

The spiral of silence theory holds that you're more likely to voice agreement than disagreement, which creates the belief that there's more agreement than there really is (because people who disagree aren't voicing their disagreement) (Noelle-Neumann, 1991). If you were talking with a group of new work colleagues, would you be more likely to voice opinions that agreed with the majority? Would you hesitate to voice opinions that differed greatly from what the others were expressing? Under what conditions are you likely to voice disagreement?

tant meanings and serves important functions (Jaworski, 1993; Johannesen, 1974). For example, silence allows the speaker time to think, time to formulate and organize his or her verbal communications. Before messages of intense conflict, as well as before those confessing undying love, there is often silence. Again, silence seems to prepare the receiver for the importance of these messages.

Some people use silence as a weapon to hurt others. We often speak of giving someone "the silent treatment." After a conflict, for example, one or both individuals may remain silent as a kind of punishment. Silence used to hurt others may also take the form of refusal to acknowledge the presence of another person, as in disconfirmation (see Chapter 5); here silence is a dramatic demonstration of the total indifference one person feels toward the other.

DEVELOPING LANGUAGE AND COMMUNICATION SKILLS

Children and Teens "Hear" What You Do, Not What You Say

Because young children are still trying to figure out social rules, they're very attuned to the behaviour and emotions of adults around them. For example, suppose you tell a child that you're happy to see her but you have a worried expression. The child will be more likely to respond to the worried expression than to the words you say. Teens (who, like preschoolers, are experiencing rapid brain growth) are also very attuned to facial expressions and nonverbal communication. Brain scans have shown that the emotional (limbic) regions in teens' brains are more active than they are in children or adults. As a result, teens tend to react more quickly and emotionally to a neutral look or an accidental bump in the school hallway than to spoken words. If you'd like to learn more, watch this video at http://greatergood.berkeley.edu/gg_live/science_meaningful_life_videos/speaker/daniel_siegel/the_purpose_of_the_teenage_brain.

Sometimes silence is used as a response to personal anxiety, shyness, or threats. You may feel anxious or shy among new people and prefer to remain silent. By remaining silent, you preclude the chance of rejection. Only when you break your silence and make an attempt to communicate with another person do you risk rejection.

Silence may also be used to prevent communication of certain messages. In conflict situations, silence is sometimes used to prevent certain topics from surfacing and to prevent one or both parties from saying things they may later regret. In such situations, silence often allows us time to cool off before expressing hatred, severe criticism, or personal attacks—which, as we know, are irreversible.

Like the eyes, face, or hands, silence can be used to communicate emotional responses (Ehrenhaus, 1988). Sometimes silence communicates a determination to be uncooperative or defiant; by refusing to engage in verbal communication, you defy the authority or the legitimacy of the other person's position. Silence is also often used to communicate annoyance, particularly when accompanied by a pouting expression, arms crossed in front of the chest, and nostrils flared. Silence may conversely express affection or love, especially when coupled with longing gazes into each other's eyes.

Silence also may be used strategically, to achieve specific effects. You may, for example, strategically position a pause before what you feel is an important comment in order to make your idea stand out. Interestingly enough, interviewers who paused about every 20 seconds were more successful in gaining compliance than were those who spoke without a pause (Swanbrow, 2011). As well, a prolonged silence after someone voices disagreement may give the appearance of control and superiority. It's a way of saying, "I can respond in my own time."

Silence is also seen in computer-mediated communication. For example, when a close friend posts a message that asks for support or help and you remain silent, you're communicating a message—perhaps you simply didn't know what to say or you weren't interested or you didn't have online access (an excuse that's becoming increasingly difficult to advance convincingly). Or when someone sends you a lengthy email and you fail to respond to its main theme (indicating that you haven't really read the email), you're communicating some message.

INTERPERSONAL CHOICE POINT

Remaining Silent

Your roommate has developed a small business selling term papers and uses your jointly owned computer to store them. You've remained silent about this for some time, but you've become increasingly uncomfortable about the situation and want to distance yourself from what you feel is unethical. How might you break your silence to distance yourself or, better, sever yourself entirely from this entire operation without creating too much trouble in the small dorm room you'll have to continue sharing for the next year?

ETHICAL MESSAGES

Silence

In the Canadian legal system, you have the right to remain silent and to refuse to reveal information about yourself that could be used against you or that might incriminate you. But you don't have the right to refuse to reveal information about, for example, the criminal activities of others that you may have witnessed. Rightly or wrongly (and this in itself is an ethical issue), psychiatrists, clergy, and lawyers are often exempt from this general rule. Similarly, a wife can't be forced to testify against her husband or a husband against his wife.

In interpersonal situations, however, there are no such written rules, so it's not always clear if or when silence is ethical. For example, most people (but not all) would agree that you have the right to withhold information that has no bearing on the matter at hand. Thus, your previous relationship history, affectional orientation, or religion is usually irrelevant to your ability to function as a doctor or police officer and may thus be kept private in most job-related situations. On the other hand, these issues may be relevant when, for example, you're about to enter a more intimate phase of a relationship—then there may be an obligation to reveal information about yourself that could have been kept hidden at earlier relationship stages.

As you consider the ethical dimensions of silence, ask yourself what types of information you can ethically withhold from, say, your relationship partner or family or best friend. What types of information would it be unethical to withhold?

Ethical Choice Point

Remaining silent after witnessing an unethical act is sometimes seen as the same as condoning it. When you witness an act of harassment or bullying, do you always speak up or are you silent? When you see someone cheating on an exam, do you speak up or are you silent? What does our culture say about breaking silence when it comes to our friends, our colleagues, or our family members? When and how would you challenge these norms?

Not all cultures view silence in the same way (Vainiomaki, 2004). In North America, for example, silence is often interpreted negatively. At a business meeting or even in informal social groups, a silent person may be seen as not listening, as having nothing interesting to add, or as not understanding the issues, when in fact he or she may be an introverted person who needs a bit more time to reflect before jumping in to speak in front of a group (Cain, 2012). Yet in First Nations culture, for example, silence is accepted as a normal part of communication, and participants don't feel pressured to fill the silence. Similarly, silence has a positive connotation in Japanese and Chinese cultures (Gendron, 2011).

Time Messages

The study of **temporal communication**, known technically as **chronemics**, concerns the use of time—how you organize it, react to it, and communicate messages through it (Bruneau, 1985, 1990, 2009/2010). Time is important in both face-to-face and computer-mediated communication. The time you take to poke someone back on Facebook or the time you take to respond to an email request for a favour or the delay in returning a phone call will all communicate varied messages. Often, as you've probably already discovered, the meanings that the sender intends to communicate aren't the same as the meanings the receiver constructs.

Before reading further about time, take a look at your own time orientation by taking the accompanying self-test. A future orientation is thought to be correlated to a more successful lifestyle and career, as it involves planning, preparing, and perseverance skills that are associated with higher levels of education and higher status careers.

Different time perspectives also account for much intercultural misunderstanding, as different cultures often teach their members drastically different time orientations. For example, people from some Latin cultures would rather be late for an appointment than end a conversation abruptly or before it has come to a natural end. So these Latin cultures may see an individual's lateness as a result of politeness. But others may see the lateness as impolite to the person with whom the individual had the appointment (Hall & Hall, 1987). Generally, it can be said that significant differences exist in the attitude toward time between Western technological cultures and non-Western cultures—and that sometimes these differences in the perception can become a barrier in the conflict-resolution process (Zakay, 2012).

TEST YOURSELF

What's Your Time?

Indicate whether each of the following statements is true (*T*) or false (*F*) as it pertains to your general attitude and behaviour.

_____ 1. I work hard today basically because of tomorrow's expected rewards.

_____ 2. I enjoy life as it comes.

_____ 3. I enjoy planning for tomorrow and the future generally.

_____ 4. I avoid looking too far ahead.

_____ 5. I'm willing to endure difficulties if there's a payoff/reward at the end.

_____ 6. I frequently put off work to enjoy the moment.

_____ 7. I prepare "to do" lists fairly regularly.

_____ 8. I'm late with assignments at least 25 percent of the time.

_____ 9. I get very disappointed with myself when I'm late with assignments.

_____10. I look for immediate payoffs/rewards.

How Did You Do? These questions were designed to raise the issue of present and future time orientation: whether you focus more on the present or more on the future. Future-oriented individuals would respond with *T* to odd-numbered statements (1, 3, 5, 7, and 9) and *F* to even-numbered questions (2, 4, 6, 8, and 10). Present-oriented individuals would respond in reverse: *F* for odd-numbered statements and *T* for even-numbered statements.

What Will You Do? As you read more about time and nonverbal communication generally, consider how these time orientations work for or against you. For example, will your time orientation help you achieve your social and professional goals? If not, what might you do about changing these attitudes and behaviours?

Similarly, the future-oriented person who works for tomorrow's goals will frequently see the present-oriented person as lazy and poorly motivated for enjoying today and not planning for tomorrow. In turn, the present-oriented person may see those with strong future orientations as obsessed with amassing wealth or rising in status.

FORMAL AND INFORMAL TIME   In Canada and in most of the world, **formal time** is divided into seconds, minutes, hours, days, weeks, months, and years. Some cultures, however, may use seasons or phases of the moon to delineate their most important time periods. In North America, if your college or university is on the semester system, your courses are divided into 50- or 75-minute periods that meet two or three times a week for 14-week periods. Eight semesters of 15 or 16 periods per week equal a college education. As these examples illustrate, formal time units are arbitrary. The culture establishes them for convenience.

In contrast, the term **informal time** refers to people's understanding of general time terms—for example, expressions such as *forever*, *immediately*, *soon*, *right away*, and *as soon as possible*. Communication about informal time creates the most problems because the terms have different meanings for different people. And this is especially true when the terms are used interculturally. For example, what does *late* mean when applied to a commuter train? Apparently, it depends on your culture. In the New York area, *late* means six minutes, and in Britain, it means five minutes. But in Japan, it could mean one minute.

Can you define and give examples of messages in each of the basic channels through which you send and receive nonverbal signals (gestures, body appearance, face, eyes, space and territory, artifacts, touch, paralanguage, silence, and time)?

NONVERBAL COMMUNICATION COMPETENCE

Throughout the discussion of nonverbal communication, you've probably deduced a number of suggestions for improving your own nonverbal communication. Here we bring together some suggestions for both receiving and sending nonverbal messages.

Perhaps the most general skill that applies to both receiving and sending is to become mindful of nonverbal messages—those of others as well as your own. Observe those whose nonverbal behaviour you find particularly effective and those you find ineffective and try to identify exactly what makes one effective and one ineffective. Consider this chapter a brief introduction to a lifelong study.

In addition to mindfulness, general suggestions can be offered for encoding (or sending) nonverbal messages and for decoding (or interpreting) nonverbal messages.

Identifying Connections Between Verbal and Nonverbal Messages

To demonstrate that the way you say something influences the meanings you communicate, try reading aloud each of the following sentences—first to communicate a positive meaning and then to communicate a negative meaning. As you communicate these meanings, try to identify the nonverbal differences between the ways you express positive meanings and the ways you express negative meanings. Look specifically at (a) how you read the statements in terms of rate, pauses, and volume and (b) how your facial and eye expressions differ.

1. Oh, yeah, I have the relationship of a lifetime.
2. I can't wait to receive my test results.
3. Did you see her Facebook profile and the new photos?
4. I had some fantastic date last night.
5. Did you see him pitch that great game last night?

You can't speak a sentence without using nonverbal signals, and these signals influence the meaning you send to the receiver.

Encoding Skills

In using nonverbal messages to express your meanings, consider these suggestions:

1. Consider your choices for your nonverbal communication just as you do for your verbal messages. Identify and think mindfully about the choices you have available for communicating what you want to communicate.
2. Keep your nonverbal messages consistent with your verbal messages; avoid sending verbal messages that say one thing and nonverbal messages that say something else—at least not when you want to be believed.
3. Monitor your own nonverbal messages with the same care that you monitor your verbal messages. If it's not appropriate to say "This meal is terrible," then it's not appropriate to have a negative expression when you're asked if you want seconds.
4. Avoid extremes and monotony. Too little nonverbal communication or too much are likely to be responded to negatively. Similarly, always giving the same nonverbal message—say, continually smiling and nodding your head when listening to a friend's long story—is likely to be seen as insincere.
5. Take the situation into consideration. Effective nonverbal communication is situational; to be effective, adapt your nonverbal messages to the specific situation. Nonverbal behaviour appropriate to one situation may be totally inappropriate in another.
6. Usually, depending on cultural considerations, maintain eye contact with the speaker—whether at a meeting, in the hallway, or on an elevator; it communicates politeness and says that you're giving the person the consideration of your full attention. Eye contact that is too focused and too prolonged is likely to be seen as invasive and impolite.
7. Avoid using certain adaptors in public—for example, combing your hair, picking your teeth, or putting your pinky in your ear; these will be seen as impolite. And, not surprisingly, the greater the formality of the situation, the greater the perception of impoliteness is likely to be. So, for example, combing your hair while sitting with two or three friends would probably not be considered impolite (or perhaps only mildly so), but in a classroom or at a company meeting, it would be considered inappropriate.
8. Avoid strong cologne or perfume. While you may enjoy the scent, those around you may find it unpleasant and intrusive. Just as others don't want to hear your cell phone conversation, they probably don't want to have their sense of smell invaded, either.
9. Be careful with touching; it may or may not be considered appropriate or polite depending on the relationship you have with the other person and on the context in which you find yourselves. The best advice here is to avoid touching unless it's part of the culture of the group or organization.

> **INTERPERSONAL CHOICE POINT**
>
> **Demonstrating Credibility**
> At work, people underestimate your competence and potential, even though you're probably as competent as anyone else. You need to increase the nonverbal credibility cues you give off. What nonverbal cues can you use to communicate your competence and ability? How might you begin to integrate these into your everyday interactions?

Decoding Skills

When you make judgments or draw conclusions about another person on the basis of her or his nonverbal messages, consider these suggestions:

1. Be tentative. Resist the temptation to draw conclusions from nonverbal behaviours. Instead, develop hypotheses (educated guesses) about what's going on, and test the validity of your hypotheses on the basis of other evidence.
2. When making judgments, mindfully seek alternative judgments. Your first judgment may be in error, and one good way to test it is to consider alternative judgments. When your romantic partner creates a greater-than-normal distance between you, it may signal an annoyance with you, but it can also signal that your partner needs some space to think something out.
3. Notice that messages come from lots of different channels and that reasonably accurate judgments can be made only when multiple channels are taken into consideration. Although textbooks (like this one) must present the areas of nonverbal communication separately, the various elements all work together in actual communication situations.

4. Even after you've explored the different channels, consider the possibility that you're incorrect. This is especially true when you make a judgment that another person is lying based on, say, eye avoidance or long pauses. These nonverbal signals may mean lots of things (as well as the possibility of lying).

5. Interpret your judgments and conclusions against a cultural context. Consider, for example, whether you interpret another's nonverbal behaviour through its meaning in your own culture. So, for example, if you interpret someone's "overly close" talking distance as intrusive or pushy because that's your culture's interpretation, you may miss the possibility that this distance is simply standard in the other person's culture or that it's a way of signalling closeness and friendliness.

6. Consider the multitude of factors that can influence the way a person behaves nonverbally; for example, a person's physical condition, personality, or particular situation may all influence his or her nonverbal communication. A sour stomach may be more influential in unpleasant expressions than any interpersonal factor. A low grade in an exam may make your normally pleasant roommate scowl and grumble. Without knowing these factors, it's difficult to make an accurate judgment.

 Can you use the suggestions to more effectively decode the nonverbal messages of others? Can you use the suggestions to more effectively encode your own nonverbal messages?

CANADIAN PROFILE: WRAP-UP

War Child Canada/ Dustin Rabin

Samantha Nutt is a medical doctor, not an entertainment celebrity, and yet her work and advocacy for children impacted by war is well known. How is it possible to use nonverbal communication techniques to build a public profile so as to be "heard" around the world or even in a local community? In what ways does simply being well known involve nonverbal communication techniques? Is this type of nonverbal influence always an ethical way of advocating and communicating?

SUMMARY OF CONCEPTS AND SKILLS

This chapter explored nonverbal communication—communication without words—and considered such areas as body language, body appearance, facial messages, eye messages, spatial and territorial communication, artifactual communication, touch communication, paralanguage, silence, time, and smell communication, and nonverbal communication competence.

Principles of Nonverbal Communication

1. Nonverbal messages often interact with verbal messages to accent, complement, contradict, regulate, repeat, or substitute.
2. Nonverbal messages help manage impressions. We present ourselves nonverbally to give people the desired impression.

3. Nonverbal messages help form relationships.
4. Nonverbal messages structure conversation.
5. Nonverbal messages can influence and deceive.
6. Nonverbal messages are crucial for expressing emotions.

The Channels of Nonverbal Messages

7. Body gestures are classified into five categories: emblems (which rather directly translate words or phrases); illustrators (which accompany and "illustrate" verbal messages); affect displays (which communicate emotional meaning); regulators (which coordinate, monitor, maintain, or control the speaking of another individual); and adaptors

(which are usually unconscious and serve some kind of need, as in scratching an itch).

8. Body appearance (for example, height and general attractiveness) communicates a variety of messages.

9. Facial movements may communicate a variety of emotions. The most frequently studied are happiness, surprise, fear, anger, sadness, and disgust/contempt. Facial management techniques enable you to control your facial expression of emotions. The facial feedback hypothesis claims that facial display of an emotion can lead to physiological and psychological changes.

10. Eye movements may seek feedback, invite others to speak, signal the nature of a relationship, or compensate for physical distance.

11. The study of proxemics investigates the communicative functions of space and spatial relationships. The four major proxemic distances are (1) intimate distance, ranging from actual touching to 46 centimetres; (2) personal distance, ranging from 46 centimetres to 1.2 metres; (3) social distance, ranging from 1.2 to 3.6 metres; and (4) public distance, ranging from 3.6 to 7.6 or more metres. Your treatment of space is influenced by such factors as status, culture, context, subject matter, sex, age, and positive or negative evaluation of the other person. Territoriality involves people's possessive reactions to particular spaces or objects.

12. Artifactual communication consists of messages conveyed by objects or arrangements created by humans; for example, by the use of colour, clothing, body adornment, space decoration, or scent/smell.

13. Touch communication, or haptics, may communicate a variety of meanings, the most important being positive affect, playfulness, control, ritual, and task-relatedness. Touch avoidance is the desire to avoid touching and being touched by others.

14. Paralanguage has to do with the vocal but nonverbal dimension of speech. It includes rate, pitch, volume, resonance, and vocal quality as well as pauses and hesitations. Based on paralanguage, we make judgments about people, sense conversational turns, and assess believability.

15. Silence communicates a variety of meanings, from anger (as in the "silent treatment") to deep emotional responses.

16. Time communication, or chronemics, consists of messages communicated by our treatment of time.

17. Cultural variations in nonverbal communication are great. Different cultures, for example, assign different meanings to gestures, facial expressions, and colours; have different spatial rules; and treat time very differently.

Nonverbal Communication Competence

18. Encoding skills (maintaining eye contact, avoiding intrusive touching) will enable you to communicate more effectively with nonverbal messages.

19. Decoding skills (being conscious of the several nonverbal channels sending messages simultaneously, interpreting messages in a cultural context) will enable you to more effectively understand the meanings being communicated with nonverbal signals.

This chapter also covered some significant nonverbal communication skills. Check those you wish to work on.

_____1. *Body movements.* Use body and hand gestures to reinforce your communication purposes.

_____2. *Facial messages.* Use facial expressions to communicate involvement. In listening, look to the emotional expressions of others as cues to their meaning.

_____3. *Eye movements.* Use eye movements to seek feedback, exchange conversational turns, signal the nature of your relationship, or compensate for increased physical distance.

_____4. *Spatial and proxemic conversational distances.* Maintain distances that are comfortable and that are appropriate to the situation and to your relationship with the other person.

_____5. *Giving space.* Give others the space they need. Look to the other person for any signs of spatial discomfort.

_____6. *Artifactual communication.* Use artifacts (for example, colour, clothing, body adornment, space decoration) to communicate desired messages.

_____7. *Touch and touch avoidance.* Respect the touch-avoidance tendencies of others; pay special attention to cultural and gender differences in touch preferences.

_____8. *Paralanguage.* Vary paralinguistic features to communicate nuances of meaning and to add interest and colour to your messages.

_____9. *Silence.* Examine silence for meanings just as you would eye movements or body gestures.

_____10. *Time cues.* Interpret time cues from the perspective of the person with whom you're interacting. Be especially sensitive to the person's leave-taking cues—remarks such as "It's getting late" or glances at the clock.

_____11. *Smell.* Avoid strong smells that might offend.

_____12. *Nonverbal communication and culture.* Interpret the nonverbal cues of others from the perspective of the other person's cultural meanings (insofar as you can).

VOCABULARY QUIZ: The Language of Nonverbal Communication

Match the terms of nonverbal communication with their definitions. Record the number of the definition next to the appropriate term.

____ emblems (125)
____ affect displays (125)
____ proxemics (129)
____ territoriality (130)
____ haptics (134)
____ paralanguage (136)
____ chronemics (139)
____ artifactual messages (132)
____ tie signs (122)
____ adaptors (125)

1. Movements of the facial area that convey emotional meaning.
2. The study of how time communicates.
3. Signals that communicate your relationship status.
4. Nonverbal behaviours that directly translate into words or phrases.
5. Communication by touch.
6. Gestures that satisfy some personal need.
7. The meanings communicated by clothing, jewellery, or buttons.
8. The study of how space communicates.
9. A possessive or ownership reaction to space or to particular objects.
10. The vocal but nonverbal aspects of speech—for example, rate and volume.

These 10 terms and additional terms used in this chapter can be found in the glossary.

CHAPTER

7

Emotional Messages

Suticha Goodman

Aaron Goodman (at left in photo) teaches at Kwantlen Polytechnic University in Surrey, B.C. Through his work as a multimedia reporter, video journalist, and documentary maker, Goodman shines a light on critical social issues, conflicts, natural disasters, and humanitarian issues across the globe.

Goodman was born in Vancouver in 1974 and grew up in Ottawa. His first international volunteer experience was at age 17 when he lived for three months in a remote village in the Sumatran rainforest in Indonesia with Canada World Youth. Witnessing the injustices of poverty firsthand in Indonesia inspired Goodman's work as a journalist. He's covered the violent crackdown

on independence supporters in East Timor by pro-Jakarta militias in 1999, the legacy of the Khmer Rouge genocide in Cambodia, the search for tens of thousands of boys and men forcibly "disappeared" by government forces in Sri Lanka, and other underreported stories. Following the earthquake in northern Pakistan that claimed more than 70 000 lives and left more than a million people homeless, Goodman trained local reporters in the disaster zone for eight months.

As founder of StoryTurns (www.storyturns.org), Goodman facilitates digital storytelling workshops for a wide range of organizations that enable people to tell powerful first-person stories, express emotions, and develop agency. As Aaron Goodman explains, "Everyone has a story to tell. Some have waited years, even decades, to tell them. Supporting people to write and create their stories is always a remarkable and enriching experience. The workshops are very supportive, collaborative, and creative. This storytelling method has been life-changing for me, and sharing it with others is so rewarding" (Aaron Goodman).

As you work through this chapter, think about how emotions can be communicated in a variety of ways. Think about how expressing emotions can produce both positive and negative results depending on how the message is communicated and how it's heard. How might digital storytelling facilitate the effective communication of emotional messages?

LEARNING OBJECTIVES *After reading this chapter, you should be able to:*

1. Explain the nine principles of emotions and emotional messages.

2. Describe the three obstacles to communicating emotions, and combat these in your own emotional communication.

3. Communicate your own emotions effectively.

4. Respond appropriately to the emotions of others.

Vladimir Mucibabic/Shutterstock

VIEWPOINTS **Strong Emotions**

Anyone who's witnessed road rage will likely agree that it's a concern. Road rage is, in fact, a growing phenomenon in Canada (Smart & Mann, 2002). It has been defined as "a situation where a driver or passenger attempts to kill, injure or intimidate a pedestrian, or another driver or passenger, or to damage their vehicle in a traffic incident" (Smart & Mann, 2002). Causes of road rage may be increasing traffic congestion or the poor driving of others, as well as personality and mental health characteristics of the aggressor (Smart et al., 2003). Being the victim of road rage can be highly distressing, and may even lead to psychiatric problems (Smart et al., 2003). What triggers your anger as you're driving? Is it drivers who are distracted, whether from texting, say, or listening to loud music? What can you do to prevent feelings of rage as you drive?

This chapter addresses this crucial topic, offers insight into the nature of emotions and emotional expression, and explores some of the obstacles to communicating emotions. With this understanding as a base, suggestions for communicating emotions and for responding to the emotions of others are offered.

Among our most difficult interpersonal communication situations are those that involve strong **emotions**. The power of expressing emotions was eloquently articulated by the American poet Maya Angelou: "I've learned that people will forget what you said, people will forget what you did, but people will never forget how you made them feel."

PRINCIPLES OF EMOTIONS AND EMOTIONAL MESSAGES

Communicating emotions is both difficult and important. It's difficult because your thinking often gets confused when you're intensely emotional. It's also difficult because the expectations for communicating emotions vary significantly in the many different contexts we're part of. Yet communicating emotions is a vital component of interpersonal relationships. Feelings constitute a great part of your meanings. If you leave your feelings out or if you communicate them inadequately, you'll fail to communicate a great part of who you are and of what is important to you. Consider what your communications would be like if you left out your feelings when talking about failing a recent test, winning the lottery, becoming a parent, getting engaged, driving a car for the first time, becoming a citizen, or being promoted to supervisor. Emotional expression is so much a part of communication that, even in our often matter-of-fact email message style, emoticons are becoming more popular.

So important is **emotional communication** that it's at the heart of what is now called "emotional intelligence" or "social intelligence" (Goleman, 1995a, 1995b). In fact, the inability to engage in emotional communication—as sender and as receiver—is part of the learning disability known as *dyssemia*, a condition in which individuals are unable to appropriately read the nonverbal messages of others or to communicate their own meanings nonverbally (Duke & Nowicki, 2005). For example, those suffering from dyssemia (often, but not always, associated with high-functioning people with Asperger's syndrome) often fail to return smiles, look uninterested, and use facial expressions that are inappropriate to the situation and the interaction. As you can imagine, people who are poor senders and receivers of emotional messages will likely have problems in developing and maintaining relationships. While there is no cure for this disability, there are many strategies to help children improve their ability to read social situations and respond appropriately. As members of Canadian society committed to inclusion, and with enhanced understanding and acceptance of people with this and other disabilities, "senders" can do much to help people who have difficulties in this area.

Hector Vivas/Jam Media/LatinContent/Getty Images

Soap operas attempt to tell stories that viewers can identify with, but that are generally more extreme. To achieve this over-the-top intensity, these stories rely heavily on emotional expression—the subject of this chapter, in which we consider the nature of emotions, the major obstacles to their expression, and how we can become more effective in both expressing our own feelings and responding to the feelings of others.

Let's look first at several general principles of emotions and emotional expression; these will establish a foundation for our consideration of the skills of emotional communication.

Emotions May Be Primary or Blended

How would you feel in each of the following situations?

- You won the lottery.
- You got the job you applied for.
- A loved one has passed away.
- Your partner is leaving you.

You'd obviously feel very differently in each of these situations. In fact, each feeling is unique. Yet amid all these differences, there are some similarities. For example, most people would claim that the feelings in the first two examples are more similar to each other than they are to the last two. Similarly, the last two are more similar to each other than they are to the first two.

To capture the similarities among emotions, many researchers have tried to identify basic or **primary emotions**. Robert Plutchik (1980) and Havlena, Holbrook, and Lehmann (1989) have developed a helpful wheel-shaped model comprising eight basic emotions (Figure 7.1): joy, acceptance, fear, surprise, sadness, disgust, anger, and anticipation. Emotions that are close to each other on this wheel are also close to each other in meaning. For example, joy and anticipation are more closely related than are joy and sadness or acceptance and disgust. Emotions that are opposite each other on the wheel are also opposite each other in their meaning. For example, joy is the opposite of sadness; anger is the opposite of fear.

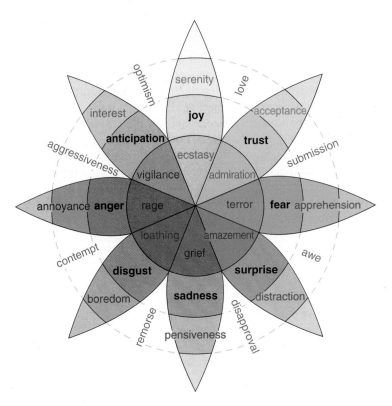

FIGURE 7.1
A Model of the Emotions
Do you agree with the basic assumptions of this model?

Source: Reprinted with permission from Annette deFerrari Design.

In this model, there are also **blended emotions**. These are emotions that are combinations of the primary emotions, and are noted outside the emotion wheel. For example, according to this model, love is a blend of joy and acceptance, and remorse is a blend of disgust and sadness.

Emotions Are Influenced by Body, Mind, and Culture

Emotion involves at least three parts: bodily reactions (such as blushing when you're embarrassed), mental evaluations and interpretations (as in calculating the odds of drawing an inside straight at poker), and cultural rules and beliefs (such as the pride parents feel when their child graduates from college or university).

Bodily reactions are the most obvious aspect of our emotional experience because we can observe them easily. Such reactions span a wide range. They include the blush of embarrassment, the sweating palms that accompany nervousness, and the playing with your hair or touching your face that goes with discomfort. When you judge people's emotions, you probably look to these nonverbal behaviours. You conclude that Munesh is happy to see you because of his smile and his open body posture. You conclude that Lisa is nervous from her damp hands, vocal hesitations, and awkward movements.

In recent years, technological advances have allowed scientists to learn much more about how emotions affect the body, and vice versa. Emotions evoke brain activity in specific regions such as the amygdala and the hippocampus (Koelsch et al., 2013). Using functional MRI scans, scientists today can pinpoint specific neural pathways and brain regions that are activated when a person experiences even complex emotions such as pride and shame (Karczmar, 2014, Roth et al., 2014) or "moral" emotions such as retribution and forgiveness (Fourie et al., 2014). Neural correlates of responses to emotions in others have also been identified (Kumfor et al., 2013). Responses can alter based on personality traits (Park et al., 2013) and on gender (Schiffer et al., 2013).

Chemicals in our bodies that mediate some emotions have now been identified. For example, oxytocin is strongly associated with pleasure and reward sensations (Scheele et al., 2013), while elevated cortisol levels are associated with stress (Jameel et al., 2014).

> ### INTERPERSONAL CHOICE POINT
>
> #### Dealing with Sadness and Joy
> The parents of your neighbour, who's lived next door to you for the past 10 years, were recently killed in a car accident. Now your neighbour, who's had many difficult financial times, will inherit a large estate. You meet in the hallway of your apartment house. What are some of the things you could say to your neighbour at this time? What would you say?

The mental or cognitive part of emotional experience involves the evaluations and interpretations you make on the basis of your behaviours. For example, psychotherapist Albert Ellis (1988; Ellis & Harper, 1975), whose insights are used throughout this chapter, claims that your evaluations of what happens have a greater influence on your feelings than what actually happens. More recent psychologists explain that while the actual emotional response to an event often lasts no more than a minute and a half, the thinking about the event, which causes further emotional reactions, can last for a very long time. Therefore, while we may not be able to control an immediate emotional reaction to an event, we can learn to stop, think about our response, and change it. For example, say you're driving and the car in front of you stops unexpectedly and almost causes an accident. Your immediate response is anger—you may be thinking, "What an idiot! People like him shouldn't drive" as your feelings of anger swell. At this point you can say to yourself, "No point in being angry—it may distract me from driving carefully," and then notice the emotional reaction subside. Or you may choose to continue to be angry—to think about how you'd like to stop that driver, give him a piece of your mind, tell him this, that, or the other. The important thing here is that you have the ability to stop and think about how you want to respond, which will affect your emotional state considerably.

The culture in which you were raised and live also gives you a framework for both expressing feelings and interpreting the emotions of others. In a study conducted by Saba Safdar at the University of Guelph (2009), rules of emotional display in Canada, the United States, and Japan were compared in terms of the expression of specific emotions and of emotional expression with different interaction partners and genders. As expected, more differences were found between the Japanese and the North American countries than between Canada and the U.S. The study attributed this to the fact that in collectivist societies such as Japan, the expression of powerful emotions such as anger and contempt could threaten harmony, whereas in individualistic societies it would be seen as self-assertive and therefore tolerated. Yet there were differences as well between Americans and Canadians; for example, the expression of contempt was considered to be less acceptable in Canadian than in American participants, a finding that Safdar and his colleagues (2009) attribute to the importance Canadians place on being agreeable.

Emotional Arousal Is a Multi-Step Process

If you were to describe the events leading up to emotional arousal, you'd probably describe three stages: (1) An event occurs. (2) You experience an emotion such as surprise, joy, or anger. (3) You respond physiologically; your heart beats faster, your face flushes, and so on. The process would look like this:

An early theory of emotion was offered by psychologist William James and physiologist Carl Lange (James, 1884). Their theory places the physiological arousal *before* the experience of the emotion. The sequence of events according to the **James–Lange theory** is as follows: (1) An event occurs. (2) You respond physiologically. And (3) you experience an emotion; for example, you feel joy or sadness. The process would look like this:

According to a third explanation, the **cognitive labelling theory**, you interpret the physiological arousal and, on the basis of this, experience joy, sadness, or any other emotion (Reisenzein, 1983; Schachter, 1971). The sequence goes like this: (1) An event occurs. (2) You respond physiologically. (3) You interpret this arousal—that is, you decide what emotion you're experiencing. And (4) you experience the emotion. Your interpretation of your arousal will depend on the situation you're in. For example, if you experience an increased pulse rate after someone you've been admiring smiles at you, you may interpret this as joy. If three suspicious-looking strangers approach you on a dark street, however, you may interpret that same increased heartbeat as fear. It's only *after* you make the interpretation that you experience the emotion; for example, the joy or the fear. The process would look like this:

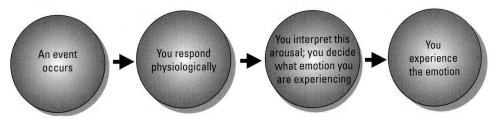

As you continue reading this chapter, consider these three alternative explanations. Although none of them explains the process fully, each offers interesting insights that help explain the nature of emotional communication.

Emotions May Be Adaptive and Maladaptive

Emotions are often adaptive and help you adjust to the situation. For example, if you feel anxious about not doing well on an exam, it might lead you to study harder. If you fear losing your partner, you might act more supportively and lovingly. If you become suspicious of someone following you down a dark street, it might motivate you to take safety precautions. All of these situations are examples of emotions aiding you in accomplishing useful goals.

At other times, emotions may be maladaptive and may get in the way of your accomplishing your goals. For example, you may be so anxious about a test that you just stop thinking and do more poorly than you would have if you had walked in totally detached. Or you might fear losing your partner and, as a result, become suspicious and accusatory, making your relationship even less likely to survive.

Another way emotions may create problems is in what some theorists have cleverly called catastrophizing (or awfulizing)—taking a problem, even a minor one, and making it into a catastrophe: "If I don't do well on this test, I'll never get into law school" or "If this relationship doesn't work, I'm doomed." As you tell yourself (and convince yourself) of these impending catastrophes, your emotional responses can easily get out of hand (Bach & Wyden, 1968; Willson & Branch, 2006).

Emotions Are Communicated Verbally and Nonverbally

Although emotions are especially salient in conflict situations and in relationship development and dissolution, they're actually a part of all messages. Emotions are always present—sometimes to a very strong extent, sometimes only mildly. Therefore, they must be recognized as a part of the communication experience. This is not to say that emotions should always be talked about or that all emotions you feel should be expressed. Emotional feeling and emotional communication are two different things. In some instances, you may want to say exactly what you feel, to reveal your emotions without any censorship. At other times, however, you may want to avoid revealing your emotions. For example, you might not want to reveal your frustration over a customer's indecision, or you might not want to share with your children your worries about finding a job.

Theorists don't agree over whether you can choose the emotions you feel. Some argue that you can; others argue that you can't. However, a growing body of evidence suggests that you have the ability to choose which emotions you wish to focus on, and that you can learn strategies to do just that. For example, if you conduct an online search using the words *happiness training*, you'll find multiple sites for organizations that base their training on the foundations of what's known as positive psychology.

You also have a choice in the ways you express your emotions. Whether or not you choose to express your emotions will depend on your own attitudes about emotional expression. You may wish to explore these by taking the self-test on the next page. While you often hear people say "I couldn't control myself" after an outburst of emotion, most people can indeed learn to control how they express emotion most of the time.

Emotional Expression Is Governed by Display Rules

As explained in Chapter 6, **display rules** govern which emotions are and are not permissible to communicate. For example, although men and women experience emotions similarly, they display them differently (Fischer & Manstead, 2000;

INTERPERSONAL CHOICE POINT

Comforting the Dying

An older, very close relative is dying and calls to ask you to spend some time with her. She says that she wants you to know how much she's always loved you, and that her only regret in dying is not being able to see you anymore. You want her to feel comforted, yet it's so emotional for you. What are some of the things you might say?

TEST YOURSELF

How Do You Feel About Communicating Feelings?

Respond to each of the following statements with a *T* if you feel the statement is a generally true description of your attitudes about expressing emotions or with an *F* if you feel the statement is a generally false description of your attitudes.

_____ 1. Expressing feelings is healthy; it reduces stress and prevents wasting energy on concealment.

_____ 2. Expressing feelings can lead to interpersonal relationship problems.

_____ 3. Expressing feelings can help others understand you.

_____ 4. Emotional expression is often an effective means of persuading others to do as you wish.

_____ 5. Expressing emotions may lead others to perceive you negatively.

_____ 6. Emotional expression can lead to greater and not less stress; expressing anger, for example, may actually increase your feelings of anger.

How Did You Do? These statements are arguments that are often made for and against expressing emotions. Statements 1, 3, and 4 are arguments made in favour of expressing emotions; 2, 5, and 6 are arguments made against expressing emotions. You can look at your responses as revealing (in part) your attitude favouring or opposing the expression of feelings. "True" responses to statements 1, 3, and 4 and "False" responses to statements 2, 5, and 6 would indicate a favourable attitude toward expressing feelings. "False" responses to statements 1, 3, and 4 and "True" responses to statements 2, 5, and 6 indicate a negative attitude.

What Will You Do? There is evidence suggesting that expressing emotions can lead to all six outcomes—the positives and the negatives—and so general suggestions for increasing your willingness to express your emotions are not offered. These potential consequences underscore the importance of critically assessing your options for emotional expression. Especially, be flexible, remembering that what will work in one situation may not work in another.

Oatley & Duncan, 1994; Wade & Tavris, 1998). Women talk more about feelings and emotions and use communication for emotional expression more than men (Barbato & Perse, 1992). Perhaps because of this, they also express themselves facially more than men. Even high school students show this gender difference.

Women are also more likely to express socially acceptable emotions than are men (Brody, 1985). Women smile significantly more than men. In fact, women smile even when smiling isn't appropriate—for example, when reprimanding a subordinate. Men, on the other hand, are more likely than women to express anger and aggression (DePaulo, 1992; Fischer, 1993; Wade & Tavris, 1998). Similarly, women are more effective at communicating happiness, and men are more effective at communicating anger (Coats & Feldman, 1996). Women also cry more than men (Metts & Planalp, 2002).

SKILL-BUILDING EXERCISE

Analyzing Cultural and Gender Emotional Display Rules

Examine each of the following situations, and identify the cultural and gender display rules that would most likely influence your emotional expression (or lack of it).

1. You're watching a movie with a group of friends, and you're emotionally moved by the film and feel like crying.
2. You've just been severely criticized by your supervisor in front of six workers you supervise. You're so stunned that the supervisor walks away before you can say anything. You're now alone with your six subordinates, and you want to scream.

3. One of your close friends accuses you of stealing money, which you didn't do. This person has told several mutual friends, who seem to believe the story. You're angry, and you want this rumour stopped.

Everyone is influenced in their emotional expression by the display rules they learned from their culture. Becoming mindful of emotional display rules will increase your understanding of the emotional expression of others and inform your own choices for emotional expression.

Emotions Can Be Used Strategically

Although you may at first think of emotional expression as honest reflections of what a person is feeling, expressions of emotions can be and often are used strategically. In **strategic emotionality**, emotions (for example, crying, ranting, screaming, and threatening to commit self-harm) are used for one's personal ends. Such emotions can take a variety of forms and serve a variety of purposes. But the basic idea behind strategic emotionality is to control the situation or the other person. For example, in a conflict situation, emotions are often used to win. If someone cries enough and loud enough, the other person may just give in. It works for the baby who wants to be picked up, and it often works for the adult and enables the person to win the fight. This strategy is more likely to be used by members of individualist cultures, which emphasize the winning of a conflict rather than compromise or negotiation (which would be more likely in collectivist cultures).

Not surprisingly, this strategy, which is essentially one of manipulation, often creates resentment and perhaps a desire to retaliate—neither of which is good for a relationship. Another negative outcome of this strategy is that the other person can never be sure how accurately your emotions reflect your true feelings, and this is likely to create communication problems whenever emotions are involved. The effect of this lack of transparency—of not knowing whether your partner is trying to manipulate you or is expressing strong and honest feelings—is likely to be greatest in intimate relationships where these expressions are likely to have long-term effects.

Javier Pierini/Digital Vision/Getty Images

VIEWPOINTS Sex Differences in Communication

Which of these theories seems the most reasonable based on your own observations of sex differences in communication (Guerrero, Jones, & Boburka, 2006)?

- *Biological theory*: Differences in brains and chemistry account for the differences in the ability to express and detect emotions in others.

- *Evolutionary theory*: Emotional expression was basic to survival; those who were good at it lived and passed on their genes to others.

- *Socialization theory*: Men and women are taught differently about emotions and have been socialized into expressing emotions as they do.

Emotions Are Contagious

Emotional messages are often contagious (Cappella & Schreiber, 2006). If you've ever watched an infant and mother interacting, you can readily see how quickly the infant mimics the emotional expressions of the mother. If the mother smiles, the infant smiles; if the mother frowns, the infant frowns. Recent research (Valliant-Molina, Bahrick, & Flom, 2013) confirms that babies as young as five months old recognize the emotions of other babies and are affected by them; other researchers point to the beginnings of emotional recognition as early as three months of age (Turati et al., 2010). As children get older, they begin to pick up more subtle expressions of emotions. For example, children quickly identify and often mimic a parent's anxiety or fear. Even among college roommates, the depression of one roommate can spread to the other over a period of just three weeks (Joiner, 1994). In short, emotions pass easily from one person to another, and women are especially prone to **emotional contagion** (Cappella & Schreiber, 2006; Doherty et al., 1995). In conversation and in small groups, the strong emotions of one person can easily prove contagious to others present; this can be positive when the emotions are productive, and less so when the emotions are unproductive.

One view of this process goes like this:

1. You perceive the emotional expression of others.
2. You mimic this emotional expression, perhaps unconsciously.
3. The feedback you get from your expressions recalls (consciously or unconsciously) the feelings you had when you last expressed yourself in this way, and this recall creates the feelings.

Another view of this process holds that it's under more conscious control. That is, you look at others who are expressing emotions to see how you should be feeling—you take nonverbal cues from those you observe—and then experience the feeling you sense you should be feeling.

Intentional emotional contagion also often occurs in attempts at persuasion. One popular appeal, which organizations use frequently in fundraising for causes related to children, is to use the emotion of pity. By showing you images of hungry and destitute children, these fundraisers hope to get you to empathize with the children's suffering and contribute to their efforts to provide aid. Another, quite different example of the contagious nature of emotions can be seen in spectator sports. Anyone who's watched a hockey game can attest to the contagious nature of the joy, anger, or disappointment that can be stirred up in the crowd.

Emotional contagion also seems to be the goal of certain organizational display rules (Ashkanasy & Humphrey, 2011). For example, it may be required (or at least expected) that the sales force cheer enthusiastically as each new product is unveiled. This cheering is extremely useful and is likely to make the sales representatives more enthusiastic about and more emotionally committed to the product than if they hadn't engage in this cheering.

Emotions Have Consequences

Like all communications, emotions and emotional expression have consequences and can affect your relationships in important ways. Generally, expression of emotion is viewed positively. Faizal H. Sahukhan, a professional counsellor, describes the power of effective communication in solidifying relationships; he emphasizes the importance of expressing feelings in an open and nonjudgmental environment as a means to promote bonding and a heightened sense of intimacy and connection, which are the basis for a range of relationships (Galea, 2012). However, revealing emotions can lead to negative consequences as well. For example, some people feel uncomfortable when others express strongly felt emotions. And if the other person isn't empathic, there is a risk of being judged as variously "too emotional," "too fanatical," "too negative," or "too enthusiastic." As well, expressions of anger can be exceedingly hurtful to others if not expressed with caution, and expressions of sadness may be considered depressing. These risks are only heightened when emotions are communicated on Facebook or other social networks.

So, while the expression of emotion is part of normal and positive relationships, and when done with reciprocity is a means of deepening a relationship, there is a need to utilize good assessment and judgment skills. It's important to assess the environment in which the emotion is to be expressed with questions such as, "How might the other person respond?" "Can I trust these people?" "Will what I say be used against me?" Then, on the basis of the answers to these questions, one can judge the appropriateness of the emotional communication.

With these principles of emotions and emotional expression as a foundation, we can now look at some of the obstacles to effective emotional expression.

> **INTERPERSONAL CHOICE POINT**
>
> **Emotional Frankness**
>
> Joe is extremely honest and open; he regularly says everything he feels without self-censorship. Not surprisingly, he often offends people. Joe is entering a new work environment and worries that his frankness may not be the best way to win friends and influence people. What are some things he can do to better understand this problem? What can he do to correct it?

Can you explain the nine principles of emotions and emotional expression? (Emotions are primary or blended; influenced by body, mind, and culture; aroused in stages; adaptive and maladaptive; communicated verbally and nonverbally; governed by display rules; can be used strategically; are contagious; and have consequences.)

OBSTACLES TO COMMUNICATING EMOTIONS

The expression of feelings is part of most meaningful relationships. Yet it's often very difficult. Three major obstacles stand in the way of effective emotional communication: (1) society's rules and customs, (2) fear, and (3) inadequate interpersonal skills. Let's look more closely at each of these barriers.

"I've been thinking—it might be good for Andrew if he could see you cry once in a while."

Robert Weber/The New Yorker Collection/www.cartoonbank.com

Social and Cultural Customs

If you grew up in Canada, you probably learned the display rule that it's inappropriate to convey strong emotions among people you don't know well, except in certain situations—including loud expressions of joy when your hockey team gets a goal. Moreover, depending on your age and gender, you may have grown up with clear expectations about the kind of emotions that are appropriate to express at all. While these norms are changing, we still hear of little boys being told that "men don't cry" and women are still not exempt from the difficulties of emotional expression. At one time, our society permitted and encouraged women to express emotions openly; however, the tide has been turning, especially for those women in executive and managerial positions who'd be unlikely to show any of the once-acceptable "soft" emotions for fear of losing the respect of their co-workers.

There are enormous variations in display rules about public expressions of love and affection, whether within couples or between parents and children. Studies have shown that what impacts expression of emotion isn't simple and straightforward, but rather based on a set of complex, interacting factors. That is, beneath the generalization that culture impacts emotional expression, we need to see that within any one culture will exist differences based on gender and the interactional partner. The study by Safdar and colleagues (2009) cited earlier, for example, noted that the effect of gender in Canada was stronger than in the United States and Japan.

For both men and women, the best advice is to express your emotions selectively. Carefully weigh the arguments for and against expressing your emotions. Consider the situation, the people you're with, the emotions themselves, and all the elements that make up the communication act. And, most important, consider your choices for communicating emotions—not only what you'll say but also how you'll say it. And realize that one choice is *not* to express your emotions.

Fear

A variety of types of fear stand in the way of emotional expression. Emotional expression exposes a part of you that makes you vulnerable to attack. For example, if you express your love for another person, you risk being rejected. When you expose a weakness, you can be more easily hurt by the uncaring and the insensitive. Or you may

ETHICAL MESSAGES

Motivational Appeals

Appeals to motives are commonplace. For example, if you want a friend to take a vacation with you, you're likely to appeal to such motives as the friend's desire for fun and excitement and perhaps to your friend's hopes of finding true love; if you look at the advertisements for cruises and vacation packages, you'll see appeals to very similar motives. Advertisers also appeal to your desire for increased attractiveness and prestige in trying to sell you everything from cosmetics and clothing to cars. Fear appeals are also common: those who want to censor online content may appeal to your fear of children accessing pornographic materials; those who want to restrict media portrayals of violence may appeal to your fear of increased violence in your community.

Ethical Choice Point

Fear appeals are often used by parents to prevent their children from actions that put them at risk. "If you eat candy, you'll get bad teeth and have to go to the dentist"; "If you aren't careful you'll get run over and have to go to the hospital"; "If you're bad, the boogy man will get you." Where would you draw a line for ethical use of fear when communicating with children?

be angry and want to say something but fear that you might hurt the person and then feel guilty. In addition, you may not reveal your emotions for fear of causing a conflict. Expressing your dislike for your new romantic partner's friends, for example, may create difficulties for the two of you, and you may not be willing to risk the argument and its aftermath. Because of fears such as these, you may deny to others and perhaps even to yourself that you have certain feelings. In fact, this kind of denial is the way many people were taught to deal with emotions.

As you can appreciate, fear can also be adaptive and may lead you to not say things you may be sorry for later. It may lead you to consider more carefully whether you should express yourself and how you might do it. However, when fear debilitates us and contradicts what logic and reason might tell us, it becomes maladaptive.

Inadequate Interpersonal Skills

Perhaps the most important obstacle to effective emotional communication is lack of interpersonal skills. Many people simply don't know how to express their feelings. Some, for example, can express anger only through violence or avoidance. Others can deal with anger only by blaming and accusing others. And many cannot express love. They literally cannot say "I love you."

Expressing negative feelings is doubly difficult. Many of us suppress or fail to communicate negative feelings for fear of offending the other person or making matters worse. But failing to express negative feelings probably won't help the relationship, especially if these feelings are concealed frequently and over a long time.

Both communicating your emotions and responding appropriately to the emotional expressions of others are as important as they are difficult (Burleson, 2003).

Can you describe the three obstacles to emotional communication (societal and cultural customs, fear, and inadequate communication skills)? Can you avoid these obstacles in your own intercultural communication?

SKILLS FOR COMMUNICATING EMOTIONS

Just as emotions are part of your psychological life, emotional expression is part of your interpersonal life; it's not something you can avoid even if you wanted to. In specific cases, you may decide to hide your emotions and not express them, but in other cases, you will want to express them—and this calls for **emotional competence**, the skills for expressing and responding to the emotions of others. We can group these under three major headings: emotional understanding, emotional expression, and emotional responding (see Table 7.1).

Emotional Understanding

Your first task is to develop self-awareness: recognizing what your feelings are, understanding why you feel as you do, and understanding the potential effects of your feelings (Stein & Book, 2011). Here you ask yourself a few pertinent questions.

- *"What am I feeling, and what made me feel this way?"* That is, understand your emotions. Think about your emotions as objectively as possible. Identify, in terms as specific as possible, the antecedent conditions that may be influencing your feelings. Try to answer the question "Why am I feeling this way?" or "What happened to lead me to feel as I do?"
- *"What exactly do I want to communicate?"* Consider also whether your emotional expression will be a truthful expression of your feelings. When emotional expressions are faked—when, for example, you smile though feeling angry or say "I forgive you"

> **INTERPERSONAL CHOICE POINT**
>
> **The Crying Child**
> A seven-year-old is crying because the other children won't play with her. What are some things you can say to make this child feel better (but without trying to solve her problems by asking the other children to play with her)?

TABLE 7.1

EMOTIONAL HAPPINESS

A somewhat different view of emotional competence would be emotional happiness; after all, if you're emotionally competent, it should contribute to your individual happiness. Here are a few "dos" (but with qualifications) for achieving emotional satisfaction, contentment, and happiness.

Do	But
Think positively.	Don't be a Pollyanna; don't gloss over problems.
Associate with positive people.	Don't avoid others because they have different ideas or backgrounds; you'll miss out on a lot.
Do what you enjoy.	Don't forget your responsibilities or ignore obligations.
Talk about your feelings.	Don't substitute talk for action or talk too much.
Imagine yourself positively.	Don't become egotistical; after all, we all have faults, and these need to be addressed if we're to improve.
Think logically; keep emotions in perspective.	Don't ignore the crucial role that emotions and emotional expression often play in interpersonal communication.

when you don't—you may actually be creating emotional and physical stress (Grandey, 2000). Remember, too, the irreversibility of communication; once you communicate something, you can't take it back.

■ *"What are my communication choices?"* Evaluate your communication options in terms of both effectiveness (what will work best and help you achieve your goal) and ethics (what is right or morally justified).

Emotional Expression

Your second step is interpersonal. Here are a few suggestions for this type of special communication. A special box on expressing anger complements this discussion (see pages 161–162).

■ *Be specific.* Consider, for example, the frequently heard "I feel bad." Does it mean "I feel guilty" (because I lied to my best friend)? "I feel lonely" (because I haven't had a date in the past two months)? "I feel depressed" (because I failed that last exam)? Specificity helps. Describe also the intensity with which you feel the emotion: "I feel so angry I'm thinking of quitting my job." "I feel so hurt I want to cry." Also describe any mixed feelings you might have. Very often feelings are a mixture of several emotions, sometimes even of conflicting emotions. Learn the vocabulary to describe your emotions and feelings in specific and concrete terms.

  Table 7.2 provides a list of terms for describing your emotions verbally. It's based on the eight primary emotions identified by Plutchik (refer to Figure 7.1, page 147). Notice that the terms included for each basic emotion provide you with lots of choices for expressing the intensity level you're feeling. For example, if you're extremely fearful, *terror* or *dread* might be appropriate, but if your fear is mild, perhaps *apprehension* or *concern* might be an appropriate term. In addition, the table provides a list of antonyms, providing additional choices for emotional expression.

■ *Describe the reasons you're feeling as you are.* "I feel lonely; I haven't had any contact with friends or family for weeks." "I'm really depressed from failing that last exam." If your feelings were influenced by something the person you're talking to did or said, describe this also. For example, "I felt so angry when you said you wouldn't help me." "I felt hurt when you didn't invite me to the party."

TABLE 7.2

Verbal Expressions of Emotion

Basic Emotion	Synonyms	Antonyms
Joy	happiness, bliss, cheer, contentment, delight, ecstasy, enchantment, enjoyment, felicity, rapture, gratification, pleasure, satisfaction, well-being	sadness, sorrow, unhappiness, woe, depression, gloom, misery, pain
Trust	confidence, belief, hope, assurance, faith, reliance, certainty, credence, certitude, conviction	distrust, disbelief, mistrust, uncertainty
Fear	anxiety, apprehension, awe, concern, consternation, dread, fright, misgiving, phobia, trepidation, worry, qualm, terror	courage, fearlessness, heroism, unconcern
Surprise	amazement, astonishment, awe, caught off-guard, eye-opener, incredulity, jolt, revelation, shock, startle, taken aback, wonder	expectation, assurance, confidence, fear, intention, likelihood, possibility, prediction, surmise
Sadness	dejected, depressed, dismal, distressed, grief, loneliness, melancholy, misery, sorrowful, unhappiness	happiness, gladness, joy, cheer
Disgust	abhorrence, aversion, loathing, repugnance, repulsion, revulsion, sickness, nausea, offensiveness	admiration, desire, esteem, fondness, liking, loving, reverence, respect
Anger	acrimony, annoyance, bitterness, displeasure, exasperation, fury, ire, irritation, outrage, rage, resentment, tantrum, umbrage, wrath, hostility	calmness, contentment, enjoyment, peace, joy, pleasantness
Anticipation	contemplation, prospect, expectancy, hope, foresight, expectation, foreboding, forecast, forethought	unreadiness, doubt, uncertainty

- *Address mixed feelings.* If you have mixed feelings—and you really want the other person to understand you—then address these mixed or conflicting feelings. "I want so much to stay with Pat and yet I fear I'm losing my identity." Or "I feel anger and hatred, but at the same time, I feel guilty for what I did."
- *Anchor your emotions in the present.* Coupled with specific description and the identification of the reasons for your feelings, such statements might look like this: "I feel like a failure right now; I've erased this computer file three times today." "I felt foolish when I couldn't think of that formula." "I feel stupid when you point out my grammatical errors."

SKILL-BUILDING EXERCISE

Communicating Emotions Effectively

The following statements are all ineffective expressions of feelings. For each statement, (1) identify why the statement is ineffective (for example, what problem or distortion the statement creates) and (2) rephrase it as a more effective statement.

1. You hurt me when you ignore me. Don't ever do that again.
2. I'll never forgive that louse. The hatred and resentment will never leave me.
3. Look. I really can't bear to hear about your problems deciding whom to date tomorrow and whom to date the next day and the next. Give me a break. It's boring. Boring.
4. You did that just to upset me. You enjoy seeing me get upset, don't you?
5. Don't talk to me in that tone of voice. Don't you dare insult me with that attitude of yours.

Learning to express emotions effectively will help you think about emotions more logically.

■ *Own your feelings; take personal responsibility for them.* Consider the following statements: "You make me angry." "You make me feel like a loser." "You make me feel stupid." "You make me feel like I don't belong here." In each of these **you-messages**, the speaker blames the other person for the way he or she is feeling. Of course, you know, upon sober reflection, that no one can make you feel anything. Others may do things or say things to you, but it's you who interprets them. That is, you develop feelings as a result of the interaction between what these people say, for example, and your own interpretations. **Owning feelings** means taking responsibility for them—acknowledging that your feelings are your feelings. The best way to own your statements is to use **I-messages** rather than the kinds of you-messages given above. With this acknowledgment of responsibility, the above statements would look like these: "I get angry when you come home late without calling." "I begin to think of myself as a loser when you criticize me in front of my friends." "I feel so stupid when you use medical terms that I don't understand." "When you ignore me in public, I feel like I don't belong here." These rephrased statements identify and describe your feelings about those behaviours; they don't attack the other person or demand that he or she change certain behaviours and consequently don't encourage defensiveness. With I-message statements, it's easier for the other person to acknowledge his or her behaviours and offer to change them.

For good or ill, some social network sites (and the same is true with blogs) make it very easy to *not* own your own messages by enabling you to send comments anonymously.

■ *Ask for what you want.* Depending on the emotions you're feeling, you may want the listener to assume a certain role or just listen or offer advice. Let the listener know what you want. Use I-messages to describe what, if anything, you want the listener to do: "I'm feeling sorry for myself right now; just give me some space. I'll give you a call in a few days." Or, more directly: "I'd prefer to be alone right now." Or "I need advice." Or "I just need someone to listen."

■ *Respect emotional boundaries.* Each person has a different level of tolerance for communication about emotions or communication that's emotional. Be especially alert to nonverbal cues signalling that boundaries are close to being broken. It's often useful to simply ask, "Would you rather change the subject?"

"So, would anyone in the group care to respond to what Clifford has just shared with us?"

Tom Cheney/The New Yorker Collection/www.cartoonbank.com

At the same time, realize that you also have a certain tolerance for revealing your own feelings as well as for listening to and responding to the emotions of others.

Table 7.3 provides a comparison and summary of effective and ineffective emotional expression.

 Can you communicate your own emotions effectively?

TABLE 7.3

INEFFECTIVE AND EFFECTIVE EMOTIONAL EXPRESSION

Effective Emotional Expression	Ineffective Emotional Expression
Specific; talks about emotions using specific terms and with specific examples and behavioural references.	**General**; talks about emotions and feelings in general terms and without specifics.
Mindful; identifies the reasons for the feelings; seeks to understand the causes of emotions.	**Mindless**; mindlessly accepts emotions without asking about their causes.
Present focused; concentrates on present feelings.	**Past focused**; concentrates on past feelings (perhaps as a way to avoid focusing on present feelings).
Uses I-messsages; demonstrates ownership of feelings and their expressions—*I feel angry, I'm hurt, I don't feel loved.*	**Uses you-messages**; attributes feelings to others—*You made me angry, you hurt me, you don't love me.*
Polite; talks about emotions (even anger) without anger and with respect for the other person and the relationship.	**Impolite**; lashes out in anger without regard for the feelings of the other person.

SKILLS FOR RESPONDING TO EMOTIONS

Expressing your feelings is only half the process of emotional communication; the other half is listening and responding to the feelings of others. Here are a few guidelines for making an often difficult process a little easier. A special box on responding to the grief-stricken complements this discussion (see pages 162–163).

- *Look at nonverbal cues to understand the individual's feelings.* For example, overly long pauses, frequent hesitations, eye-contact avoidance, or excessive fidgeting may be a sign of discomfort that it might be wise to talk about. Similarly, look for inconsistent messages, as when someone says that "everything is okay" while expressing facial sadness; these are often clues to mixed feelings. But be sure to use any verbal or nonverbal cues as hypotheses, never as conclusions. Check your perceptions before acting on them. Treat inferences as inferences and not as facts.
- *Look for cues as to what the person wants you to do.* Sometimes, all the person wants is for someone to listen. Don't equate "responding to another's feelings" with "solving the other person's problems." Instead, provide a supportive atmosphere that encourages the person to express his or her feelings.
- *Use active listening techniques.* These will encourage the person to talk should he or she wish to. Paraphrase the speaker. Express understanding of the speaker's feelings. Ask questions as appropriate.

isifa Image Service s.r.o./Alamy

VIEWPOINTS Decoding Emotions

Research finds that sleep deprivation hinders your ability to accurately recognize the emotions expressed facially by others (Gordon, 2010). What other factors (about yourself, the context, your relationship to the other person, and so on) might influence your ability to accurately detect the emotions of others?

INTERPERSONAL CHOICE POINT

The Break-In

Fellow students have just had their dorm room broken into, their computers stolen, and their furnishings trashed. They come to you to tell you what happened. Your room wasn't touched. What might you say? What should you be sure you don't say?

- *Empathize.* See the situation from the point of view of the speaker. Don't evaluate the other person's feelings. For example, comments such as "Don't cry; it wasn't worth it" or "You'll get promoted next year" can easily be interpreted to mean "Your feelings are wrong or inappropriate."
- *Focus on the other person.* Interjecting your own similar past situations is often useful for showing your understanding, but it may create problems if it refocuses the conversation away from the other person. Show interest by encouraging the person to explore his or her feelings. Use simple encouragers like "I see" or "I understand." Or ask questions to let the speaker know that you're listening and that you're interested.
- *Remember the irreversibility of communication.* Whether expressing emotion or responding to the emotions of others, it's useful to recall the irreversibility of communication. You won't be able to take back an insensitive or disconfirming response. Responses to another's emotional expressions are likely to have considerable impact, so be especially mindful to avoid inappropriate responding.

Can you use the suggestions offered here to respond appropriately to the emotions of others?

SKILL-BUILDING EXERCISE

Responding to Emotions

Responding appropriately to emotions is one of the most difficult of all communication tasks. Here are some situations to practise on. Visualize yourself in each of the following situations, and respond as you think an effective communicator would.

1. A friend of yours has betrayed your trust by talking publicly about something you told her in confidence. You're angry and disappointed, but don't want to lose the friendship.

2. A young child who's a relative of yours comes to you in tears because his pet dog has died. What would you say to him?

3. Neighbours who've lived next door to you for the past 10 years and who've had many difficult financial times have just won the lottery worth several million dollars. You meet in the hallway of your apartment house; they're glowing.

Communicating emotions is difficult, but often there is no alternative.

HANDLING ANGER: A SPECIAL CASE ILLUSTRATION

As a kind of summary of the guidelines for expressing your emotions, this section looks at anger. **Anger** is one of the eight basic emotions identified in Plutchik's model (Figure 7.1). It's also an emotion that can create considerable problems if not managed properly. Anger varies from mild annoyance to intense rage; increases in pulse rate and blood pressure usually accompany these feelings.

Anger isn't necessarily always bad. In fact, anger may help you protect yourself, energizing you to fight or flee. Often, however, anger does prove destructive—as when, for example, you allow it to obscure reality or to become an obsession.

Anger doesn't just happen; you make it happen by your interpretation of events. Yet life events can contribute mightily. There are the road repairs that force you to detour so that you wind up late for an important appointment. There are the moths that attack your favourite sweater. There's the water leak that ruins your carpet. People, too, can contribute to your anger: the driver who tailgates, the clerk who overcharges, the supervisor who ignores your contributions to the company. But it's you who interprets these events and people in ways that stimulate you to generate anger.

Writing more than a hundred years ago, Charles Darwin observed in *The Expression of the Emotions in Man and Animals* (1872) that "The free expression by outside signs of an emotion intensifies it . . . the repression, as far as this is possible, of all outside signs softens our emotions. He who gives way to violent gestures will increase his rage." Popular psychology ignored Darwin's implied admonition in the 1960s and 70s, when the suggested prescription for dealing with anger was to "let it all hang out" and "tell it like it is." Express your anger, many people advised, or risk its being bottled up and eventually exploding. This idea is called the **ventilation hypothesis**—the notion that expressing emotions allows you to ventilate your negative feelings and that this will have a beneficial effect on your physical health, your mental well-being, and even your interpersonal relationships (Kennedy-Moore & Watson, 1999; Spett, 2004).

Later thinking has returned to Darwin, however, and suggests that venting anger may not be the best strategy (Tavris, 1989). Expressing anger doesn't get rid of it but makes it grow: angry expression increases anger, which promotes more angry expression, which increases anger, and on and on. Some support for this idea that expressing emotions makes them stronger comes from a study that compared (a) participants who only felt emotions such as happiness and anger with (b) participants who both felt and expressed these emotions. The results of the study indicated that people who both felt and expressed the emotions became emotionally aroused faster than did those who only felt the emotions (Hess et al., 1992). And of course this spiral of anger can make conflicts all the more serious and all the more difficult to manage.

A better strategy seems to be to reduce the anger. With this principle in mind, here are some suggestions for managing and communicating anger.

Anger Management: SCREAM Before You Scream

Perhaps the most popular recommendation for dealing with anger is to count to 10. The purpose is to give you a cooling-off period, and the advice isn't bad. A somewhat more difficult but probably far more effective strategy, however, would be to use that cooling-off period not merely for counting but for mindfully analyzing and ultimately managing your anger. The **anger management** procedure offered here is similar to those available in popular books on anger management but is couched in a communication framework. It's called SCREAM, an acronym for the major components of the communication process that you need to consider:

1. *Self.* How important is this matter to you? Is it worth the high blood pressure and the general aggravation? Are you interpreting the "insult" as the other person intended, or could you be misperceiving the situation or the intent? Are you confusing factual with inferential knowledge? Are you sure that what you think happened really happened?
2. *Context.* Is this the appropriate time and place to express your anger? Do you have to express your anger right now? Do you have to express it right here? Might a better time and place be arranged?
3. *Receiver.* Is this person the one to whom you wish to express your anger? For example, do you want to express your anger to your life partner if you're really angry with your supervisor for not recommending your promotion?
4. *Effect (immediate).* What effect do you want to achieve? Do you want to express your anger to help you get the promotion? To hurt the other person? To release pent-up emotions? To stand up for your rights? Each purpose would obviously require a different communication strategy. Consider, too, the likely effect of your anger display. For example, will the other person also become angry? And if so, is it possible that the entire situation will snowball and get out of hand?
5. *Aftermath (long-range).* What are the likely long-term repercussions of this expression of anger? What will be the effects on your relationship? Your continued employment?

HANDLING ANGER: A SPECIAL CASE ILLUSTRATION (continued)

6. *Messages.* Suppose that after this rather thorough analysis, you do decide to express your anger. What messages would be appropriate? How can you best communicate your feelings to achieve your desired results? This question brings us to the subject of anger communication.

Anger Communication

Anger communication is not angry communication. In fact, it might be argued that the communication of anger ought to be especially calm and dispassionate. Here, then, are a few suggestions for communicating your anger in a non-angry way.

- *Get ready to communicate calmly and logically.* First, relax. Try to breathe deeply; think pleasant thoughts; perhaps tell yourself to "take it easy," "think rationally," and "calm down." Try to get rid of any unrealistic ideas you may have that might contribute to your anger. For example, ask yourself whether this person's revealing something about your past to a third party is really all that serious or was really intended to hurt you.
- *Examine your communication choices.* In most situations, you'll have a range of choices. There are lots of different ways to express yourself, so don't jump to the first possibility that comes to mind. Assess your options for the form of the communication—should

you communicate face to face? By email? By telephone? Similarly, assess your options for the timing of your communication, for the specific words and gestures you might use, for the physical setting, and so on.

- *Consider the advantages of delaying the expression of anger.* For example, consider writing the email but sending it to yourself, and waiting at least until the next morning. Then the options of revising it or not sending it at all will still be open to you.
- *Remember that different cultures have different display rules*—norms for what is and isn't appropriate to display. Assess the culture you're in as well as the cultures of the other people involved, especially these cultures' display rules for communicating anger.
- *Apply the relevant skills of interpersonal communication.* For example, be specific, use I-messages, avoid generalizations, avoid polarized terms, and in general communicate with all the competence you can muster.
- *Recall the irreversibility of communication.* Once you say something, you won't be able to erase or delete it from the mind of the other person.

These suggestions aren't going to solve the problems of road rage, gang warfare, or domestic violence. Yet they may help—a bit—in reducing some of the negative consequences of anger and perhaps even some of the anger itself.

COMMUNICATING WITH THE GRIEF-STRICKEN: A SPECIAL CASE ILLUSTRATION

Communicating with people who are experiencing grief, a common but difficult type of communication interaction, requires special care (Zunin & Zunin, 1991). Consideration of this topic also will offer a useful recap of some of the principles of responding to the emotions of others.

A person may experience grief because of illness or death, the loss of a job or highly valued relationship (such as a friendship or romantic breakup), the loss of certain physical or mental abilities, the loss of material possessions (a house fire or stock losses), or the loss of some ability (for example, the loss of the ability to have children or to play the piano). Each situation seems to call for a somewhat different set of dos and don'ts.

We sometimes experience discomfort when in contact with a person who is grieving. Your response will depend on many things—how well you know the person, the nature of your relationship, and the state of the person who is grieving.

Here are some suggestions for communicating effectively with the grief-stricken.

- *Confirm the other person and the person's emotions.* A simple "You must be worried about finding another position" or "You must be feeling very alone right now" confirms the person's feelings. This type of expressive support lessens feelings of grief (Reed, 1993). (Be careful, however, not to make assumptions.)
- *Give the person permission to grieve.* Let the person know that it's acceptable and okay with you if he or she grieves in the ways that feel most comfortable—for example, crying or talking about old times. Don't try to change the subject or interject too often. As long as the person is talking and seems to be feeling better for it, be supportive.
- *Avoid trying to focus on the bright side.* Avoid expressions such as "You're lucky you have some vision left" or "It's better this way; Pat was suffering so much."

COMMUNICATING WITH THE GRIEF-STRICKEN: A SPECIAL CASE ILLUSTRATION (continued)

These expressions may easily be seen as telling people that their feelings should be redirected, that they should be feeling something different.

- *Encourage the person to express feelings and talk about the loss.* Most people will welcome this opportunity. On the other hand, don't try to force people to talk about experiences or feelings they may not be willing to share.
- *Be especially sensitive to leave-taking cues.* Behaviours such as fidgeting or looking at a clock and statements such as "It's getting late" or "We can discuss this later" are hints that the other person is ready to end the conversation. Don't overstay your welcome.
- *Let the person know that you care and are available.* Saying you're sorry is a simple but effective way to

let the person know you care. Express your empathy; let the grief-stricken person know that you can feel (to some extent) what he or she is going through. But don't assume that your feelings, however empathic you are, are the same in depth or in kind. At the same time, let the person know that you're available—"If you ever want to talk, I'm here" or "If there's anything I can do, please let me know."

Even when you follow the principles and do everything according to the book, you may find that your comments aren't appreciated or are not at all effective in helping the person feel any better. Use these cues to help you readjust your messages.

CANADIAN PROFILE: WRAP-UP

Suticha Goodman

Aaron Goodman uses digital media to help people tell their stories, stories that are often hard to tell or that are deeply personal and emotional. If you had the opportunity to create a digital story, what would you share? How do you think producing your digital story would affect you or others? How might digital storytelling support those who may not feel they have a voice?

SUMMARY OF CONCEPTS AND SKILLS

This chapter explored the nature and principles of emotions in interpersonal communication, the obstacles to meaningful emotional communication, and some guidelines that will help you communicate your feelings and respond to the feelings of others more effectively.

Principles of Emotions and Emotional Messages

1. Emotions consist of a physical part (our physiological reactions), a cognitive part (our interpretations of our feelings), and a cultural part (our cultural traditions' influence on our emotional evaluations and expressions).
2. Emotions may be primary or blends. The primary emotions, according to Robert Plutchik, are joy, acceptance, fear, surprise, sadness, disgust, anger, and anticipation. Other emotions, such as love, awe, contempt, and aggressiveness, are blends of primary emotions.

3. There are different views as to how emotions are aroused. One proposed sequence is this: an event occurs, you respond physiologically, you interpret this arousal, and you experience emotion based on your interpretation.
4. Emotions are communicated verbally and nonverbally, and the way in which you express emotions is largely a matter of choice.
5. Cultural and gender display rules identify what emotions may be expressed, where, how, and by whom.
6. Emotions are often contagious.

Obstacles to Communicating Emotions

7. Among the obstacles to emotional expression are societal rules and customs, the fear of appearing weak or powerless, and not knowing how to express emotions.

Skills for Communicating Emotions

8. Develop self-awareness: recognize what your feelings are, understand why you feel as you do, and understand the potential effects of your feelings.
9. Practise the skills for effective verbal and nonverbal expression; for example, be specific and own your own messages.

Skills for Responding to Emotions

10. Learn what the other person is feeling by understanding his or her verbal and nonverbal cues.

This chapter also covered a wide variety of skills for more effective emotional communication. Check those you wish to work on.

_____ 1. *Understanding feelings.* Understand your feelings. Understand what you're feeling and what has made you feel this way.

_____ 2. *Communication goals.* Formulate a communication goal. What exactly do you want to accomplish when expressing emotions?

_____ 3. *Consider choices.* Identify your communication choices and evaluate them, and only then make your decision as to what to say.

_____ 4. *Communicating feelings.* Describe your feelings as accurately as possible, identify the reasons for your feelings, anchor your feelings and their expression to the present time, own your own feelings, and handle your anger as appropriate.

_____ 5. *Emotional cues.* Look for cues to understanding the person's feelings.

_____ 6. *Emotional wants.* Look for cues as to what the person wants you to do, and try to be responsive to these wants.

_____ 7. *Active listening.* Use active listening techniques.

_____ 8. *Empathize.* See the situation from the other person's perspective.

_____ 9. *Other-focus.* Focus on the other person; avoid changing the focus to yourself.

_____ 10. *Irreversibility.* Remember the irreversibility of communication; once something is said, it can't be unsaid.

VOCABULARY QUIZ: The Language of Emotions

Match the following terms of emotional communication with their definitions. Record the number of the definition next to the appropriate term.

_____ blended emotions (148)
_____ display rules (150)
_____ strategic emotionality (152)
_____ emotional communication (146)
_____ ventilation hypothesis (161)
_____ emotional contagion (152)
_____ primary emotions (147)
_____ anger (161)
_____ emotional competence (155)
_____ anger management (161)

1. Using emotions to achieve some personal end.
2. The idea that expressing emotions allows you to express your negative feelings and that this will have beneficial effects.
3. Combinations of the basic emotions.
4. The process by which the strong emotions of one person can be easily transferred to others present.
5. Acrimony, annoyance, bitterness, displeasure, exasperation, fury, ire, irritation, outrage, rage, resentment, tantrum, umbrage, wrath, hostility.
6. Norms for what is and isn't appropriate to express.
7. The most basic of emotions, often thought to consist of joy, acceptance, fear, surprise, sadness, disgust, anger, and anticipation.
8. The process by which you handle anger.
9. The expression of feelings—for example, feelings of guilt, happiness, or sorrow.
10. The skills for expressing and responding to the emotions of others.

These 10 terms and additional terms used in this chapter can be found in the glossary.

8

Conversation Messages

CANADIAN PROFILE: Stephen Lewis

Eric Miller Africapictures.net/Newscom

Born in Ottawa in 1937, Stephen Lewis has been a teacher, politician, diplomat, ambassador, journalist, labour arbitrator, author, and tireless advocate for human rights and HIV/AIDS in Africa and around the globe. After teaching English in Africa, he became an active member of Ontario's New Democratic Party. His work with the United Nations spanned more than two decades, beginning in 1984 when he was named Canada's ambassador to the UN. From there he became deputy executive director of UNICEF and was later named the UN secretary-general's special envoy for HIV/AIDS in Africa.

Lewis is a passionate, articulate advocate for the plight of those around the globe suffering from poverty, war, and the AIDS pandemic. Throughout his life he's had countless conversations with a wide range of people—from students to international leaders to village people in Africa. He's had to adapt his communication style and vocabulary depending on who he's talking to; a conversation with an African grandmother who's raising children orphaned by AIDS is very different from a conversation with UN leaders. Lewis uses what he's learned from his many conversations to hold yet more conversations with those he hopes can truly make a change in our world.

Those who've been privileged to hear Lewis speak may have heard him begin with the heart-wrenching words, "I have spent many years of my life watching people die" (Stephen Lewis). He tells stories of the people he's met, of their children and families, and of the pain of losing them to the AIDS pandemic. He uses language that is simple yet powerful, evoking pictures in the mind that can't be forgotten. Stephen Lewis claims that one of his greatest challenges is how to arouse people not just to pity and horror but to action.

As you work through this chapter, think about how you use conversation to give and receive important messages. Think too about the many different people with whom you speak and how you adjust both your conversational techniques and your vocabulary. What techniques does the chapter discuss that might help you have meaningful conversations with a wide variety of people?

LEARNING OBJECTIVES *After reading this chapter, you should be able to:*

1. Explain the stages of conversation, its dialogic nature, and the roles of turn-taking and politeness.

2. Define *self-disclosure*, disclose with recognition of the associated rewards and dangers, and use the suggestions to respond to the disclosures of others and to resist the pressure to self-disclose.

3. Communicate effectively in making small talk, introductions, and apologies and in giving compliments and advice.

4. Describe the differences between technology-mediated conversation and face-to-face conversation.

The TV show *Blue Bloods* features amazingly effective conversation around the family dinner table. Although these aren't likely to be representative of most family meals, we can learn a great deal from observing how conversations are managed and made more effective—the subject of this chapter.

Definitions of the word *conversation* vary slightly, but it's generally understood to mean an exchange of thoughts, feelings, and ideas between two or more people, and usually entails both verbal and nonverbal communication. Good conversation is considered to be a highly valued social skill. It seems to come naturally to many people; however, it can also be learned. Examining the art of conversation provides an excellent opportunity to look at verbal and nonverbal messages as they're used in day-to-day communications and thus serves as a useful culminating discussion for this second part of the text. In this chapter, we look at three aspects of conversation: (1) principles of conversation, (2) conversational disclosure, in which you reveal yourself to others, and (3) some special types of conversations, grouped under the heading "Everyday Conversations." The general purpose of this discussion is to increase your understanding of the conversation process and to enable you to engage in conversations with greater comfort, effectiveness, and satisfaction.

The main body of knowledge and the theories related to conversation were developed prior to the prevalence of technology-mediated communication, and are based on the assumption that conversations take place face to face. There is some concern today that the multitude of methods available to us for "connecting" are actually negatively impacting the art of conversation as well as the intimate relationships that evolve as a result of these conversations. Sherry Turkle, in a highly debated *New York Times* article, argues that although email, Twitter, and Facebook have their place in human relationships, politics, and business, they're not a substitute for face-to-face conversations—conversations in which we attend to tone and nuance and are "called upon to see things from another's point of view" (Turkle, 2012). For Turkle, the waning of face-to-face communication short-changes the very nature of interpersonal relationships. This view is shared by many scholars of communication; Thiebaud (2010), for example, argues that such technology has, over the years, caused us to forget, or leave behind, the interpersonal interactions that are the very essence of our humanity.

We may or may not agree with these views, but we do need to understand whether and how non-face-to-face conversation differs from face to face, and even whether the principles of conversation need to be revised to better reflect the incorporation of conversations that are conducted through technological means.

PRINCIPLES OF CONVERSATION

Although conversation is an everyday process and one we seldom think about, it is, like most forms of communication, governed by several principles.

The Principle of Process: Conversation Is a Developmental Process

Conversation is best viewed as a process rather than as an act. It's convenient to divide up this process into stages and to view each stage as requiring a choice as to what you'll say and how you'll say it. Here we divide the sequence into five steps: opening, feedforward, business, feedback, and closing. These stages and the way people follow them will vary depending on the personalities of the communicators, their culture, the context in which the conversation occurs, the purpose of the conversation, and the entire host of factors considered throughout this text.

- *Opening.* The first step is to open the conversation, usually with some kind of greeting: "Hi. How are you?" "Hello, this is Joe." The greeting is a good example of what's known as *phatic communion*—a message that establishes a connection between two people and opens up the channels for more meaningful interaction. Openings, of course, may be nonverbal as well as verbal. A smile, kiss, or handshake may be as clear an opening as "Hello." Greetings are so common that they often go unnoticed. But when they're omitted—as when the doctor begins the conversation by saying, "What's wrong?"—you may feel uncomfortable and thrown off guard.

- *Feedforward.* At the second step, you (usually) provide some kind of **feedforward**, which gives the other person a general idea of the conversation's focus: "I've got to tell you about Jack," "Did you hear what happened in class yesterday?," or "We need to talk about our vacation plans." Feedforward also may identify the tone of the conversation ("I'm really depressed and need to talk with you") or the time required ("This will just take a minute") (Frentz, 1976; Reardon, 1987). Conversational awkwardness often occurs when feedforwards are used inappropriately; for example, using overly long feedforwards or omitting feedforward before a truly shocking message.

INTERPERSONAL CHOICE POINT

Prefacing to Extremes

A friend whom you talk to on the phone fairly regularly seems to take an inordinate amount of time in giving you a preview of what the conversation is going to be about—the preface is so long that it makes you want to get off the phone, and frequently you make excuses to do just that. What are some things you might do to change this communication pattern?

- *Business.* The third step is the "business," the substance or focus of the conversation. The term *business* is used to emphasize that most conversations are goal directed. That is, you converse to fulfill one or several of the general purposes of interpersonal communication: to learn, relate, influence, play, or help (see Chapter 1). The term is also sufficiently general to incorporate all kinds of interactions. In general, the business is conducted through an exchange of speaker and listener roles. Brief, rather than long, speaking turns characterize most satisfying conversations. In the business stage, you talk about Jack, what happened in class, or your vacation plans. This is obviously the longest part of the conversation and the reason for the opening and the feedforward.

- *Feedback.* The fourth step is **feedback**, the reverse of the second step. Here you (usually) reflect back on the conversation in order to signal that, as far as you're concerned, the business is completed: "So you want to send Jack a get-well card," "Wasn't that the craziest class ever?," or "I'll call for reservations, and you'll shop for what we need."

- *Closing.* The fifth and last step, the opposite of the first step, is the closing, the goodbye, which often reveals how satisfied the participants were with the conversation: "I hope you'll call soon" or "Don't call us, we'll call you." The closing may also be used to schedule future conversations: "Give me a call tomorrow night" or "Let's meet for lunch at noon."

When closings are indefinite or vague, conversation often becomes awkward; you're not quite sure if you should say goodbye or wait for something else to be said.

Remember that the steps described above would represent a conversation at its best—and that many

Pearson

VIEWPOINTS Gender Differences in Communication

One of the stereotypes about gender differences in communication is that women talk more than men. However, one study of 396 college students found that women and men talk about the same number of words per day, about 16 000 (Mehl et al., 2007). Do your own experiences support the stereotype, or do they support this research finding?

conversations in our day-to-day life are much more rushed, and may not include all of these stages. Consider this exchange—"Do we need to buy eggs?" "No, not today." "Okay, see you tonight"—whose context, purpose, and nature of the relationship may eliminate the need for some of the above steps. Conversations between two people using technology will also often miss certain stages and can become quite informal: "Hey Taylor, did u pick up my class notes for me?" "Yep." Words and sentences are often shortened and texting abbreviations used to the point of being indecipherable to some: "KK! TY, TTYL, Raj" ("Okay! Thank you, Talk to you later").

DEVELOPING LANGUAGE AND COMMUNICATION SKILLS

Learning the Uses of Conversation

When children start school, they learn new uses for conversation and begin to develop more complex conversational strategies. For example, if an adult refuses a child's request the first time, the child learns to rephrase the request more politely a second time. School-aged children are also more sensitive than preschoolers to the distinctions between what people say and what they mean (for example, if Mom says that the garbage smells, the child understands that Mom really wants him to take the garbage out). As well, schoolmates help each other learn to communicate clearly. While adults may often simply accept what children have to say because they're not really listening, peers will challenge and demand clarification.

The Principle of Dialogue: Conversation Is Dialogic

Often the term *dialogue* is used as a synonym for *conversation*. However, **dialogue** connotes a deeper level of engagement than conversation, one in which the input of each participant is highly valued (Yau-fai Ho et al., 2001). In dialogue, each person is both speaker and listener, sender and receiver, with a concern for the other person and the relationship between the two. The objective of dialogue is usually to achieve mutual understanding and empathy.

"Conversation? I thought we were just meeting for coffee."

Opening and Closing a Conversation

Effectively opening and closing conversations can often be challenging. Consider, first, a few situations in which you might want to open a conversation. For each situation, develop a possible opening message in which you seek to accomplish one or more of the following: (a) telling others that you're accessible and open to communication, (b) showing that you're friendly, or (c) showing that you like the other person.

1. You're one of the first guests to arrive at a friend's party and are now there with several other people to whom you've only just been introduced. Your friend, the host, is busy with other matters.
2. You're in the cafeteria eating alone. You see another student who's also eating alone and whom you recognize from your English literature class. But you're not sure whether this person has noticed you in class.

Here are two situations in which you might want to bring a conversation to a close. For each situation, develop a possible closing message in which you seek to accomplish one or more of the following: (a) end the conversation without much more talk, (b) leave the other person with a favourable impression of you, or (c) keep the channels of communication open for future interaction.

1. You and a friend have been talking on the phone for the past hour, but not much new is being said. You have a great deal of work to do and want to wrap it up. Your friend just doesn't seem to hear your subtle cues.
2. You're at a party and are anxious to meet a person with whom you've exchanged eye contact for the past 10 minutes. The problem is that another person is demanding all your attention. You don't want to insult this person, but you need to end the conversation in order to make contact with the other person.

Opening and closing conversations are often difficult; your handling of these steps will help create an impression that's likely to be long lasting and highly resistant to change.

Monologue, conversely, is communication in which one person speaks and the other listens—there's no real interaction between participants. The monologic communicator is focused only on his or her own goals and has no real concern for the listener's feelings or attitudes; this speaker is interested in the other person only insofar as that person can serve his or her purposes.

To increase dialogue and decrease monologic tendencies, try the following:

- *Be respectful and acknowledge the presence and importance of the other person.* Ask for suggestions, opinions, and clarification to ensure that you understand what the other person is saying from that person's poiont of view.
- *Avoid negative criticism* ("I didn't like that explanation") and negative judgments ("You're not a very good listener, are you?"). Instead, practise using positive criticism ("I like those first two explanations best; they were really well reasoned").
- *Keep the channels of communication open* by displaying a willingness to listen. Give cues (nonverbal nods, brief verbal expressions of agreement, paraphrasing) that tell the speaker you're listening.
- *Avoid manipulating the conversation* to get the person to say something positive about you or to force the other person to think, believe, or behave in any particular way.

The Principle of Turn Taking: Conversation Is a Process of Turn Taking

The defining feature of conversation is **turn taking** (introduced briefly in Chapter 6), where the speaker and listener exchange roles throughout the interaction. You accomplish this through a wide variety of verbal and nonverbal cues that signal conversational turns—the changing or maintaining of the speaker or listener role during the conversation. In hearing people, turn taking is regulated by both audio and visual signals. Among blind speakers, turn taking is governed in larger part by audio signals and often touch.

Among deaf speakers, turn-taking signals are largely visual and also may involve touch (Coates & Sutton-Spence, 2001). By combining the insights of a variety of communication researchers (Burgoon, Guerrero, & Floyd, 2010; Duncan, 1972; Pearson & Spitzberg, 1990), let's look more closely at conversational turns in terms of cues that speakers use and cues that listeners use.

SPEAKER CUES   As a speaker, you regulate conversation through two major types of cues: turn maintaining and turn yielding. **Turn-maintaining cues** help you maintain the speaker's role. You can do this with a variety of cues; for example, by continuing a gesture to show that you haven't completed the thought, avoiding eye contact with the listener so that there's no indication that you're passing on the speaking turn, or sustaining your intonation pattern to indicate that you intend to say more (Burgoon, Guerrero, & Floyd, 2010; Duncan, 1972). In most cases, speakers are expected to maintain relatively brief speaking turns and to turn over the speaking role willingly to the listener, when so signalled by the listener.

With **turn-yielding cues**, you tell the listener that you're finished and wish to exchange the role of speaker for that of listener. For example, at the end of a statement, you might add some paralinguistic cue such as "eh?" that asks one of the listeners to assume the role of speaker. You can also indicate that you've finished speaking by dropping your intonation, by prolonged silence, by making direct eye contact with a listener, by asking some general question, or by nodding in the direction of a particular listener.

LISTENER CUES   As a listener, you can regulate the conversation by using a variety of cues. **Turn-requesting cues** let the speaker know that you'd like to take a turn as speaker. Sometimes you can do this by simply saying, "I'd like to say something," but often you do it more subtly through some vocalized "er" or "um" that tells the mindful speaker that you'd now like to speak. This request to speak is also often made with facial and mouth gestures. You can, for example, indicate a desire to speak by opening your eyes and mouth widely as if to say something, by beginning to gesture with your hand, or by leaning forward.

You can also indicate your reluctance to assume the role of speaker by using **turn-denying cues**. For example, intoning a slurred "I don't know" or a brief grunt signals you have nothing to say. Other ways to refuse a turn are to avoid eye contact with the speaker who wishes you to take on the role of speaker or to engage in some behaviour that's incompatible with speaking—for example, coughing or blowing your nose.

BACKCHANNELLING CUES   **Backchannelling cues** (introduced in Chapter 4) are used to communicate various types of information back to the speaker *without* your assuming the role of speaker; these cues are generally supportive and confirming, and show that you're listening and are involved in the interaction (Kennedy & Camden, 1988). You can communicate a variety of messages with these backchannelling cues; here are four of the most important (Burgoon, Guerrero, & Floyd, 2010; Pearson & Spitzberg, 1990).

■ *To indicate agreement or disagreement.* Smiles, nods of approval, brief comments such as "Right" and "Of course," or a vocalization like "uh-huh" signal agreement. Frowning, shaking your head, or making comments such as "No" or "Never" signal disagreement.
■ *To indicate degree of involvement.* An attentive posture, forward leaning, and focused eye contact tell the speaker that you're involved in the conversation. An inattentive posture, backward leaning, and avoidance of eye contact communicate a lack of involvement.
■ *To pace the speaker.* You ask the speaker to slow down by raising your hand near your ear and leaning forward or to speed up by repeatedly nodding your head. Or you may cue the speaker verbally by asking the speaker to slow down or to speed up.

■ *To ask for clarification.* Puzzled facial expressions, perhaps coupled with a forward lean, or the direct interjection of "Who?," "When?," or "Where?" signal your need for clarification.

INTERRUPTIONS In contrast to backchannelling cues, **interruptions** are attempts to take over the role of the speaker. These are not supportive and are often disconfirming. Interruptions are often interpreted as attempts to change the topic to a subject that the interrupter knows more about or to emphasize the person's authority. Interruptions are often seen as attempts to assert power and to maintain control. Not surprisingly, research finds that superiors (bosses and supervisors) and those in positions of authority (police officers and interviewers) interrupt those in inferior positions more than the other way around (Ashcraft, 1998; Carroll, 1994). In fact, it would probably strike you as strange to see a worker repeatedly interrupting a supervisor.

Another and even more often studied aspect of interruption is that of gender difference. Early research studies (Anderson et al., 1998) seemed to confirm the popular belief that men interrupt more than women, but a more recent review (Bell & McCarthy, 2012) suggests that the evidence points to very little, if any, difference.

INTERPERSONAL CHOICE POINT

Interrupting

You're supervising a group of six people who are working to revise your college's website. But one member of the group interrupts so much that other members have simply stopped contributing. It's become a one-person group, and you can't have this. What are some of the things that you might say to correct this situation without coming across as the bossy supervisor?

The Principle of Politeness: Conversation Is (Usually) Polite

Not surprisingly, conversation is expected (at least in many cases) to follow the principle of politeness. Norms for what is considered polite behaviour in conversation vary considerably from culture to culture, and even within cultures. What is considered impolite in any one group—whether it's a demographic, social class, or ethnic group—may be acceptable in another. The following six rules (referred to as maxims) of politeness were identified by linguist Geoffrey Leech (Leech, 1983). As you read these, ask yourself whether they apply as much today as they did in 1983; what, if anything has changed; and what might be some cultural differences in relation to these rules. Before reading about these maxims, take the accompanying self-test to help you personalize the material that follows.

TEST YOURSELF

How Polite Are You?

Try estimating your own level of politeness. For each of the statements below, indicate how closely it describes your typical communication behaviour. Avoid giving responses that you feel might be considered "socially acceptable"; instead, give responses that accurately represent your typical communication behaviour. Use a 10-point scale, with 10 being "very accurate description of my typical conversation" and 1 being "very inaccurate description of my typical conversation."

____ 1. I tend not to ask others to do something or to otherwise impose on others.

____ 2. I tend to put others first, before myself.

____ 3. I maximize the expression of approval of others and minimize any disapproval.

____ 4. I seldom praise myself but often praise others.

____ 5. I maximize the expression of agreement and minimize disagreement.

____ 6. I maximize my sympathy for another and minimize any feelings of antipathy.

How Did You Do? All six statements characterize politeness, so higher scores (8–10) would indicate politeness and lower scores (1–4) would indicate impoliteness.

What Will You Do? As you read the following rules for politeness, personalize them with examples from your own interactions, and try to identify specific situations in which increased politeness might have been more effective.

Lisa Sakulensky

VIEWPOINTS Potential Barriers

What potential barriers—for example, cultural barriers, age barriers—might work against the ready flow of meaningful communication among two or more people? How might these barriers be overcome?

1. *Be tactful* (statement 1 in self-test). This helps maintain the other's autonomy. Using tact in conversation means that you don't impose on others or challenge their right to do as they wish. For example, if you wanted to ask someone a favour, using the maxim of tact, you might say something like, "I know you're very busy but . . . " or "I don't mean to impose but . . . " Not using the maxim of tact, you might say something like, "You have to lend me your car this weekend" or "I'm going to use your ATM card."

2. *Be considerate or generous* (statement 2). This helps confirm the other person's importance; for example, the importance of the person's time, insight, or talent. Using the maxim of generosity, you might say, "I'll walk the dog; I see you're busy," whereas in violating the maxim, you might say, "I'm really busy, why don't you walk the dog? You're not doing anything important."

3. *Use positive acknowledgment* (referred to as *approbation*) (statement 3). This involves praising or complimenting the person in some way (for example, "I was really moved by your poem") and minimizing any expression of criticism or disapproval (for example, "For a first effort, that poem wasn't half bad").

4. *Be modest* (statement 4). This minimizes any praise or compliments *you* might receive. At the same time, you might praise and compliment the other person. For example, you might say something like, "Well, thank you, but I couldn't have done this without your input; that was the crucial element."

5. *Find areas of agreement* (statement 5). This refers to your seeking out areas of agreement and expressing them ("That colour you selected was just right; it makes the room exciting") and at the same time avoiding and not expressing (or at least minimizing) disagreements ("It's an interesting choice, very different"). In violation of this maxim, you might say "That colour—how can you stand it?"

6. *Express sympathy or empathy where appropriate* (statement 6). This refers to the expression of understanding, sympathy, empathy, supportiveness, and the like for the other person. Using this maxim, you might say, "I understand your feelings; I'm so sorry." If you violated this maxim, you might say, "You're making a fuss over nothing" or "You get upset over the least little thing; what is it this time?"

An awareness of these several principles will likely lead to more effective and more satisfying conversations. Table 8.1 provides a different perspective on conversational effectiveness and satisfaction.

? Can you explain the stages of conversation, its dialogic nature, and the roles of turn taking and politeness? Can you effectively converse in conversation that is dialogic (rather than monologic), operates with appropriate turn taking, and is generally polite?

TABLE 8.1

Unsatisfying Conversational Partners and How Not to Become One

As you read this table, consider your own conversations. Have you met any of these people? Have you ever been one of these people?

Unsatisfying Conversational Partners	How Not to Become One
The **Detour Taker** begins to talk about a topic and then goes off pursuing a totally different subject.	Follow a logical pattern in conversation, and avoid frequent and long detours.
The **Monologist** gives speeches rather than engaging in dialogue.	Dialogue; give the other person a chance to speak and keep your own "lectures" short.
The **Complainer** has many complaints and rarely tires of listing each of them.	Be positive; emphasize what's good before what's bad.
The **Moralist** evaluates and judges everyone and everything.	Avoid evaluation and judgment; see the world through the eyes of the other person.
The **Inactive Responder** gives no reaction regardless of what you say.	Respond overtly with verbal and nonverbal messages; let the other person see and hear that you're listening.
The **Storyteller** tells stories, too often substituting them for two-way conversation.	Talk about yourself in moderation; be other-oriented.
The **Egotist** talks only about topics that are self-related.	Be other-oriented; focus on the other person; listen as much as you speak.
The **Thought Completer** "knows" exactly what you're going to say and so says it for you.	Don't interrupt; assume that the speaker wants to finish her or his own thoughts.
The **Self-Discloser** discloses more than you need or want to hear.	Disclose selectively, in ways appropriate to your relationship with the listener.
The **Adviser** regularly and consistently gives advice, whether you want it or not.	Don't assume that the expression of a problem is a request for a solution.

CONVERSATIONAL DISCLOSURE: REVEALING YOURSELF

One of the most important forms of interpersonal communication you can engage in is talking about yourself, or self-disclosure. **Self-disclosure** refers to communicating information about yourself (usually information that you normally keep hidden) to another person. It may involve information about (1) your values, beliefs, and desires ("I believe in reincarnation"); (2) your behaviour ("I shoplifted but was never caught"); or (3) your self-qualities or characteristics ("I'm dyslexic"). Overt and carefully planned statements about yourself as well as slips of the tongue would be classified as self-disclosing communications.

Similarly, you could self-disclose nonverbally by, for example, wearing gang colours, a wedding ring, or a shirt with slogans that reveal your political or social concerns, such as "Pro-choice" or "Go green."

Self-disclosure occurs in all forms of communication, not just interpersonal. It frequently occurs in small group settings, in public speeches, and even on television talk

CJG - Technology/Alamy

VIEWPOINTS Disinhibition

Some researchers have pointed to a "disinhibition effect" that occurs in online communication. We seem less inhibited in communicating in email or in chat groups, for example, than we do face to face. Among the reasons for this seems to be the fact that in online communication there is a certain degree of anonymity and invisibility (Suler, 2004). Does your relative anonymity in online communication lead you to self-disclose differently than you do in face-to-face interactions?

shows. Self-disclosure also, of course, takes place online. On social network sites, for example, a great deal of self-disclosure goes on (verbally as well as in images), just as it does when people reveal themselves in personal emails, newsgroups, and blog posts.

You probably self-disclose for a variety of reasons. Perhaps you feel the need for catharsis—a need to get rid of guilty feelings or to confess some wrongdoing. You might also disclose to help the listener—to show the listener, for example, how you dealt with an addiction or succeeded in getting a promotion. And you may self-disclose to encourage relationship growth, to maintain or repair a relationship, or even as a strategy for ending a relationship. If we view disclosure as a developing process, we can see how self-disclosure changes as the relationship changes; for example, as a relationship progresses from initial contact through involvement to intimacy, the self-disclosures increase. If the relationship deteriorates and perhaps dissolves, the disclosures will decrease.

Self-disclosure involves at least one other individual; it cannot be an intrapersonal communication act. To qualify as self-disclosure, the information must be received and understood by another individual.

Influences on Self-Disclosure

Many factors influence whether you disclose, what you disclose, and to whom you disclose. Among the most important factors are who you are, your culture, your gender, who your listeners are, and what your topic is.

- *Your personality.* Highly sociable and extroverted people self-disclose more than those who are less sociable and more introverted. People who are apprehensive about talking in general also self-disclose less than do those who are more comfortable in communicating.
- *Your culture.* Studies conducted in the 1980s found significant cultural differences with regard to disclosure (Barnlund, 1989; Gudykunst, 1983; Hall & Hall, 1987). Yet a later study of American, Japanese, and Korean young adults found that self-disclosure across cultures didn't differ as much as one would expect (Yum & Hara, 2005). In terms of disclosure on social networks, one study (Wu & Lu, 2010) found that, on the whole, those from individualistic cultures, such as Canada, the United States, and Germany, tend to disclose more than those from collectivist cultures. Among individualistic cultures, Americans disclose more than do Germans. According to another study (Kisilevich & Mansmann, 2010), Russians tend to disclose less information on social networking sites and were more concerned about privacy than were users in Western countries.
- *Your gender.* Earlier research found a great amount of self-disclosure between women, a moderate amount in opposite-sex dyads, and the least amount between men (Aries, 2006; Dindia & Allen, 1992). But more recent research (Wu & Lu, 2010) suggests that there may be much less of a difference in self-disclosure between men and women than previously thought, and no gender differences at all in online forums (Barak & Gluck-Ofri, 2007) or online chatting (Cho, 2007). However, other studies have found that women discuss more topics in a more intimate manner with their exclusive Facebook friends and face-to-face friends than do men, but that men disclose more with new or recently added Facebook friends than do women. Overall, women generally disclose more than men in existing relationships, but men disclose more in new relationships. This could suggest that women require the development of trust for disclosure more than men do (Sheldon, 2013).
- *Your listeners.* In face-to-face communication, disclosure occurs more between people who have an open relationship (with a desire to divulge information) than a closed relationship (with a desire to be private) (Zhao, Hinds, & Gao, 2012). Because you disclose on the basis of the support you receive, you disclose to people you like (Collins & Miller, 1994; Derlega et al., 2004) and to people you trust and

love (Sprecher & Hendrick, 2004; Wheeless & Grotz, 1977). You also come to like those to whom you disclose (Sprecher et al., 2013). And, not surprisingly, age plays a role in self-disclosure (Goodstein, 2007).

■ *Your topic.* You're more likely to disclose about some topics than others. For example, some people are very open about their sexual preferences but would never reveal personal financial information, while for others the opposite may be true. Culture plays a role in the ease with which people are willing to discuss their religion, political opinions, and a range of other topics. You're also more likely to disclose favourable than unfavourable information. Generally, the more personal and negative the topic, the less likely you are to self-disclose.

■ *The medium.* The widespread belief that disclosure of personal information is more frequent online than in face-to-face communication is being contested by recent research (Nguyen, Bin, & Campbell, 2012). The relationship between the communicators, the specific mode of communication, and the context of the interaction seem to be the most influential factors related to the degree of disclosure. Different amounts and degrees of disclosure have been found between different social networking sites. For example, one study (Fogel & Nehmad, 2009) found that Facebook engenders a higher level of trust than other social media popular at the time (MySpace), while another study (Frye & Dornisch, 2010) found that more information is disclosed when the communication tools are perceived to offer a high level of privacy.

Rewards and Dangers of Self-Disclosure

Research shows that self-disclosure has both significant rewards and dangers. In making choices about whether to disclose, consider both.

REWARDS OF SELF-DISCLOSURE   Self-disclosure is a key part of a trust-building relationship. When you disclose something about yourself to another person, you're saying, "I trust you with this information" and "I can be trusted with information you share about yourself." Brain research conducted at Harvard University suggests that human beings are "wired" to find self-disclosure pleasurable, and that the tendency to disclose one's thoughts and beliefs may be an adaptive advantage because it engenders social bonds and alliances between people, results in obtaining feedback which enhances self-knowledge, and helps shape our behaviour (Tamir & Mitchell, 2012). This may explain the propensity to self-disclose on social media and why so many people are willing to share intimate details of their lives on talk shows with millions of viewers. In mentoring and therapeutic relationships, appropriate disclosure is thought to promote rapport and positive feelings of the client (Spencer, 2014).

Big Cheese Photo/Big Cheese/AGE Fotostock

VIEWPOINTS Remaining Mysterious

"The more you reveal about yourself to others, the more areas of your life you expose to possible attack. Especially in the competitive context of work, and even romance, the more others know about you, the more they'll be able to use against you." While there is some truth to these statements, they also portray a fairly negative view of human interaction. Perhaps the best advice is to use disclosure cautiously, as a way of enhancing interpersonal relationships. What would be some advantages of conveying an image of yourself that is slightly mysterious as opposed to exposing your "real self"?

DANGERS OF SELF-DISCLOSURE   There are also, of course, personal, relational, and professional risks to self-disclosure. Disclosing unfavourable aspects of your past or current behaviour may result in the loss of esteem among friends or colleagues, and could damage even close personal relationships or prospects for employment (Fesko, 2001).

In making your choice between disclosing and not disclosing, keep in mind—in addition to the advantages and dangers already noted—the irreversible nature of communication. Regardless of how many times you may try to qualify something or take it back, once you've disclosed something, you can't undisclose it. You can't erase the conclusions and inferences listeners have made on the basis of your disclosures.

Guidelines for Self-Disclosure

Because self-disclosure is so important and so delicate a matter, guidelines are offered here for (1) deciding whether and how to self-disclose, (2) responding to the disclosures of others, and (3) resisting pressures to self-disclose.

GUIDELINES FOR MAKING SELF-DISCLOSURES The following guidelines will help you raise the right questions before you make a choice that must ultimately be your own.

INTERPERSONAL CHOICE POINT

To Disclose or Not
You decided to leave your current place of employment because you were passed over for a promotion. You're currently preparing for an interview with a new employer. During your interview, how much would you disclose about why you left your current job?

■ *Disclose out of appropriate motivation.* Self-disclosure should be motivated by a concern for the relationship, for the others involved, and for oneself.
■ *Disclose in the appropriate context.* Before making any significant self-disclosure, ask whether this is the right time and place. Could a better time and place be arranged? Ask, too, whether this self-disclosure is appropriate to the relationship. Generally, the more intimate the disclosures, the closer the relationship should be.
■ *Disclose gradually.* During your disclosures, give the other person a chance to reciprocate with his or her own disclosures. If reciprocal disclosures aren't made, reassess your own self-disclosures. It may be a signal that, for this person at this time and in this context, your disclosures are not welcome or appropriate.
■ *Disclose without imposing burdens on yourself or others.* Carefully weigh the potential problems you may incur as a result of your disclosure. Can you afford to lose your job if you disclose your arrest record? Are you willing to risk relational difficulties if you disclose your infidelities?

GUIDELINES FOR FACILITATING AND RESPONDING TO SELF-DISCLOSURES When someone discloses to you, it's usually a sign of trust and affection. In serving this most important receiver function, keep the following guidelines in mind. These guidelines will also help you facilitate the disclosures of another person.

■ *Practise the skills of effective and active listening.* The skills of effective listening are especially important when you're listening to another person's self-disclosures: listen actively, listen for different levels of meaning, listen with empathy, and listen with an open mind. Express an understanding of the speaker's feelings to allow him or her the opportunity to see them more objectively and through the eyes of another. Ask questions to ensure your own understanding and to signal your interest and attention. And if for any reason you feel that you shouldn't be listening to someone's disclosure, gently inform the person that you're unable to continue this conversation, and direct him or her to the person who can help.

INTERPERSONAL CHOICE POINT

Unwanted Disclosure
You're close friends with both members of a couple who are currently undergoing divorce proceedings. One of them begins to tell you something very negative about her partner. How might you communicate your lack of willingness to hear negative information about a close friend?

■ *Support and reinforce the discloser.* Express support for the person during and after the disclosures. Concentrate on understanding and empathizing with (rather than evaluating) the discloser. Make your supportiveness clear through your verbal and nonverbal responses: maintain eye contact, lean toward the speaker, ask relevant questions, and echo the speaker's thoughts and feelings.
■ *Be willing to reciprocate.* When you make relevant and appropriate disclosures of your own in response to the other person's disclosures, you're demonstrating your understanding of the other's meanings and at the same time showing a willingness to communicate on this meaningful level.

■ *Keep the disclosures confidential.* When people disclose to you, it's because they want you to know their feelings and thoughts. If you reveal these disclosures to others, negative outcomes are inevitable, and your relationship is almost sure to suffer for it.

GUIDELINES FOR RESISTING SELF-DISCLOSURE   You may, on occasion, find yourself in a position where a friend, colleague, or romantic partner pressures you to self-disclose. In such situations, you may wish to weigh the pros and cons of self-disclosure and then make your decision as to whether and what you'll disclose. If your decision is not to disclose and you're still being pressured, then you need to say something. Here are a few suggestions.

■ *Don't be pushed.* Although there may be certain legal or ethical reasons for disclosing, generally, if you don't want to disclose, you don't have to. Don't be pushed into disclosing because others are doing it or because you're asked to.
■ *Be indirect and move to another topic.* Avoid the question, and change the subject. This is a polite way of saying, "I'm not talking about it," and it may be the preferred choice in certain situations. Most often people will get the hint and understand your refusal to disclose.
■ *Delay a decision.* If you don't want to say no directly but still don't want to disclose, delay the decision, saying something like, "That's pretty personal; let me think about that before I make a fool of myself" or "This isn't really a good time (or place) to talk about this."
■ *Be assertive in your refusal to disclose.* Say, very directly, "I'd rather not talk about that now" or "Now is not the time for this type of discussion." More specific guidelines for communicating assertiveness are offered in Chapter 5.

> **INTERPERSONAL CHOICE POINT**
>
> **Refusing to Self-Disclose**
> You've met with someone three or four times, and each time this person self-discloses quite a lot, with the expectation that you'll do likewise. But you're just not ready to talk about personal topics, at least not at this early stage of the relationship. What are some of the things you can say or do to resist this pressure to self-disclose? What might you say to discourage further requests that you reveal yourself?

Can you define *self-disclosure*? Can you apply the guidelines for making, facilitating, and resisting self-disclosure?

EVERYDAY CONVERSATIONS

Here we discuss a variety of everyday conversation situations: making small talk, introducing other people or ourselves, apologizing, complimenting, and giving advice. When reading and thinking about these, keep in mind that not everyone speaks with the fluency and ease that many textbooks often assume. Speech and language disorders, for example, can seriously disrupt the conversation process when some elementary guidelines aren't followed. Table 8.2 offers suggestions for making such conversations run more smoothly.

Small Talk

Small talk is pervasive; all of us engage in it. Sometimes we use small talk as a preface to big talk. For example, before a conference with your boss or even an employment interview, you're likely to engage in some preliminary small talk: "How are you doing?" "I'm pleased this weather has finally cleared up." "That's a great-looking jacket." The purpose of much of this face-to-face small talk is to ease into the major topic or the big talk. (On Facebook and Twitter, however, small talk may actually be an end in itself—simply a way of letting your "friends" know that you went to the movies last night and not necessarily to get into an extended discussion of the movie.)

TABLE 8.2

INTERPERSONAL COMMUNICATION TIPS BETWEEN PEOPLE WITH AND WITHOUT SPEECH AND LANGUAGE DISORDERS

Speech and language disorders vary widely—from fluency problems such as stuttering, to indistinct articulation, to difficulty in finding the right word (aphasia). Following a few simple guidelines can facilitate communication between people with and without speech and language disorders.

If you're the person without a speech or language disorder:

Generally	Specifically
Avoid finishing another's sentences.	Finishing the person's sentences may communicate the idea that you're impatient and don't want to spend the extra time necessary to interact effectively.
Avoid giving directions to the person with a speech disorder.	Saying "slow down" or "relax" will often seem insulting and will make further communication more difficult.
Maintain eye contact.	Show interest and at the same time avoid showing any signs of impatience or embarrassment.
Ask for clarification as needed.	If you don't understand what the person said, ask him or her to repeat it. Don't pretend that you understand when you don't.
Don't treat people who have language problems like children.	A person with aphasia who has difficulty with names or nouns is in no way childlike. Similarly, a person who stutters is not a slow thinker; in fact, stutterers differ from non-stutterers only in their oral fluency.

If you're the person with a speech or language disorder:

Let the other person know what your special needs are.	If you stutter, you might tell others that you have difficulty with certain sounds and so they need to be patient.
Demonstrate your own comfort.	Show that you have a positive attitude toward the interpersonal situation. If you appear comfortable and positive, others will also.
Be patient.	For example, have patience with those who try to finish your sentences; they're likely just trying to be helpful.

Sources: These suggestions were drawn from a variety of sources including the websites of the National Stuttering Association, the National Aphasia Association, the United States Department of Labor, and the American Speech and Hearing Association, all accessed May 9, 2012.

At other times, small talk is a politeness strategy and a bit more extensive way of saying hello as you pass a co-worker in the hallway or run into a classmate at the post office. And so you might say, "Good seeing you, Jack. You're ready for the big meeting?" or "See you in geology this afternoon."

Sometimes your relationship with another person revolves solely around small talk, perhaps with your barber or hairdresser, a colleague at work, your next-door neighbour, or a student you sit next to in class. In these relationships, neither person makes an effort to deepen the relationship, and it remains on a small-talk level.

Before reading about the guidelines for effective small talk, take the accompanying self-test to start thinking about how you engage in small talk.

TEST YOURSELF

How Do You Small Talk?

Examine your small-talk communication by responding to the following questions.

_____ 1. On an elevator with three or four strangers, I'd be most likely to
a. seek to avoid interacting.
b. respond to another but not initiate interaction.
c. be the first to talk.

_____ 2. When I'm talking with someone and I meet a friend who doesn't know the person I'm with, I'd be most apt to
a. avoid introducing them.
b. wait until they introduce each other.
c. introduce them to each other.

_____ 3. At a party with people I've never met before, I'd be most likely to
a. wait for someone to talk to me.
b. indicate nonverbally that I'm receptive to someone interacting with me.
c. initiate interaction with others nonverbally and verbally.

_____ 4. When confronted with someone who doesn't want to end the conversation, I'd be most apt to

a. just stick it out and listen.
b. tune out the person and hope time goes by quickly.
c. end it firmly myself.

_____ 5. When the other person monologues, I'd be most apt to
a. listen politely.
b. try to change the focus.
c. exit as quickly as possible.

How Did You Do? The _a_ responses are unassertive, the _b_ responses are indirect (not totally unassertive but not assertive, either), and the _c_ responses are direct and assertive. Very likely, if you answered with four or five _c_ responses, you're comfortable and satisfied with your small-talk experiences. Lots of _a_ responses would indicate some level of dissatisfaction and discomfort with the experience of small talk. If you had lots of _b_ responses, you probably experience both satisfaction and dissatisfaction with small talk.

What Will You Do? If your small talk experiences aren't satisfying to you, read on. The entire body of interpersonal skills will prove relevant here, as will a number of suggestions unique to small talk.

Although "small," this talk still requires the application of the interpersonal communication skills for "big" talk. Keep especially in mind that the best topics are noncontroversial and that most small talk is relatively brief. Here are a few additional guidelines for more effective small talk.

■ _Be positive._ No one likes a negative doomsayer.
■ _Talk about noncontroversial topics._ If there are wide differences of opinion on a topic, it's probably not appropriate for small talk.
■ _Be sensitive to leave-taking cues._ Small talk is necessarily brief, but at times one person may want it to be a preliminary to big talk and another person may see it as the sum of the interaction.
■ _Talk in short sequences_; dialogue, don't monologue.
■ _Stress similarities_ rather than differences; this is a good way to ensure that this small talk is noncontroversial.
■ _Answer questions with enough elaboration_ to give the other person information that can then be used to interact with you. Let's say someone notices a book you're carrying and says, "I see you're taking an interpersonal communication course." If you simply say yes, you haven't given the other person anything to talk with you about. Instead, if you say, "Yes, it's a great course; I think I'm going to major in communication," then you've given the other person information that can be addressed. Of course, if you don't want to interact, then a simple one-word response will help you achieve your goal.

INTERPERSONAL CHOICE POINT

Making Small Talk

You're on an elevator with three other people from your office building. The elevator gets stuck without any indication of when the power will go back on. What are some of your options for initiating small talk? What would your first sentence be?

ETHICAL MESSAGES

The Ethics of Gossip

Gossip is social talk that involves making evaluations about persons who aren't present during the conversation; it generally occurs when two people talk about a third party (Eder & Enke, 1991; Wert & Salovey, 2004). As you obviously know, a large part of our conversation at work and in social situations, whether face to face or online, is spent gossiping (Carey, 2005; Lachnit, 2001; Waddington, 2004). In fact, one study estimates that approximately two-thirds of people's conversation time is devoted to social topics, and that most of these topics can be considered gossip (Dunbar, 2004). And, not surprisingly, gossip occupies a large part of online communication (Morgan, 2008).

Gossip serves a number of purposes. For example, it bonds people together and solidifies their relationship; it creates a sense of camaraderie (Greengard, 2001; Hafen, 2004). At the same time, of course, it helps to create an in-group (those doing the gossiping) and an out-group (those being gossiped about). Gossip also teaches people which behaviours are acceptable (from positive gossip) and which are unacceptable (from negative gossip) (Baumeister, Zhang, & Vohs, 2004; Hafen, 2004).

As you might expect, gossiping often has ethical implications, and in many instances, gossip would be considered unethical. The following list identifies some instances that are generally considered to be unethical (Bok, 1983). As you read these, consider whether there are other types of gossip that you might consider unethical.

- When gossip is used to unfairly hurt another person; for example, spreading gossip about an office romance or an instructor's past indiscretions.
- When you know that what you're saying isn't true; for example, lying to make another person look bad.
- When no one has the right to such personal information; for example, revealing the income of neighbours to others or revealing another student's poor grades to other students.
- When you've promised secrecy; for example, revealing something that you vowed not to repeat to others.

Ethical Choice Point

You've overheard some gossip about a colleague's inappropriate use of the computer during work hours. You have no direct knowledge about whether or not this is true. Would you share what you've heard with anyone?

Introducing People

Conversations between strangers usually begin with introductions. While on the surface introductions seem straightforward, people often aren't sure how they should introduce both themselves or other people. Such uncertainty includes the following questions:

- Do you use first names or last names and titles (Dr., Ms., Mrs., Mr.)?
- If you're not sure how to pronounce someone's name, or have forgotten their name, how do you handle this?
- When you introduce yourself to a stranger, how much information do you provide?
- How can you ensure culturally appropriate behaviour when introducing people from cultures different from your own? (For example, handshakes between men and women would not be appropriate for many people).
- How do differences in age or social and positional status affect the manner in which you introduce yourself and others?
- Which verbal and nonverbal gestures are appropriate when introductions are being conducted?

INTERPERSONAL CHOICE POINT

Introducing Yourself

You're in class early with a few students; no one knows anyone. What are some of the ways you can introduce yourself and engage in small talk? What would you say?

Rules and norms that provide answers to these questions change over time; they also vary significantly between cultures, within different groups and cultures, and in different contexts (for example, business versus informal social events). Therefore, rather than provide a how-to list, we recommend that you reflect on the preceding questions, discuss them with peers and classmates, and try to gain a better understanding of the kinds of introductions that are appropriate in different contexts and with different people.

In Canada and the United States, the handshake is a common gesture of introduction. In Muslim cultures, people hug same-sex people but not those of the opposite sex. In Latin America, South America, and the Mediterranean, people are more likely to hug (and perhaps kiss on the cheek) than are Northern Europeans, Asians, and North Americans. Asians are more reluctant to extend their hands, and more often they bow, with lower bows required when people of lower status meet someone of higher status; for example, an intern meeting a company executive or a private meeting a general. In the past, handshaking was more common among men than women, but as women have entered the world of business, they've adopted the handshake as a standard greeting. (Handshaking is an almost exclusively adult greeting; one seldom sees young people shaking hands.) Generally, the advice given for handshaking is to engage with the person through eye contact and smiling while shaking his or her hand; use your right hand, firmly but not so much that it will be uncomfortable, and shake two or three times.

During the SARS epidemic in Canada, people were hesitant to shake hands for fear of contagion, and some adopted the Eastern bow as an alternative greeting. Some even said that they preferred this kind of a greeting; for example, it eliminates the worry about sweaty hands, or hands improperly dried when no towel is available.

John Boykin/PhotoEdit

VIEWPOINTS Conversation Openers

Depending on your relationship with the people you encounter, your greeting will differ, whether it's a merely a nod, or perhaps a handshake or a hug. How would you open a conversation if you were already friends? How does that differ from how you'd open the conversation if you were new to the group?

Apologies

Despite your best efforts, there are times when you'll say or do the wrong thing and an apology may be necessary. An **apology** is an expression of regret or sorrow for having done what you did or for what happened; it's a statement that you're sorry. And so, the most basic of all apologies is simply "I'm sorry." In popular usage, the apology includes some admission of wrongdoing on the part of the person making the apology. Sometimes the wrongdoing is acknowledged explicitly ("I'm sorry I lied") and sometimes only by implication ("I'm sorry you're so upset"). In many cases, the apology also includes a request for forgiveness ("Please forgive my lateness") and some assurance that you won't repeat the behaviour ("Please forgive my lateness; it won't happen again").

An effective apology must be crafted for the specific situation. Effective apologies to a longtime lover, to a parent, or to a new supervisor are likely to be very different because the individuals are different and your relationships are different. And so the first rule of an effective apology is to take into consideration the uniqueness of the situation—the people, the context, the cultural rules, the relationship, the specific wrongdoing—for which you might want to apologize. Each situation will call for a somewhat different message of apology. Nevertheless, we can offer some general recommendations.

- *Admit wrongdoing* (if indeed wrongdoing occurred). Accept responsibility. Own your own actions; don't try to pass them off as the work of someone else. Instead of "Smith drives so slow that it's a wonder I'm only 30 minutes late," say "I should have taken traffic into consideration."
- *Be apologetic.* Say (and mean) the words "I'm sorry." Don't justify your behaviour by mentioning that everyone does it; for example, "Everyone leaves work early on

"What flower says you're sorry without admitting wrongdoing?"

Mike Twohy/The New Yorker Collection/www.cartoonbank.com

Corbis Cusp/Alamy

VIEWPOINTS Acceptable versus Unacceptable Apologies

What kinds of apologies do you hear most often from your peers? Can you identify what makes some apologies acceptable and others unacceptable?

Friday." And don't justify your behaviour by saying that the other person has done something equally wrong: "So I play poker; you play the lottery."

- *Be specific.* State, in specific rather than general terms, what you've done. Instead of "I'm sorry for what I did," say "I'm sorry for flirting at the party."
- *Empathize.* Express understanding of how the other person feels and acknowledge the legitimacy of those feelings; for example, "You have every right to be angry; I should have called." Express your regret that this has created a problem for the other person: "I'm sorry I made you miss your appointment." Don't minimize the problem this may have caused. Avoid such comments as "So the figures arrived a little late. What's the big deal?"
- *Give assurance* that it won't happen again. Say, quite simply, "It won't happen again" or, better and more specifically, "I won't be late again." And, whenever possible, offer to correct the problem: "I'm sorry I didn't clean up the mess I made; I'll do it now."
- *Avoid excuses.* Be careful not to include excuses with your apology; for example, "I'm sorry the figures are late, but I had so much other work to do." An excuse often takes back the apology and says, in effect, "I'm really not sorry because there was good reason for what I did, but I'm saying 'I'm sorry' to cover all my bases and to make this uncomfortable situation go away."
- *Choose the appropriate channel.* Don't take the easy way out and apologize through email (unless the wrongdoing was committed in email or if email is your only or main form of communication). Generally, it's preferable to use a more personal mode of communication—face-to-face or phone, for example. It's harder, but it's more effective.

Complimenting

A **compliment** is a message of praise, flattery, or congratulations. It's the opposite of criticism, insult, or complaint. It can be expressed in face-to-face interaction or on social media sites when, for example, you retweet someone's post or indicate "like" or "+1" or when you comment favourably on a blog post. The compliment functions as a kind of interpersonal glue; it's a way of relating to another person with positiveness and immediacy. It's also a conversation starter: "I like your watch; may I ask where you got it?" In online communication—when you poke, tag, +1, or retweet, for example—it's a reminder that you're thinking of someone (and being complimentary). Another purpose the compliment serves is to encourage the other person to compliment you—even if not immediately (which often seems inappropriate).

A *backhanded compliment* is really not a compliment at all; it's usually an insult masquerading as a compliment. For example, you might give a backhanded compliment if you say "That beautiful red sweater takes away from your pale complexion; it makes you look less washed out" (complimenting the colour of the sweater but criticizing the person's complexion) or "Looks like you've finally lost a few pounds, am I right?" (complimenting a slimmer appearance but pointing out that the person is overweight).

Yet compliments are sometimes difficult to express and even more difficult to respond to without discomfort or embarrassment. Fortunately, there are easy-to-follow guidelines.

GIVING A COMPLIMENT   Here are a few suggestions for giving compliments.

- *Be real and honest.* Say what you mean, and omit giving compliments you don't believe in. They'll likely sound insincere and won't serve any useful purpose.
- *Compliment in moderation.* A compliment that is too extreme (say, for example, "This is the best decorated apartment I've ever seen in my life") may be viewed as dishonest. Similarly, don't compliment at every possible occasion; if you do, your compliments will seem too easy to win and not really meaningful.
- *Be entirely complimentary.* Avoid qualifying your compliments. If you hear yourself giving a compliment and then adding a "but" or a "however," be careful; you're likely going to qualify your compliment. Unfortunately, in such situations, many people will remember the qualification rather than the compliment, and the entire compliment-plus-qualification will appear as a criticism.
- *Be specific.* Direct your compliment at something specific rather than something general. Instead of saying something general, such as "I like your design," you might say something more specific, such as "I like your design; the colours and fonts are perfect."
- *Be personal in your own feelings.* For example, say "Your song really moved me; it made me recall so many good times." At the same time, avoid any compliment that can be misinterpreted as overly sexual.

RECEIVING A COMPLIMENT   In receiving a compliment, people generally take either one of two options: denial or acceptance.

Many people deny the compliment ("It's nice of you to say, but I know I was terrible"), minimize it ("It isn't as if I wrote the great Canadian novel; it's just an article no one will read"), change the subject ("So, where should we go for dinner?"), or say nothing. Each of these responses creates problems. When you deny the legitimacy of the compliment, you're saying that the person isn't being sincere or doesn't know what he or she is talking about. When you minimize it, you say, in effect, that the person doesn't understand what you've done or what he or she is complimenting. When you change the subject or say nothing, again, you're saying that the compliment isn't having any effect; you're ignoring it because it isn't meaningful.

Accepting the compliment seems the much better alternative. An acceptance might consist simply of (1) a smile with eye contact—avoid looking at the floor; (2) a simple "thank you," and, if appropriate, (3) a personal reflection where you explain (very briefly) the meaning of the compliment and why it's important to you (for example, "I really

Dmitriy Shironosov/Shutterstock

VIEWPOINTS Giving Advice

When in conversation with someone, knowing whether to give advice or simply express empathy can sometimes be difficult to determine. Sometimes both are required. When a problem or a question is put to you, are you more likely to try to solve the problem or to express empathy for the speaker? How do you determine what is the most appropriate response in each situation?

appreciate your comments; I worked really hard on that design, and it's great to hear it was effective"). Depending on your relationship with the person, you might use his or her name; people like to hear their names spoken, and doubly so when it's associated with a compliment.

Advice Giving

Advice is the process of giving another person a suggestion for thinking or behaving, usually to change his or her thinking or ways of behaving. The popularity of the "Dear Abby" type of columns—in print, in online newspapers and magazines, and in the many websites that offer advice on just about everything—attests to our concern with asking for and getting advice.

In many ways, you can look at advice giving as a suggestion to solve a problem. So, for example, you might advise friends to change their ways of looking at broken love affairs or their financial situations or their career paths. Or you might advise someone to do something, to behave in a certain way; for example, to start dating again or to invest in certain stocks or to go back to school and take certain courses.

Keep in mind that you can give advice in at least two ways. One way is to give specific advice, and another is to give **meta-advice**, or advice about advice. Thus, you can give advice to a person that addresses the problem or issue directly—buy that condo, enroll in this course, or take that vacation in Hawaii. Or you can give advice about advice; for example, by suggesting that the person explore additional options and choices, seek professional help, or delay a decision until more information becomes available.

APPROACHES TO GIVING ADVICE   Here are a few suggestions for giving specific advice:

- *Listen.* This is the first rule for advice giving. Listen to the person's thoughts and feelings. Listen to what the person wants—the person may actually want support and active listening and not advice. Or the person may simply want to vent in the presence of a friend.
- *Empathize.* Try to feel what the other person is feeling. Perhaps you might recall similar situations you were in or similar emotions you experienced. Think about the importance of the issue to the person, and, in general, try to put yourself in the position, the circumstance, or the context of the person asking your advice.
- *Be tentative.* If you give advice, give it with the qualifications it requires. The advice seeker has a right to know how sure (or unsure) you are of the advice or what evidence (or lack of evidence) you have that the advice will work.
- *Ensure understanding.* People seeking advice are often emotionally upset and may not remember everything in the conversation. So seek feedback after giving advice, for example, "Does that make sense?" "Is my suggestion workable?"
- *Keep the interaction confidential.* Often advice seeking is directed at very personal matters, so it's best to keep such conversations confidential, even if you're not asked to do so.
- *Avoid "should" statements.* People seeking advice still have to make their own decisions rather than being told what they should or shouldn't do. So it's better to say, for example, "You *might* do X" or "You *could* do Y" rather than "You *should* do Z." Don't demand—or even imply—that the person has to follow your advice. This attacks the person's need for autonomy.

INTERPERSONAL CHOICE POINT

Unwanted Advice

One of your close friends has the annoying habit of trying to give you advice, which you don't want. What are some of your options for dealing with this problem? What are some of the things you might say to your friend?

RESPONDING TO ADVICE Responding appropriately to advice is an often difficult process. Here are just a few suggestions for making the reception of advice more effective.

- *Accept the advice.* If you asked for the advice, then accept what the person says. Accepting advice doesn't mean you have to follow it; you just have to listen to it and process it.
- *Avoid negative responses.* Even if you didn't ask for advice (and don't like it), resist the temptation to retaliate or criticize the advice giver. Instead of responding with "Well, your hair doesn't look that great either," consider whether the advice has any merit.
- *Interact with the advice.* Talk about it with the advice giver. A process of asking and answering questions is likely to produce added insight into the problem.
- *Express appreciation.* Express your appreciation for the advice. It's often difficult to give advice, so it's only fair that the advice giver receive some words of appreciation.

In each of these everyday conversations, you have choices in terms of what you say and how you respond. Consider these choices mindfully, taking into consideration the variety of influencing factors discussed throughout this text and their potential advantages and disadvantages. Once you lay out your choices in this way, you'll be more likely to select effective ones.

Can you communicate effectively in small talk? In making introductions? In apologizing? In giving compliments? In advice giving?

CANADIAN PROFILE: WRAP-UP

Eric Miller Africapictures.net/Newscom

Stephen Lewis has engaged in conversations with people all over the globe, from the most powerful to the most underprivileged and unheard. He then crafts potent messages to share with others to urge them to take action. How does understanding processes and techniques of conversational messages help Lewis in his work? How successful do you think you are in participating in meaningful conversations and then crafting powerful messages for others? What would you like to take from this chapter to allow you to become an even more powerful communicator?

SUMMARY OF CONCEPTS AND SKILLS

This chapter reviewed the principles of conversation, conversational disclosure, and some everyday conversation situations.

Principles of Conversation

1. Conversation can be viewed as a developmental process, consisting of a series of stages: opening, feedforward, business, feedback, and closing.
2. Conversation is best viewed as dialogic.
3. Conversation is a process of turn taking.
4. Conversation is, at least usually, a polite interaction.

Conversational Disclosure: Revealing Yourself

5. Self-disclosure involves revealing hidden information about yourself to others, and is influenced by a variety of factors: who you are, your culture, your gender, your listeners, and your topic and channel.
6. Among the rewards of self-disclosure are self-knowledge, ability to cope, communication effectiveness, meaningfulness of relationships, and physiological health. Among the dangers are personal risks, relational risks, professional risks, and the fact that communication is irreversible (once something is said, you can't take it back).

Everyday Conversations

7. Small talk is pervasive and noncontroversial and often serves as a polite way of introducing oneself or a topic.

8. How you introduce one person to another, or yourself to others, will vary with your culture.

9. Apologies are expressions of regret or sorrow for having done what you did or for what happened.

10. A compliment is a message of praise, flattery, or congratulations and often enables you to interact with positiveness and immediacy.

11. Advice—telling another person what he or she should do—can be specific or general (meta-advice). In addition, this chapter covered a variety of conversational skills. Check those you wish to work on.

____1. *Dialogue.* Engage in conversation as dialogue rather than as monologue.

____2. *Turn-taking cues.* Be responsive to the turn-taking cues you give and that others give.

____3. *Politeness.* Follow the maxims of politeness: tact, generosity, approbation, modesty, agreement, and sympathy.

____4. *Self-disclosing.* In self-disclosing, consider your motivation, the appropriateness of the disclosure to the person and context, the disclosures of others (the dyadic effect), and the possible burdens that the self-disclosure might impose on yourself or on others.

____5. *Responding to disclosures.* In responding to the disclosures of others, listen effectively, support and reinforce the discloser, keep disclosures confidential, and don't use disclosures as weapons.

____6. *Resisting self-disclosure.* When you wish to resist self-disclosing, don't be pushed; try indirectness or delaying the disclosures, or be assertive in your determination not to disclose.

____7. *Small talk.* Engage in small talk in a variety of situations with comfort and ease by keeping the conversation noncontroversial.

____8. *Introductions.* Introduce people to each other and yourself to others in any interaction that looks as if it will last for more than a few minutes.

____9. *Apologies.* Formulate effective apologies, and use them appropriately (and ethically) in interpersonal interactions.

____10. *Complimenting.* Extend and receive a compliment graciously, honestly, and without avoidance.

____11. *Advising.* Give advice carefully and mindfully, considering the advantages of meta-advice (when you're not an expert).

VOCABULARY QUIZ: The Language of Conversation

Match the following conversation-related terms with their definitions. Record the number of the definition next to the appropriate term.

____ backchannelling cues (170)
____ compliment (183)
____ apology (181)
____ meta-advice (184)
____ feedback (167)
____ interruption (171)
____ self-disclosure (173)
____ turn taking (169)
____ monologue (169)
____ small talk (177)

1. Reflecting back on a conversation to signal that its business is completed.

2. Attempts to take over the speaker's role.
3. Revealing information about yourself (usually information that you normally keep hidden) to another person.
4. The exchanging of roles between speaker and listener.
5. A message of praise, flattery, or congratulations.
6. Noncontroversial talk that is usually short in duration.
7. Conversational cues that communicate information back to the speaker.
8. An expression of regret or sorrow for having done what you did or for what happened.
9. Communication in which one person speaks and the other listens.
10. Advice about advice.

These 10 terms and additional terms used in this chapter can be found in the glossary.

CHAPTER

9

Interpersonal Relationships

CANADIAN PROFILE: Chris Hadfield

Rex Features/CP Images

Astronaut Chris Hadfield became a global celebrity in 2013 during his five months aboard the International Space Station. Many of you will have watched his performance in space of David Bowie's "Space Oddity," which attracted over 7 million viewers in the first few days after it was posted.

Growing up on a farm in Sarnia, Ontario, Hadfield dreamed of becoming an astronaut. He pursued his life dream relentlessly, first in the Air Cadets and then in the Canadian Air Force, where he flew fighter jets. He trained with both the United States and Canadian Air Forces, was a test pilot in both countries, and did research for NASA.

When Canada began its own space program in 1992, Hadfield was one of only four Canadian astronauts chosen from among 5330 applicants. Since then he's flown several space missions. He was the first Canadian to do a space walk and the first Canadian to command the International Space Station. "To be able to command the space station, yes, it's professional, and yes, I'll take it seriously, and yes, it's important for Canada, but for me, as just a Canadian kid, it makes me want to shout and laugh and do cartwheels" (Chris Hadfield, n.d.).

Hadfield is a pioneer not only in terms of his space accomplishments but also in his desire to form relationships with everyday Canadians and help them learn more about space travel. His Twitter feeds and his YouTube videos about such topics as how to brush your teeth or sleep in space ensured that millions of Canadians followed his adventures and felt a personal connection to him. Hadfield became a master at using social media to reach out to Canadians who might otherwise have never connected with him or with the Canadian space program.

As you work through this chapter, think about how you build interpersonal relationships using various forms of communication, both in person and through social media. Which of the techniques discussed in this chapter do you think Hadfield used successfully?

LEARNING OBJECTIVES *After reading this chapter, you should be able to:*

1. Describe the advantages and disadvantages of interpersonal relationships and assess your own relationships in light of these.

2. Define *jealousy, bullying,* and *relationship violence* and discuss how you might use the suggestions for managing the dark sides of relationships.

3. Explain changing family structures, family characteristics, and the influence of culture, gender, and technology in the family.

4. Describe the "POSITIVE" approach to improving relationship communications.

Martin Novak/Alamy

VIEWPOINTS Negative Turning Points

Turning points are often positive, but they can also be negative. For example, the first realization that a partner has been unfaithful or has lied about past history, or the moment when he or she reveals a debilitating condition, would likely be a significant turning point for many relationships. What have been your experiences with negative relationship turning points?

Relationships come in many forms, as you'll see throughout this chapter. Central to friendships, romantic relationships, family relationships—and in fact to all kinds of relationships—is communication. In fact, the term **relationship communication** is almost synonymous with interpersonal communication.

Although most relationships are face-to-face interactions, online relationships are widespread in Canada and around the world. Many people are turning to the internet to find a friend or a romantic partner. Some use the internet as their only means of interaction; others use it as a way of beginning a relationship before moving to a face-to-face meeting.

The quality that makes a relationship interpersonal is *interdependency*: one person's actions have consequences for the other person. The actions of a stranger—for example, a person working overtime or flirting with a colleague—may have no impact on you; you and the proverbial stranger are independent and your actions have limited effect on each other. If, however, you're in an interpersonal relationship and your partner works overtime or flirts with a co-worker, these actions will affect you and the relationship in some way.

ADVANTAGES AND DISADVANTAGES OF INTERPERSONAL RELATIONSHIPS

All relationships have advantages and disadvantages, and it's helpful to consider what these may be.

A good way to begin the study of interpersonal relationships is to examine your own relationships (past, present, or those you look forward to) by asking yourself what your relationships do for you. What are the advantages and the disadvantages? Focus on your own relationships in general (friendship, romantic, family, and work), on one particular relationship (say, your life partner or your child or your best friend), or on one type of relationship (say, friendships), and respond to the following statements by indicating the extent to which your relationship(s) serve each of these functions. Visualize a 10-point scale in which 1 indicates that your relationship(s) never serves this function, 10 indicates that your relationship(s) always serves this function, and the numbers in between indicate levels between these extremes. You may wish to do this twice—once for your face-to-face relationships and once for your online relationships.

_____ 1. My relationships help to lessen my loneliness.
_____ 2. My relationships help me gain in self-knowledge and in self-esteem.
_____ 3. My relationships help enhance my physical and emotional health.
_____ 4. My relationships maximize my pleasures and minimize my pains.
_____ 5. My relationships help me to secure stimulation (intellectual, physical, and emotional).

Let's elaborate just a bit on each of these commonly accepted advantages of interpersonal communication.

1. One of the major benefits of relationships is that they help to lessen loneliness (Rokach, 1998; Rokach & Brock, 1995). They make you feel that someone cares, that someone likes you (the popularity of the "like" button on Facebook and +1 on

Google+ attests to the importance of this benefit), that someone will protect you, that someone ultimately will love you.

2. Through contact with others you learn about yourself and see yourself from different perspectives and in different roles—as a child or parent, as a co-worker, as a student, as a best friend. This function is significantly strengthened by the availability of so many international relationship sites that can expose you to widely varied ways of viewing yourself and relationships. Healthy interpersonal relationships also help enhance self-esteem and self-worth. Simply having a friend or romantic partner (at least most of the time) makes you feel desirable and worthy.

3. Research consistently shows that interpersonal relationships contribute significantly to physical and emotional health (Goleman, 1995; Pennebacker, 1991; Rosen, 1998; Rosengren, 1993) and to personal happiness (Berscheid & Reis, 1998). Without close interpersonal relationships, it's possible to become depressed—and this depression, in turn, can contribute to physical illness. Relationship isolation, in fact, contributes as much to mortality as high blood pressure, high cholesterol, obesity, smoking, or lack of physical exercise (Goleman, 1995).

4. The most general function served by interpersonal relationships, and the function that encompasses all the others, is that of maximizing pleasure and minimizing pain. Your good friends, for example, will make you feel even better about your good fortune and less hurt when you're confronted with hardships.

5. Just as plants are heliotropic and orient themselves to light, humans are stimulotropic and orient themselves to sources of stimulation (Davis, 1973). Human contact is one of the best ways to secure this stimulation—intellectual, physical, and emotional. Even an imagined relationship seems better than none.

allOver photography/Alamy

VIEWPOINTS Online Relationship Advantages

Virtual or online relationships can expose you to many different ways of viewing yourself and your relationships. Among the advantages of online relationships is that they reduce the importance of physical characteristics and instead emphasize such factors as rapport, similarity, and self-disclosure and in the process promote relationships that are based on emotional connection rather than physical attraction (Cooper & Sportolari, 1997). What do you see as the main advantages of online relationships?

Now respond to these sentences as you did to the above.

_____ 6. My relationships put uncomfortable pressure on me to expose my vulnerabilities.
_____ 7. My relationships increase my obligations.
_____ 8. My relationships prevent me from developing other relationships.
_____ 9. My relationships scare me because they may be difficult to dissolve.
_____10. My relationships hurt me.

These statements express what most people would consider disadvantages of interpersonal relationships.

6. Close relationships put pressure on you to reveal yourself and to expose your vulnerabilities. While this is generally worthwhile in the context of a supporting and caring relationship, it may backfire if the relationship deteriorates and these weaknesses are used against you.

7. Close relationships increase your obligations to other people, sometimes to a great extent. Your time is no longer entirely your own. And although you enter relationships to spend more time with these special people, you also incur time (and perhaps financial) obligations with which you may not be happy.

8. Close relationships can lead you to abandon other relationships. Sometimes the other relationship involves someone you like but your partner can't stand. More often, however, it's simply a matter of time and energy; relationships take a lot of both and you have less to give to these other relationships.

Cherishing Behaviours

Cherishing behaviours are those small gestures you enjoy receiving from your friend or partner (a smile, a wink, a phone call, an email saying "I'm thinking of you," a kiss). They are (1) specific and positive; (2) focused on the present and future; (3) capable of being performed daily; and (4) easily executed. Cherishing behaviours are an especially effective way to affirm another person and build the strength of your relationship (Lederer, 1984).

Prepare a list of 10 cherishing behaviours you would like to receive from a friend or partner. After the two of you prepare lists, exchange them and, ideally, perform the desired cherishing behaviours. At first, these behaviours may seem self-conscious and awkward. In time, however, they'll become a normal part of your interaction, which is exactly what you want.

Lists of cherishing behaviours—yours or your partner's—will also give you insight into your relationship needs and the kind of communicating partner you want.

9. The closer your relationships, the more emotionally difficult they are to dissolve, a feeling that may be uncomfortable for some people. If a relationship is deteriorating, you may feel distress or depression. In some cultures and religions, societal pressures may prevent married couples from separating.

10. And, of course, your partner may break your heart. Your partner may leave you—despite all your pleading and promises. Your hurt will be in proportion to how much you care for your partner. If you care a great deal, you're likely to experience great hurt; if you care less, the hurt will be less—it's one of life's little ironies.

Can you describe the major advantages and disadvantages of interpersonal relationships? Can you assess and evaluate your own relationships in terms of its advantages and disadvantages?

CULTURAL INFLUENCES ON INTERPERSONAL RELATIONSHIPS

Cultural factors play important roles in the formation of relationships. In most of North America, interpersonal friendships are drawn from a relatively large pool. Out of all the people with whom you come into regular contact, you choose relatively few as friends. In rural areas and in small villages throughout the world, however, people have very few choices. The two or three other children closest to your age become your friends; there's no real choice. In some cultures, children's friends are primarily members of their extended family.

Most cultures assume that relationships should be permanent or at least long lasting. Consequently, it's assumed that people want to keep relationships together and will exert considerable energy to maintain them. Because of this perspective, there is little research about how to move effortlessly from one intimate relationship to another or how to do this more effectively and efficiently.

Culture influences heterosexual relationships by assigning different roles to men and women. In North America, men and women are supposed to be equal—at least, that's the stated ideal. As a result, both men and women can initiate relationships and both can dissolve them. Both men and women are expected to derive satisfaction from their interpersonal relationships and, when that satisfaction isn't present, either partner may seek to exit the relationship. However, in many countries, only the man has the right to dissolve a marriage without giving reasons. For example, in Jordan, it was only relatively recently (2002) that the first woman was granted a divorce; before this only husbands could obtain divorces (*New York Times*, May 15, 2002, p. A6).

In some cultures, homosexual relationships are accepted while in others they are condemned. In Canada, federal legislation has been passed to approve same-sex marriage; however, this legislation remains highly contested in some areas of the country and among certain religious groups. In the United States, same-sex marriage is legal in more than half the states, while in other jurisdictions, formally registered "domestic partnerships" grant gays, lesbians, and (in some cases) unmarried heterosexuals rights that were formerly reserved only for married couples—such as health insurance benefits and one partner's right to make decisions when the other is incapacitated. In Norway, Sweden, and Denmark, same-sex relationship partners have the same rights as married partners.

> **INTERPERSONAL CHOICE POINT**
>
> **Meeting the Parents**
>
> You're dating someone from a very different culture and have been invited to meet the parents and have a traditional ethnic dinner. What are some of the things you might do to make this potentially different situation go smoothly?

INFLUENCES OF TECHNOLOGY ON INTERPERSONAL RELATIONSHIPS

Online communication is used intensively for interpersonal relationships. In fact, evidence suggests that interpersonal communication is an important use of the internet, if not *the most* important use (Cummings et al., 2002). What is less clear is the impact of online communication on the quality of social relationships.

Studies have shown that teens, for example, use online communication to maintain social relationships with family and friends that were initially developed face to face and also to create new relationships completely online (Mesch & Talmud, 2006). Mesch and Talmud (2006) argue that the quality of social relationships depends on the length of the relationship and on the topics and activities that are shared.

Whereas online relationships have the same potential advantages and disadvantages as face-to-face relationships, conflicting evidence exists about the potential quality of a fully online relationship. Some research suggests that online relationships can be meaningful and deep; however, other data suggest that people don't value their online relationships to the same degree that they value their face-to-face ones, perhaps because there are often so many of the former (Cummings, Butler, & Kraut, 2002). As well, time spent online reduces the amount of time spent with family and friends and has been shown to diminish social involvement and psychological well-being (Cummings, Butler, & Kraut, 2002). It would seem that the key issue in determining the effect of online communication on interpersonal relationships is whether it's used to supplement or to substitute for face-to-face communication with friends and family.

Women, it seems, are more likely to form relationships on the internet than men. An early study showed that about 72 percent of women and 55 percent of men had formed personal relationships online (Parks & Floyd, 1996). And women are more likely to use the internet to deepen their interpersonal relationships (Fallows, 2005).

As relationships develop on the internet, network convergence occurs; that is, as a relationship between two people develops, they begin to share their network of other communicators with each other (Parks, 1995; Parks & Floyd, 1996). This, of course, is similar to relationships formed through face-to-face contact. Online work groups also are on the increase and have been found to be more task-oriented and more efficient than face-to-face groups (Lantz, 2001). Online groups can provide a sense of belonging that may once have been thought possible only through face-to-face interactions (Silverman, 2001).

Advantages of Online Relationships

Online relationships have some advantages over face-to-face relationships. For example, in some face-to-face relationships, physical appearance outweighs personality; online communication allows the person's inner qualities to be

The Bachelor Canada (the Canadian version of the American reality show) involves a group of women competing for the affection of a man who's looking for a marriage partner. The show sends strong messages about what to look for in a partner and what the important quality are for a relationship. Do you agree with these messages? Why do you think this show is so popular given that more and more people seem to be developing relationships online?

"I can't wait to see what you're like online."

Paul Noth/The New Yorker Collection/www.cartoonbank.com

shared without the physical distractions. It is a boon to those who are shut-ins or very shy, or for whom meeting others in a more traditional way is difficult. Another obvious advantage is that the number of people you can meet online is vast compared with the number you can meet in person. This increases the opportunity to meet people with whom you may share common interests.

Disadvantages of Online Relationships

However, online relationships also have their own unique disadvantages. These relationships allow people to present a false self with little chance of detection. For example, minors may present themselves as adults and adults may present themselves as children for illicit and illegal sexual communications. Similarly, an online partner can present as rich, mature, or serious and committed when none of these characteristics hold true.

Increasingly, it seems that young people prefer to communicate with one another online, a preference that has been called *hyperpersonal communication* (Tidwell & Walther, 2002). Tidwell and Walther (2002) consider three elements of interpersonal conversation that are impacted through online connections: idealized perception, selective self-perception, and reduced cues.

Idealized perception can occur with the limited information that is often provided online, when users may come to perceive the other as the "perfect person." In the process of *selective self-perception*, what is presented can be the idealized person, what one wants the other to think, without having to address characteristics of the physical self such as age, gender, or appearance. Because online users can't see each other (other than posted pictures which may or may not be real) and can't hear the other's voice (including expressions, tone, accent, and so on), they must rely solely on the *reduced verbal cues* provided (Tidwell & Walther, 2002), which may lead to a false impression of who the other really is. This, of course, is changing as people use Skype and other video technologies more frequently.

INTERPERSONAL CHOICE POINT

Coming Clean

You're getting ready to meet someone you've communicated with only online and you're going to have to admit that you weren't completely honest about your age and a few other things. What are the things about which you'd have to come clean with most immediately? What are your options for expressing this? What seems the best option for disclosure?

While online communication may encourage, permit, or help to develop interpersonal relationships, McQuillen (2003) cautions that these relationships could be compared to interactions at a costume party. Party-goers become the characters represented by the costumes they're wearing because they can choose what to disclose to others through what they present to others. If what one person chooses to present to the other is more a function of perception than of reality, the relationship may be disconfirming. Some research has found that, in seeking relationships online, you may become more discriminating, less forgiving of minor imperfections, and less willing to work out differences because the field of available people is so vast (Cohen, 2001).

One study found that among people who met online, those who met in places of common interest, who communicated over a period of time before they met in person, who managed barriers to greater closeness, and who managed conflict well were more likely to stay together than couples who did not follow this general pattern (Baker, 2002). Based on your own experiences, how would you predict which couples would stay together and which would break apart? Can you describe cultural and technological influences on interpersonal communication? How might you use the discussion of the advantages and disadvantages of online communication to review your own online communications?

INTERPERSONAL CHOICE POINT

Virtual Infidelity

You discover that your partner of the past 15 years is being unfaithful with someone online (and in another country). You believe that infidelity often results from a failure in communication (Young et al., 2000). You want to discover the extent of this online relationship and your partner's intentions. What choices do you have for opening up this topic for honest conversation without making your partner defensive and hence uncommunicative?

ETHICAL MESSAGES

Your Obligation to Reveal Yourself

If you're in a close relationship, your influence on your partner is considerable, so you may have an obligation to reveal certain things about yourself. Conversely, you may feel that the other person—because he or she is so close to you—has an ethical obligation to reveal certain information to you.

Ethical Choice Point

Consider: At what point in a relationship—if any—do you feel you would have an ethical obligation to reveal each of the 10 items of information listed here? Visualize a relationship as existing on a continuum from initial contact at 1 to close intimacy at 10, and use the numbers from 1 to 10 to indicate at what point you'd feel your romantic partner or close friend has a right to know each type of information about you. If you feel you'd never have the obligation to reveal this information, use 0.

As you respond to these items, ask yourself, what gives one person the right to know personal information about another person? What principle of ethics requires another person to disclose this information in a relationship?

At what point do you have an ethical obligation to reveal ...	Romantic Partner	Close Friend
Age		
History of family genetic disorders		
HIV status		
Past sexual experiences		
Marital history		
Annual salary and net financial worth		
Affectional orientation		
Attitudes toward other races and nationalities		
Religious beliefs		
Past criminal activity or incarceration		

Inmagine/Alamy

VIEWPOINTS Gender Differences in Breaking Up

Popular myth would have us believe that most heterosexual love affairs break up as a result of the man's outside affair, but the research does not support this (Blumstein & Schwartz, 1983; Janus & Janus, 1993). When surveyed as to the reason for breaking up, only 15 percent of the men indicated that it was their interest in another partner, whereas 32 percent of the women noted this as a cause of the breakup. These findings are from 1983 and 1993 and are, therefore, dated. What do you think we'd find if the same survey were done today? More important, why do you think differences exist at all?

THE DARK SIDE OF INTERPERSONAL RELATIONSHIPS

Although relationships serve a variety of vital functions and provide enormous advantages, as already noted not all relationships are equally satisfying and productive. Consequently, it's necessary to explore this "dark" side. Here we consider three such dark sides: jealousy, bullying, and violence in close relationships.

Relationship Jealousy and Envy

We often use the terms *envy* and *jealousy* interchangeably, since in both cases we experience a negative emotion about our relationship. But the two are actually very different. Envy is an emotion we experience when we desire what someone else has or has more of than we do. For example, we might feel envious of a friend who has lots of friends or romantic partners or money when we have significantly less. When we feel **envy**, we may feel that we are inferior to or of lesser importance than someone else. **Jealousy**, on the other hand, is a type or form of anger we experience when we feel that our relationship is in danger due to some rival. Jealousy is a reaction to a relationship threat: if you feel that someone is moving in on your relationship partner, you may experience jealousy—especially if you feel that this interloper is succeeding. The rival is usually a potential romantic partner but could also be a close friend or a job that occupies all our partner's time and thoughts. When we feel jealousy, we may feel angry and anxious.

COMPONENTS OF JEALOUSY   Jealousy has at least three components (Erber & Erber, 2011): cognitive, emotional, and behavioural.

- *Cognitive jealousy* involves suspicious thinking, worrying, and imagining the different scenarios in which your partner may be interested in another person.
- *Emotional jealousy* involves the feelings you have when you see your partner, say, laughing or talking intimately with or kissing a rival. It includes "emotional infidelity"—feelings of love and arousal.
- *Behavioural jealousy* refers to what you actually do in response to the jealous feelings and emotions; for example, reading your partner's email, looking on Facebook for incriminating photos, or going through the back seat of the car with the proverbial fine-tooth comb.

INTERPERSONAL CHOICE POINT

Privacy and Emotional Closeness

In face-to-face relationships, emotional closeness compromises privacy; the closer you become, the less privacy you have. In online relationships, however, because you're more in control of what you reveal, you can develop close emotional relationships but also maintain your privacy (Ben-Ze'ev, 2003). Do you find this to be true for you? If not, how would you express the relationship between emotional closeness and privacy?

Much research has reported that heterosexual men and women experience jealousy for different reasons, and that these reasons are rooted in our evolutionary development (Buller, 2005; Buss, 2000; Buunk & Dijkstra, 2004). Basically, research finds that men experience jealousy when their partner is *physically* intimate with another man, whereas women experience jealousy when their partner is *emotionally* intimate with another woman. The evolutionary reason researchers give is that men provided food and shelter for the family and would resent their partner's physical intimacy with another because they would then be providing food and shelter for another man's child. Women, because they depended on men for food and shelter, became especially jealous when their partner was emotionally intimate with another because this might mean he might leave her and she'd thus lose the food and shelter protection.

There is some evidence that feelings of jealousy are culturally determined rather than based on evolutionary roots as described above (Harris, 2003). For example, among Chinese men, only 25 percent reported physical infidelity to be the more distressing while 75 percent reported emotional infidelity to be more distressing.

Another commonly assumed gender difference is that jealous men are more prone to respond with violence. This assumption, however, does not seem to be the case; apparently, men and women are equally likely to respond with violence (Harris, 2003).

DEALING WITH JEALOUSY   So what do you do when you experience jealousy (instead of responding with violence)? Rather than succumbing to popular but generally negative responses (Dindia & Timmerman, 2003; Guerrero et al., 1995), try to work things out with your partner using the following "integrative communication" skills:

- disclosing your feelings
- being honest
- practising effective conflict management
- listening actively

David Grossman/The Image Works

"Falling out of love is very enlightening; for a short while, you see the world with new eyes."—Iris Murdoch

Bullying

Bullying, whether in a close relationship, the workplace, or the playground, consists of abusive acts repeatedly committed by one person (or a group) against another. Bullying is behaviour that has become a pattern; it's repeated frequently rather than being an isolated instance. On the playground, bullying often involves physical abuse, whereas in the workplace or at college or university, bullying is generally verbal.

An alarming and rapidly increasing form of bullying is cyberbullying. This form of bullying can take place through any online medium—Facebook, Twitter, email, instant messages, blog posts, sexting—and can take the form of sending threatening messages or images, posting negative comments, revealing secrets, lying about another person, or sexual harrassment. In one 2009 survey of 13- to 18-year-olds, 15 percent said they had been cyberbullied, and in another study of 12- to 17-year-olds, one-third said they had been threatened or embarrassed by things said about them online. In another study, 88 percent of teenagers said they witnessed other people being mean or cruel on the sites and 15 percent say they were the targets of such meanness (Lenhart et al., 2011). In recent years, Canadian media has highlighted several cases of teen suicide linked back directly to forms of cyberbullying.

Cyberbullying is so serious because it can occur at any time; the messages, photos, and videos can be distributed quickly and widely; and the bully can hide behind false names. Websites, in fact, will do this for you and send messages anonymously. Cyberbullying attacks—because they occur electronically and the perpetrator doesn't need to attack in person—are often more cruel than those made in face-to-face attacks (Hinduja & Patchin, 2008).

AF archive/Alamy

VIEWPOINTS Bullying

Bullying can sometimes be a part of the organization's culture; for example, new recruits or employees may be treated unfairly and may be abused by their superiors. Sometimes it's perpetrated by a group who perhaps bully the newcomers or those who do less creative jobs. What's the status of bullying in organizations with which you're familiar?

Victims of bullying may suffer significant mental and physical problems, including high stress, financial problems, reduced self-esteem, sleep and digestion disturbances, depression, and suicidal ideations. From the point of view of the student or friend being bullied, it obviously creates tension, perhaps a desire to avoid going to school, or a preoccupation with the bullying rather than the positive aspects of life. Researcher Danah Boyd (2014) uses the term *frenemy* to refer to supposed friends who bully online. From an ethical point of view, bullying destroys a person's right to personal dignity and a school or environment free from intimidation.

DEALING WITH BULLYING   Among the actions recommended for combating bullying are the following:

1. Ensure that everyone in the classroom, school, group, or organization understands what behaviours actually constitute bullying; for example, ensure that everyone recognizes the distinction between everyday conflict and bullying.
2. Be clear that bullying is not tolerated, whether face to face or online.
3. Explore and understand why online bullying is so traumatic, why it is often more harmful than the face-to-face kind.
4. Know how to take action when you or someone else is being bullied. If someone comes to you with concerns about bullying, listen and support the other while you gather further evidence.

Relationship Violence

Perhaps the most obvious dark side of relationships are the varied forms of relationship violence. Before reading about this important but often neglected topic, take the following self-test.

Four types of relationship violence may be distinguished: physical abuse, verbal or emotional abuse, sexual abuse, and economic abuse (Rice, 2007).

■ *Physical abuse* includes threats of violence as well as acts such as pushing, hitting, slapping, kicking, choking, throwing things, or breaking things.

TEST YOURSELF

Is Violence Part of Your Relationship?

Based on your present relationship or one you know, respond to the following questions with *yes* or *no*.

Do either of you

_____ 1. get angry to the point of making the other person fearful?

_____ 2. engage in behaviour that could be considered humiliating to the other person?

_____ 3. verbally abuse the other?

_____ 4. threaten the other with violence?

_____ 5. engage in slapping, hitting, or pushing the other?

_____ 6. throw things in anger?

_____ 7. make accusations of sexual infidelity?

_____ 8. force the other to have sex?

_____ 9. use abusive sexual terms in reference to the other?

_____10. withhold cash or hide credit cards from the other?

_____11. require the other to ask for money and justify household expenses?

How Did You Do? These eleven items are all signs of a violent relationship (note that it takes only one item to make a relationship violent). Items 1–3 are examples of verbal or emotional abuse, 4–6 of physical abuse, 7–9 of sexual abuse, and 10–11 of economic abuse—which are explained more fully below.

What Will You Do? If any of these items applies to your relationship, you may wish to seek professional help (which is likely available on your campus). Additional suggestions are offered in the text and are readily available online.

Source: These questions were drawn from a variety of websites, including those from SUNY at Buffalo Counseling Services; The American College of Obstetricians and Gynecologists, Women's Heath Care Physicians; and the University of Texas at Austin, Counseling and Mental Health Center.

- *Verbal or emotional abuse* includes humiliating, isolating, criticizing, or stalking the partner.
- *Sexual abuse* includes touching that is unwanted, accusations of sexual infidelity without reason, forced sex, or referring to a partner with abusive sexual terms.
- *Economic abuse* includes controlling the partner's finances or preventing the partner from working.

Dating Violence

A body of research has focused on the prevalence of abuse experienced in dating relationships of Canadian post-secondary students. Warthe and Tutty (2008) added some questions exploring dating violence to the National College Health Assessment (NCHA) and found that in the 12 months prior to completing the survey, 9 percent of women and 4.8 percent of men had experienced some form of dating violence in their relationships. The most common forms of violence reported were being made to "feel inferior and incompetent" (37 percent) and being "yelled at" (37.8 percent). The study found that 3.9 percent of respondents had been forced to participate in an unwanted sexual activity. For those who experienced physical abuse, 0.6 percent required medical attention. There were significant gender differences with regard to dating expectations, the effects of violence, and the ability to access support. The most common reported effect of dating violence was that the individual felt "embarrassed and emotionally upset."

Dealing with Relationship Violence

Whether you're the victim of relationship violence or a friend of a victim, it's important to have some basic strategies at hand. According to the Canadian Women's Foundation website (www.canadianwomen.org), 67 percent of the general population knows of someone who is in a violent relationship—equivalent to almost seven out of ten people. More importantly for those at college or university, 66 percent of these women are under the age of 24.

What should you do if you know someone who is in a violent relationship? The Canadian Women's Foundation (www.canadianwomen.org) has this advice:

- If she is in immediate danger, call 911.
- Put her safety first. Be careful not to alert her partner.
- Don't be judgmental—there are many reasons why it can be difficult to leave a violent relationship. Often this decision can be a dangerous one, so respect her for her decisions.
- Listen to her if she wants to talk. If she doesn't, reassure her that you're always there for her.
- Learn about the services and resources in your area. Consider becoming a volunteer.

If you are in a violent relationship, the Alberta Council of Women's Shelters (www.acws.ca) offers this advice:

- Learn about the services and resources in your area, but check them out safely. Keep you and your children safe while searching by not bookmarking sites and being sure to close the browser if searching from home.
- Cover your tracks. For example, the page on the ACWS website has a button that will immediately take you to the Weather Network if you're afraid someone will see what page you're checking out.
- When you have made the decision to leave, call for help safely. Don't use your home phone or even your cell phone as your partner can track these. Use a phone at work or somewhere your partner may not know about.
- Try to remember that this is not your fault, and that violence is not part of love.
- Violence affects your children, even if they are not abused themselves. Don't feel you need to hold a violent relationship together for the sake of the children.

TABLE 9.1

VIOLENT AND NONVIOLENT RELATIONSHIPS

Here are some characteristics that distinguish a nonviolent from a violent relationship, drawn largely from the University of Texas website on relationship violence.

Violent Relationships	Nonviolent Relationships
Emotional abuse	Fairness; you look for resolutions to conflict that will be fair to both of you.
Control and isolation	Communication that makes the partner feel safe and comfortable expressing himself or herself.
Intimidation	Mutual respect, mutual affirmation, and valuing of each other's opinions.
Economic abuse	The partners make financial decisions together.
Threats	Accountability—each person accepts responsibility for his or her own behaviour.
Power over the other	Fair distribution of responsibilities.
Sexual abuse	Trust and respect for what each person wants and is comfortable with.

INTERPERSONAL CHOICE POINT

Verbal Abuse

On your way to work, you witness a father verbally abusing his three-year-old child. Your first impulse is to speak up and tell this man that verbal abuse can have lasting effects on the child and often leads to physical abuse. At the same time, you don't know what's been happening prior to what you're seeing and you don't want to interfere with his right to speak to his child. You certainly don't want to make him angrier. What are some things you might say or do in this difficult situation?

While the pronoun *she* has been used here, remember that men, too, can be the victims of violent relationships. Violence in homosexual relationships is also often overlooked—and for bystanders it can often present a more complicated situation, since they won't likely know whom to contact or where to get help. As well, they have to be careful not to "out" someone before they're ready.

Relationship violence is not an inevitable part of interpersonal relationships; in fact, it occurs in a minority of relationships. Yet it's important to know that there is the potential for violence in all relationships, just as there is potential for friendship, love, support, and all the positive things we look for in a relationship. Knowing the difference between productive and destructive relationships (see Table 9.1) seems the best way to make sure that your own relationships are as you want them to be.

 Can you define *jealousy and envy,* bullying, and *relationship violence?* How might you use the suggestions offered here to help you effectively deal with such relationships in your own personal or workplace life?

RELATIONSHIP TYPES

In this section we look at friendship and family relationships, and their various types. Workplace relationships will be discussed in detail in Chapter 11.

Friendship Relationships

Friendship is an *interpersonal relationship* between two people that is mutually productive and characterized by mutual positive regard. Friends react to each other as complete persons—as unique, genuine, and irreplaceable individuals (Wright, 1978, 1984).

In online friendships, people often have friends numbering in the hundreds. In a 2011 survey, Facebook users had an average of 229 friends, with many having friends numbering in the thousands (Hampton et al., 2011). Facebook's friends lists and Google+'s circles enable you to group your friends based on degree of closeness—or any other grouping you find useful.

Note that in the preceding definition friendships must be *mutually productive*; in other words, they cannot be destructive to either person. Once destructiveness enters into a relationship, it no longer qualifies as friendship. A relationship in which one person intimidates, controls, or ridicules the other can hardly be called a friendship. Romantic relationships, marriage relationships, parent–child relationships, and just about any other possible relationship can be either destructive or productive. But true friendship must enhance the potential of each person and be productive.

Friendships are also characterized by *mutual positive regard*. Liking people is essential if we are to call them friends. Three major characteristics of friendship—trust, emotional support, and sharing of interests—testify to this positive regard (Blieszner & Adams, 1992). And, of course, the "like" and "+1" icons on social media sites make the expression of this positive regard easy, though perhaps given lightly.

The closer friends are, the more interdependent they become; that is, when friends are especially close, the actions of one will more significantly affect the other than they would if the friends were just casual acquaintances. Similarly, the friends of one may become the friends of others—more easily on social media sites but also in face-to-face friendships. Close friends are less influenced by the societal rules that govern more casual relationships. Close friends are likely to make up their own rules for interacting with each other; they decide what they will talk about and when, what they can say to each other without offending and what they can't, when and for what reasons one friend can call the other, and so on.

INTERPERSONAL CHOICE POINT

Friend Request

You get a request to be friends with someone you really don't want to have in your network. Assuming you don't want to create animosity, what are some of your options in this case?

SKILL-BUILDING EXERCISE

Identifying Friendship Functions in Social Media

Understanding the functions that friendships serve will help you communicate more effectively. Friendships serve a variety of functions or needs. The following five functions were identified in a pre–social media communication environment and are based largely on face-to-face friendships (Reiner & Blanton, 1997; Wright, 1978, 1984). However, these functions are also served by social media friendships. In the column on the right, indicate the specific means used (and specific examples) in social media communication to serve each of these five needs/functions.

Function	Generally	In Social Media
Utility	Friends can do useful things for you; for example, helping you get a better job or introducing you to a possible romantic partner.	
Affirmation	Friends can affirm your personal value and help you to appreciate your qualities.	
Support	Friends can be supportive, encouraging, and complimentary, helping you develop a healthy sense of self.	
Stimulation	Friends can introduce you to new ideas and new ways of seeing the world.	
Security	Friends can come to your aid when you need them, supportively and nonjudgmentally.	

Radoslaw Korga/Shutterstock

VIEWPOINTS **Social Information Processing**

Social information processing (SIP) theory claims that whether you're communicating face-to-face or online, you can communicate the same degree of personal involvement and develop similar close relationships (Walther, 2011). Communicators are clever people; they will make whatever adjustments are needed to communicate what they want and to develop the relationships they want. In short, communication and relationships can be as personal online as face-to-face. In what ways do you adjust your online communication to make it resemble face-to-face communication? What do you think of this theory?

Friendship, Culture, Gender, and Technology

Your friendships and the way you look at friendships will be influenced by your culture, gender, and the technology around us.

CULTURE   In North America, you can be friends with someone yet never really be expected to go much out of your way for the other person. Yet many from the Middle East, Asia, and Latin America would consider going significantly out of their way an absolutely essential ingredient in friendship; if you're not willing to sacrifice for your friend, then this person is not really your friend (Dresser, 2005).

Generally, friendships are closer in collectivist cultures than in individualist cultures (see Chapter 2). In their emphasis on the group and on cooperating, collectivist cultures foster the development of close friendship bonds. Members of collectivist cultures are expected to help others in the group, certainly a good start for a friendship. Members of individualist cultures, on the other hand, are expected to look out for themselves. Consequently, they're more likely to compete and to try to do better than each other—conditions that don't generally support the development of close friendships.

GENDER   Gender also influences your friendships—who becomes your friend and the way you look at friendships. Women engage in significantly more affectional behaviours with their friends than do males; this difference may account for the greater difficulty men experience in beginning and maintaining close friendships (Hays, 1989). Perhaps the best documented finding, already noted in the section on self-disclosure in Chapter 3, is that women typically self-disclose more than men (e.g., Dolgin, Meyer, & Schwartz, 1991). Women engage in more casual communication; they also share greater intimacy and more confidences with their friends than do men. Communication, in all its forms and functions, seems a more important dimension of women's friendships.

Men's friendships are often built around shared activities—attending a ball game, playing cards, working on a project at the office. Women's friendships, on the other hand, are built more around a sharing of feelings, support, and "personalism." Similarity in status, willingness to protect a friend in uncomfortable situations, and academic major have been found to be significantly related to the relationship closeness of male–male friends but not of female–female or female–male friends (Griffin & Sparks, 1990).

TECHNOLOGY   Whereas not so many years ago, friends met at school, at work, or in their neighbourhood, today online friendships in some form are a major part of our relationship life. Social networking sites make it increasingly easy and interesting both to meet new friends and to keep in touch with old friends. Establishing and maintaining friendships, in fact, are the major reasons for online communication among college students and among teens (Lenhart et al., 2007).

INTERPERSONAL CHOICE POINT

Given the information discussed above, perhaps similarity is a criterion for male friendships but not for female or mixed-sex friendships. Do you think gender differences are changing with increased online communication? Do you see the differences between men and women increasing or decreasing? What do you see as the major difference between men and women in their attitudes and beliefs about friendship? About family relationships?

 Can you explain the roles of culture, gender, and technology in friendships?

Family Relationships

Years ago, if you were asked to define the word *family*, you might have said that a family consisted of parents and one or more children. If pressed, you might have added that families could consist of other relatives such as grandparents, aunts and uncles, in-laws, perhaps even pets. But today, other forms of family are increasingly common and accepted.

DEVELOPING LANGUAGE AND COMMUNICATION SKILLS

The "Me" Generations: Toddlers and Teens

Toddlers are learning developmentally that they're separate from the adult caregivers in their lives. It's a time when everything is about them: all toys belong to them, they want to do everything by themselves, and they don't understand when others have differ- ent schedules or needs. Teens also go through a developmental period of separation from the adults in their lives and start relying more on peers. This is an important process in which their brains are restructuring to enable them to become independent, ready to strike out on their own as adults themselves. While communication isn't easy at either stage, neither toddlers nor teens are deliberately being selfish; their brains are simply get- ting ready for the next important stages of their lives as individuals and coming adults. If you'd like to learn more, see http://dalailamacenter.org/learn/daniel-siegel-teenage-brain.

The Changing Family

Divorce rate statistics provide significant information about the changing nature of the typical two-parent family. Consider these 2003 figures from Statistics Canada:

- In 1973, 5.4 percent of divorces involved husbands who had been divorced before. In 2003, this number had dramatically increased to 16.2 percent.
- In 1973, the same number of divorces involved wives who had been divorced before. In 2003, this number showed a slightly lower increase to 15.7 percent.
- Overall in Canada, there was an increase of 1 percent in the number of divorces between 2001 and 2002, which roughly corresponded to the general increase in population.
- However, Newfoundland and Labrador showed a major decrease of 21.4 percent in the number of divorces in the same period.
- The peak divorce rate occurs after three years of marriage, when 26.2 out of every 1000 marriages will fail. After that crucial time, the risk of divorce decreases slightly with each year.
- However, 38.3 percent of all marriages in Canada will end in divorce before the 30th wedding anniversary.

Canadian data indicate that an increasing number of children under the age of 18 are living in single-parent families (Statistics Canada, 2001). Data from the 2001 census include the following:

- The overwhelming majority (84.3 percent) of children live in two-parent homes.
- This number has dropped only slightly since 1999, when 85.9 percent of children lived in two-parent homes.
- Approximately 12.6 percent (down from 13.5 percent in 1999) of children are being raised in female-headed families.
- In a dramatic rise from 0.6 percent in 1999, 2.9 percent of children are being raised in male-headed families.
- Between 1971 and 2001, lone-parent families increased from 9.4 percent of all fami- lies to 15% of all families.

Another example of changing family relationships involves partners who aren't married but live together in an exclusive relationship. For the most part, these cohabitants live as

Rachel Epstein/The Image Works

"Although all those who fall in love do so in the same way, not all fall in love for the same reason. There is no single quality which is universally loved." —José Ortega y Gasset

if they were married: there is an exclusive sexual commitment; there may be children; and financial responsibilities, time, and space are shared. These relationships often mirror traditional marriages, except that in marriage the union is recognized by a religious body, the state, or both, whereas in a relationship of cohabitants the relationship is not generally recognized this way. Again, data from the 2001 census indicate the following:

- In Canada, common-law unions have increased steadily since 1981.
- In Quebec, the rates rose to 25 percent in 2001 from 8 percent in 1981.
- In the rest of Canada, common-law unions have increased at a lesser but still steady rate, to 13.7percent in 2001, up from 6 percent in 1981.
- In 2001, 530 900 common-law families had at least one child living at home; 261 970 of those families were located in Quebec.

Another example of the changing family is the same-sex couple who have all the same characteristics of family. Many of these couples have children from previous heterosexual unions, through artificial insemination, or by adoption. Although accurate statistics are difficult to secure, couplehood among gays and lesbians seems more common than the popular media might lead us to believe.

Characteristics of Families

All primary relationships and families have several qualities that further characterize this relationship type: defined roles, recognition of responsibilities, shared history and future, and shared living space.

- *Defined roles.* Some heterosexual couples still divide their roles rather traditionally, with the man as primary wage earner and maintenance person and the woman as primary cook, child rearer, and housekeeper. This is less true among more highly educated couples and those in the higher socioeconomic classes, where changes in traditional role assignments are seen first. However, among same-sex couples, clear-cut, stereotypical male and female roles are not found (Cloud, 2008; Peplau, 1988).
- *Recognition of responsibilities.* Family members see themselves as having certain obligations and responsibilities to one another. For example, individuals have an obligation to help each other financially. There are also emotional responsibilities: to offer comfort when family members are distressed, to take pleasure in their pleasures, to feel their pain, to raise their spirits.
- *Shared history and future.* Primary relationship partners have a shared history and the prospect of a shared future. For a relationship to become primary, there must be some history, some significant past interaction. Despite Canada's rate of divorce sitting at just over 38 percent, most couples entering a relationship such as marriage view it—ideally, at least—as permanent.
- *Shared living space.* Most Canadian families share their living space. There is, however, a growing minority of couples who retain their original apartments or houses but spend substantial time apart. For example, there are a growing number of divided families as one partner, say from Newfoundland or the Maritimes, moves to Alberta for work on the oil sands for large parts of the year. These relationships, it should be stressed, are not necessarily less satisfying. After a thorough review of the

research, one researcher concluded that "there is little, if any, decrease in relationship satisfaction, intimacy, and commitment as long as [partners] are able to reunite with some frequency (approximately once a month)" (Rohlfing, 1995, pp. 182–183). In some traditional cultures, in fact, men and women don't share the same living space; the women may live with the children while the men live together in a communal arrangement (Harris, 1993).

■ *Communication rules.* All families teach rules for communication. Some of these are explicit, such as "Don't contradict the family in front of outsiders" or "Never talk finances with outsiders." Other rules are unspoken; you deduce them as you learn the communication style of your family. For example, if financial issues are always discussed in secret and in hushed tones, then you can infer that you shouldn't tell others about family finances. Family communication research points to the importance of rules in defining the family (Galvin, Bylund, & Brommel, 2004). These rules concern three main interpersonal communication issues (Satir, 1983):

1. What can you talk about? Can you talk about Grandpa's drinking? Your sister's lifestyle?
2. In what way can you talk about a given topic? Can you joke about your brother's disability? Can you directly address questions of family history or family skeletons?
3. To whom can you talk? Can you talk openly to extended family members such as cousins, aunts, and uncles? Can you talk to close neighbours about family health issues?

> **INTERPERSONAL CHOICE POINT**
>
> **Couple Types**
>
> Your current relationship—which is a good one for the most part—is becoming too "separate" for your liking. You'd like it to be more "traditional." What are some of your options for changing your couple type? What would you do or say to begin this transformation?

Not surprisingly, the rules a family develops are greatly influenced by both home (or traditional) culture and the wider host culture. Although there are many similarities among families throughout the world, there are also differences (Georgas et al., 2001). For example, members of collectivist cultures (see Chapter 2) are more likely to restrict family information from outsiders as a way of protecting the family. Many women will not report spousal abuse because of a desire to protect the family image—a need to not let others know that things aren't perfect at home (Dresser, 2005).

Families, Culture, Gender, and Technology

Families vary from one culture to another, are viewed differently by men and women, and are influenced by technology.

CULTURE AND FAMILIES In Canada, it's assumed that you have the right to exit an undesirable relationship. But in some cultures, you cannot simply dissolve a relationship once it's formed or there are children. More important, there may be such issues as "How do you maintain a relationship that has problems?" "What can you do to survive in this unpleasant relationship?" or "How can you repair a troubled relationship?" (Moghaddam, Taylor, & Wright, 1993).

Further, your culture will influence the difficulty you undergo when relationships do break up. For example, married persons whose religion forbids divorce and remarriage will experience religious disapproval and condemnation as well as the same economic and social

Dmitrii Kotin/Getty Images

VIEWPOINTS Marriage and Culture

Men and women from different cultures were asked the following question: "If a man (woman) had all the other qualities you desired, would you marry this person if you were not in love with him (her)?" Results varied from one culture to another (Levine et al., 1994). For example, 50 percent of the respondents from Pakistan said yes and 49 percent of those from India said yes. At the other extreme were those from Japan (only 2 percent said yes) and the United States (only 3.5 percent said yes). How would you answer this question? How is your answer influenced by your culture?

Amanda Wesson

VIEWPOINTS Establishing Family Communication Rules

Some millennials spend up to 6.5 hours a day using some form of electronic media (Wallis, 2006). However, much of this time is spent multitasking—simultaneously attending to additional media, such as television, music, and books, while working on the computer. While parents are encouraged to set limits on their children's computer usage, as well as monitor content, what are the advantages to these forms of technology? Can you think of some ways that technology could be used to enhance communication in relationships?

difficulties everyone else goes through. In Canada, child custody often goes to the woman, which presents added emotional burdens for the man. In other countries, the law requires that child custody goes to the man, which presents added emotional burdens for the woman.

GENDER AND FAMILIES   In Canada, both men and women can initiate relationships and both can dissolve them. Both men and women are expected to derive satisfaction from their interpersonal relationships and, when that satisfaction isn't present, either person may seek to exit the relationship. In other cultures, on the other hand, only the man has the right to dissolve a marriage.

Same-sex families are accepted in some cultures and condemned in others. In Canada, same-sex couples are able to legally marry. In the United States, some states allow same-sex couples to legally marry, whereas in other states, "domestic partnerships" grant same-sex couples and (in some cases) unmarried heterosexuals rights that were formerly reserved only for married couples, such as health insurance benefits and the right to make decisions when one member is incapacitated.

TECHNOLOGY AND FAMILIES   You know from your own family interactions that technology has greatly changed communication among family members. Cell phones enable parents and children to keep in close touch in case of emergencies or just to chat. College and university students can stay in closer touch with their parents and friends at home with cell phones and Skype as well as through other forms of social media.

On the other hand, some people—in some cases parents, in most cases children—become so absorbed in their online communities that they have little time for face-to-face interactions with friends or family. Many educators and psychologists are now encouraging parents to help their children reduce their compulsion for technology in order to spend more time in the physical company of family and friends (Wallis, 2006). They challenge parents to lead by example, to slow down and unplug once in a while. However, family psychologist Edward Hallowell (as cited in Wallis, 2006) says that technology itself is not the problem. "The problem is . . . that you are not having family dinner, you are not having conversations, you are not debating whether to go out with a boy who wants to have sex on the first date, you are not going on a family ski trip or taking time just to veg. It's not so much that the video game is going to rot your brain, it's what you are not doing that is going to rot your life."

As Wallis (2006) concludes, "Generation M [millennials] has a lot to teach parents and teachers about what new technology can do. But it's up to grownups to show them what it can't do and that there's life beyond the screen."

 Can you define family characteristics and explain the influence of culture, gender, and technology in family interactions?

A POSITIVE APPROACH TO IMPROVING RELATIONSHIP COMMUNICATION

There seems little doubt that effective communication is at the heart of effective interpersonal relationships. Without effective communication, such relationships are likely to be a lot less meaningful and satisfying than they could be. The acronym POSITIVE stands for general principles of effective communication that enhance all interpersonal relationships: positiveness, openness, supportiveness, interest, truthfulness, involvement, value, and equality.

Positiveness

Positiveness in conversation, as discussed in Chapter 8, entails both a positive attitude toward a specific communication and an expression of positiveness toward the other person. In relationship effectiveness, positiveness toward the relationship is required, both toward the other (your partner, friend, or colleague) and also about the other when interacting with third parties.

Don't confuse positiveness with agreement. You don't necessarily need to agree with everything your partner says or does, but you do need to be able to talk about it without prejudging.

As well, don't confuse positiveness with perfection. Whether influenced by the media, by a self-commitment to have a relationship better than their parents', or by a mistaken belief that other relationships are better than their own, people sometimes look for and expect perfection. But this sets up unrealistic expectations; it's almost sure to result in dissatisfaction and disappointment with existing relationships and, in fact, with any relationship that's likely to come along.

Openness

Openness entails a variety of attitudes and behaviours. It means really listening—closing down both your verbal and inner talk so that you can focus on the other. It means listening to the anxieties, worries, and feelings of the other, even when you honestly believe these are minor issues that will go away tomorrow.

Openness also involves a willingness to empathize with the other—to seek to experience the feelings of the other and to see the world as they do. It doesn't mean that you should take on the other's feelings or even necessarily be in agreement with those feelings, but rather that you should try to understand them as the other experiences them.

Openness recognizes that, throughout any significant relationship, there will be numerous changes in each of the individuals and in the relationship itself. Because people in relationships are interconnected, with each having an impact on the other, changes in one person may require changes in the other. Your willingness to be responsive to such changes, to be adaptable and flexible, is likely to enhance relationship satisfaction (Noller & Fitzpatrick, 1993). Openness thus entails a willingness to consider new ideas, new ways of seeing the other and your relationship, and new ways of interacting.

Supportiveness

In relationship communication, being supportive includes encouraging the other person to be the best he or she can be. Supportiveness recognizes that a relationship entails both of you or, when the family includes children, all of you. It requires that you find ways to be together to make decisions, to plan, to move forward as a family. So, for example, while you enjoy attending your children's soccer games, it's also important that your partner and children support you when you run your half marathon. Supportiveness is mutual; what you do for the other should be joyfully returned by the other.

Supportiveness also means being there when your partner or other family members are struggling with concerns, anxieties, uncertainties, or making decisions. Rather than imposing your own ideas of how things should be resolved, supportiveness means engaging in open discussion, really listening to the other. Families who talk openly about what's important to them as a family unit learn how to make decisions that can be accepted and supported by every member. No family member ever needs to feel that he or she is alone; there should always be someone in the family ready to listen.

Interest

The more interested you are in the other person, the more likely it is that the other will be interested in you. But be sure that this is a real interest in the other, and not a face or a front. Developing shared interests—learning new skills or hobbies together, learning to appreciate new music, or even something as simple as going to the movies once a week to share the experience together—may help two people learn about each other's likes and dislikes, values and interests, emotions and motivations. In the process, each of you is likely to become a more interesting person, which contributes further to enhancing your communication.

Children and pets may be joint interests that partners come to experience as a couple. In some cases, as parents share child-rearing and its accompanying joys and problems, they grow closer as a couple. At least, that's the common wisdom, and often why couples choose to have a baby—to bring the couple closer together. However, long-term studies in Western countries show that a couple's happiness can begin to slip away with the birth of their first child and continue downward through the child's 14th year (Pruett & Pruett, 2009). Through the experience of raising children, couples come to know each other better because they see each other in a new set of circumstances—for better or for worse.

Truthfulness

Honesty and truthfulness do not mean revealing every thought and desire you may have; everyone has a right to some privacy. As already stressed, in any decision concerning self-disclosure, the possible effects on the relationship should be considered (see Chapter 3). Total self-disclosure, in fact, may not be effective or appropriate (Noller & Fitzpatrick, 1993). Ethical issues should also be considered—specifically, the other person's right to know about behaviours and thoughts that might influence the choices he or she will make.

The truthful sharing of feelings helps a great deal in enabling each person to empathize with the other; each comes to understand the other's point of view better when some level of self-disclosures are made. Truthfulness, as a quality of effective relationship communication, means that what you do reveal will be an honest reflection of what you feel rather than an attempt to manipulate your partner's feelings to achieve a particular or perhaps selfish goal.

Involvement

Involvement means active participation in the relationship. Simply being there or going through the motions isn't sufficient. Relationship involvement calls for active sharing in the other person's life (although not to the point of intrusion) and in the other person's goals. It includes active nurturing of the relationship—taking responsibility for its maintenance, satisfaction, and growth. As discussed in Chapter 10 on conflict resolution, withdrawal and silence are generally unfair conflict strategies. In contrast, actively listening to the other's complaints, searching for solutions to problems and differences, and working to incorporate these solutions into your everyday lives are all part of relationship involvement.

Value

When you fall in love or develop a close friendship, you probably do so because you see value and worth in the other person. You're attracted to this person because of some inner qualities you feel this person has. Sometimes this sense of appreciation is lost over the years and you may eventually come to take the other person for granted or wonder why you were so attracted initially—situations that can seriously damage an interpersonal relationship. So it's often helpful to renew and review your reasons for establishing the relationship in the first place and perhaps to focus on the values that originally brought you together. Very likely these qualities haven't changed; what may have changed instead is that they're no longer as salient as they once were. Your task is to bring these values, along with new values, to the forefront again and learn to appreciate them anew.

Equity

Equity entails sharing power and decision making in conflict resolution, as well as in any significant relationship undertaking. **Equity theory** holds that you develop and maintain relationships in which your "cost–benefit ratio" is approximately equal to the other's (Messick & Cook, 1983; Walster et al., 1978). An equitable relationship is one in which each party derives rewards that are proportional to what he or she gives. If you contribute more to the relationship than the other, then equity requires that you get greater rewards. If you each work equally hard, then equity demands that you each get approximately equal rewards. Conversely, inequity exists in a relationship if you give more (for example, if you do more of the unpleasant tasks) but the other enjoys more of the rewards. Inequity also exists if you and the other work equally hard but one of you gets more of the rewards.

Be very careful here, though, as equity issues are often ones of perception. There are some interesting popular surveys, for example, which suggest that husbands think they're contributing more to household maintenance (chores, cleaning, cooking, and so on) than their wives give them credit for. What this says is that partners, in friendships or in families, need to be able to openly discuss what their expectations are of the other and how they're feeling. Perceptions need to be carefully handled; it's possible that they aren't based on what's really happening but are nonetheless strongly held. It's possible that the discussion may be less about what's actually happening than how one partner is feeling.

Can you explain the POSITIVE approach to improving communication effectiveness in relationships? How might you use these suggestions in a current relationship?

CANADIAN PROFILE: WRAP-UP

Chris Hadfield made excellent use of both social media and music to connect with Canadians. Did you become connected in any way to Hadfield and to space as a result of his efforts? How have you used social media to build interpersonal relationships? Have you ever felt a connection with another as a result of music or other forms of artistic communication?

SUMMARY OF CONCEPTS AND SKILLS

This chapter explored the advantages and disadvantages of relationships; the dark side of relationships, including jealousy, bullying, and violence; changing family structures, the characteristics of families, and the impact of culture, gender, and technology on families; and the POSITIVE approach to relationship communication.

Advantages and Disadvantages of Interpersonal Relationships

1. Interpersonal relationships have both advantages and disadvantages. Among the advantages are that they stimulate you, help you learn about yourself,

and generally enhance your self-esteem. Among the disadvantages are that they require you to expose your vulnerabilities, make demands on your time, and may cause you to abandon other relationships.

Cultural Influences on Interpersonal Relationships

2. Cultural factors have an important influence on the formation of relationships, on the roles assigned to men and women, and on the acceptance of same-sex relationships.

Influences of Technology on Interpersonal Relationships

3. Although online communication is used intensively for interpersonal relationships, the quality of these relationships seems to depend on whether they're used to enhance or to replace face-to-face relationships.

The Dark Side of Interpersonal Relationships

4. Jealousy is a feeling that a relationship is in danger due to some rival and may be cognitive, emotional, and/or behavioural.
5. Bullying consists of abusive acts repeatedly committed by one person or group against another; cyberbullying is becoming an increasingly worrying trend, especially among teens and young adults.
6. Relationship violence may be verbal, physical, sexual, and/or economic.

Relationship Types

7. Friendship is an interpersonal relationship between two people; it is mutually productive and characterized by mutual positive regard. Our relationship to friends, like our relationship with family, is influenced by our culture, our gender, and our technological landscape.
8. Family relationships are those existing between two or more people who have defined roles, recognize their responsibilities to one another, have a shared history and a prospect of a shared future, and interact with a shared system of communication rules.

A POSITIVE Approach to Improving Relationship Communication

9. A communication enhancement approach to relationship effectiveness can be spelled out with the acronym POSITIVE: positiveness, openness, supportiveness, interest, truth, involvement, value, and equity.

This chapter also considered a variety of skills. As you review these skills, check those you wish to work on.

_____1. *Advantages and disadvantages of relationships.* Be willing to carefully explore all of your relationships, current and future, in light of both advantages and disadvantages and consider how to effectively manage these.

_____2. *Jealousy.* Recognize the generally unproductive nature of jealousy and seek ways to manage it.

_____3. *Bullying.* Become aware of the tactics of bullies and ways to combat them. Review your own actions to ensure that you don't become a bully.

_____4. *Violence in relationships.* Become sensitive to the development of violence in a relationship and learn ways to deal with this problem, should it arise.

_____5. *The POSITIVE approach to relationship communication.* Understand and practise strategies that support positive and supportive interpersonal relationships.

VOCABULARY QUIZ: The Language of Interpersonal Relationships

Match the following terms of interpersonal relationships with their definitions. Record the number of the definition next to the appropriate term.

_____ relationship communication (188)
_____ envy (194)
_____ jealousy (194)
_____ bullying (195)
_____ equity (207)

1. The feeling of being inferior to or of lesser importance than someone else.
2. Abusive acts repeatedly committed by one person (or group) against another.
3. Communication between or among intimates or those in close relationships.
4. The sharing of power and decision making in a relationship.
5. A form of anger when we feel our relationship is in danger from a rival.

These five terms can be found in the glossary.

CHAPTER

10

Interpersonal Communication and Conflict

CANADIAN PROFILE: Roméo Dallaire

Patrick Doyle/CP Images

As Canadians, we have long prided ourselves on the role of our international peacekeeping troops. More recently, we've also become aware of the impact of war on members of our Canadian Armed Forces when they participate as active battle troops. One of the most well-known Canadian soldiers is Roméo Dallaire, a retired lieutenant-general, retired senator, and celebrated humanitarian.

In 1993, Dallaire was appointed force commander for the United Nations Assistance Mission for Rwanda, where he witnessed the country descend into chaos and genocide, leading to the deaths of more than 800 000

Rwandans in less than 100 days. Since his retirement from the Armed Forces, Dallaire has spoken openly about his complete sense of disempowerment and inability to call the world into action in Rwanda. He has also spoken openly about his post-traumatic stress disorder (PTSD), which has made the past 20 years of his life a struggle. He has addressed his own personal demons by becoming an outspoken advocate for human rights, genocide prevention, mental health, and war-affected children.

Dallaire founded the Roméo Dallaire Child Soldiers Initiative, an organization committed to ending the use of child soldiers worldwide. He is a powerful advocate for human rights, particularly for war-affected children, women, First Nations, and military veterans. Roméo Dallaire has also written two bestselling books: *Shake Hands with the Devil: The Failure of Humanity in Rwanda* (which was made into the movie *Hotel Rwanda*) and *They Fight Like Soldiers; They Die Like Children: The Global Quest to Eradicate the Use of Child Soldiers*.

As you work through this chapter, think about the role of communication in either accelerating or reducing conflict. How well do you think you use communication skills in resolving conflict? Do you see a role in addressing conflict peacefully using communication?

LEARNING OBJECTIVES *After reading this chapter, you should be able to:*

1. Define *interpersonal conflict* and identify some popular myths about conflict.

2. Explain the characteristics of interpersonal conflict.

3. Describe different approaches to resolving conflict, identify your strengths, and discuss how you might use these in resolving interpersonal conflicts.

4. Define and distinguish between the ways to manage conflict: avoiding versus confronting conflict, defensiveness versus supportiveness, face-attacking versus face-enhancing, and verbal aggressiveness versus argumentativeness.

The profile of Roméo Dallaire provides one example of conflict taken to an extreme. While the vast majority of conflicts fortunately don't reach that extreme, each of us encounters conflict at some level almost daily. Often, conflict is a matter of a misunderstanding or a difference of opinion that can be readily addressed. However, because we work and live together, we all need to improve our skills in reducing and resolving conflict.

Therefore, among the most important of all your interpersonal interactions are those involving conflict. Interpersonal conflict can create uncertainty, anxiety, and problems for any relationship, but it also provides opportunities for improving and strengthening a relationship. Understanding interpersonal conflict and mastering skills to reduce and resolve conflict—the subject of this chapter—will prove immensely effective in making your own interpersonal interactions more satisfying and more productive.

WHAT IS INTERPERSONAL CONFLICT?

Interpersonal conflict is disagreement between or among connected individuals—co-workers, close friends, partners, or family members. The word *connected* emphasizes the transactional nature of interpersonal conflict—the fact that each person's position affects the other person. The positions in interpersonal conflicts are to some degree both interrelated and incompatible (Cahn & Abigail, 2007; Folger, Poole, & Stutman, 2013; Hocker & Wilmot, 2007). More specifically, interpersonal conflict occurs when people

- *are interdependent* (they're connected in some significant way); what one person does has an effect on the other person.
- *are mutually aware of incompatible goals;* if one person's goal is achieved, then the other person's goal may not be achieved. For example, if one person wants to buy a new car and the other person wants to pay down the mortgage, there is conflict.
- *perceive each other as interfering* with the attainment of their own goals. For example, you may want to study but your roommate may want to party; the attainment of either goal would interfere with the attainment of the other goal.

One of the implications of this concept of interdependency is that the greater the interdependency, (1) the greater the number of issues on which conflict can centre, and

ETHICAL MESSAGES

Libel, Slander, and More

The Canadian Charter of Rights and Freedoms states that everyone has the following fundamental freedoms:

- freedom of conscience and religion
- freedom of thought, belief, opinion, and expression, including freedom of the press and other media of communication
- freedom of peaceful assembly
- freedom of association

However, expressions of thought, belief, and opinion are not always free. Some kinds of speech, for example, are unlawful and unethical. It's generally both illegal and unethical to defame another person—to falsely attack his or her reputation, causing damage. When this attack is done in print or in pictures, it's called *libel*; when done through speech, it's called *slander*.

People are becoming increasingly sensitive to and respectful of cultural differences. Whereas a few decades ago it may have been considered acceptable to use racist, sexist, or homophobic terms in conversation or to tell jokes at the expense of various cultural groups, most Canadians now consider these forms of speech inappropriate. Today most Canadians disapprove of speech demeaning another person because of that person's gender, age, race, nationality, affectional orientation, or religion, and most people avoid speaking in cultural stereotypes—fixed images of groups that promote generally negative pictures.

Ethical Choice Point

At the office water cooler, you join two of your colleagues only to discover that they're exchanging racist jokes. You don't want to criticize them for fear that you'll become unpopular and that these colleagues will make it harder for you to get ahead. At the same time, you don't want to remain silent for fear it would imply that you're accepting of this type of talk. What would you do in this situation?

(2) the greater the impact of the conflict on the individuals and on the relationship. Looked at in this way, it's easy to appreciate how important understanding interpersonal conflict and the strategies of effective conflict management are to your life with others.

Myths About Conflict

Many people have problems dealing with conflict because they hold false assumptions about what conflict is and what it means. Think about your own assumptions of interpersonal and small group conflict; these were probably derived from the communications you witnessed in your family and in your social interactions. For example, do you think the following are true or false?

- Conflict is best avoided. Time will solve the problem; it will all blow over.
- If two people experience relationship conflict, it means their relationship is in trouble.
- Conflict damages an interpersonal relationship.
- Conflict is destructive because it reveals our negative selves—our pettiness, our need to be in control, our unreasonable expectations.
- In any conflict, there has to be a winner and a loser. Because goals are incompatible, someone has to win and someone has to lose.

These are myths and, as we'll see in this chapter, they can interfere with your ability to deal with conflict effectively. Some methods of approaching conflict can resolve difficulties and differences and can actually improve a relationship. Other reactions to conflict can hurt the relationship; they can destroy self-esteem, create bitterness, and foster suspicion. Conflict doesn't mean that someone has to lose and someone has to win; both parties can win. Your task, therefore, is not to try to create relationships that will be free of conflict but rather to learn appropriate and productive ways of managing conflict so that neither person can be considered a loser.

Can you define *interpersonal conflict* and identify the popular myths about conflict?

CHARACTERISTICS OF INTERPERSONAL CONFLICT

Interpersonal conflict is a process that is complex and often difficult to understand. The following characteristics will help you better understand how interpersonal conflict works:

- Conflict is inevitable—you can't avoid it but you can reduce it.
- Conflict can centre on content and/or relationship issues.
- Conflict can have positive as well as negative effects.
- Conflict is heavily influenced by gender, culture, and technology.
- The styles of conflict you use will have significant effects on your relationship.

Conflict Is Inevitable

Conflict is part of every interpersonal relationship, between parents and children, brothers and sisters, friends, partners, and co-workers. In fact, one study found that people have approximately seven conflicts per week at work, school, or home (Benoit & Benoit, 1990).

The very fact that people are different, have had different histories, and have different goals will invariably produce differences. If the individuals are interdependent, as discussed above, these differences may well lead to conflicts and, if so, they can focus on a wide variety of issues and be extremely personal. Of course, some people have greater tolerance for disagreement and are more likely to let things slide and not become

WavebreakMediaMicro/Fotolia

How might conflict at work or school differ from conflict at home or with family members?

emotionally upset or hostile than are those with little tolerance for disagreement (Teven, Richmond, & McCroskey, 1998; Wrench, McCroskey, & Richmond, 2008). Others have developed techniques for deflating potential conflicts.

Conflict Can Centre on Content and/or Relationship Issues

Using concepts developed in Chapter 1, we can distinguish between *content conflict* and *relationship conflict*. Content conflict centres on objects, events, and persons in the world that are usually, though not always, external to the parties involved in the conflict. Content conflicts have to do with the millions of issues about which we disagree and argue every day—the merit of a particular movie, what to watch on television, the fairness of the last exam or job promotion, the way to spend our savings.

Relationship conflicts are equally numerous and include clashes between, for example, a younger brother who refuses to listen to his older brother when their parents are out, two partners who want to go to different vacation locations, or a mother and daughter who each want to have the final word concerning the daughter's lifestyle. Here the conflicts are concerned not so much with some external object as with the relationships between the individuals—with such issues as who is in charge, how equal the members in a family relationship are, or who has the right to set down rules of behaviour.

Content and relationship dimensions are always easier to separate in a textbook than they are in real life, in which many conflicts contain elements of both. For example, you can probably imagine both content and relationship dimensions in each of the content issues mentioned earlier. Yet certain issues seem oriented more toward one dimension than the other. For example, differences on political and social issues are largely content focused, whereas intimacy and power issues are largely relational.

In the workplace, conflicts also centre on both content and relationship issues. As you can appreciate, conflict is an especially important issue in the workplace because of its many potential negative effects such as personnel leaving the job (necessitating new recruitment and retraining), low morale, and decreasing desire to perform at top efficiency. Workplace conflicts, according to one study, centre on such issues as the following, a clear mix of both content and relationship issues (Psychometrics, 2010):

- personality differences and resulting clashes (86 percent)
- ineffective leadership (73 percent)
- lack of openness (67 percent)
- physical and emotional stress (64 percent)
- differences in values and resulting clashes (59 percent)

Chapter 11 focuses on many aspects of workplace communication.

Conflict Can Be Negative or Positive

Although interpersonal conflict is always stressful, it's important to recognize that it has both negative and positive aspects.

INTERPERSONAL CHOICE POINT

Escalating to Relationship Conflict

Your own interpersonal conflicts often seem to start out as content conflicts but then somehow degenerate into relationship conflicts. You want to find ways to keep your arguments and the eventual resolutions focused on the content. What are some things you can say to prevent this move to relationship conflict?

NEGATIVE ASPECTS OF INTERPERSONAL CONFLICT   Conflict often leads to increased negative regard for the other. One reason for this is that many conflicts involve unfair methods and are focused largely on hurting the other person. When one person hurts the other, increased negative feelings are inevitable; even the strongest relationship has limits.

At times, too, conflict may lead you to close yourself off from the other person. When you hide your true self from another, you prevent meaningful communication from taking place. Because the need for openness and closeness is so strong, one or both parties may then seek this closeness elsewhere. This often leads to further conflict, mutual hurt, and resentment—qualities that add heavily to the costs carried by the relationship. Meanwhile, rewards may become difficult to exchange. In this situation, the costs increase and the rewards decrease, which may result in the relationship deteriorating and even dissolving.

POSITIVE ASPECTS OF INTERPERSONAL CONFLICT   The major value of interpersonal conflict is that it forces you to examine a problem and work toward a potential solution. If the participants use productive conflict strategies, the relationship may well emerge from the encounter stronger, healthier, and more satisfying than before. And you may emerge stronger, more confident, and better able to stand up for yourself (Bedford, 1996).

Through conflict and its resolution, we can also stop resentment from increasing and let our needs be known. For example, suppose one partner needs lots of attention when he or she comes home from work but the other partner needs to review and get closure on the day's work. If both partners can appreciate the legitimacy of these needs, then they can find solutions.

Consider, too, that when you try to resolve conflict within an interpersonal relationship, you're saying that the relationship is worth the effort; otherwise, you would walk away from such a conflict. Usually, confronting a conflict indicates commitment and a desire to preserve the relationship.

> **INTERPERSONAL CHOICE POINT**
>
> **Politeness**
> Canadians are known to be polite, and you try to be polite with everyone you meet. However, one of your colleagues argues that, because of the many immigrants coming to Canada from all over the world, politeness is no longer the norm for Canadians. What do you say? Do you agree? If this norm is indeed changing, does it bother you? Why or why not?

Conflict Is Influenced by Culture, Gender, and Technology

As in other areas of interpersonal communication, it helps to view conflict in light of culture, gender, and technology. All three exert powerful influences on how people view and resolve conflicts.

CONFLICT AND CULTURE   Notice how the following three Canadians responded to the question, "What did you learn about culture from your family?"

■ Anna is a member of the Métis nation. Her father is Cree. "When I was a child, the kids would try to get me to fight by calling me a half-breed. 'Make them laugh,' said my father. 'Laughing is stronger than fighting.'"

■ Hadassah is an immigrant to Canada from Israel. Her grandparents were Holocaust survivors who used to say to her, "Always keep one step ahead of those who would hurt you. Outsmart them. Use your head, not your fists, to deal with conflict."

■ Erin's family is of British origin and has been in Canada for several generations. "Conflict? What's that?" she said. "We don't like to even acknowledge that conflict exists."

Many conflicts arise as a result of the cultural orientation of the individuals involved. In collectivist cultures, conflicts are more likely to centre on violations of collective or group norms and values; for example, failing to provide for family members or publicly disagreeing with a superior. Conversely, in individualist cultures, conflicts are more likely to occur when people violate individual norms; for example, not defending a position in the face of disagreement (Ting-Toomey, 1985).

A good example of these cultural differences is a story told by process facilitator Adam Kahane (2007) about his move from Britain to South Africa. During his first months there, if he was lost he would stop someone and, trying to be polite, would come straight to the point. "Excuse me. Can you please tell me how to get to such and such a place?" Every time he did this, the person would look at him with shock. Eventually, an older man helped him understand his social gaffe by looking him straight in the eye and saying, "Hello! How are you?"

Another example comes from a study that asked North American and Chinese students to analyze a conflict episode between a mother and daughter (Goode, 2000). North American students were more likely to decide in favour of either the mother or the daughter—to see one side as right and one side as wrong. The Chinese students, however, were more likely to see the validity of both sides; both mother and daughter were right but both were also wrong. This finding is consistent with the Chinese preference for proverbs that contain a contradiction (for example, "Too modest is half boastful")—and North Americans' reactions to these proverbs as "irritating."

The ways in which members of different cultures express conflict also differ. In Japan, for example, it's especially important that you not embarrass the person with whom you are in conflict, especially if the disagreement occurs in public. This face-saving principle prohibits the use of such strategies as personal rejection or verbal aggressiveness. In North America, men and women, ideally at least, are both expected to express their

---

INTERPERSONAL CHOICE POINT

Cultural Conflict Resolution

You feel that there's often much to be learned from how others settle conflict. However, some new Canadians are demanding that their cultural and religious rules be accommodated within Canadian law, and you feel that these rules conflict with the Charter of Rights and Freedoms. If you were a leader/politician in this situation, what would you need to learn more about in order to consider this demand? What personal beliefs (your own cultural and religious rules, perhaps) would you use to try to understand this situation? Would your personal beliefs create barriers to your understanding or would they assist you?

---

desires and complaints openly and directly. Many Middle Eastern and Pacific Rim cultures, however, would discourage women from such expressions; rather, a more agreeable and submissive posture would be expected.

CONFLICT AND GENDER Not surprisingly, research finds significant gender differences in interpersonal conflict. For example, some research has shown that men are more apt to withdraw from a conflict situation than are women. It's been argued that this may be due to the fact that men become more psychologically and physiologically aroused during conflict (and retain this heightened level of arousal much longer) than do women, and so they may try to distance themselves and withdraw from the conflict to prevent further arousal (Goleman, 1995b; Gottman & Carrere, 1994). Another position would argue that men withdraw because the culture has taught them to avoid conflict, and still another would claim that withdrawal is an expression of power.

This research also shows that women, on the other hand, want to get closer to the conflict; they want to talk about it and resolve it. Even adolescents reveal these differences. In research on boys and girls aged 11 to 17, boys withdrew more than girls (Heasley, Babbitt, & Burbach, 1995; Lindeman, Harakka, & Keltikangas-Jarvinen, 1997). Other research has found that women are more emotional and men are more logical when they argue. Women have been defined as conflict "feelers" and men as conflict "thinkers" (Sorenson, Hawkins, & Sorenson, 1995). Women have also been found to be more apt to reveal their negative feelings than are men (Canary, Cupach, & Messman, 1995; Schaap, Buunk, & Kerkstra, 1988).

It's important to note, however, that other research does not support these gender differences in conflict style. For example, several studies dealing with both post-secondary students and men and women in business found no significant differences in the ways men and women engage in conflict (Canary & Hause, 1993; Gottman & Levenson, 1999;

Wilkins & Andersen, 1991). All of us can cite examples of men wanting to be very clear about situations and clarifying misunderstandings whereas women seem to want to keep relationships intact by moving around or avoiding conflict. As with all aspects of conflict, gender plays a role, but it's not a set role—it depends.

CONFLICT AND TECHNOLOGY   In large part, the same conflicts you experience in face-to-face relationships can also arise in online communication. Yet there are a few issues that may lead to conflict and that seem to be unique to online communication, whether in email, social networking sites such as Facebook, or blog postings. For example:

- hitting "reply all" often fills people's inboxes with unnecessary replies that not everyone needs to see
- sending commercial messages to those who didn't request them
- sending a message to an entire listserv when it's relevant to only one member
- sending unsolicited mail (spamming)
- repeatedly sending the same mail
- posting the same message in lots of newsgroups, especially when the message is irrelevant to the focus of one or more groups
- putting out purposefully incorrect information or outrageous viewpoints to watch other people correct you or get emotionally upset by your message (trolling)
- making and taking cell phone calls at inappropriate times
- calling someone at work just to chat
- criticizing someone unfairly or posting an unflattering photo on social network sites
- cyberbullying (as discussed in Chapter 9), an increasingly alarming form of online conflict.

A major impact of technology is that conflict is not mediated face to face. This can sometimes make it easier for people to say what they feel they need to say to the other. Taking the time to write out your concerns and perspectives allows you to be clearer, more precise, and less emotional. This is especially true if you give yourself time to calm down before sending, for example, an angrily worded email.

On the other hand, the fact that online communication is not face to face can cause harm. Again, it's much easier to say things that you'd never say face to face. It's all too easy to send off a quick text without really thinking about the consequences. In verbal communication, we use body language and tone to determine the emotional state of the other. Because these cues are generally

---

SKILL-BUILDING EXERCISE

Resolving Online Conflicts

Resolving an online conflict can sometimes require different approaches than face-to-face conflicts. Suler (as cited in Munro, 2002) has proposed a series of suggestions for resolving online conflict.

- Don't respond to the post (email, text, and so on) right away.
- Read it again, later, when you're past your initial emotional reaction.
- Discuss the post, in person, with someone you know.
- Choose if you want to respond.
- Assume people mean well.
- Clarify what was meant.
- Think about what you want to accomplish with your communication. Do you want to connect with the person? Do you want to understand them or want to be understood yourself?
- Verbalize what you want to accomplish.
- Use "I" statements, such as "I feel..." rather than "you" statements such as "You made me feel..."
- Use strictly "feeling" statements.
- Place yourself in the other person's shoes.
- Use emoticons to express tone.
- Start and end the post with positive statements.

Which of these suggestions have you used? Were they successful? Why? Which didn't work for you? Why not? Do you have other suggestions to add to the list?

INTERPERSONAL CHOICE POINT

Preventing Conflicts in Social Media

In a variety of social media sites, you can disable comments on a post that might be causing conflict, prevent it from being shared, or remove your post entirely. In what ways might these abilities be applied to face-to-face conflict?

missing in written communication, the communication may be misunderstood or misinterpreted. As with all forms of conflict, the use of technology can be either positive or negative in starting and resolving a conflict.

Suler (as cited in Munro, 2002, n.p.) refers to what he calls the "disinhibition effect" when communicating online. He writes that disinhibition "is a double-edged sword. Sometimes people share very personal things about themselves. They reveal secret emotions, fears, wishes. Or they show unusual acts of kindness and generosity. On the other hand, the disinhibition effect may not be so benign. Out spills rude language and harsh criticisms, anger, hatred, even threats."

Conflict Styles Have Consequences

The way in which you engage in conflict has consequences for the resolution of the conflict and for the relationship between the conflicting parties. Here we consider five basic styles (Blake & Mouton, 1985), as summarized in Figure 10.1. As you read through these styles, try to identify your own conflict style as well as the styles of those with whom you have close relationships.

COMPETING: I WIN, YOU LOSE   The competitive conflict style involves thinking more about my own needs and desires and little about yours. As long as my needs are met, the conflict has been dealt with successfully (for me). In conflict motivated by competitiveness, I'm likely to be verbally aggressive and to blame you.

This style represents an *I win, you lose* philosophy. This style might be appropriate in a courtroom or at a used car lot, two settings where one person benefits from the other person's losses. But in interpersonal situations, this philosophy can lead to resentment on the part of the person who loses, which can easily cause additional conflicts. Further, the fact that I win and you lose probably means that the conflict hasn't really been resolved but only concluded (for now).

AVOIDING: I LOSE, YOU LOSE   In avoiding conflict, I am relatively unconcerned with my own or with your needs or desires. I avoid any real communication about the problem, change the subject when the problem is brought up, and generally withdraw from the scene both psychologically and physically.

The avoiding style does little to resolve any conflicts and may be viewed as an *I lose, you lose* philosophy. Interpersonal problems rarely go away of their own accord; rather, they need to be faced and dealt with effectively. Avoidance merely allows the conflict to fester and probably grow, only to resurface in another guise.

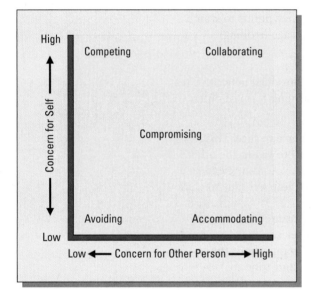

FIGURE 10.1

The Five Conflict Styles

Source: R. R. Blake & J. S. Mouton, *The Managerial Grid III.* Gulf Publishing Company, 1985. Reprinted by permission of Grid International, Inc.

In the popular cooking show *Chopped*, four chefs attempt to create the winning dish with previously unseen ingredients. The stakes are high and the pressure to perform—under excruciating time constraints and in front of millions of viewers—is intense. There is one goal and only one chef can win. It's a zero-sum game: one wins and three lose. In contrast, the kind of interpersonal conflict we discuss in this text isn't a zero-sum game, in that both parties can win or both can lose. What are you learning about how you can achieve win-win outcomes?

Generating Win–Win Solutions

To get into the habit of looking for win–win solutions, consider the following conflict situations. For each situation, generate as many win–win solutions as you can—solutions in which both people win. After you complete your list, explain what you see as the major advantages of win–win solutions.

1. For their vacation, Pat wants to go to the shore and relax by the water; Chris wants to go hiking and camping in the mountains.
2. Pat hangs around the house in underwear. Chris really hates this and they argue about it almost daily.
3. Pat wants to pool their income whereas Chris wants to keep each person's income and savings separate.
4. Pat wants Chris to commit to their relationship and move in together. Chris wants to wait to make sure that this is the right thing.

Win–win solutions exist for most conflict situations (though not necessarily all); with a little effort, win–win solutions can be identified for most interpersonal conflicts.

ACCOMMODATING: I LOSE, YOU WIN   In accommodating, I sacrifice my needs for your needs. My major purpose is to maintain harmony and peace in the relationship or group. This style may help maintain peace and may satisfy the opposition, but it does little to meet my own needs, which are unlikely to go away.

Accommodation represents an *I lose, you win* philosophy. And although this conflict style may make you happy (at least on this occasion), it's not likely to prove a lasting resolution to an interpersonal conflict. I'll eventually sense unfairness and inequality and may easily come to resent you and perhaps even myself.

COLLABORATING: I WIN, YOU WIN   In collaborating, I address both my own and your needs. This conflict style, often considered the ideal, takes time and a willingness to communicate—and especially to listen to your perspectives and needs.

Ideally, collaboration enables each person's needs to be met, an *I win, you win* situation. This is obviously the style that, in an ideal world, most people would choose for interpersonal conflict.

COMPROMISING: I WIN AND LOSE, YOU WIN AND LOSE   The compromising style is in the middle: there's some concern for my own needs and some concern for your needs. Compromise is the kind of strategy that might be referred to as "meeting each other halfway" or "give and take." This strategy is likely to result in maintaining peace, but there will be a residue of dissatisfaction over the inevitable losses that each side has to accept.

Compromise represents an *I win and lose, you win and lose* philosophy. There are lots of times when we can't both get exactly what we want. We can't both get a new car if the available funds allow for only one. And yet we might each get a better used car than the one we now have. So, each of us might win something, though not everything.

Can you explain the characteristics of interpersonal conflict (that it's inevitable; can centre on content and/or relationship issues; can be positive or negative; is influenced by culture, gender, and technology; and that conflict styles have consequences)?

WAYS TO MANAGE CONFLICT

Since many factors will influence how you deal with conflict (Koerner & Fitzpatrick, 2002), understanding these factors may help you select more effective strategies to manage conflict with success.

Wavebreakmedia ltd/Shutterstock

VIEWPOINTS Social Network Conflicts

How would you compare interpersonal conflicts that occur in face-to-face encounters and online? Are the issues argued about the same? Are the strategies for resolving the conflict the same?

- The *goals* (short-term and long-term) you wish to achieve. Depending on the situation (for example, a casual friendship or a temporary connection), you may want to simply give in and ignore the difficulty. On the other hand, if you want to build a long-term relationship, you may want to fully analyze the cause of the problem and choose cooperative strategies.
- Your *emotional state*. When you're sorry, you're likely to use conciliatory strategies designed to make peace; when you're angry, you're more likely to use strategies that express this anger, perhaps by lashing out at the other person. If you're frightened, you may do your best to avoid either creating or addressing a conflict; if tired, you may actually escalate a conflict.
- Your *assessment* of the situation. For example, your attitudes and beliefs about what is fair and equitable will influence your readiness to acknowledge the fairness in the other person's position. Your own assessment of who (if anyone) is the cause of the problem will also influence how you consider the conflict.
- Your *personality and communication competence*. If you're shy and unassertive, you may want to avoid a conflict rather than confronting it. If you're extroverted and have a strong desire to state your position, you may be more likely to be confrontational and argue forcefully.
- Your *family history*. If your parents argued about money or gave each other the silent treatment when conflict arose, you're likely to repeat these patterns yourself if you aren't mindful of your conflict orientation.

Before examining the various conflict-management strategies, take the following self-test and examine your own resolution behaviours.

TEST YOURSELF

Conflict Resolution Strengths

Conflict resolution strengths identifies 11 conflict resolution behaviours. In order to be able to practise these behaviours consistently, you need to know how well you can do each of them. Once you know how well (or whether) you practise each one, you'll understand your conflict resolution strengths and be able to explore how to become even more effective at peacefully resolving conflicts.

Step 1: Take the Conflict Resolution Survey.

Try to recall the typical interactions you have with a particular person when the two of you disagree. Use the survey below to improve your conflict resolution skills by indicating how you behave with the person you have identified. The more honest you can be on the survey, the more valuable it will be to you. Use the following scale to respond: 5 = almost always, 4 = often, 3 = sometimes, 2 = infrequently, 1 = rarely, and 0 = never.

_____ 1. When I disagree, I'm honest about the fact that I disagree and why.

_____ 2. When proven wrong, I admit it rather than deny it or try to cover my tracks.

_____ 3. In verbal exchanges I let the other person talk first; I don't have to get in my two cents' worth before he or she speaks.

_____ 4. Before I respond to the other person's assertions, I ask questions or attempt to paraphrase his or her points to make certain I understand what was said.

_____ 5. I stay calm and rational, being careful not to engage in name-calling or to say anything I'll regret later.

_____ 6. When I do allow myself to get angry, I talk about that anger rather than what the person did to elicit it.

TEST YOURSELF (continued)

_____ 7. I'm careful to direct my attacks at issues, not people. I address the other's claims without condemning him or her for making them.

_____ 8. Even if I disagree with the person's assertions, I recognize the validity of his or her feelings.

_____ 9. I direct our attention to *fixing the future* rather than rehashing the past.

_____10. I keep the focus on our potentially disparate needs, *not our opposing positions*, so that we can search for creative ways to meet both sets of needs and reach a common ground.

_____11. I use *we, us,* and *our,* rather than *I, me,* and *you,* when discussing the issue.

Step 2: Circle All Scores Below a 4.

Are these items more a reflection of your relationship with this particular person or more a reflection of your personal conflict resolution style? One way to answer this question is to complete the survey for other people in your life with whom you have disagreements. Note which items tend to be scored differently (a reflection of the specific relationship) and which items are scored the same. What do these scores suggest you do differently the next time you come into conflict with this person or someone else?

Step 3: Choose How to Become Even Better at Conflict Resolution.

These recommendations that might improve your problem-solving skills are matched by number to the items in the survey.

1. Honesty. When you disagree with someone, what is the trigger that brings your disagreement into discussion? Is it because you say something like "We have a problem"? Or does the discussion begin only after the other person calls you on your different behaviour or attitude? Do you admit your disagreement or do you sulk? When you have something to say but choose not to, you engage in a form of passive-aggressive behaviour. You're being unfair to the other person, to your team, and to yourself.

2. "I was wrong." Unfortunately, many people believe that admitting error is a sign of weakness that will compromise their position in a disagreement. Quite the opposite is true. When you admit to having been wrong about something, you're in the best position to ask other people to reciprocate in some way. Admitting wrong also happens to be the right thing to do.

3. Speak second. In an argument, there are at least four reasons why you should let the other speak while you listen. First, letting other people "get it all out" will help to calm them down and defuse their

anger. Second, your willingness to wait is a sign of respect. Third, by listening carefully (open listening) to their assertions, you'll gain clues to what the basis of the conflict might actually be (such as a misunderstanding or different values). Finally, only after others have emptied themselves of their ideas, emotions, and anger are they likely to pay much attention to yours (active listening).

4. Make sure you understand. The single greatest cause of interpersonal conflict is little more than misunderstanding. Don't take a chance that miscommunication is at the root of a disagreement you have with someone. Ask clarifying questions and listen with empathy. When possible, encourage the playing of the "paraphrasing game." The first person starts by stating his or her position. The second person must paraphrase to the first person's satisfaction what he or she just said before earning the right to respond. Continue the entire conversation in this manner, with permission to talk always tied to a successful paraphrase. You'll be amazed at the results.

5. Bite your tongue and think before you speak. A number of years ago, 100 people aged 95 and older were asked the question "If you could live your life over again, what would you do differently?" The most frequent response was that, in many situations, they should have taken the time to think more carefully before they spoke.

6. Talk about your anger. Much of the advice in this survey is intended to limit your anger. However, if you do lose your temper, try to talk about why. Describe your emotions, your pain, your fear. Only when you've vented completely should you then talk about the incident you became angry about. Don't talk about what the person did to make you angry—remember that people don't have the ability to make you angry without your full cooperation.

7. Focus on the issue, not the person. Attack issues with full force while letting people escape unscathed. This is especially important with children—remember that the child's behaviour is what angers you, never the child. Pinpoint the behaviour or the issue and state what your needs are in regard to it.

8. Allow for feelings. All feelings are valid and part of human nature. We should avoid saying something like "You have no right to feel that way." Some people have a powerful need to discuss their feelings as a prelude to resolving the conflict into which those feelings are woven. Give them every opportunity to

do that even if you don't share that need. You'll increase your chances for a win–win outcome.

9. Fix the future. Why do we seek to resolve conflict? To prevent more of the same in the future. The ideal position to take is described by the question "What can we do to keep this from happening again?" At some point two people in conflict need to stop talking about the behaviour that has contributed to the clash, and even to stop talking about the feelings that have resulted. One trick for getting both of you on track to a solution is to invoke the 30-minute rule. It works like this: "Let's agree that for the rest of this discussion neither one of us will talk about anything that happened more than a half hour ago."

10. Meet needs; don't take positions. Two people in a disagreement often take opposite positions on an issue. As the debate flares, they harden their stances. This approach leaves little in the way of resolution possibilities other than compromise. A fragile peace is won only after both sides are willing to retreat from their positions to a middle ground that neither side likes but both realize they must accept. A more satisfying outcome for both parties is possible when they define their differences in terms of needs rather than positions. When each person has the opportunity to say "This is what I want to accomplish by taking this position" or "These are the values and beliefs I have that lead me to this conclusion," then you can engage in problem solving.

11. Favour cooperative pronouns. Pronouns like *I, me,* and *mine* represent the language of a position taker. Pronouns like *we, our,* and *us* encourage collaboration and mutual problem solving.

How Did You Do? What did you learn about your own conflict resolution style when you completed the survey the first time? Did any of your scores change when you completed the survey for other people in your life with whom you have disagreements? What do you think that tells you about your conflict resolution behaviours?

What Will You Do? What changes would you like to see in how you manage conflict? Which of the 11 conflict resolution behaviours do you think you could reasonably adopt and make your own? Why did you choose the ones you chose?

Source: Power tools: 33 management inventions you can use today by Deep, Samuel D.; Sussman, Lyle Reproduced with permission of Addison-Wesley in the format Republish in a book via Copyright Clearance Center.

Avoidance Versus Confronting Conflict

Psychologists talk about three ways of dealing with extreme distress or trauma: fight, flight, or dissociation. Conflict **avoidance** may involve actual physical flight: you may leave the scene of the conflict (walk out of the apartment or go to another part of the school or shop), fall asleep, or blast the stereo to drown out all conversation. It may also take the form of emotional or intellectual avoidance, in which you may leave the conflict psychologically by not dealing with any of the arguments or problems raised (dissociation). In this case, you may view the conflict as a bystander, from outside of yourself.

Nonnegotiation is a special type of avoidance. Here you refuse to discuss the conflict or to listen to the other person's argument. At times, nonnegotiation takes the form of hammering away at your own point of view until the other person gives in—this is called *steamrolling*.

Another form of avoidance is **gunnysacking**. A gunnysack is a large bag, usually made of burlap. As a conflict strategy, gunnysacking is the unproductive practice of storing up grievances so as to unload them at another time (Bach & Wyden, 1968). The immediate occasion for unloading may be relatively simple (or so it may seem at first); for example, you come home late one night without calling. Instead of arguing about this, the gunnysacker pours out all past grievances: the birthday you forgot, the time you arrived late for dinner, the hotel reservations you forgot to make. As you probably know from experience, gunnysacking often begets gunnysacking. When one person unloads the gunnysack, the other person starts to unload his/her own gunnysack.

The result is that we have two people dumping their stored-up grievances on each other. Frequently the trigger problem never gets addressed. Instead, resentment and hostility escalate.

Instead of avoiding the issues, consider some of these ideas:

- *Take an active role* in your interpersonal conflicts and involve yourself actively as both speaker and listener. Turn off the phone, television, or computer; face the other person. Devote your total attention to the other person. However, many parents talk about how addressing conflict with their teenager is often more successful when they raise the issue in the car or when watching a movie together. It seems that sometimes not facing the person but instead sitting side by side can be less threatening and provide space for open expression of thoughts and feelings.
- *Voice your feelings and listen carefully* to the voicing of the other person's feelings. When appropriate, consider taking a time-out. Be careful to keep these feelings between the two of you; avoid writing on the person's Facebook wall, for example, and thus airing the conflict for your entire network to read.
- *Own your thoughts and feelings*. For example, when you disagree with your partner or find fault with her or his behaviour, take responsibility for these feelings, saying, for example, "I disagree with…" or "I don't like it when you…" Avoid statements that deny your responsibility; for example, "Everybody thinks you're wrong about…" or "Chris thinks you shouldn't…"
- *Focus on the present*, on the here and now, rather than on an issue that occurred two months ago.
- *Focus your conflict on the behaviour or concerns of the person* with whom you're fighting, not on the person's mother, child, or friends.
- *Express your support, empathy, and agreement.* When you show that you're trying to understand and respect the other's feelings and needs, you're opening the door to a win–win solution. " I know you're feeling overwhelmed with school, work, and the baby. How can I help?"

DEVELOPING LANGUAGE AND COMMUNICATION SKILLS

Positive, Tolerable, and Toxic Stress

We can't avoid stress in our lives. In fact, some types are considered *positive stress*, such as when we meet new people or start college, university, or a new job; we can benefit from these experiences by learning new skills and building our confidence. What's known as *tolerable stress* is more serious, such as when we experience a car accident or an illness; however, if we have caring people around to support us, we can cope. *Toxic stress* is severe, chronic, and ongoing, such as abuse or neglect, and isn't mediated by caring others. Toxic stress in early childhood is actually built into the structure of the developing brain, weakening it and causing lifelong issues such as poor health and difficulties in school and at work. Conflict, like stress, is often unavoidable, but if we develop ways to mediate conflict and treat one another respectfully, it doesn't need to become toxic. If you'd like to learn more, go to http://developingchild.harvard.edu and look for the "Toxic Stress" section.

Force Versus Talk

When confronted with conflict, many people would rather not deal with the issue but instead force their position on the other person. The force may be emotional (for example, compelling a partner to give in by provoking feelings of guilt or sympathy) or physical. In either case, the issues are avoided; the person who "wins" is the one who exerts the most force. This is the technique of warring nations, quarrelling children, and even some normally sensible and mature adults. The only real alternative to force is talking and listening openly, reflectively, and with empathy and respect.

Defensiveness Versus Supportiveness

Unfortunately, not all talk is equally productive in conflict resolution. One of the best ways to look at destructive versus productive talk is to look at how the style of your communications can create unproductive **defensiveness** (characterized by threats, fear, or domination) or a productive sense of **supportiveness** (characterized by openness, absence of fear, and a genuine feeling of equality) (Gibb, 1961). The type of talk that generally proves destructive and sets up defensive reactions in the listener is talk that is evaluative, controlling, strategic, indifferent or neutral, superior, and certain.

EVALUATION   When you evaluate or judge another person or what that person has done, that person is likely to become resentful and defensive and perhaps to respond by being equally evaluative and judgmental. In contrast, when you describe how you feel or what you want, you generally don't create defensiveness and may be seen as supportive. The distinction between **evaluation** and description can be seen in the differences between you-messages and I-messages.

Evaluative You-Messages	**Descriptive I-Messages**
You never reveal your feelings.	I'd like to hear how you feel about this.
You just don't plan ahead.	I need to know what our schedule for the next few days will be.
You never call me.	I'd enjoy hearing from you more often.

If you put yourself in the role of the listener hearing these statements, you'll probably be able to feel the resentment or defensiveness that the evaluative messages (you-messages) would create and the supportiveness from the descriptive messages (I-messages).

CONTROL   When you try to control the behaviour of the other person, when you order the other person to do this or that, or when you make decisions without mutual discussion

---

Responding to Confrontations

Sometimes you'll be confronted with an argument that you can't ignore and that you must respond to in some way. Here are a few examples of confrontations. For each statement below, write a response in which you (a) let the person know that you're open to her or his point of view and that you view this perspective as useful information (listening openly), (b) show that you understand both the thoughts and the feelings that go with the confrontation (listening with empathy), and (c) ask the person what he or she would like you to do about it.

1. You're calling these meetings much too often and much too early to suit us. We'd like fewer meetings scheduled for later in the day.

2. There's a good reason why I don't say anything—you never listen to me anyway.

3. I'm tired of having all the responsibility for the kids—volunteering at their school, driving to soccer practice, checking homework, making lunch.

Confrontations can give you valuable feedback that will help you improve; if responded to appropriately, confrontations can actually improve your relationship.

and agreement, defensiveness is a likely response. Control messages deny the legitimacy of the person's contributions and in fact deny his or her importance. They say, in effect, "You don't count; your contributions are meaningless." In other words, you're not seeing the other as a fellow human. When, on the other hand, you focus on the problem at hand—not on controlling the situation or getting your own way—defensiveness is much less likely. This problem orientation invites mutual participation and recognizes the significance of each person's contributions.

MANIPULATION   When you try to get around other people or situations using manipulation—especially when you conceal your true purposes—others are likely to feel resentful and respond defensively. But when you act openly and with spontaneity, you're more likely to create an atmosphere that is equal and honest.

NEUTRALITY   When you demonstrate **neutrality**—seeming to show a lack of empathy or interest in the thoughts and feelings of the other—it's likely to create defensiveness. Neutrality is especially damaging when partners and family members are in conflict. When, on the other hand, you demonstrate empathy and open listening, defensiveness is unlikely to occur.

SUPERIORITY   When you present yourself as superior to the other person, you're implying that the other is inferior. It's a violation of the implicit equality contract that people in a close relationship have—namely, the assumption that each person is equal.

CERTAINTY   The person who appears to know it all is likely to be resented, so **certainty** often sets up a defensive climate. After all, there is little room for negotiation or mutual problem solving when one person already has the right answer. An attitude of openness— "Let's explore this issue together and try to find a solution"—is likely to be much more productive than closed-mindedness.

Face-Attacking Versus Face-Enhancing Strategies: Politeness in Conflict

In Chapter 3 we introduced the concepts of face and politeness. Face-attacking strategies involve treating the other person as incompetent or untrustworthy, as unable or bad (Donahue & Kolt, 1992). Such attacks can vary from mildly embarrassing to severely damaging to the other's ego or reputation. When such attacks become extreme, they may become verbal aggression and abuse.

One common face-attacking strategy is called **beltlining** (Bach & Wyden, 1968). Like fighters in a ring, each of us has a "beltline." When you hit someone below his or her emotional beltline, you can inflict serious injury. When you hit above the belt, however, the person is able to absorb the blow. With most interpersonal relationships, especially those of long standing, you know where the beltline is and it's your responsibility to never hit below that line. Another face-attacking strategy is **blame**. Instead of focusing on a solution to a problem, some try to affix blame on the other person. Blame is also used when people are unwilling to accept responsibility for their own actions or when they're

DAJ/Amana Images inc./Alamy

VIEWPOINTS The Importance of Saving Face

Cultures vary widely in how important they consider saving face. How important is it to maintain face in a conflict situation in your culture and the cultures with which you're familiar?

unable to respond with empathy. Whether or not blame does in fact belong with the other, it is unproductive; it diverts attention away from the problem and from its potential solution, and it creates resentment that is likely to be responded to with additional resentment.

Face-enhancing techniques involve helping the other maintain a positive self-image—the image of a person who is competent and trustworthy, able and good. Strategies that enhance a person's self-image and acknowledge a person's autonomy will be respectful and likely effective in resolving conflict.

Verbal Aggressiveness Versus Argumentativeness

An especially interesting perspective on conflict has emerged from work on verbal aggressiveness and argumentativeness, concepts developed by communication researchers that have quickly spread to other disciplines such as psychology, education, and management, among others (Infante, Rancer, & Avtgis, 2010; Rancer & Avtgis, 2006). Understanding these two concepts will help you understand some of the reasons why things go wrong and some of the ways in which you can use conflict to improve rather than damage your relationships.

VERBAL AGGRESSIVENESS **Verbal aggressiveness** is an unproductive conflict strategy in which a person tries to win an argument by inflicting psychological pain, attacking the other person's self-concept, and seeking to discredit the individual's view of self (Infante & Wigley, 1986; Rancer & Avtgis, 2006). Atkin et al. (2002) suggest that verbal aggression is widespread in North American society. Further, they suggest that committing and experiencing verbal aggression is reciprocal and that there is a strong relationship between verbal and physical aggression.

ARGUMENTATIVENESS **Argumentativeness** refers to your willingness to argue for a point of view, your tendency to speak your mind on significant issues. It's the mode of dealing with disagreements that is the preferred alternative to verbal aggressiveness.

As you can appreciate, argumentativeness differs greatly from verbal aggressiveness (see Table 10.1). Argumentativeness is constructive; the outcomes are positive in a variety of communication situations (interpersonal, group, organizational, family, and intercultural). Verbal aggressiveness is destructive; the outcomes are negative.

Argumentativeness leads to relationship satisfaction in a family and can enhance relationships in other situations such as work or school. Aggressiveness, on the other hand, leads to relationship dissatisfaction and, in an organization, can demoralize workers on many levels of the hierarchy.

Argumentative individuals are generally seen as having greater credibility; they're considered more trustworthy, committed, and dynamic than their aggressive counterparts. In addition, argumentativeness is likely to increase your power of persuasion and will also increase the likelihood that you'll be seen as a leader.

Warren Goldswain/Shutterstock

VIEWPOINTS **Relationship Violence**

One of the most puzzling findings on relationship violence is that many victims interpret it as a sign of love. For some reason, they see being beaten or verbally abused as a sign that their partner is fully in love with them. Moreover, many victims blame themselves for the violence (Gelles & Cornell, 1985). Why do you think this is so? Does force or violence play a role in conflicts in your own interpersonal relationships?

INTERPERSONAL CHOICE POINT

Talking Aggressively

Your partner is becoming more and more verbally aggressive, and you're having trouble with this new communication pattern. Regardless of what the conflict is about, your partner seems to deliberately attack your sense of self. You want to stop this kind of attack, change this pattern of communication, and preserve the relationship. What are your options for communicating in this situation? What would you say?

TABLE 10.1

DIFFERENCES BETWEEN VERBAL AGGRESSIVENESS AND ARGUMENTATIVENESS

As discussed above, there are numerous differences between argumentativeness and verbal aggressiveness. Here is a brief summary (Infante & Rancer, 1996; Rancer & Atvgis, 2006).

Verbal Aggressiveness	Argumentativeness
Is destructive; the outcomes are negative in a variety of interpersonal communication situations	Is constructive; the outcomes are positive in a variety of interpersonal communication situations
Leads to relationship dissatisfaction, not surprising for a strategy that aims to attack another's self-concept	Leads to relationship satisfaction
May lead to relationship violence	May prevent relationship violence, especially in domestic relationships
Damages organizational life and demoralizes workers on various levels	Enhances organizational life; subordinates prefer supervisors who encourage argumentativeness
Prevents meaningful parent–child communication; makes corporal punishment more likely	Enhances parent–child communication and enables parents to use positive discipline effectively
Decreases the user's credibility, in part because it's seen as a tactic to discredit the opponent rather than address the argument	Increases the user's credibility; the user is seen as trustworthy, committed, and dynamic
Decreases the user's power of persuasion	Increases the user's power of persuasion; the user is more likely to be seen as a leader

ETHICAL MESSAGES

Ethical Conflict

As we've discussed, all communication strategies have an ethical dimension; the same is true for conflict resolution strategies. Think about the following situations:

- Does conflict avoidance have an ethical dimension? For example, can it be unethical for one relationship partner to refuse to discuss disagreements or to walk out of an argument?
- Are face-attacking strategies inherently unethical or might it be appropriate to use them in certain situations?
- What are the ethical implications of verbal aggressiveness?
- Is it ethical to deceive another in order to resolve an interpersonal conflict?
- Can the use of physical force by one person in order to influence another ever be ethical? Do you feel the same when the physical force is used by an adult over

a child? In a broader context, can the use of physical force by one country to compel another country to accept a religious or political orientation be ethical? Do you see a difference between the use of physical force between individuals and between countries? Why or why not?

Ethical Choice Point

Over the past few years, news outlets have been embedding journalists into armed forces in order to provide more immediate and, perhaps, more accurate coverage of a given conflict. Do you think embedded journalists and immediate social media reports of international conflicts affect Canadian perceptions of both the cultures involved and the conflict itself? Given the risks these journalists must take being so close to danger, do you think this is an ethical form of reporting?

Can you define and distinguish among the ways to manage conflict (avoidance versus confronting conflict, defensiveness versus supportiveness, face-attacking versus face-enhancing, and verbal aggressiveness versus argumentativeness)? Which recommendations for managing conflict effectively are strengths for you and which would you like to add to your repertoire?

THREE SPECIFIC APPROACHES TO RESOLVING CONFLICTS

In this section we look at three conflict-resolution approaches that represent Western, Eastern, and global traditions, respectively. As you read about these different approaches, think about your own traditions of conflict resolution, where your strengths lie, and how you might improve your current methods.

Interest-Based Relational (IBR) Approach

The Interest-Based Relational (IBR) approach (Mind Tools, n.d.) is especially useful when there's time to plan how best to mediate a conflict; for example, one that has developed while working on a group project. This type of rational conflict resolution respects individual differences while helping people avoid becoming too entrenched in a fixed position. The goal of this approach is to get to underlying interests, needs, and concerns to find a common solution. IBR follows three guiding principles: be calm, be patient, and be respectful.

- *Ensure that your relationship is the first priority.* As much as possible, stay calm and acknowledge the mutual respect you hold for each other. Do your best to be courteous and keep your comments constructive.
- *Keep people and problems separate.* Recognize that in many cases the other person isn't just being difficult; real and valid differences can lie behind conflicting positions. By separating the problem from the person, issues can be debated without attacking and damaging relationships.
- *Pay attention to the issues being presented by the other person.* By listening carefully you'll most likely understand why the other person feels the way he or she does.
- *Listen first; talk second.* To solve a problem effectively, it's important to understand where the other person is coming from before you begin to defend your own position.
- *Set out the facts of the conflict.* Work together to understand and agree on what the conflict is really about. Try to avoid bringing in extraneous issues that don't pertain to this specific conflict.
- *Explore options together.* Be open to the idea that a third position may exist and that you can get to this idea jointly.

The IBR approach requires the use of active listening and an assertive (as opposed to either an aggressive or submissive) approach; when successful, it will result in a win–win situation. If this approach seems suitable for the conflict situation you're facing, follow these steps:

- *Step 1: Set the scene.* Use active listening skills to hear the other person's concerns, perceptions, and beliefs. Use your skills of restating, paraphrasing, and summarizing what you hear.
- *Step 2: Gather information.* In this step, you're trying to identify what's really causing the conflict in the first place. Use your skills of listening with empathy, using "I" statements, clarifying feelings, and remaining flexible and open.
- *Step 3: Agree on the problem.* This may sound obvious, but sometimes conflicts develop over something entirely different from what's really causing the problem. Use your skills of active listening and avoid common conflict negatives such as downloading (that is, saying what we usually say or what we think we're supposed to say; see Chapter 1) and personal attacks.
- *Step 4: Brainstorm possible solutions.* Consider any number of possible solutions to the conflict, including those you may have tried before or have already discarded. A new conflict may require old solutions or totally new innovative ones. Use your skills of openness to consider all possibilities.
- *Step 5: Negotiate a solution.* This may be easier than you initially thought, and will result in the working out of a win–win solution. Alternatively, this step may show that there are true differences that need to be negotiated; in this case, a compromise solution may be necessary and beneficial.

Negotiating Group Projects

You've likely been assigned many group projects during your career as a student. Teachers reason that because most jobs require that you work with a team, it's important that you learn how to negotiate and complete a project together. The primary benefits of teamwork are encapsulated in the maxims "Two (or more) minds are better than one" and "Many hands make light work." When these maxims hold true, teamwork can be fun, challenging, and rewarding. However, group projects can also be frustrating; you've probably been in at least one group that was dysfunctional, whether because someone didn't complete his or her portion of the project, or personalities clashed, or the group couldn't decide on a single direction. And when group projects are assigned grades, they become very important to each of the members and can cause increased tension.

Chances are you'll be assigned a group project this year. How can you ensure that the project will successful and relatively stress free? One approach is to begin with a group-project charter that outlines the scope and objectives for the project and assigns each person a role and responsibilities (Hicks, 2011). Consider appointing a project manager whose role will be to check in on everyone's progress and keep the group heading in the same direction. Also lay out the groundwork process for successful conflict resolution; after all, in group projects or endeavours of any kind, conflict should be seen as a group problem, not an individual problem (Hicks, 2011).

Have you ever been given a charter by an instructor when assigned a group project? Have you ever completed one as a group? What's important to include in such a charter? Which of the concepts discussed in this chapter and throughout the text would you want to include? For further guidance, go to www.beyondintractability.org and search for "Group Projects."

"Solving Tough Problems"

Adam Kahane, the author of *Solving Tough Problems* (2007), is a social innovator who facilitates processes in order to address major global problems; this section summarizes his approach to resolving conflicts.

Kahane's four ways of talking and listening—downloading, debating, reflective dialogue, and generative dialogue—were introduced in Chapter 1. Kahane reflects these four ideas when he discusses how we talk with others.

Avoid assuming that there's only one right answer. Many conflicts develop because people on all sides believe that theirs is the only way forward. It takes willingness, openness, and commitment to accept that other people may have good ideas and potential solutions.

Recognize unproductive ways of talking. Four ways of talking with others can lead to conflict:

- Sometimes we dictate to others; instead of presenting our idea as an option, we put forth our opinion as the only viable solution.
- Sometimes we're too polite when we talk. We worry about offending others, and this can constrain us from speaking openly and productively.

"This isn't really about the beagles, is it."

Paul Noth/The New Yorker Collection/www.cartoonbank.com

■ Sometimes we're too submissive or shy and we don't speak up, meaning that others can't know how we're feeling or what's bothering us.

■ Sometimes we only talk and neglect to actively listen to others.

Understand effective ways of listening. The other side of talking is, of course, listening. There are many ways to listen, and Kahane provides ways that can help address conflict situations.

■ *Listening openly.* "If talking openly means being willing to expose to others what is inside of us, then listening openly means being willing to open ourselves to hearing something new from others" (Kahane, 2007, p. 73). Sometimes people don't really listen and are instead preparing to jump in with a story of their own, in a kind of one-upmanship. When this happens, active, open listening is not happening. Kahane suggests that open listening, by contrast, is the basis for all creativity and resolution and requires that we listen to those who seem different, who are on the opposite side of a conflict, or who are seen as the enemy.

■ *Listening reflectively.* Sometimes we may think we're listening but are instead "reloading old tapes" (Kahane, 2007, p. 79); reflective listening, on the other hand, means being receptive to new ideas and willing to be influenced and changed by them. For example, in the heat of a conflict, if you believe that the only possible resolution is the one you've proposed, you aren't using your skills of reflection and open listening to consider new possibilities.

■ *Listening with empathy.* While listening openly and reflectively are good beginnings, we miss the essence of a conversation if we don't listen with empathy. Kahane describes a conventional greeting in Zulu, *sawu bona*, which means "I see you" and is returned with "I am here. I see you." This greeting goes beyond the customary North American "Hi. How are you?," which is equivalent to a mere polite hello. When we truly see the other, we see a fellow human, not an enemy, a partner in conflict, or someone beneath our notice.

■ *Committing to a resolution.* If all parties in a conflict truly want to solve tough problems or even a minor conflict, they need to be committed to finding a solution. That commitment needs to be shared by all parties in the conflict (in which there are often many sides). In other words, they will be in a process of co-creating a solution, a process that requires strong interpersonal skills.

■ *Listening by not talking.* This involves not speaking out loud, of course, but also closing down our internal talk. While we're listening, we're often busy reacting, projecting, judging, anticipating, and even drifting off. In our multitasking world, it's often difficult to shut down our internal chatter. And when we allow that chatter to continue, it's difficult to listen intently and with empathy.

Use the "closed fist, open palm." This ancient sacred hand gesture, noted in the *I Ching*, is sometimes used at the end of a Tai Chi or martial arts session. In this gesture, the left hand, which gently holds the right, represents the yin or feminine and refers to the ability to be receptive (open listening). The right hand, softly closed in a fist, represents the yang and refers to the ability to act (open talking). The hand gesture signifies that we can't solve problems by only listening or only talking; we need to do both in turn, respectfully and with a commitment to finding a solution.

INTERPERSONAL CHOICE POINT

Parent–Teacher Confrontation

You're a student teacher at an elementary school. One of the children in the class has been doing poorly and has created all sorts of discipline problems. Her parents complain that she dislikes school and isn't learning anything. They want her transferred to another class with another teacher. What are some of the strategies you might use to lessen their anger so that you can work together to find a solution?

INTERPERSONAL CHOICE POINT

Confronting a Problem

Your next-door neighbour never puts out the garbage in time for pickup. As a result, the garbage—often broken into by stray animals—remains until the next pickup. You're fed up with the rodents and birds the garbage draws, the smell, and the horrible appearance. What strategies might you use to help resolve this conflict?

SKILL-BUILDING EXERCISE

Solving Tough Problems Using the "Open Way"

Here are 10 suggestions (Kahane, 2007, pp. 129–130) for opening up in order to become unstuck and create solutions:

1. Pay attention to your state of being and how you're both talking and listening.
2. Speak up.
3. Remember that you don't really know the truth about the facts of the conflict; it's really only your opinion.
4. Engage with and listen to others who have a stake in the conflict.
5. Reflect on your own role in the conflict.
6. Listen with empathy.
7. Listen to what's being said not just by yourself and others but through all of you as a whole.
8. When listening, stop talking both verbally and internally.
9. Be fully present.
10. Try out these suggestions and see what happens.

You may want to practise these techniques in a discussion about how to complete a group project for class, in a conversation about how to spend the evening with a group of friends, or while working to resolve a conflict with your partner. What skills have you learned throughout this text that can help you with these suggestions? Which of these suggestions are new for you? Which are easier for you to use? Which ones would you like to work on more?

"A Peaceful Personal Space"

The "Peaceful Personal Space" approach to defusing conflict situations before they escalate combines Eastern practices of mindfulness and meditation with the science of brain development. More specifically, these Eastern practices have been found to improve the functioning of the prefrontal cortex, an area of the brain that allows you to efficiently take on multiple tasks: to make decisions, stay focused and ignore distractions, set goals, and change direction when necessary. It also helps regulate your emotions, meaning that you're better able to acknowledge and to express these emotions in socially appropriate ways. Vancouver's Dalai Lama Center for Peace Education (Dalai Lama Center, 2008) offers not a conflict-resolution process per se, but rather the following strengths-based suggestions for maintaining a positive frame of mind, thus reducing potential conflicts; and when conflicts do arise, for resolving them peacefully.

- Be curious—collect information before making decisions.
- Create a positive future story—be optimistic.
- Deny the drama—avoid participating in gossip and school/office politics.
- Experience nature.
- Keep a gratitude journal.
- Meditate.
- Notice pleasant and beautiful things.
- Offer and receive physical contact—including hugs.
- Practise deep breathing.
- Separate your roles—take a shower or change clothes after school or work.
- Slow your pace.
- Stimulate/challenge yourself—find things that interest and engage you.
- Volunteer.

> ### INTERPERSONAL CHOICE POINT
>
> **Resolving Conflict**
>
> Your dorm mate is very popular and has an open-door policy. So, throughout the day and evening, friends drop by to chat, borrow a book, arrange a time to go out for a drink, and do a range of things—all of which prevents you from studying. You need to resolve this problem. What strategies might you use to begin to resolve this conflict?

Can you explain the three approaches to conflict resolution (Interest-Based Relational, "Solving Tough Problems," and "A Peaceful Personal Space")? Which approaches would you like to add to improve your own conflict-resolution abilities?

Patrick Doyle/CP Images

While many people believe that global conflict and resulting human rights violations are inevitable, Roméo Dallaire firmly believes otherwise: "Now is the time," he has declared, "to take up the cause of the advancement of human rights for all and the moment is yours to grasp" (www.romeodallaire.com). Can you see yourself stepping outside of your comfort zone to grasp this moment as Dallaire challenges us? How can you practise for this larger mission by learning to address your personal conflicts head-on and peacefully?

SUMMARY OF CONCEPTS AND SKILLS

This chapter examined the nature and characteristics of interpersonal conflict, ways to manage conflict, and three specific approaches for resolving conflict.

What Is Interpersonal Conflict?

1. Interpersonal conflict is disagreement between or among connected individuals. The positions in interpersonal conflicts are to some degree interrelated and incompatible.

Characteristics of Interpersonal Conflict

2. Interpersonal conflict is inevitable. If a relationship exists, conflict in some form will also exist.
3. Interpersonal conflict may focus on content and/or relationship issues.
4. Interpersonal conflict can be negative or positive; any conflict encounter may be destructive or constructive.
5. Interpersonal conflict is influenced by culture, gender, and technology.
6. Interpersonal conflict may be approached with different styles, each of which has different consequences.

Ways to Manage Conflict

7. Managing conflict can include both unproductive and productive conflict strategies, such as avoidance versus confronting conflict, defensiveness versus supportiveness, face-attacking versus face-enhancing strategies, and verbal aggressiveness versus argumentativeness.
8. Managing conflict has ethical dimensions.

Three Specific Approaches to Resolving Conflicts

9. The Interest-Based Relational (IBR) approach is a Western problem-solving approach to conflict resolution that requires all involved to be calm, patient, and respectful.
10. "Solving Tough Problems," an approach developed from working on difficult global issues, suggests

ways to listen and talk openly, reflectively, and with empathy.
11. The "Peaceful Personal Space" approach, combining techniques from ancient Eastern traditions with the modern neuroscience of brain development, offers insights into how to prevent conflicts from developing and, if they do, how to resolve them peacefully.

This chapter also focused on the major skills for managing interpersonal conflict. Check those you wish to work on.

_____1. *Negatives and positives of conflict.* Approach conflict to minimize its negative aspects and to maximize the positive benefits of conflict and its resolution.

_____2. *Conflict, culture, and gender.* Approach conflict with the understanding of the cultural and gender differences in attitudes toward what constitutes conflict and how it should be pursued.

_____3. *Conflict styles.* Choose your conflict style carefully; each style has consequences. In relationship conflict, look for win–win solutions rather than solutions in which one person wins and the other loses.

_____4. *Content and relationship conflicts.* Analyze conflict messages in terms of content and relationship dimensions, and respond to each accordingly.

_____5. *Problem-solving conflicts.* Deal with interpersonal conflicts systematically as problems to be solved: define the problem, examine possible solutions, test a solution, evaluate the solution, and accept or reject the solution.

_____6. *Active interpersonal conflict.* Engage in interpersonal conflict actively, be appropriately revealing, and listen to your partner.

_____7. *Supportive conflict.* Engage in conflict using a supportive approach so as not to create defensiveness; avoid messages that evaluate or control, that are strategic or neutral, or that express superiority or certainty.

_____8. *Face-saving strategies.* Use strategies that allow your opponents to save face; avoid beltlining, or hitting opponents with attacks that they will have difficulty absorbing and will resent.

_____9. *Open expression in conflict.* Try to express your feelings openly rather than resorting to silence or avoidance.

_____10. *Present-focus conflict.* Focus your conflict resolution messages on the present; avoid gunnysacking, or dredging up old grievances and unloading these on the other person.

_____11. *Argumentativeness.* Avoid aggressiveness (attacking the other person's self-concept); instead, focus logically on the issues, emphasize finding solutions, and work to ensure that what is said will result in positive self-feelings for both individuals.

VOCABULARY QUIZ: The Language of Conflict

Match the terms of interpersonal conflict with their definitions. Record the number of the definition next to the appropriate term.

_____ avoidance (220)
_____ certainty (223)
_____ argumentativeness (224)
_____ gunnysacking (220)
_____ beltline (223)
_____ verbal aggressiveness (224)
_____ defensiveness (222)
_____ nonnegotiation (220)
_____ interpersonal conflict (210)
_____ evaluation (222)

1. A disagreement between connected individuals.
2. An unproductive conflict strategy of storing up grievances and holding these in readiness to dump on the person with whom one is in conflict.
3. A person's level of tolerance for absorbing a personal attack.
4. A tendency or willingness to argue for a point of view.
5. A style of communication characterized by threats, fear, or domination.
6. The refusal to discuss a conflict or to listen to the other person's argument.
7. A tendency to defend your position even at the expense of another person's feelings.
8. Closed-mindedness; appearing to "know it all."
9. Physical, emotional, or intellectual flight.
10. You-messages that judge another person or that person's behaviour.

These 10 terms and additional terms used in this chapter can be found in the glossary.

CHAPTER

11

Interpersonal Communication and the Workplace

CANADIAN PROFILE: Sharon Carry

Sharon Carry/Bow Valley College

Every single employee influences the tone and effectiveness of communication in their workplace, but when leaders set an example by being thoughtful and purposeful in the way they communicate, it can have a profound impact on the entire work environment. Calgary's Bow Valley College has been recognized as one of Alberta's top employers, and while many people share the credit for this honour, much can be attributed to the leadership provided by its president and CEO, Sharon Carry.

Carry ensures effective communication in part by using multiple avenues, including regular email announcements,

print material, webinars, social media, and informal and formal meetings among the college's departments. She engages frequently with students and staff, listening to their ideas, their concerns, and their stories. "It's a good day," she has said, "if I can talk to at least one student."

Sharon Carry's vision of how practical, real-world education can change the lives of adult learners has guided her work over the last four decades and earned her national and international acclaim. In 2014 she was invested with the Alberta Order of Excellence and was among those named by the Women's Executive Network as Canada's Most Powerful Women: Top 100 Award Winner. "When you transform lives for a living you get a lot of heartfelt and powerful stories. The unspoken reality that binds our organization together is the sense that we all really love what happens here. When you have that sense of shared excitement for what you accomplish as a group, communication simply becomes a matter of reflecting that emotional engagement back to the very people who live it daily."

As you work through this chapter, think about the how the concepts presented fit with Sharon Carry's philosophy of communication. Which of these concepts do you see reflected in your college or workplace? Are the communication strategies in your workplace positive or negative?

LEARNING OBJECTIVES *After reading this chapter, you should be able to:*

1. Understand the ranges of diversity within the workplace.

2. Describe the culture of a particular workplace.

3. Use different modes of workplace communication to become more effective in your place of employment.

4. Establish positive relationships with peers, supervisors, and people whom you supervise.

5. Use appropriate leadership skills.

6. Understand the principles of power in the workplace.

7. Use assertiveness when appropriate.

This chapter examines the principles of workplace communication and will help you become more effective in your place of employment. While the principles of communication are similar in both personal and work settings, workplace communication presents a unique set of challenges. Understanding these challenges will better enable you to establish positive relationships with peers, supervisors, and people whom you supervise. Strong workplace communication will lead to career success; as indicated in the Skill-Building Exercise, verbal and written communication skills rank number 1 among the 10 top characteristics employers seek.

DIVERSITY IN THE WORKPLACE

Work settings today encompass many kinds of diversity. Distinct cultures are found in professional groups as well as in individual organizations. Some studies have shown that professions have unique characteristics that suit the definition of culture; for example, we talk about the culture of the nursing profession, of business culture, and of the common traits of accountants. With organizations, one could find, for example, two colleges in the same city with very different cultures: one may have a formal, hierarchical structure while the other may be more informal. As a professor once remarked, "I worked at one college for 20 years and never so much as exchanged greetings with the president. Then I moved to a less formal institution and found myself having lunch in the staff cafeteria chatting with the president."

Workplaces today have also been described as multigenerational, with each generation having unique cultural characteristics. A workplace could well include older baby boomers, Generation Xers, and young people in their 20s ("millennials"). While stereotyping is unhelpful, each generation has been found to differ in values and communication styles. As well, most workplaces in Canada include employees from very different cultural backgrounds and with varying levels of ability.

Given this vast diversity in the workplace, how do we manage to be effective communicators? We begin by defining aspects of this diversity, and then look at strategies that can be applied and adapted to these contexts. Included are discussions of telephone, electronic, and written communication, as well as networking, mentorship, and teamwork. The chapter ends with a discussion of leadership and powerful communication.

The Multigenerational Workforce

It's common to speak of the "generation gap" when looking at family dynamics, but only recently has the idea of the generation gap moved to the workplace. Indeed, today there can be as many as four or five generations working together in one setting. The first of these four groups has been described as "traditionalists," the "silent generation," or the "veterans" (Jennings, 2000)—those people who were born before 1946. The second group, known as **baby boomers**, were born between 1946 and 1965. The third group, known as **Generation Xers** or the baby bust, were born between 1966 and 1979. The fourth group, known as the **millennials** (also referred to as Generation Y or Generation Next), were born after 1980.

wavebreakmedia/Shutterstock

VIEWPOINTS The Many Kinds of Diversity

A diverse workforce can often be a more productive workforce. The term *diversity*, after all, refers to more than just cultural or ethnic diversity. What other kinds of diversity could contribute to a productive workplace, and why is this important?

SKILL-BUILDING EXERCISE

Speaking and Writing Skills

Given that so much of our working time is spent in some form of communication, strong communication skills are critical to career success. In fact, verbal and written communication skills rank number one in the top 10 list of qualities employers seek. Here we'll look at the ways in which to improve those skills.

Speaking Skills

The ability to deliver an effective talk is one of the most valuable skills you can cultivate, and yet most people are afraid to speak in front of a group. Some people panic and their minds go blank while others may get an upset stomach. But with careful preparation and a fair amount of practice, nearly anyone can become a competent speaker.

- *Be prepared.* One way to overcome pre-speech jitters is to know what you're talking about. Research your subject area thoroughly until you know your topic inside out. Organize the information and then write one or two summary sentences that clearly define the purpose of your presentation. Next, create an outline to give your speech direction and ensure that you don't leave out key points. Keep in mind that listeners get overwhelmed if you try to tell them too much—two or three main points are usually sufficient. Finally, rehearse your presentation several times so that you can become comfortable with your talk and improve your delivery.
- *Understand your audience.* What do your listeners want to know? How much do they already know about the subject? Once you know your audience, you can better determine what direction your presentation should take.
- *Overcome stage fright.* Channel your nervous energy and get your body involved in what you're saying. Gesture with your hands to reinforce key points, move about a little, and take deep breaths to calm your nerves. It also helps to concentrate on just a couple of people instead of the entire group. And remember, your audience wants you to succeed. If

they learn something (anything) of value, they'll consider their time spent with you worthwhile.

Writing Skills

In the workplace you'll be expected to write memos, letters, and proposals. Many people just start writing and hope for the best. But, as in speaking, before you begin writing you must first organize your thoughts, understand your intended reader, and clearly define your purpose.

Most writing is done either to persuade, describe, or explain. But no matter what your purpose, writing should always be

- concise
- compelling
- clear
- correct

Managers are bombarded with messages every day, and they often don't have time to read all of them. If a piece of correspondence doesn't capture their interest quickly, there's a good chance it won't be read—and this is especially true with cover letters and résumés. In today's job market, a company may receive up to 300 résumés for a single job opening. To narrow down the selection, some employers put the one-page résumés in one pile and the two-page résumés in the trash.

If your writing is clear and simple and you follow these tips, chances are your correspondence won't end up in the basket.

- Understand your intended reader.
- Put the most important information at the start of your correspondence.
- Don't use big, fancy words.
- Keep sentences short.
- Use active verbs.
- Leave out unrelated information.
- Proofread everything you write.

INTERPERSONAL CHOICE POINT

Becoming Clearer

Following their presentations, students often feel that they haven't communicated their ideas clearly enough. What advice would you give to a peer on how to communicate more effectively?

While generalizations about any group can lead to stereotyping, understanding key characteristics of each generation can help to foster positive and effective communication. Keep in mind that the following descriptions are based largely on North American research, and that these differences in intergenerational workplace communication have been shown to vary between Western and non-Western countries (McCann & Giles, 2006).

TRADITIONALISTS   The traditional generation is characterized by their patriotism, hard work, frugality, and faith in the organizations and institutions of their society. They are described as loyal. They respect discipline, law, and order and tend to be oriented in the past.

BOOMERS   Boomers were brought up in a more affluent, opportunity-filled world. They are highly competitive, idealistic, and optimistic. They're used to being the centre of attention and look for personal gratification. It's been estimated that by 2025, one in three workers is likely to be a boomer.

GENERATION XERS   These are the children of the boomers. They tend to be skeptical; they're also resourceful, money-oriented, and independent, and don't like to be micromanaged. They were the generation that experienced the soaring divorce rates and decline in the security of family, in addition to the downsizing of corporations and the general decline in job security. They look for balance and a sense of family. They prefer informality and want to be self-reliant.

THE MILLENNIALS   This group has been described as bold, brazen, and "the cockiest in recent history, with an unprecedented sense of entitlement" (McLaren, 2005). Many were brought up in homes where parents treated children as equals, which some think has resulted in a generation that has little respect for the wisdom and experience of older people. The self-confidence that seems typical of this generation has been described as a two-edged sword. On the one hand, their self-confidence, competence (especially in technology), and high expectations bode well; on the other hand, an overestimated sense of self-worth can have negative effects on relationships and lead to unrealistic expectations of one's ability: "In the age of self-esteem, where everybody, not just the best and the brightest, gets gold stars beside their name in school, no one expects to start at the bottom" (McLaren, 2005).

As we can see, there are significant differences between these groups, and each group has its strengths, its attitudes toward work (and to the technology that has become central to most work), and its needs in workplace relationships. Consider, for example, the different values associated with job changing. Traditionalists tend to view changing jobs as a stigma, whereas boomers tend to stay in the same job "to make a difference." Generation Xers have been labelled as "job hoppers" who try to get as many skills and experiences as possible on a résumé, while the millennials see "job changing as part of normal routine" (Armour, 2005).

> **INTERPERSONAL CHOICE POINT**
>
> **Generational Differences in Communication**
>
> You want to express appreciation to a colleague who's helped you out, or you want to convey your dissatisfaction with a particular event at work. What differences might you consider in how you communicate to members of different generations? For example, how formal would you be? Would you use slang? Would you communicate in person or via technology?

THE CULTURE OF THE WORKPLACE

Understanding organizational cultures can help you communicate more effectively within the work setting. As we've seen, organizations have distinct cultures (Handy, 1985; Harrison & Carroll, 2006; Manzoni, 2012). These workplace cultures, like other cultures, revolve around shared values, attitudes, and experiences that validate the culture (Holmes & Marra, 2002). The workplace culture is learned and shared through expectations for behaviour, customs, and ceremonies. Workplaces often have their own jargon, traditions, and stories, which communicate cultural values and provide cues to new employees regarding expected behaviour. Employee recognition ceremonies, sports competitions, fundraisers, and family outings are all examples of organizational traditions and ceremonies (Holmes & Marra, 2002). The culture of organizations has been described in four main categories (Handy, 1985): role culture, achievement culture, power culture, and people culture.

In a **role culture** organization, there is general conformity to expectations, clear regulations and procedures, and clearly defined tasks. Often strategies exist, usually in the form of financial rewards and bonuses, that encourage employees to perform according to expectations. These kinds of strategies are referred to as *extrinsic motivation*.

Many government or civil service offices fit this description. **Power culture** is described as having clear authority, high expectations for loyalty, and measures in place to ensure accountability. Traditional banks are examples of organizations in this category. **Achievement culture** fosters creativity, competition, and independence in its employees. Less formal rules and structures exist, and employees seem to have more intrinsic motivation to perform. Small high-tech startup companies fit this category. Finally, organizations that have a strong **people culture** emphasize relationships, sharing, and friendship; employees are motivated intrinsically through job satisfaction rather than through external rewards.

What are some differences in the communication styles that fit these different organizational cultures? For example, in a role culture organization, one would probably be less inclined to share personal information and be open about difficulties than in an organization that has a people culture. In a role culture or power culture organization, communication would likely be more formal; employees would be expected to follow procedures regarding who they talk to as well as when and how they talk. In organizations that have an achievement culture, competition may be such that employees tend not to share ideas, but communication might tend to be less structured and formal. In a people culture, we would expect communication to be quite open and relaxed, and employees encouraged to share their concerns with their colleagues and supervisors.

In a small group, discuss the types of cultures you've been exposed to in the workplace. Of the four organizational cultures, which suits you best? Why?

Like any other culture, organizational culture isn't static. Organizations merge, new employees bring new aspects to the culture, and the culture often needs to adapt to changing markets and changing needs. The increasing role of women in the workplace is also reshaping business culture (Walsh, 2005). Yet strong organizational cultures are important for the success of organizations, and understanding the culture of the organization will help you become more successful in your communications and interpersonal relationships in the workplace.

The Culture of the Professions

Just as organizations have identifiable cultures, so do many occupational groups such as engineers, teachers, or nurses (Rochester, 2002; Suominen et al., 1997). Professional cultures evolve as societal needs change (Beauschene & Patsdaughter, 2005), and organizations often employ a multidisciplinary workforce. Canadian researchers have shown that, with specialization increasing, professional cultures can actually form barriers to effective communication in the workplace (Hall, 2005). Thus, understanding the culture of the professions involved is important for effective communication within organizations.

MESSAGES IN THE MEDIA

Hand-out/Cbc Television/ Newscom

Dragons' Den is a Canadian television reality show in which aspiring entrepreneurs pitch business ideas to a panel of venture capitalists in the hope of securing business financing. Watch how the hopeful contestants communicate their ideas to the panel. How thoughtful do they seem in the manner they choose to convey their messages? What can you learn about the culture of entrepreneurship from this show?

Professional culture isn't easy to define, but it represents a shared experience that other groups don't have, often reinforced by professional associations (Rochester, 2002). The culture of professions is impacted by the people who make up the profession and by the skills they use in practice. For example, Rochester (2002) describes the engineering profession as practical, problem-solving, and detail-oriented, claiming that the people who enter the profession tend to like to work with things or ideas more than with people. Indeed, one of the most noticeable differences between occupations is based on whether they're focused on objects or things or involved directly in helping or healing people. While architects and engineers would likely argue that one of the goals of their work is to help people or society, they do so by creating objects (buildings, bridges) rather than by directly helping people. One profession is no less important than the other; however, the type of work seems to be a factor in the culture that has evolved around these groups.

Some professions focus as much on process as they do on outcome. For example, in early childhood education, the goal of each interaction with a child is to enhance and support his or her healthy development. So while the goal and the desired outcome are clear, professionals are generally assessed on the basis of their ongoing interactions with the children. Compare this with architects or engineers, whose work is assessed based on the quality of the product they develop. Nonetheless, it's important not to oversimplify. A performance appraisal of an engineer or an architect would likely include her ability to communicate effectively. In fact, one report (Darling & Dannels, 2003) observed that "communication is the life blood" of engineers and recommended much more emphasis on communication training in the curriculum of university engineering programs. Conversely, requiring that practitioners in health and human service professions evaluate their work on the basis of measurable outcomes is a growing trend in those fields.

Health and human service occupations have been described as the caring professions, and clearly there are similarities between occupations such as nursing, social work, and psychology. The focus on helping, healing, and supporting has led to a strategy of communication with clients, called *therapeutic* or *supportive communication*, which is the basis for counselling (Horsfall, 1998). Therapeutic communication includes active listening, reflection on content and feeling, clarifying, paraphrasing, questioning, providing information, and the constructive confronting of communicative contradictions. There are also cultural differences within the health and human service professions; one manifestation of this has been found in the varying suicide rates in particular branches of nursing (Wilson et al., 2005; Yamaguchi, 2004).

Diverse Personalities in the Workplace

Of course, diversity isn't found solely in the culture of organizations or professions, or even in an individual's culture or ability. People are simply different—they have different likes, dislikes, personalities, and temperaments. And while we have some choice in our private lives about who we wish to spend time with, this is not the case at work. Understanding your own learning style, personality, and temperament can help you

Dmitriy Shironosov/Shutterstock

VIEWPOINTS Hedging

Research shows that hedging (making tentative statements) reflects negatively on both male and female speakers when it indicates a lack of certainty or conviction resulting from some inadequacy on the speaker's part (Pearson, West, & Turner, 1995). The hedging will be more positively received, however, if listeners feel that it reflects the speaker's belief that tentative statements are the only kind a person can reasonably make. What are some of the implications of this for effective workplace communication?

SKILL-BUILDING EXERCISE

Communicating in an Emergency

Emergency responders must be extraordinarily competent communicators to get the information they need as quickly as possible and help the patient be calm. Here are some of the guidelines they use:

Do

- Pay attention to first impressions—be neat and clean, maintain an overall demeanor that is calm, capable and trustworthy
- Be confident, not arrogant
- Be respectful considerate as you enter another person's home
- Get down to a patient's level if a child or seated person is involved
- Maintain an open stance where possible
- Remove sunglasses and use eye contact as much as possible
- Use an appropriate compassionate touch to show concern and support
- Use open ended and direct questions (not leading questions); ask one question at a time and listen to the complete response before asking th next question

- Use language the patient can understand and avoid interruptions

Don't

- Provide false assurances
- Give unwanted advice
- Use avoidance behaviour
- Use professional jargon
- Ask "why"
- Interrupt

Then and Now

Have you ever been in an emergency situation where you have had to either give or get information? Did the person who was getting information from you use the techniques described above? What behaviours were used that contributed to a feeling of safety and comfort, or stress and discomfortable?

Source: Adapted from Bledsoe et al. Essentials of Paramedic Care: Division I 2006 Pearson Education, Inc. Uper Saddle River, N.J.

become more aware of how you affect others in your workplace. Just as important, learning to recognize the characteristics of the people you work with can help you become a more effective communicator.

For example, Susan Cain (2012), in her book *Quiet: The Power of Introverts in a World That Can't Stop Talking* (and the related TED talk that has received over 8 million views), reminds us that in a culture where being outgoing is valued more than anything else, being an introvert can be very difficult, and that we miss out on the extraordinary talents and abilities many introverts bring to the world by not giving them the space and quiet they need to perform optimally in the workplace.

Many employers use personality tests either as part of a selection process for new employers or as a tool for professional development. The best known of these is the Myers Briggs Type Indicator, which has been thoroughly researched and tested and is used worldwide. However, numerous other tests are also available. A somewhat simpler and more enjoyable test of personalities is based on five personality traits: openness, conscientiousness, extroversion, agreeableness, and negative emotionality or neuroticism.

These tests can be useful in assessing yourself, your colleagues, and your supervisors, and in using this knowledge to adapt and enhance your workplace communication. For example, although new employees often come into an organization with new ideas and are motivated to share them, their ideas may be either dismissed

Comstock/Getty Images

VIEWPOINTS **The Culture of Health Care**

Recall a time when you or a family member met with a health care professional (doctor, nurse, or counsellor). Did you feel that you were being listened to? Did you feel that you were being understood? Did you feel comfortable and safe to disclose information? If so, what behaviours made you feel listened to, understood, and safe? If not, what behaviours prevented this?

or simply ignored by those making the decisions. Understanding a bit about the character of the decision makers will help you frame your communication in a way that's more likely to be heard. For example, you'd probably use one approach with a manager who likes having control and power over people and a rather different approach with a leader who's more easygoing, warm, and cooperative.

Cultural Diversity in the Workplace

Workforce population trends in North America have increased the number and kinds of culturally diverse people who work together (Chao & Moon, 2005). Therefore, the same understanding and awareness that are required for sensitive, appropriate, and effective intercultural communication (see Chapter 2) apply to work settings as well.

In the business sector, cultural differences lend complexity to interactions and negotiations. For example, different meanings attributed to business ethics, different interpretations of the right to privacy, and different meanings of body language, status, and time, if not understood, can interfere greatly with successful business practice (Moon & Williams, 2000). Furthermore, different cultures have different approaches to power, authority, and acceptable public behaviour. Styles of confrontation, levels of assertiveness, and differing expressions of warmth are just some of the factors that need to be considered in a multicultural workplace.

Gender and the Workplace

Considerable research has been conducted on differences in communication styles between men and women and the impact these have in both personal and professional settings. And yet most of the research on gender differences in work-related communication was conducted with the boomers or Generation Xers—there is little available research on the younger generation at work. It could well be that these differences are diminishing, but to date we can only speculate. Research suggests that women managers still face difficulty in being accepted by males in the workplace (Bongiorno & David, 2003), and still face barriers to acceptance in work arenas that were traditionally male (Irizarry, 2004; Merchant, 2012).

Deborah Tannen (1990) described how the different communication styles related to gender may put women at a disadvantage for being taken seriously at work. For example, women tend to apologize more, not necessarily because they think they did something wrong but as a way of smoothing out the conversation. Men tend to say "I'm sorry" infrequently, and tend to interpret women's use of apology as a weakness, or as accepting blame for a situation.

Similarly, women tend to use the phrase "thank you" differently from men. For women, "thanks" is often a ritualized way of closing a conversation or an email communication. Men tend to interpret "thank you" as gratitude for something they've done. As well, women tend to ask for more input than do men. They do that as a way of fostering a sense of collaboration in which everyone's opinion is valued. Men, on the other hand, tend to see this effort at collaboration as indecisive behaviour—the inability to do things independently.

Moreover, men tend to take more oppositional stances than do women; women tend to take these stances as personal attacks. Often, however, the intention is to debate issues or present another view rather than to attack. Humour is reportedly also used differently by men and women, with women tending to use self-putdowns more frequently and men tending to use teasing and mock hostile attacks (Tannen, 1990).

Monkey Bussiness Images/Shutterstock

VIEWPOINTS Gender Differences in Communication

Do you notice differences in the ways men and women communicate at work? How do these compare with what Deborah Tannen described in 1990? Do you think there are fewer gender differences today? Can you give concrete examples to back up your position?

Diversity in Ability

In every workplace there may be employees with a broad range of abilities. Progressive workplaces are hiring people today who may have previously been considered unemployable. With the proper support for people with disabilities, employees can enjoy the benefits of job satisfaction and a sense of belonging. Furthermore, workplaces that have purposefully provided support to people with developmental disabilities have commented on the benefits to the organization (L'Arche Canada, 2005).

However, communication with employees with disabilities requires thoughtfulness, consideration, and an effort to understand the barriers that these employees may face. For example, Holmes (2003) described the difficulties that people with developmental disabilities may face in participating in small talk at work (so-called water cooler communication). Small talk may not seem complex, but recognizing what's acceptable and what's not—how frequently it can be engaged in, on which occasions, and in which contexts—actually entails sophisticated judgments that may not be easy for workers with developmental disabilities. An employer who wants to foster the success of a worker with a developmental disability will pay attention to managing small talk and to raising awareness of how to include people with disabilities in the formal and informal interactions at work.

Just as employers have an obligation to make accommodations for people with physical disabilities, efforts should be made to accommodate employees with lower levels of cognitive functioning, as specified in the Canadian Human Rights Act. For more information on this topic, visit the Canadian Human Rights Commission at www.chrc-ccdp.ca.

In summary, how can an understanding of these differences help you communicate more effectively at work? First, you can better understand how others may interpret your own communication style. This doesn't necessarily mean that you have to change your style, but rather that it's important to understand your style's potential impact. If your natural communication style tends to be very informal, but you work in a role culture organization and report to a manager from the traditionalist generation, you may have to adapt your style. If you're very introverted and don't show excitement readily, you may want to ensure that your co-workers don't perceive your introversion as disinterest. And if you're working with people who have developmental disabilities, you may want to ensure that you adapt your language accordingly.

Learning to adapt your communication style to become more effective at work doesn't change who you are. Consider communication strategies as the palette of an artist: using a richer variety of colours and textures allows for more elaborate and effective expression.

TEST YOURSELF

What Kind of Workplace Appeals to You?

Indicate how important each of the following characteristics is to you in a potential workplace. Use a scale in which **5** = very important; **4** = important; **3** = neither important or unimportant; **2** = unimportant; and **1** = totally unimportant.

____ Good salary
____ Respectful atmosphere
____ Clear rules and expectations
____ Autonomy
____ Diversity
____ Lots of opportunity for group work
____ Lots of opportunity to work alone
____ High ethical standards
____ Competitive atmosphere
____ Collaborative atmosphere

____ Lots of socializing
____ Minimum need to socialize
____ Innovation rewarded
____ Following procedures rewarded

How Did You Do? There are no correct or incorrect answers to these, and people will respond differently perhaps according to age, gender, culture, and personality.

What Will You Do? Knowing what's important to you in a workplace will help you make choices that are right for you. It isn't always possible to find a job that reflects all the characteristics you chose above, but understanding your own preferences will be an important part of developing your career path.

WORKPLACE COMMUNICATION

Telephone Communication

Much communication in the workplace takes place over the phone. Answering the phone isn't a difficult physical task, but using it in a businesslike and professional manner isn't so straightforward. Being effective, as well as staying calm and controlled, can be quite demanding. Good telephone manners at work include techniques such as introducing yourself with your first and last name, company name and department; developing rapport by using a friendly tone of voice; answering questions promptly and efficiently; and asking both open-ended questions for general information and closed questions for clarifying the facts. Take notes to help you remember the content of the call, check back with the caller to make sure you have the correct information, and end the call on a positive note. While it's important to remain polite at all times, keep in mind that you're entitled to be spoken to respectfully, even if the speaker is angry or upset. If a caller becomes abusive, it's your right to terminate the conversation.

Computer-Mediated Communication

Technology is radically changing the environment of our workplaces, not only in how we conduct business and communicate at work but also from where we can work. Videoconferencing, online collaboration, smartphones, email, instant messaging, blogs, and Wifi are all leading to the creation of virtual teams and even virtual companies. However, while many see technology as a boon to the bottom line, it also poses some challenges. One observation made over two decades ago—that the promised paperless office is drowning in paper, and that proposed savings are eaten up by the costs of planning, implementing, and continually upgrading labour-saving technology (Grosch, 1994)—may still at least partially reflect today's reality.

There are many ways in which employees communicate in the workplace. Email has long been touted as the darling of workplace communication, but it's been losing favour—almost being seen as the new snail mail (Irvine, 2006). Like home mailboxes that are often cluttered with advertising flyers, email inboxes are increasingly saturated with spam, prolonging the job of sorting through new emails to weed out what can be deleted and what should be addressed. Employees complain that they're often days or even weeks behind in their email. Nonetheless, email can still be very useful for many tasks, including sending and receiving attachments, keeping in touch with parents or teachers, conducting informal correspondence, or sending a message or document from one to many.

 In what ways might email enable you to avoid conflict more than a face-to-face situation might? Alternatively, in what ways might email enable you to engage in conflict more actively than a face-to-face situation might? In what other ways does conflict through email differ from face-to-face conflict?

Today many workplaces are increasingly turning to social networking and collaborative communication tools like instant messaging (IM) and blogging for their flexibility, their personal approach, and their ability to send and receive in real time, to integrate into existing internal systems, and to reach and engage clients and employees.

Cameron and Webster (2005) highlight the challenges of integrating IM into workplace communication; for example, IM may be viewed as less rich than face-to-face communication, and as interruptive, distracting, and unfair in its perceived requirement of immediacy throughout the duration of the workday. If integrated and used appropriately, however, the benefits of integrating IM into the workplace are evident in an overall decrease in the cost of communication, in facilitating collaboration over many geographic zones, and in its potential positive impact on workplace performance (Macdonald & Poniatowska, 2011).

Blogging in the workplace has the potential to become a key tool for both communication and workplace learning. Miller (2003) sees two main potential applications for blogs: to be used externally by companies to communicate with potential customers, and to be used internally to distribute information that changes on a regular basis. However, blogging is not without its challenges, especially if employees are the ones blogging and negative or sensitive information is inadvertently or purposefully published (Ostrander, 2007).

Many employers today use webinars as a substitute for face-to-face meetings or professional development. This saves time and money and allows employees to participate from a distance.

In summary, for many workplaces now, it's a question of choosing the most appropriate communication and collaboration tool. For example, you might text-message during a meeting when you need to be quiet or you might choose to discuss a sensitive issue over the phone so that there's no written record. Matthew Felling (as cited in Irvine, 2006), a former spokesman for the Centre for Media and Public Affairs in Washington and an admitted "serial-texter," claims that technology is fast becoming the "ultimate social crutch to avoid personal communication. Don't want to see someone? Call them. Don't want to call someone? Email them. Don't want to take the trouble of writing sentences? Text them."

Multitasking

All of this new technology in the workplace encourages—or perhaps requires—employees to become experts at multitasking. It's not unusual to see an employee talking on the phone while reading an email and checking a calendar entry on a smartphone as a colleague waits at the office door for a quick word. The developers of technology often sell their products with the promise of increased efficiency; however, can communication and collaboration technologies really enable one employee to do the work of two?

Psychology professor Hal Pashler (cited in Wallis, 2006) explains that when the brain is asked to multitask, it actually performs the actions sequentially, one task at a time. Sequential processing occurs in the prefrontal cortex of the brain, which is one of the last areas to mature and one of the first to decline with aging. This means that young children and adults over 60 don't multitask well (Wallis, 2006). However, even for younger people, multitasking has its limits. When people try to alternate rapidly between two or more activities, both the time needed to complete the tasks and the errors may increase (Cherry, 2014a).

DEVELOPING LANGUAGE AND COMMUNICATION SKILLS

Following Instructions
Children's brains develop rapidly in the first five years of their lives. However, it takes some time for them to develop the cognitive abilities to hear, remember, and follow a series of instructions. When children are two or three years old, they need to be given one instruction at a time: "Please take off your shoes; now you can put them on the mat beside the door." By the time children are ready to start school, they should be able to follow instructions that have two, three, or even more steps: "It's time to go! Please put on your sweater, grab your bag, and meet me at the front door." Be sensitive to adults who are learning English or have developmental delays, as they may also need to have the steps of complex instructions broken down.

In fact, researchers are suggesting that multitasking short-circuits attention spans and induces an "air traffic controller–like" stress that can actually increase the time it takes to accomplish tasks by up to 50 percent (Lauer, 2004). Harvard Medical School psychiatrist Edward Hallowell (as cited in Lauer, 2004) describes an epidemic that he refers to as ADT: attention deficit trait. Constant electronic communication and the immediate demands it makes on employees are diluting performance and increasing irritability. Thus, those who used to be well organized and efficient are increasingly becoming disorganized underachievers.

This phenomenon is leading many concerned workplaces to order a technology vacation for its workers every so often, perhaps an afternoon a week without using any technological devices—no email, no IM, no iPads or smartphones, no voicemail. It's hoped that these vacations will allow employees to give their brains the rest and recovery time they need to process and consolidate information—as well as provide the time to enjoy one another's company and have face-to-face conversations. More common, though, is the ever-increasing number of etiquette guidelines for the polite integration and use of collaborative communication technology in the workplace (Waldeck et al., 2012).

Technology Confrontations

Computer-mediated communication (CMC) is often used as a way for people to resolve personal conflicts—to say things to one another that might not be possible or comfortable to say face to face. The workplace is no different. However, a survey by VitalSmarts (as cited in Grenny, 2005) found that 87 percent of those polled indicated that email, voicemail, or text messages may actually amplify a workplace conflict. Furthermore, 89 percent of those polled say that CMC actually gets in the way of good workplace communication. This is especially true when news is bad or sensitive, when negative feedback is being delivered, or when differing opinions are involved and nonverbal signals are important in accurately deciphering the message.

Now that CMC is in such wide use, many corporations are formulating policies that prevent inappropriate use and reduce exposure to liability (Sipior & Ward, 1999). Such policies include restricting email use to business only, prohibiting inappropriate language and conduct, and reserving the right to monitor communication. However, as companies begin to institute surveillance and monitor the work of their employees—specifically the use of email, listservs, and the web—concerns increase about the violation of employees' right to privacy (Miller & Weckert, 2000).

Written Communication in the Workplace

With the growing use of electronic communication, it's easy to forget that messages written on paper still have an important function in many workplaces. As with other nonverbal messages, the layout and general appearance of a letter or memo communicate an impression before any words have been read. The very fact that someone has taken the time to format a letter and send it in the mail, rather than send a quick email, is a message in itself. There are many guides available for business letters; one such resource can be found at www.usingenglish.com (search for "Formal Letter Writing").

Written communication extends the opportunity to plan and review the information being sent before it reaches the receiver. Read and review memos and letters carefully, correct any grammar or spelling errors, and ensure that the format is impressive before sending the communication because, as with verbal communication, written communication is irreversible. So take some time before sending a written communication in order to ensure that the message sent reflects the message you intend.

Negative Workplace Communication

Negative communication can take place in any context. In the workplace, the effect of negative communication can lead to a decline in staff morale, in productivity, and in service. Four notable kinds of negative communication are rumours, gossip, anonymous communication, and outright lying.

RUMOURS   Rumours have been defined as "public communications that reflect private hypotheses," or as attempts to make sense of unclear or uncertain situations (Rosnow, 1988). Consider the following event. Dania, who had worked in the office for six years, suddenly didn't show up to work and didn't let anyone know she wasn't coming. Several days later, an email welcoming her replacement went out to all employees. No official reason was given for Dania's termination of employment, and so rumours started to circulate: "She was caught stealing company property" and "She's suffering from a sudden illness." Then people started to talk and provide rationale for each hypothesis: "She *had* been acting rather secretively" or "She hasn't really looked well for a while." Such rumours were an attempt to find explanations where there was a vacuum of information from a reliable source.

Rumours may, in fact, be true. Often they're not, although there may be a grain of truth in a rumour. Essentially, a rumour is information that is disseminated without official verification. The potential of rumours to damage the workplace and individuals is very real (Difonzo et al., 1994; Robertson, 2005). Not surprisingly, negative rumours tend to be more prevalent than positive rumours in work settings (Bordia et al., 2003). And when anxieties and uncertainties prevail, rumours tend to proliferate. For example, if a company is downsizing, or a merger is expected, or a change in leadership occurs, rumours will likely circulate until (and even after) the facts are known.

Although it's impossible to prevent or stop rumours in the workplace, managers and leaders can take steps to avoid the initiation and spread of rumours.

GOSSIP   Gossip and rumours are closely related. Gossip can often be detected by examining the motive of the person spreading it. For example, private but true information about a co-worker often takes the form of gossip. Gossip has been defined as "small talk about personal affairs and people's activities with or without a known basis in fact" (Rosnow & Fine, 1976). Similarly, if private information about a co-worker is disseminated without his or her knowledge or consent, this too can be seen as gossip.

Negative gossip can empower the gossiper and disempower the person being gossiped about (Kurland & Pelled, 2000), although gossip can also backfire and harm the gossiper.

Gossip, like rumour, has been referred to as "grapevine communication." One study (Baker & Jones, 1996) highlighted the fact that although many organization leaders say they prefer direct means of communicating, employees often depend on the grapevine within organizations to receive and deliver information.

There is no simple solution to gossip in the workplace. Sometimes it's easiest just to ignore it. But if gossip is hurtful, damaging, and persistent, action needs to be taken. Many of the strategies for preventing rumours apply to gossip as well. It may be helpful to consider the gossiper as a sort of bully or harasser. In that context, the victim needs to be protected from gossip at the workplace just as he or she would from any form of harassment.

ANONYMOUS COMMUNICATION   Many organizations oppose or ignore anonymous communication. For example, accusations against supervisors or co-workers are often not seen as legitimate unless the source is known. But in reality the issue is not that simple. The old-fashioned suggestion box, replaced today by a variety of new communication technologies, gives workers more opportunity to communicate ideas and concerns without identifying themselves. Anonymity allows people in an organization to say what they think, communicate about sensitive topics, and generally interact more openly (Scott & Rains, 2005).

Under what circumstances is anonymous communication acceptable or even preferred? Most colleges and universities distribute anonymous questionnaires in order for students to evaluate their instructors. This seems fair, since students may fear retribution if they negatively evaluate an instructor. Similarly, organizations may introduce an anonymous questionnaire to receive feedback on a manager or supervisor. It's difficult to avoid the conclusion that the greater the power differential and the greater the lack of security and trust between people in an organization, the more likely it is that they'll prefer anonymous communication. However, the solution to a worker's dissatisfaction often lies in direct communication between the worker and her supervisor. This solution isn't possible when communication is anonymous.

INTERPERSONAL CHOICE POINT

Conflict with Supervisors

Conflict with supervisors can have a detrimental effect on your career, and yet you may disagree strongly with your supervisor on an issue that is important to you. In this case, how would you approach a potential conflict situation in a way that minimizes the possibility of negative repercussions? In what situations might you choose to avoid the conflict altogether?

Anonymous communication can be most effective when it's part of organizational surveys or assessments (Scott & Rains, 2005). Anonymous communication may allow workers who feel powerless to express views that may, in fact, benefit the organization. Organizations that use anonymous communication need to provide clear guidelines to employees regarding appropriate and inappropriate uses of anonymous communication. Clearly, the spread of rumours and gossip through anonymous communication should be considered unacceptable.

UNTRUTHFUL COMMUNICATION   An article in *Maclean's* magazine (Righton, 2006) began with the following sentence: "Prospective employers take note: In the business world, honesty is rarely the best policy." Simply put, lying seems to be so inherent in our workplaces (as in other realms of life) that those who don't lie are often disadvantaged. We are reminded (Righton, 2006) that most people lie an average of six times a day, from "real whoppers to slight obfuscations, omissions, false compliments and exaggerations," and often these lies are considered essential for getting ahead in the workplace. Typical lies include falsifying a résumé and taking credit for someone else's work to get a promotion.

People generally discriminate between lies that are harmless and used to smooth over social situations, and those that are hurtful, damaging, or callous. Thus, a mildly untruthful response—"Fine, thank you" to the question "How are you today?" when you really aren't fine—seems to be acceptable. Falsifying information that would impact a person's decision (for example, accident details on a used car that's for sale) is seen by many as unacceptable.

While the trend in business seems to be that lying isn't always serious, and that the focus should instead be on cheating, stealing, or telling callous lies about co-workers, we may want to consider another approach. Just as workplaces today take measures to prevent the spread of the common cold—putting up signs reminding people to wash their hands and installing air filters, automatic taps, and doors that open with a foot pedal—so could workplaces act to limit lying. Like a cold, such lying usually isn't fatal, but it's also usually not healthy. We can encourage truthful communication by modelling it, by reminding people of its value, and by being careful not to disadvantage the truthful communicator.

WORKPLACE RELATIONSHIPS

Workplace relationships are becoming more and more important as more of our time is spent in work situations, whether face to face in the traditional office or online. Let's look at several kinds of workplace relationships: mentoring, networking, and working in teams.

Mentoring Relationships

In a **mentoring relationship**, an experienced individual helps train a person who is less experienced. An accomplished teacher, for example, might mentor a young teacher who is newly arrived in a school or who has never taught before. The mentor guides the new person through the ropes, teaches the strategies and techniques for success, and otherwise communicates his or her accumulated knowledge and experience to the mentored.

The mentoring relationship provides an ideal learning environment. It's usually a supportive and trusting one-on-one relationship between expert and novice. There's a mutual and open sharing of information and thoughts about the job. The relationship enables the novice to try out new skills under the guidance of an expert, to ask questions, and to obtain the feedback so necessary to the acquisition of complex skills. Mentoring is perhaps best characterized as a relationship in which the experienced and powerful mentor empowers the novice, giving the novice the tools and techniques for gaining the same power the mentor now holds. Few mentoring relationships have as much potential for personal growth as the relationship between a manager and an employee (Brown, 2003).

Monkey Business Images/Shutterstock

VIEWPOINTS **Online Mentoring**

Not surprisingly, today mentoring is frequently conducted online. One great advantage of ementoring is the flexibility it allows for communication—email messages, for example, can be sent and received at times that are convenient for the individuals involved (Stewart, 2006). Further, it's possible to have mentor–protégé relationships with people who are far away or who can't readily travel (Burgstahler, 2007).

At the same time, the mentor benefits from clarifying his or her thoughts, from seeing the job from the perspective of a newcomer, and from considering and formulating answers to a variety of questions. Just as a teacher learns from teaching, a mentor learns from mentoring.

Networking Relationships

Networking is more than a technique for securing a job. It is a broad process of enlisting the aid of other people to help you solve a problem or to offer insights that bear on your problem—for example, on how to publish your manuscript, where to go for low-cost auto insurance, how to find an apartment, or how to empty your cache (Heenehan, 1997). Here are a few principles for effective networking, which have special application to the workplace but which you'll find generally useful. Serious networking would include social media networking sites such as LinkedIn or Plaxo. They offer opportunities for networking that are simply not available offline.

Start your networking with people you already know. You'll probably discover that you know a great number of people with specialized knowledge who can be of assistance (Rector & Neiva, 1996). You can also network with people who know the people you know. Thus, you may contact a friend's friend to find out whether the firm where he or she works is hiring. Or you may contact people with whom you have no connection. Perhaps you've read something the person wrote or heard the person's name raised in connection with an area in which you're interested and you want to get more information. With email addresses so readily available, it's now quite common to email individuals who have particular expertise and ask your questions. Newsgroups and chat rooms are other obvious networking avenues.

> **INTERPERSONAL CHOICE POINT**
>
> **Networking**
>
> You want to establish a small mail-order business selling framed prints; you plan to buy the frames and prints separately and inexpensively at yard sales, restore them, and sell them. What types of network connections might be appropriate in this situation? How would you go about the actual networking?

Try to establish relationships that are mutually beneficial. If you can provide others with helpful information, it's more likely that they'll provide helpful information for you. In this way, you establish a mutually satisfying and productive network.

Be proactive; initiate contacts rather than waiting for them to come to you. If you're also willing to help others, there's nothing wrong in asking these same people to help you. If you're respectful of your contacts' time and expertise, it's likely that they'll respond favourably to your networking attempts. Following up your requests with thank-you notes—the polite thing to do—will help you establish networks that can be ongoing relationships.

Working in Teams

Much workplace communication today takes place in teams. Team approaches to planning, problem solving, and getting the work done seem to be gaining recognition and popularity in organizations. Two main premises apply to teamwork: "Several heads are better than one" and "The sum is greater than all its parts." Teams develop over time as people work together, and the stages of team development are often described (MacMillan, 2001) as

- forming (becoming oriented)
- storming (struggling over purpose and goals)
- norming (resolving concerns, building trust)
- performing (working productively towards shared goals)
- transforming (bringing about change, celebrating accomplishments)

Team members carry out different functions. Some members play a significant role in keeping spirits up and providing emotional support, some play devil's advocate by challenging views and sometimes seeming negative, while others may play the more instrumental role of actually getting the tasks done. Most teams have a designated leader, but different members of the team will often take on leadership roles at various times.

General guidelines for effective communication are equally applicable to a team setting, but given that teams often have specific tasks and timelines in which to achieve these tasks, some features of effective communication stand out. Useful tips can be found in the "Teams" section at www.effectivemeetings.com. They include the following:

- Communicate, communicate, communicate.
- Listen actively.
- Do not blame others.
- Support group members' ideas.
- Get involved.
- No bragging.
- Be positive.

In addition, it is vital to be sensitive to the diversity issues described earlier in this chapter—personality, gender, culture, ability, organizational culture, and professional culture. The team can be seen as a micro-organization within an organization, and therefore all these factors come into play.

LEADERSHIP IN THE WORKPLACE: BEING A POWERFUL COMMUNICATOR

Effective leadership in the workplace is a rapidly growing field of study; numerous books, articles, and courses now define leadership and provide advice on how to be effective as a leader. Leaders can be managers or CEOs or have other titles that give them the power to make decisions and influence people. Both formal and informal leadership roles exist in organizations. Formal leaders may have responsibilities for a range of domains, from multi-site industries to small departments within an organization. Informal leaders may also sometimes be influential in organizations. These informal leaders are people without official titles or offices, but who are respected because of personal wisdom or a willingness to share (Anderson, 1997). Informal leaders are often role models who take on mentoring roles with colleagues.

So what is the essence of leadership, whether it's formal or informal? Leadership consists of having the ability to affect and influence others and bring about change. In short, leaders have the power to influence others, whether through force or through more acceptable means such as modelling, persuasion, and developing a common vision and goals.

The most respected kind of leader is referred to as the "transformational leader" (Riggio, 2009) who is empathic rather than confrontational. The transformational leader shares power with others and values collaboration. Usually the transformational leader becomes a source of inspiration to others, considers others' needs, and stimulates them to look at the world from new perspectives. The transformational leader has the trust of those who work with him, fosters creativity, and provides inspirational motivation (Cherry, 2014b).

INTERPERSONAL CHOICE POINT

Giving Everyone a Turn

How would you ensure that the team you're leading is respectful of the diversity of its members? How would you ensure that the introvert is able to contribute in a meaningful way? What about the novice, who may not yet have the confidence to speak in front of the group? How would you request that someone who is dominating the meeting give others a chance to participate as well?

Leadership and Power

Sometimes we think of power negatively—as if it connotes the use of power to dominate others. In fact, good leaders influence others through powerful communication. Good leaders share power and empower others. Understanding how to communicate powerfully in the workplace will help make you a better member of the team and the organization, as well as a better leader.

The next section examines the principles of power, and focuses especially on how you can increase your own interpersonal power in the workplace.

PRINCIPLES OF POWER

Interpersonal power is what enables the individual with power to influence the behaviours of others, and is governed by a few important principles. These principles spell out the basic characteristics of power. They help explain how power works interpersonally and how you may more effectively deal with power.

Power Varies from Person to Person

Some people are born with assets that empower them, but anyone can increase his or her interpersonal power. You can, for example, learn the principles of effective communication and increase your power to persuade.

Confidence communicates power. One of the clearest ways you can communicate power is by demonstrating confidence through your verbal and nonverbal behaviours. The confident communicator is relaxed (rather than rigid); flexible in voice and body (rather than locked into one or two ranges of voice or body movement); and controlled (rather than shaky or awkward). A relaxed posture is more likely to portray confidence and sense of control, status, and power than would the appearance of tension or rigidity.

Here are a few additional suggestions for communicating confidence:

- Take the initiative in introducing yourself to others and in introducing topics of conversation; try not to wait for others to act first. When you react, rather than act, you're more likely to communicate a lack of confidence and control over the situation.
- Use open-ended questions to involve the other person in the interaction (as opposed to questions that merely ask for a yes or no answer). Follow up these questions with appropriate comments or additional questions.
- Use you-statements. These are statements that directly address the other person—they're not accusatory, but instead signal a direct and personalized focus on the other person, such as "Do you agree?" or "How do you feel about that?"
- Avoid various forms of powerless language, such as statements that express a lack of conviction or that are self-critical. Starting a communication with "I may be wrong but…" is an example of powerless language.

Record yourself making a short presentation, and then play it back. Do you observe evidence of powerless speech behaviours? What behaviours do you observe that showed confidence?

Power Is a Part of All Interpersonal Messages

Chapter 1 introduced the key principle that it's impossible to *not* communicate. By the same token, you can't communicate without making some implicit comment on your power or lack of it. When interacting, therefore, recognize that on the basis of your verbal and nonverbal messages, people will assess your power—along with your competence, trustworthiness, honesty, openness, and so on.

The ways in which people communicate powerfulness and powerlessness through speech have received lots of research attention (Dillard & Marshall, 2003; Johnson, 1987; Kleinke, 1986; Molloy, 1981). Generally, research finds that men use more powerful language forms than do women (Lakoff, 1975; Timmerman, 2002). Listed below are the major characteristics of powerless speech. As you consider this list, think of your own speech. Do you avoid the following speech behaviours?

- *Hesitation* makes you sound unprepared and uncertain. Example: "I . . . er . . . want to say that . . . ah . . . this one is . . . er . . . the best, you know?"
- Too many *intensifiers* make your speech monotonous and don't allow you to stress what you do want to emphasize. Example: "Really, this was the greatest; it was truly phenomenal."
- *Disqualifiers* signal a lack of competence and a feeling of uncertainty. Examples: "I didn't read the entire article, but . . ." or "I didn't actually see the accident, but . . ."
- *Tag questions* ask for another's agreement and therefore may signal your need for agreement—and your own uncertainty. Examples: "That was a great movie, wasn't it?" or "She's brilliant, don't you think?"
- *Self-critical statements* signal a lack of confidence and may make public your own inadequacies. Examples: "I'm not very good at this" or "This is my first public speech."
- *Slang and vulgar language* suggest low social class and hence little power. Examples: "@*+#?$!!" or "No problem!"

AVAVA/Shutterstock

Research finds that men are generally perceived to have higher levels of *legitimate power* (based on the belief that by virtue of their position they have the right to influence or control others' behaviour). Women, by contrast, are generally perceived to have higher levels of *referent power* (based on others' desire to identify with or be like that individual).

NONVERBAL COMMUNICATION OF POWER   Just as you communicate your power (or lack of power) verbally, you also communicate it nonverbally—for example, through the things you wear and own. Truly powerful people have no time for new trends that come and go every six months. Further, they don't wear or have anything cheap because they have money to buy the real thing.

Nonverbal communication takes on a key role in the workplace environment. The norms for nonverbal communication will be impacted by all the factors reviewed at the beginning of this chapter relating to diversity. Dress code norms, for example, may be challenged by younger workers who may emphasize casual attire, tattoos, or body piercing.

Touching, which is a major aspect of nonverbal communication, can also be an expression of power. Touching takes on great complexity in workplace settings. The interpretation of touching is strongly influenced by one's own culture, gender, and the culture of the profession. It's probably better to err on the side of caution and avoid touching, hugging, or patting on the back, unless you're certain that it will be interpreted as you intended.

Nonverbal behaviour can convey a lack of power, as when someone fidgets at a meeting, indicating discomfort. A powerful person may be bored but will not appear uncomfortable or ill at ease.

Territory also reflects a person's power. It's difficult for the junior executive who operates out of a cubbyhole in the basement of some huge office complex to appear powerful with an old metal desk and beat-up filing cabinet. Often, however, you're more in control of your space than you may realize. Clutter can signify a lack of power—and can easily be eliminated to communicate a more powerful image.

But perhaps the most important part of communicating power is demonstrating your knowledge, your preparation, and your organization in relation to whatever you're doing. If you can exhibit control over your own responsibilities, people will generally conclude that you can and do exhibit control over other aspects of life.

EMPOWERING OTHERS   While it's important to understand and learn the strategies that will enhance your own power, remember that empowering others is just as important. People who feel confident of their own power tend to make more efforts to help others feel empowered. And while empowering others is certainly a characteristic of effective leaders, it's also part of collegial relationships at work.

Power Is Frequently Used Unfairly

Although it would be nice if power were always wielded for the good of all, it's often used selfishly and unfairly in the workplace. We see unethical uses of power in interpersonal relationships more frequently than we would wish. Here we look at two serious examples of the unethical use of power: sexual harassment and power plays.

SEXUAL HARASSMENT   Harassment of any kind, particularly sexual harassment, is an extreme form of abuse of power. Sexual harassment violates Canadian law and the Canadian Human Rights Act. There are two general categories of sexual harassment. In one, employment opportunities (as in hiring and promotion) are made dependent on the granting of sexual favours. Reprisals and various negative consequences can result from the failure to grant such sexual favours.

The other category is hostile-environment harassment, which is broader and includes all sexual behaviours (verbal and nonverbal) that make a worker uncomfortable. Putting sexually explicit pictures on the bulletin board, using sexually explicit screen savers, telling sexual jokes and stories, and using sexual and demeaning language or gestures all constitute hostile environment harassment.

Although most cases brought to public attention are committed by men against women, women may also harass men. Anyone in an organization can be guilty of sexual harassment, although most cases of harassment involve people in authority who harass subordinates. And sexual harassment isn't limited to business organizations, of course; it can occur in schools, in hospitals, and in social, religious, and political organizations.

For those who think they may be a victim of sexual harassment, a good guideline is available from the Student Legal Services of Edmonton (www.slsedmonton.com). The most important thing to remember is that rather than worrying whether what you're experiencing may or may not "qualify" as harassment, consult with an adviser for support and advice.

POWER PLAYS   **Power plays** are patterns of communication (not isolated instances) that take unfair advantage of another person (Steiner, 1981). These are less obvious abuses of power that can be disempowering to others. When someone constantly ignores you or what you say, you can feel disempowered. When someone constantly reminds you that you "owe them" for a past favour, they're exerting unfair power. Or if someone constantly turns everything into a joke, this can be an attempt to take your power away.

When you feel trapped in a power play, try the following:

- *Express your feelings.* Tell the person that you're angry, annoyed, or disturbed by his or her behaviour.
- *Describe the behaviour to which you object.* Tell the person—in language that describes rather than evaluates—the specific behaviour you object to; for example, reading your mail, coming into your office without knocking, persisting in trying to hug you.
- *State a cooperative response that you can both live with comfortably.* Tell the person—in a cooperative tone—what you want; for example, "I want you to knock before coming into my office."

INTRAPERSONAL POWER: SELF-ESTEEM

How much do you like yourself? How valuable a person do you think you are? How competent do you think you are? The answers to these questions will reflect your **self-esteem**, the value that you place on yourself.

Success breeds success. When you feel good about yourself—about who you are and what you're capable of doing—you will perform better. When you think like a success, you're more likely to act like a success. When you think you're a failure, you're more likely to act like a failure. Increasing self-esteem will, therefore, help you function more effectively in interpersonal relationships and in careers. Here are a few suggestions for increasing self-esteem. Recognize, though, that too much self-esteem can be detrimental and can become arrogance (Baumeister et al., 2000; Hewitt, 1998), especially if based on an unrealistic appraisal of yourself (Bower, 2001).

Attack Self-Destructive Beliefs

Actively challenge those beliefs you have about yourself that you find are unproductive or that make it more difficult for you to achieve your goals. Examples of unproductive beliefs are the feeling that you have to succeed in everything you do and believing that you have to be loved by everyone. Replace these self-destructive beliefs with more productive ones, such as "I succeed in many things; I don't have to succeed in everything" and "It would be nice to be loved by everyone, but it isn't necessary to my well-being or my happiness."

Seek Out Positive People

Some people criticize and find fault with just about everything. Others are positive and optimistic—they reward us, they stroke us, they make us feel good about ourselves. To enhance your self-esteem, seek out these people. At the same time, avoid negative people, those who don't make you feel good about yourself.

Secure Affirmation

Remind yourself of your successes. Focus on your good deeds, your positive qualities, strengths, and virtues, and keep your last positive performance appraisal in your desk so that you can refer to it occasionally.

Affirm yourself by trying to honestly appraise your strengths, and then focus on them. For example, you could affirm yourself by stating:

- I am a reliable employee.
- I have made positive contributions to the sales campaign.
- I helped most of my clients find employment.

Work on Projects That Will Result in Success

Try to consciously select projects that will result in success. Each success will help build self-esteem and make the next success a little easier.

When a project does fail, recognize that this doesn't mean you're a failure. Everyone fails somewhere along the line. Failure is something that happens—it's not necessarily something you've created and it's not something inside you. Further, your failing once doesn't mean that you'll fail the next time. So put failure in perspective. Don't make it an excuse for not trying again.

"So, when he says, 'What a good boy am I,' Jack is really reinforcing his self-esteem."

INTERPERSONAL POWER: ASSERTIVENESS

If you disagree with other people in a group, do you speak your mind? Do you allow others to take advantage of you because you're reluctant to say what you want? Do you feel uncomfortable when you have to state your opinion in a group? Questions such as these revolve around your degree of **assertiveness**.

Assertive Versus Nonassertive and Aggressive Messages

BEHAVING ASSERTIVELY   Assertive behaviour—behaviour that enables you to act in your own best interests *without* denying or infringing on the rights of others—is the generally desired alternative to nonassertiveness or aggressiveness. Assertive people operate with an "I win, you win" philosophy; they assume that both people can gain something from an interpersonal interaction, even from a confrontation.

Assertive people are willing to assert their own rights. Unlike their aggressive counterparts, however, they don't hurt others in the process. Assertive people speak their minds and welcome others' doing likewise.

COMMUNICATING ASSERTIVELY   Assertive messages contrast with aggressive messages (as discussed in Chapter 6), which are hurtful or disrespectful to others, and with nonassertive messages, in which one's own rights aren't asserted. This can result in a "You win, I lose" situation (Lloyd, 2001). In order to communicate assertively, here's a generally effective pattern to follow:

- *Describe the problem; don't evaluate or judge it.* "We're all working on this advertising project together. You're missing half our meetings, and you still haven't produced your first report."
- *State how this problem affects you.* Be sure to use I-messages and to avoid messages that accuse or blame the other person. "Our jobs depend on the success of this project and I don't think it's fair that I have to do extra work to make up for what you're not doing."
- *Propose solutions that are workable and that allow the person to save face.* "If you can get your report to the group by Tuesday, we'll still be able to meet our deadline. And I could give you a call an hour before the meetings to remind you."
- *Confirm understanding.* "Is it clear that we just can't produce this project if you're not going to pull your own weight? Will you have the report to us by Tuesday?"

COMMUNICATING POLITELY   Communicating assertively also means communicating politely. From your initial interview to your first day on the job and throughout your progression up the organizational ladder, politeness on the job is critical. The same general rules for effective interpersonal interaction stressed throughout this text apply here as well, of course: be positive, be expressive, listen carefully, and so on. There are, however, certain rules for polite interaction that take on special importance in the workplace. Moreover, each organization—much like each culture—will have somewhat different rules for what is considered polite. Nevertheless, here are a few general suggestions for politeness on the job, which seem near universal:

- *Be respectful of a colleague's time.* Don't copy those who don't need to be copied, don't tag people just for the sake of tagging, be brief and organized, respond to requests as soon as possible, and, when not possible, alert the other person; for example, "The figures will be sent as soon as they arrive, probably by the end of the day."
- *Be respectful of a person's territory.* Don't invade another's office or desk space; don't overstay your welcome. Treat another's work space as his or her private territory into which you must be invited.

- *Follow the rules for effective electronic communication.* Discover and adhere to the rules governing the use of emails, internet game playing, cell phones, social networking, and instant messaging.
- *Discard your Facebook grammar.* Abbreviations, acronyms, and smileys—so common in social media—are best avoided here. These may be seen as not showing sufficient respect or seriousness of purpose.
- *Use the appropriate medium for sending messages.* Generally, the rule is to respond in kind—for example, if a question is texted to you, text back; if it's been emailed, answer it in email.
- *Avoid touching except in shaking hands.* Touching is often interpreted as a sexual overture, so it's best avoided on the job. Touching may also imply a familiarity that the other person may not welcome. Your best bet is to avoid initiating touching.
- *Treat everyone politely,* even the newest intern, as if that person will one day be your boss. Follow the organization's rules of politeness; for example, in answering phones, addressing management, dress, lateness, and desk materials.

?

Can you explain the nature of work relationships (mentoring, networking, and the issues involved in power and communication)?

CANADIAN PROFILE: WRAP-UP

Sharon Carry/Bow Valley College

As a college president, Sharon Carry has made it a focus of her work to integrate strong communication strategies into college life. In your current or past place of employment, who were the key people who influenced the tone and effectiveness of communication? Were those influences positive or negative? After reading this chapter, what recommendations would you have to enhance the communication in your current work setting?

SUMMARY OF CONCEPTS AND SKILLS

This chapter explored aspects of workplace communication, including diversity in the workplace; modes of communication at work; negative communication patterns such as rumours, gossip, and untruthful communication; and personal power, self-esteem, and assertiveness.

Diversity in the Workplace

1. Workplace settings today are complex and diverse. Understanding the diversity of the workplace will help us become more effective communicators. This diversity includes a multigenerational workforce and staff from diverse cultures, with different abilities and temperaments.

The Culture of the Workplace

2. Organizations have their own culture, and often include different subcultures. Similarly, occupational groups and professions usually have marked cultures.

Workplace Communication

3. Electronic and written communication are important aspects of workforce communication.

Workplace Relationships

4. Positive communication and work can take place in teams, in mentoring relationships, and through networks.
5. Understanding the sources and reasons for negative communication in the workplace, such as gossip, rumours, and untruthfulness, can help deal with these issues.

Leadership in the Workplace: Being a Powerful Communicator

6. Effective leadership, whether it's formal or informal, is based on the ability to influence others and bring about change.

Principles of Power

7. Five principles govern power in interpersonal relationships: power varies from person to person, power is a part of all interpersonal messages, and power is often used unfairly.

Intrapersonal Power: Self-Esteem

8. Self-esteem is the way you see yourself, the value you place on yourself.

Interpersonal Power: Assertiveness

9. Assertive people stand up for their rights without denying or infringing upon the rights of others. To communicate assertively, begin by describing the problem, then state how it affects you, propose workable solutions, and confirm understanding. Communicating assertively also involves communicating politely.

In addition to the above concepts, this chapter covered several interpersonal skills. As you read over the list, place a check beside those you feel you'd like to work on:

——1. *Recognition*. Recognize the existing diversity in my own workplace.
——2. *Adaptation*. Adapt my communication to the diversity in my workplace.
——3. *Understanding*. Understand the culture of my organization.
——4. *Multiple modes*. Practise effective workplace communication—verbal, nonverbal, electronic, and written.
——5. *Affirmation*. Engage in self-affirmation.
——6. *Power management*. Manage power through verbal and nonverbal messages.
——7. *Harassment avoidance*. Avoid behaviours that could be interpreted as sexually harassing.
——8. *Strategic responses*. Respond to power plays with appropriate strategies.
——9. *Assertiveness*. Communicate assertively when it's appropriate to the situation.

VOCABULARY QUIZ: **The Language of Workplace Communication**

Match the terms of workplace communication with their definitions. Record the number of the definition next to the appropriate term.

——— self-esteem (251)
——— mentoring relationship (245)
——— assertiveness (252)
——— role culture (235)
——— networking (246)
——— millennials (233)
——— power play (250)
——— achievement culture (236)
——— confidence (248)
——— baby boomers (233)

1. Connecting with people who can help you accomplish a goal or find information.
2. An organizational culture marked by conformity, clear regulations, and defined tasks.
3. The ability to state your feelings, describe the behaviour you object to, and state a response both you and the other person will find acceptable.
4. The generation born between 1946 and 1965.
5. The value you place on yourself.
6. An organizational culture that's marked by less formal rules and that fosters creativity.
7. A relationship in which an experienced person helps train someone less experienced.
8. A comfortable, at-ease feeling in interpersonal communication situations.
9. The generation born after 1980.
10. A pattern of communication that takes unfair advantage of another person.

These 10 terms and additional key terms from this chapter can be found in the glossary.

GLOSSARY OF INTERPERSONAL COMMUNICATION CONCEPTS AND SKILLS

Listed here are definitions of the technical terms of interpersonal communication—the words that are peculiar or unique to this discipline—along with relevant skills where applicable (in *italics*). These definitions and skill statements should make new or difficult terms a bit easier to understand and should serve as reminders of the skills discussed throughout this text. All boldface terms within the definitions appear as separate entries in the glossary.

Abstract terms   Words that refer to concepts and ideas that have no physical dimensions (friendship, value, fear). *See also* **concrete terms**. *Use both abstract and concrete language when describing or explaining.*

Acculturation   The process by which one culture is modified or changed through contact with or exposure to another culture.

Active listening   The process by which a listener expresses his or her understanding of the speaker's total message, including the verbal and nonverbal, the thoughts and feelings. *Be an active listener: paraphrase the speaker's meaning, express understanding of the speaker's feelings, and ask questions when necessary.*

Adaptors   Nonverbal behaviours that, when engaged in, either in private or in public, serve some kind of need and occur in their entirety—for example, scratching one's head until the itch is relieved. *Generally, avoid adaptors; they may make you appear uncomfortable or ill at ease.*

Adjustment, principle of   The principle of verbal interaction that claims that effective communication depends on the extent to which communicators share the same system of signals.

Advice   Messages that tell another person what he or she should do.

Affect displays   Movements of the facial area that convey emotional meaning, such as anger, fear, and surprise.

Affinity-seeking strategies   Behaviours designed to increase interpersonal attractiveness.

Ageism   Discrimination based on age, usually against older people.

Alter-adaptors   Body movements you make in response to your current interactions—for example, crossing your arms over your chest when someone unpleasant approaches or moving closer to someone you like.

Ambiguity   The condition in which a message or relationship may be interpreted as having more than one meaning.

Anger management   The methods and techniques by which anger is controlled and managed. *Calm down as best you can; then consider your communication options and the relevant communication skills for expressing your feelings.*

Anonymous messages   Messages in which the author is not identified. Opposed to **onymous messages**.

Apology   An expression of regret or sorrow for having done what you did or for what happened.

Argumentativeness   A willingness to argue for a point of view, to speak one's mind. Distinguished from **verbal aggressiveness**. *Avoid aggressiveness (attacking the other person's self-concept); instead, focus logically on the issues, emphasize finding solutions, and work to ensure that what is said will result in positive self-feelings for both individuals.*

Artifactual messages   Messages conveyed by objects that are made by human hands. Art, colour, clothing, jewellery, hairstyle, and smell are all examples of artifactual messages. *Use artifacts to communicate desired messages and avoid those that may communicate negative or unwanted meanings.*

Assertiveness   A willingness to stand up for one's rights but with respect for the rights of others. *Increase assertiveness (if desired) by analyzing the assertive and non-assertive behaviours of others, analyzing your own behaviours in terms of assertiveness, recording your behaviours, rehearsing assertive behaviours, and acting assertively in appropriate situations. Secure feedback from others for further guidance in increasing assertiveness.*

Asynchronous communication   Communication in which the individuals send and receive messages at different times (as in email communication). Opposed to **synchronous communication**.

Attribution theory   A theory concerned with the processes involved in attributing causation or motivation to a person's behaviour. *In attempting to identify the motivation for behaviours, examine consensus, consistency, distinctiveness, and controllability. Generally, low consensus, high consistency, low distinctiveness, and high controllability identify internally motivated behaviour; high consensus, low consistency, high distinctiveness, and low controllability identify externally motivated behaviour.*

Avoidance   An unproductive conflict strategy in which you take mental or physical flight from the actual conflict.

Baby boomers   The generation born after the Second World War, characterized as competitive, idealistic, searching for self-gratification.

Backchannelling cues   Responses that a listener makes to a speaker (while the speaker is speaking) but that do not ask for the speaking role; for example, interjections such as "I understand" or "You said what?" *Generally, give backchannelling cues to show that you're listening actively.*

Beltlining   An unproductive conflict strategy in which one person hits the other at a vulnerable level—the level at which the other person cannot withstand the blow.

Blame   An unproductive conflict strategy in which we attribute the cause of the conflict to the other person or devote our energies to discovering who is the cause, avoiding talking about the issues at hand. *Avoid it; generally, it diverts attention from solving the problem and serves only to alienate the other person.*

Blended emotions   Emotions that are combinations of the primary emotions; for example, disappointment is a blend of surprise and sadness.

Blind self   In the Johari window model, this self represents all the things about yourself that others know but of which you're ignorant.

Boundary marker   A marker that sets boundaries around or divides one person's territory from another's—for example, a fence.

Bullying   Abusive acts repeatedly committed by one person (or a group) against another.

Central marker   A marker or item that is placed in a territory to reserve it for a specific person—for example, the sweater thrown over a library chair to signal that the chair is taken.

Certainty   An attitude of closed-mindedness that creates defensiveness among communicators.

Channel   The vehicle or medium through which signals are sent; for example, the vocal–auditory channel. *Assess your channel options (for example, face-to-face, email, leaving a voicemail message) before communicating important messages.*

Chronemics   The study of the communicative nature of time, of how a person's or a culture's treatment of time reveals something about the person or culture. Often divided into psychological and cultural time.

Civil inattention   Polite ignoring of others (after a brief sign of awareness) so as not to invade their privacy.

Closed-mindedness   An unwillingness to receive certain communication messages.

Code   A set of symbols used to translate a message from one form to another.

Cognitive labelling theory   A theory of emotions that holds that emotional feelings begin with the occurrence of an event; you respond physiologically to the event, then you interpret the arousal (you in effect decide what it is you're feeling), and then you experience (give a name to) the emotion.

Collectivist culture   A culture in which the group's goals are given greater importance than the individual's and in which, for example, benevolence, tradition, and conformity are given special emphasis. Opposed to **individualist culture**.

Communication accommodation theory   A theory of communication holding that conversationalists adjust to (or accommodate to) the speaking styles of each other.

Compliment   A message of praise, flattery, or congratulations.

Concrete terms   Words that refer to objects, people, and happenings that you perceive with your senses of sight, smell, touch, hearing, or taste. *See also* **abstract terms**.

Confidence   A quality of interpersonal effectiveness (and a factor in interpersonal power); a comfortable, at-ease feeling in interpersonal communication situations.

Confirmation   A communication pattern that acknowledges another person's presence and indicates an acceptance of this person, this person's self-definition, and the relationship as defined or viewed by this other person. Opposed to **rejection** and **disconfirmation**. *When you wish to be confirming, acknowledge (verbally and/or nonverbally) others in your group and their contributions.*

Conflict   A disagreement or difference of opinion; a form of competition in which one person tries to bring a rival to surrender; a situation in which one person's behaviours are directed at preventing something or at interfering with or harming another individual. *See also* **interpersonal conflict**. *Engage in interpersonal conflict actively—be appropriately revealing, see the situation from your partner's perspective, and listen to your partner. Approach conflict with an understanding of the cultural and gender differences in attitudes toward what constitutes conflict and how it should be pursued.*

Connotation   The feeling or emotional aspect of a word's meaning; generally viewed as consisting of evaluation (for example, good–bad), potency (strong–weak), and activity (fast–slow) dimensions. Opposed to **denotation**. *Clarify your connotative meanings if you have any concern that your listeners might misunderstand you; as a listener, ask questions if you have doubts about the speaker's connotations.*

Consistency   A tendency to maintain balance in your perception of messages or people; because of this process, you tend to see what you expect to see and to be uncomfortable when your perceptions run contrary to expectations.

Content and relationship dimensions   Two aspects to which messages may refer: the world external to both speaker and listener (content) and the connections existing between the individuals who are interacting (relationship). *Listen to both the content and the relationship aspects of messages, distinguish between them, and respond to both. Analyze conflict messages in terms of content and relationship dimensions, and respond to each accordingly.*

Context of communication   The physical, psychological, social, and temporal environment in which communication takes place. *Adjust your messages to the physical, cultural, social-psychological, and temporal context.*

Contrast, principle of   A principle of perception according to which items that are very distinct from each other are seen as separate and not belonging to the same group.

Credibility   The degree to which people see a person as believable; competence, character, and charisma (dynamism) are major factors in credibility.

Cultural display   Signs that communicate a person's cultural identification, such as clothing or religious jewellery.

Culture   The lifestyle of a group of people; their values, beliefs, artifacts, ways of behaving, and ways of communicating. Culture includes everything that members of a social group have produced and developed—their language, ways of thinking, art, laws, and religion—and that is transmitted from one generation to another through communication rather than genes. *Look at cultural differences not as deviations or deficiencies but as the differences they are. Recognizing different ways of doing things, however, does not necessarily mean accepting them. Communicate with an understanding that culture influences communication in all its forms. Increase your cultural sensitivity by learning about different cultures, recognizing and facing your fears, recognizing relevant differences, and becoming conscious of the cultural rules of other cultures.*

Culture shock   The reactions people experience when in a culture very different from their own and from what they are used to.

Dating statements   An extensional device used to emphasize the notion of constant change and symbolized by a subscript; for example, John Smith$_{2010}$ is not John Smith$_{2014}$. *Date your statements to avoid thinking of the world as static and unchanging. Reflect the inevitability of change in your messages.*

Decoder   Something that takes a message in one form (for example, sound waves) and translates it into another form (for example, nerve impulses) from which meaning can be formulated. In human communication, the decoder is the auditory mechanism; in electronic communication, the decoder is, for example, the telephone earpiece. Decoding is the process of extracting a message from a code—for example, translating speech sounds into nerve impulses. *See also* **encoder**.

Defensiveness   An attitude of an individual or an atmosphere in a group characterized by threats, fear, and domination; messages evidencing evaluation, control, strategy, neutrality, superiority, and certainty are thought to lead to defensiveness. Opposed to **supportiveness**.

Denotation   The objective or descriptive aspect of a word's meaning; the meaning you'd find in a dictionary. Opposed to **connotation**.

Dialogue   A form of communication in which each person is both speaker and listener; communication characterized by involvement, concern, and respect for the other person. Opposed to **monologue**.

Direct speech   Speech in which the speaker's intentions are stated clearly and directly.

Disconfirmation   The process by which someone ignores or denies the right of another individual even to define himself or herself. Opposed to **rejection** and **confirmation**. *Generally, avoid disconfirmation along with sexist, heterosexist, racist, and ageist language, which is insulting and invariably creates communication barriers.*

Display rules   Rules or customs (of a culture or an organization) that govern what is and what is not permissible communication.

Earmarker   A marker that identifies an item as belonging to a specific person—for example, a nameplate on a desk or initials on an attaché case. *Observe the markers of others; they often reveal a person's thinking about his or her territory.*

Effect   The outcome or consequence of an action or behaviour; communication is assumed always to have some effect.

Emblems   Nonverbal behaviours that directly translate words or phrases—for example, the signs for okay and peace.

Emotion   The feelings we have—for example, our feelings of guilt, anger, or love.

Emotional communication   The expression of feelings—for example, feelings of guilt, happiness, or sorrow. *Identify and describe emotions (both positive and negative) clearly and specifically. Learn the vocabulary of emotional expression. Communicate emotions effectively: confront the obstacles to emotional expression; describe your feelings, identifying the reasons behind them; anchor feelings to the present; and own your feelings and messages.*

Emotional contagion   The process by which the strong emotions of one person are taken on by another person; the assumption that, like the flu, emotions may be contagious.

Empathy   A quality of interpersonal effectiveness that involves sharing others' feelings; an ability to feel or perceive things from others' points of view. *Communicate empathy when appropriate: resist evaluating the person, focus on the person, express active involvement through facial expressions and gestures, reflect back the feelings you think are being expressed, self-disclose, and address mixed messages.*

Encoder   Something that takes a message in one form (for example, nerve impulses) and translates it into another form (for example, sound waves). In human communication, the encoder is the speaking mechanism; in electronic communication, the encoder is, for example, the telephone mouthpiece. Encoding is the process of putting a message into a code—for example, translating nerve impulses into speech sounds. *See also* **decoder**.

Enculturation   The process by which culture is transmitted from one generation to another.

Equity theory   A theory claiming that people experience relational satisfaction when there is an equal distribution of rewards and costs between the two persons in the relationship.

Ethics   The branch of philosophy that deals with the rightness or wrongness of actions; the study of moral values; in communication, the morality of message behaviour.

Ethnic identity   The commitment to the beliefs and philosophy of one's culture; the degree to which a person identifies with his or her cultural group.

Ethnocentrism   The tendency to see others and their behaviours through your own cultural filters, often as distortions of your own behaviours; the tendency to evaluate the values and beliefs of your own culture more positively than those of another culture. *Recognize your own ethnocentric thinking, and be aware of how it influences your verbal and nonverbal messages.*

Evaluation   A process whereby we place a value on some person, object, or event.

Facial feedback hypothesis   The hypothesis or theory that your facial expressions can produce physiological and emotional effects via a feedback mechanism.

Fact–inference confusion   A misevaluation in which a person makes an inference, regards it as a fact, and acts upon it as if it were a fact. *Distinguish facts (verifiably true past events) from inferences (guesses or hypotheses), and act on inferences with tentativeness.*

Feedback   Information that is given back to the source. Feedback may come from the source's own messages (as when you hear what you're saying) or from the receiver(s)—in forms such as applause, yawning, puzzled looks, questions, letters to the editor of a newspaper, or increased or decreased subscriptions to a magazine. *Listen to both verbal and nonverbal feedback—from yourself and from others—and use these cues to help you adjust your messages.*

Feedforward   Information that is sent before a regular message, telling the listener something about what is to follow; messages that are prefatory to more central messages. *Use feedforward when you feel your listener needs background or when you want to ease into a particular topic, such as bad news.*

Feminine culture   A culture that encourages both men and women to be modest, oriented to maintaining the quality of life, and tender. Feminine cultures emphasize the quality of life and so socialize their people to be modest and to emphasize close interpersonal relationships. Opposed to **masculine culture**.

Formal time   Temporal divisions that are measured objectively, such as seconds, minutes, hours, days, weeks, months, and years.

Fundamental attribution error   The tendency to overvalue and overweight the contribution of internal factors (i.e., a person's personality) to behaviour and to undervalue and underweight the contribution of external factors (i.e., the situation the person is in or the surrounding events). *Avoid the fundamental attribution error, whereby you attribute someone's behaviour solely to internal factors while minimizing or ignoring situational forces.*

Generation Xers   The generation born following the baby boomers, characterized as showing self-reliance and preferring balance of family and workplace.

Gunnysacking   An unproductive conflict strategy of storing up grievances—as if in a gunnysack—and holding them in readiness to dump on the other person in the conflict. *Avoid it; it leads you away from considering a workable solution to a problem.*

Halo effect   The tendency to generalize a person's virtue or expertise from one area to other areas. *Beware of this tendency; it can lead you to misperceive a situation or person.*

Haptics   The study of touch or tactile communication.

Heterosexism   Negative attitudes and beliefs about gay men and lesbians; the belief that all sexual behaviour that is not heterosexual is unnatural and deserving of criticism and condemnation.

Heterosexist language   Language that denigrates lesbians and gay men. *Avoid it; it will make you appear a bigot or, at best, ill informed.*

Hidden self   In the Johari window model, this self contains all that you know of yourself that you keep secret.

High-ambiguity tolerant cultures   Cultures that are accepting of ambiguity and do not feel threatened by unknown situations; uncertainty is a normal part of life, and people accept it as it comes.

High-context culture   A culture in which much of the information in communication messages is left implied; it's "understood." Much information is considered to be in the context or in the person rather than explicitly coded in the verbal messages. Collectivist cultures are generally high context. Opposed to **low-context culture**. *Adjust your messages and your listening in light of the differences between high- and low-context cultures.*

High-power distance culture   Cultures in which power is concentrated in the hands of a few and there's a great difference between the power held by these people and the power of the ordinary citizen. *See* **low-power distance culture**.

Illustrators   Nonverbal behaviours that accompany and literally illustrate verbal messages—for example, upward movements of the head and hand that accompany the verbal "It's up there."

Image-confirming strategies   Techniques you use to communicate or to confirm your self-image, the image you want others to see.

I-messages   Messages in which the speaker accepts responsibility for personal thoughts and behaviours and states his or her point of view explicitly. Opposed to **you-messages**. *Use I-messages when communicating your feelings; take responsibility for your own feelings rather than attributing them to others.*

Immediacy   A quality of interpersonal effectiveness that conveys a sense of contact and togetherness, a feeling of interest in and liking for the other person. *Maintain immediacy through close physical distances and eye contact and by smiling, using the other person's name, and focusing on the other's remarks.*

Impostor phenomenon   The tendency to disregard outward signs of success and to consider yourself an "impostor," a fake, a fraud, one who doesn't really deserve to be considered successful.

Impression formation   The process by which you perceive another person and ultimately come to some kind of evaluation or interpretation of this person.

Impression management   The process you go through to communicate the impression you want the other person to have of you. Some writers use the term "self-presentation" or "identity management."

Inclusion, principle of   The principle of verbal interaction holding that all members should be a part of (included in) the interaction.

Index   An extensional device symbolized by a subscript and used to emphasize the assumption that no two things are the same; for example, even though two people may both be politicians, politician1$_{[Smith]}$ is not politician2$_{[Jones]}$. *Use the index to remind yourself that even though people are covered by the same label, they are each individuals.*

Indirect speech   Speech that hides the speaker's true intentions; speech in which requests and observations are made indirectly. *Use indirect messages when a more direct style might prove insulting or offensive, but be aware that indirect messages may also create misunderstanding.*

Indiscrimination   A misevaluation that results when you categorize people, events, or objects into a particular class and respond to them only as members of the class; a failure to recognize that each individual is unique. *Treat each situation and each person as unique (when possible), even when they're covered by the same label.*

Individualist culture   A culture in which the individual's rather than the group's goals and preferences are given greater importance. Opposed to **collectivist culture**. *Adjust your messages and your listening with an awareness of differences between individualist and collectivist cultures.*

Indulgence   A cultural orientation that emphasizes the gratification of desires and a focus on having fun and enjoying life. Opposed to **restraint**.

Inevitability   A principle of communication holding that communication cannot be avoided; all behaviour in an interactional setting is communication.

Influencing strategies   Strategies designed to influence the attitudes or behaviours of others.

Informal time   Temporal divisions that are approximate and that are referred to with such general terms as, for example, *forever, immediately, soon, right away, as soon as possible. Clarify your informal time terms; ask others for clarification when they use such terms, as appropriate.*

Information overload   A condition in which the amount or complexity of information is too great to be dealt with effectively by an individual, group, or organization.

Interpersonal communication Communication between two persons or among a small group of persons and distinguished from public or mass communication; communication of a personal nature and distinguished from impersonal communication; communication between or among connected persons or those involved in a close relationship.

Interpersonal competence The knowledge of and the ability to communicate effectively in interpersonal interactions.

Interpersonal conflict A disagreement between two connected people. *To engage in more productive interpersonal conflict, (1) state your position directly and honestly; (2) react openly to the messages of your opponent; (3) own your thoughts and feelings; (4) address the real issues causing the conflict; (5) listen with and demonstrate empathic understanding; (6) validate the feelings of your interactant; (7) describe the behaviours causing the conflict; (8) express your feelings spontaneously rather than strategically; (9) state your position tentatively; (10) capitalize on agreements; (11) view conflict in positive terms to the extent possible; (12) express positive feelings for the other person; (13) be positive about the prospects of conflict resolution; (14) treat your opponent as an equal, avoiding ridicule or sarcasm; (15) involve yourself in the conflict; play an active role as both sender and receiver; (16) grant the other person permission to express himself or herself freely; and (17) avoid power tactics that may inhibit freedom of expression.*

Interpersonal perception The perception of people; the processes through which you interpret and evaluate people and their behaviour.

Interruptions Verbal and nonverbal attempts to take over the role of the speaker.

Intimate distance The closest distance in proxemics, ranging from touching to 46 centimetres.

Irreversibility A principle of communication holding that communication cannot be reversed; once something has been communicated, it cannot be uncommunicated.

Just world hypothesis The belief that the world is just, that good things happen to good people (because they are good), and that bad things happen to bad people (because they are bad).

Kinesics The study of the communicative dimensions of facial and bodily movements.

Listening An active process of receiving aural stimuli consisting of five stages: receiving, understanding, remembering, evaluating, and responding. *Be especially flexible when listening in a multicultural setting, realizing that people from other cultures give different listening cues and may operate with different rules for listening.* The process of receiving, understanding, remembering, evaluating, and responding to verbal and/or nonverbal messages.

Long-term memory The memory that holds an unlimited amount of information indefinitely.

Long-term orientation A cultural orientation that promotes the importance of future rewards; for example, members of these cultures are more apt to save for the future and to prepare for the future academically. Opposed to **short-term orientation**.

Low-ambiguity tolerant cultures Cultures that are uncomfortable with ambiguity, do much to avoid uncertainty, and

have a great deal of anxiety about not knowing what will happen next.

Low-context culture A culture in which most of the information in communication is explicitly stated in the verbal message rather than being left implied or assumed to be "understood." Low-context cultures are usually individualist cultures. Opposed to **high-context culture**.

Low-power distance culture Culture in which power is relatively evenly distributed throughout the citizenry. *See* **high-power distance culture**.

Lying The act of sending messages with the intention of giving another person information you believe to be false.

Masculine culture A culture that views men as assertive, oriented to material success, and strong; such a culture views women, on the other hand, as modest, focused on the quality of life, and tender. Masculine cultures emphasize success and so socialize their people to be assertive, ambitious, and competitive. Opposed to **feminine culture**.

Mentoring relationship A relationship in which an experienced individual helps train someone who is less experienced; for example, an accomplished teacher might mentor a younger teacher who is newly arrived or who has never taught before.

Message Any signal or combination of signals that serves as a stimulus for a receiver.

Meta-advice Advice about advice; for example, suggesting that someone seek more expert advice.

Metamessage A message that makes reference to another message, such as "Did I make myself clear?" or "That's a lie."

Millennials The generation born after 1980, characterized as having very high self-esteem and confidence and little respect for the wisdom and experience of previous generations.

Mindfulness A mental state achieved by focusing one's awareness on the present moment while calmly acknowledging and accepting one's feelings, thoughts, and bodily sensations. *Although it's used as a therapeutic technique for stress reduction, practising mindfulness will help you become a more effective listener and thus enhance your communication effectiveness.*

Mindlessness A lack of conscious awareness of the logic or reasons behind your thoughts or behaviours. *Increase your mindfulness by creating and re-creating categories and being open to new information and points of view; also, beware of relying too heavily on first impressions.*

Monologue A form of communication in which one person speaks and the other listens; there's no real interaction among participants. Opposed to **dialogue**.

Negative face The desire to be autonomous, to have the right to do as you wish.

Networking Connecting with people who can help you accomplish a goal or help you find information related to your goal; for example, to your search for a job. *Establish a network of relationships to provide insights into issues relevant to your personal and professional life, and be willing to lend your expertise to others.*

Neutrality A response pattern lacking in personal involvement; encourages defensiveness. Opposed to **empathy**.

Noise   Anything that interferes with your receiving a message as the source intended the message to be received. Noise is present in communication to the extent that the message received is not the message sent. *In managing noise, reduce physical, physiological, psychological, and semantic noise as best you can; use repetition and restatement, and, when in doubt, ask if you're clear.*

Nonverbal communication   Communication without words; communication by means of space, gestures, facial expressions, touching, vocal variation, or silence, for example.

Object-adaptors   Movements that involve manipulation of some object; for example, punching holes in a Styrofoam coffee cup, clicking a ballpoint pen, or chewing on a pencil.

Oculesics   The study of the messages communicated by the eyes.

Olfactory communication   Communication by smell. *Become mindful of your own scent messages; they can serve as attractants and as repellants.*

Onymous messages   Messages that are signed; messages for which the author is identified or known. Opposed to **anonymous messages**.

Open self   In the Johari window model, this self represents all the information, behaviours, attitudes, feelings, desires, motivations, and ideas that you and others know.

Overattribution   The tendency to attribute to one or two characteristics most or even all of what a person does. *Avoid overattribution; rarely is any one factor an accurate explanation of complex human behaviour.*

Owning feelings   The process of taking responsibility for your own feelings instead of attributing them to others. *Do it.*

Paralanguage   The vocal but nonverbal aspects of speech. Paralanguage consists of voice qualities (for example, pitch range, resonance, tempo); vocal characterizers (laughing or crying, yelling or whispering); vocal qualifiers (intensity, pitch height); and vocal segregates ("uh-uh" meaning "no," or "shh" meaning "silence"). *Vary paralinguistic features to communicate nuances of meaning and to add interest and colour to your messages.*

People culture   A workplace culture that emphasizes relationships, sharing, and friendship.

Perception   The process by which you become aware of objects and events through your senses. *Increase accuracy in interpersonal perception by identifying the influence of your physical and emotional states, making sure that you're not drawing conclusions from too little information, and checking your perceptions.*

Perception checking   The process of verifying your understanding of some message, situation, or feeling. *Increase accuracy in perception by checking your perceptions: describe what you see or hear and the meaning you assign to it, and ask the other person if your perceptions are accurate.*

Perceptual accentuation   A process that leads you to see what you expect or want to see—for example, seeing people you like as better looking and smarter than people you don't like.

Personal distance   The second closest distance in proxemics, ranging from 46 centimetres to 1.2 metres.

Physiological noise   Interference within the sender or receiver of a message, such as visual impairments, hearing loss, articulation problems, and memory loss.

Pitch   In relation to voice qualities, the highness or lowness of the vocal tone.

Polarization   A form of fallacious reasoning in which only two extremes are considered; also referred to as black-and-white or either/or thinking or as a two-valued orientation. *Avoid thinking and talking in extremes by using middle terms and qualifiers. But remember that too many qualifiers may make you appear unsure of yourself.*

Positive face   The desire to be viewed positively by others, to be thought of favourably.

Power culture   A workplace culture in which authority is clear, a high degree of loyalty is expected, and measures are in place to ensure accountability.

Power play   A consistent pattern of behaviour in which one person tries to control the behaviour of another. *Respond to power plays with cooperative strategies: express your feelings, describe the behaviour to which you object, and state a cooperative response.*

Primacy and recency effects   Giving more importance to that which occurs first (primacy) or to that which occurs last or more recently (recency).

Primacy and recency   Primacy refers to giving more credence to an event that occurs first; recency refers to giving more credence to an event that occurs last (that is, most recently). *Be aware that a first impression can act as a filter that prevents your perception of another person's perhaps contradictory behaviour, changes in situation, and especially, changes in that person. Recognize the normal tendency for first impressions to leave lasting impressions and to colour both what we see later and the conclusions we draw. Be at your very best in first encounters. Also, take the time and effort to revise your impressions of others on the basis of new information.*

Primary emotions   Basic emotions; usually identified are joy, acceptance, fear, surprise, sadness, disgust, anger, and anticipation.

Primary territory   Areas that you consider your exclusive preserve—for example, your room or office.

Proxemics   The study of the communicative function of space; the study of how people unconsciously structure their space—the distance between people in their interactions, the organization of space in homes and offices, and even the design of cities. *Maintain distances that are comfortable and that are appropriate to the situation and to your relationship with the other person.*

Proximity   As a principle of perception, the tendency to perceive people or events that are physically close as belonging together or representing some unit; physical closeness—one of the qualities influencing interpersonal attraction.

Public distance   The farthest distance in proxemics, ranging from 3.6 metres to 7.6 metres or more.

Public territory   Areas that are open to all people—for example, restaurants or parks.

Pygmalion effect   The condition in which you make a prediction of success, act as if it is true, and thereby make it come true (as when, for example, acting toward students as if they'll be successful influences them to become successful); a type of self-fulfilling prophecy.

Racism   Negative attitudes and beliefs that individuals or a society as a whole hold about specific ethnic groups.

Racist language   Language that denigrates, demeans, or is derogatory toward members of a particular ethnic group.

Rate   In relation to voice qualities, the speed at which you speak, generally measured in words per minute.

Receiver   Any person or thing that takes in messages. Receivers may be individuals listening to or reading a message, a group of persons hearing a speech, a scattered television audience, or machines that store information.

Regulators   Nonverbal behaviours that regulate, monitor, or control the communications of another person.

Rejection   A response to an individual that acknowledges the person but expresses disagreement. Opposed to **confirmation** and **disconfirmation**.

Relationship communication   Communication between or among intimates or those in close relationships; the term is used by some theorists as synonymous with interpersonal communication.

Restraint   A cultural orientation that fosters the curbing of immediate gratification and regulates it by social norms. Opposed to **indulgence**.

Reverse halo effect   The tendency to judge a person you know to have several negative qualities to also have other negative qualities (that you have not observed); also known as the "horns" effect. *See also* **halo effect**.

Rhythm   The recurring patterns of emphasis in a stream of speech.

Role culture   A workplace culture wherein there is general conformity to expectations, clear regulations and procedures, and clearly defined tasks.

Schemata   Ways of organizing perceptions; mental templates or structures that help you organize the millions of items of information you come into contact with every day as well as those you already have in memory; general ideas about groups of people or individuals, about yourself, or about types of social roles. The word *schemata* is the plural of *schema*.

Script   A type of schema; an organized body of information about some action, event, or procedure. A script provides a general idea of how some event should play out or unfold, the rules governing the events and their sequence.

Secondary territory   An area that does not belong to you but that you've occupied and that is therefore associated with you—for example, the seat you normally take in class.

Selective attention   The tendency to attend to those things that you want to see or that you expect to see.

Selective exposure   The tendency to expose your senses to certain things and not others, to actively seek out information that supports your beliefs and to actively avoid information that contradicts these beliefs.

Selective perception   The tendency to perceive certain things and not others; includes selective attention and selective exposure.

Self-adaptors   Movements that usually satisfy a physical need, especially to make you more comfortable; for example, scratching your head to relieve an itch, moistening your lips because they feel dry, or pushing your hair out of your eyes.

Self-awareness   The degree to which you know yourself. *Increase self-awareness by listening to others, increasing your open self, and seeking out information to reduce blind spots.*

Self-concept   Your self-image, the view you have of who you are. *To increase your understanding of self, try to see yourself, as objectively as you can, through the eyes of others; compare yourself to similar (and admired) others; examine the influences of culture; and observe and evaluate your own message behaviours.*

Self-disclosure   The process of revealing something about yourself to another; usually refers to information you'd normally keep hidden. *When thinking of disclosing, consider the legitimacy of your motives, the appropriateness of the disclosure, the listener's responses (is the dyadic effect operating?), and the potential burdens such disclosures might impose.*

Self-esteem   The value (usually, the positive value) you place on yourself; your self-evaluation. *Increase your self-esteem by attacking self-destructive beliefs, seeking out nourishing people, working on projects that will result in success, and securing affirmation.*

Self-fulfilling prophecy   The situation in which you make a prediction or prophecy and fulfill it yourself—for example, expecting a person to be hostile, you act in a hostile manner toward this person, and in doing so elicit hostile behaviour in return, thus confirming your prophecy that the person will be hostile. *Take a second look at your perceptions when they correspond very closely to your initial expectations; the self-fulfilling prophecy may be at work.*

Self-monitoring   Manipulating the image you present to others in interpersonal interactions so as to create the most favourable impression of yourself.

Self-monitoring strategies   Techniques you use to carefully monitor (self-censor) what you say or do.

Self-serving bias   A bias that operates in the self-attribution process, leading you to take credit for the positive consequences of your behaviours and to deny responsibility for the negative consequences. *Become mindful of giving too much weight to internal factors (when explaining your positives) and too little weight to external factors (when explaining your negatives).*

Sexism   Negative attitudes and beliefs about a particular gender; prejudicial attitudes and beliefs about men or women based on rigid beliefs about gender roles.

Sexist language   Language derogatory to members of one gender, generally women.

Short-term memory   The memory you use to remember information you need immediately or temporarily; for example, remembering a phone number just long enough to dial it.

Short-term orientation   A cultural dimension in which people look more to the past and the present; these cultural members spend their resources for the present and want quick results from their efforts. Opposed to **long-term orientation**.

Signal-to-noise ratio   A measure of the relationship between meaningful information (signal) and interference (noise).

Silence The absence of vocal communication; often misunderstood to refer to the absence of communication. *Examine silence for meanings just as you would eye movements or body gestures.*

Similarity, principle of A principle of perception in which things that are physically similar (looking alike) are perceived to belong together and to form a unit. Opposed to **contrast**.

Small talk Noncontroversial talk that is usually short in duration and often serves as a polite way of introducing one's self or a topic. Talk that is brief and serves largely to pass a short amount of time in pleasant interaction. Sometimes, small talk is a preface to big talk.

Social distance The next-to-farthest distance in proxemics, ranging from 1.2 metres to 3.6 metres; the distance at which business is usually conducted.

Source Any person or thing that creates messages—for example, an individual speaking, writing, or gesturing or a computer solving a problem.

Static evaluation An orientation that fails to recognize that the world is constantly changing; an attitude that sees people and events as fixed rather than as ever changing.

Stereotype In communication, a fixed impression of a group of people through which we then perceive specific individuals. Stereotypes are most often negative but may also be positive. *To avoid stereotypes, focus on the individual rather than on the individual's membership in one group or another.*

Strategic emotionality A condition in which emotions are used to achieve some specific end (usually to control the behaviour of another person) rather than to reveal one's true feelings.

Stress The relative emphasis that is put on a word in a sentence and that can often change the meaning of the sentence.

Supportiveness An attitude of an individual or an atmosphere in a group that is characterized by openness, absence of fear, and a genuine feeling of equality. Opposed to **defensiveness**.

Synchronous communication Communication that takes place in real time; sending and receiving take place at the same time (as in face-to-face communication). Opposed to **asynchronous communication**.

Tactile communication Communication by touch; communication received by the skin. *Use touch when appropriate to express positive affect, playfulness, control, and ritualistic meanings, and to serve task-related functions; avoid touching that may be unwelcome.*

Temporal communication The messages conveyed by your time orientation and treatment of time. *Interpret time cues from the point of view of the other's culture rather than your own.*

Territoriality A possessive or ownership reaction to an area of space or to particular objects. *Establish and maintain territory nonverbally by marking or otherwise indicating temporary or permanent ownership. Become sensitive to the territorial behaviour of others.*

Tie signs Signals (generally nonverbal) that communicate your relationship status, the ways in which your relationship is tied together.

Touch avoidance The tendency to avoid touching and being touched by others. *Recognize that some people may prefer to avoid touching and being touched. Avoid drawing too many conclusions about people from the way they treat interpersonal touching.*

Truth bias The assumption most people operate under that the messages they hear are truthful.

Turn-denying cues Signals (generally nonverbal) that indicate your reluctance to assume the role of speaker.

Turn-maintaining cues Signals that help you maintain the speaker's role. *You can do this with a variety of cues; for example, by continuing a gesture to show that you haven't completed the thought, avoiding eye contact with the listener so there's no indication that you're passing on the speaking turn, or sustaining your intonation pattern to indicate that you intend to say more.*

Turn-requesting cues Signals (generally nonverbal) that let the speaker know that you'd like to take a turn as speaker.

Turn-taking cues Signals (generally nonverbal) that indicate you're ready to speak, to listen, or to comment on what the speaker just said.

Turn-yielding cues Signals (generally nonverbal) that tell the listener you're finished and wish to exchange the role of speaker for that of listener.

Unknown self In the Johari window model, this self represents truths about yourself that neither you nor others know.

Ventilation hypothesis The assumption that expressing emotions (that is, giving vent to the emotions) lessens their intensity.

Verbal aggressiveness A method of arguing in which one person attacks the other person's self-concept.

Volume In relation to voice qualities, the relative loudness of the voice.

You-messages Messages in which you deny responsibility for your own thoughts and behaviours; messages that attribute your perception to another person; messages of blame. Opposed to **I-messages**. *Avoid using you-messages that blame or accuse; invariably these will be resented and may easily cut off further communication.*

REFERENCES

Abel, G. G., & Harlow, N. (2001). *The stop child molestation book*. Philadelphia: Xlibris.

Accessibility Directorate of Ontario. (2009). *Communication access for people who have communication disabilities*. Toronto: The Queens Printer for Ontario. Retrieved from http://www.mcss.gov.on.ca/documents/en/mcss/accessibility/DevelopingStandards/Communication_Access_ENG_no_ack.pdf

Adams-Price, C. E., Dalton, W. T., & Sumrall, R. (2004). Victim blaming in young, middle-aged, and older adults: Variations on the severity effect. *Journal of Adult Development, 11*, 289–295.

Afifi, W. A. (2007). Nonverbal communication. In B. B. Whaley & W. Samter (Eds.), *Explaining communication: Contemporary theories and exemplars* (pp. 39–60). Mahwah, NJ: Lawrence Erlbaum.

Albas, D. C., McCluskey, K. W., & Albas, C. A. (1976, December). Perception of the emotional content of speech: A comparison of two Canadian groups. *Journal of Cross-Cultural Psychology, 7*, 481–490.

Alberti, R. (Ed.). (1977). *Assertiveness: Innovations, applications, issues*. San Luis Obispo, CA: Impact.

Altman, I., & Taylor, D. A. (1973). *Social penetration: The development of interpersonal relationships*. New York: Holt, Rinehart & Winston.

Andersen, P. A., & Leibowitz, K. (1978). The development and nature of the construct touch avoidance. *Environmental Psychology and Nonverbal Behavior, 3*, 89–106.

Andersen, P. A. (1991). Explaining intercultural differences in nonverbal communication. In P. A. Andersen (2004), *The complete idiot's guide to body language*. New York: Penguin Group.

Anderson, M. (1997). *Nursing leadership, management, and professional practice for the LPN/LVN*. Philadelphia: FA Davis Co.

Anderson, K. J. et al. (1998). Meta-analysis of gender effects on conversational interruption: Who, what, when, where, and how. *Sex Roles, 39 (August)*, 225–252.

Angelou, M. quoted in Worth Repeating: More Than 5,000 Classic and Contemporary Quotes (2003) by Bob Kelly, p. 263. Kregel Publications.

Angier, N. (1999). *Women: An intimate geography*. New York: Houghton Mifflin Harcourt.

Argyle, M. (1988). *Bodily communication* (2nd ed.). New York: Methuen.

Argyle, M., & Ingham, R. (1972). Gaze, mutual gaze and distance. *Semiotica, 1*, 32–49.

Aries, E. (2006). Sex differences in interaction: A reexamination. In K. Dindia & D. J. Canary (Eds.), *Sex differences and similarities in communication* (2nd ed., pp. 21–36). Mahwah, NJ: Erlbaum.

Armour, S. (2005, November 7). Generation Y: They've arrived at work with a new attitude. *USA Today*.

Aronson, E., Wilson, T. D., & Akert, R. M. (2013). *Social psychology: The heart and the mind* (8th ed.). Boston: Pearson.

Aronson, J., Cohen, J., & Nail, P. (1998). Self-affirmation theory: An update and appraisal. In E. Harmon-Jones & J. S. Mills (Eds.), *Cognitive dissonance theory: Revival with revisions and controversies* (pp. 127–147). Washington, DC: American Psychological Association.

Asch, S. (1946). Forming impressions of personality. *Journal of Abnormal and Social Psychology, 41*, 258–290.

Ashcraft, M. H. (1998). *Fundamentals of cognition*. New York: Longman.

Ashkanasy, N. M., & Humphrey, R. H. (2011). Current emotion research in organizational behavior. *Emotion Review, 3*, 214–224.

Atkin, C. et al. (2002). Correlates of verbally aggressive communication in adolescents. *Journal of Applied Communication Research, 3*, 251–269.

Axtell, R. E. (1990). *Do's and taboos of hosting international visitors*. New York: Wiley.

Axtell, R. E. (1994). *Do's and taboos around the world* (3rd ed.). New York: Wiley.

Axtell, R. E. (2007). *Essential do's and taboos: The complete guide to international business and leisure travel*. Hoboken, NJ: Wiley.

Bach, G. R., & Wyden, P. (1968). *The intimate enemy*. New York: Avon.

Baker, A. (2002). What makes an online relationship successful? Clues from couples who met in cyberspace. *CyberPsychology and Behavior, 5*, 363–375.

Baker, J. S., & Jones, M. A. (1996). The poison grapevine: How destructive are gossip and rumour in the workplace? *Human Resource Development Quarterly, 7*, 75–86.

Barak, A., & Gluck-Ofri, O. (2007). Degree and reciprocity of self-disclosure in online forums. *CyberPsychology and Behavior, 10*(3), 407–417.

Barbato, C. A., & Perse, E. M. (1992). Interpersonal communication motives and the life position of elders. *Communication Research, 19*, 516–531.

Barker, L. L., & Gaut, D. (2002). *Communication* (8th ed.). Boston: Allyn & Bacon.

Barna, L. M. (1997). Stumbling blocks in intercultural communication. In L. A. Samovar & R. E. Porter (Eds.), *Intercultural communication: A reader* (7th ed., pp. 337–346). Belmont, CA: Wadsworth.

Barnlund, D. C. (1975). Communicative styles in two cultures: Japan and the United States. In A. Kendon, R. M. Harris, & M. R. Key (Eds.), *Organization of behavior in face-to-face interaction* (pp. 427–456). The Hague, the Netherlands: Mouton.

Barnlund, D. C. (1989). *Communicative styles of Japanese and Americans: Images and realities*. Belmont, CA: Wadsworth.

Barrett, L., & Godfrey, T. (1988). Listening. *Person Centered Review, 3*, 410–425.

Baumeister, R. F., Bushman, B. J., & Campbell, W. K. (2000, February). Self-esteem, narcissism, and aggression: Does violence result from low self-esteem or from threatened egotism? *Current Directions in Psychological Science, 9,* 26–29.

Baumeister, R. F., Zhang, L., & Vohs, K. D. (2004). Gossip as cultural learning. *Review of General Psychology, 8* (June), 111–121.

Beatty, M. J. (1988). Situational and predispositional correlates of public speaking anxiety. *Communication Education, 37,* 28–39.

Beauchesne, M. A., & Patsdaughter, C. A. (2005). Primary care for the underserved conference: The evolution of an emerging professional culture. *Journal of Cultural Diversity, 12,* 77–88.

Bedford, V. H. (1996). Relationships between adult siblings. In A. E. Auhagen & M. von Salisch (Eds.), *The diversity of human relationships* (pp. 120–140). New York: Cambridge University Press.

Beebe, S. A., Beebe, S. J., & Redmond, M. V. (2008). *Interpersonal communication,* 5th ed. Boston: Pearson Education.

Bell, C. M., & McCarthy, P. M. (2012). Using LIWC and Coh-Metrix to investigate gender differences in linguistic styles. IGI Global. Retrieved from http://www.igi-global.com/chapter/using-liwc-coh-metrix-investigate/61070

Bell, R. A., & Daly, J. A. (1984). The affinity-seeking function of communication. *Communication Monographs, 51,* 91–115.

Bennett, D. (2014, June 28). Mayor Nenshi has captured Calgary's heart, but the worst, at least politically, is yet to come. *The Globe and Mail.* Retrieved from http://www.theglobeandmail.com/news/national/mayor-nenshi-has-captured-calgarys-heart-but-the-worst-at-least-politically-is-yet-to-come/article12884159

Ben-Ze'ev, A. (2003). Primacy, emotional closeness, and openness in cyberspace. *Computers in Human Behavior, 19,* 451–467.

Benoit, W. L., & Benoit, P. J. (1990). Memory for conversational behavior, *Southern Communication Journal, 55,* 17–23.

Berger, C. R., & Bradac, J. J. (1982). *Language and social knowledge: Uncertainty in interpersonal relations.* London: Edward Arnold.

Berry, J. W., Poortinga, Y. H., Segall, M. H., & Dasen, P. R. (1992). *Cross-cultural psychology: Research and applications.* New York: Cambridge University Press.

Berscheid, E., & Reis, H. T. (1998). Attraction and close relationships. In D. Gilbert, S. Fiske, & G. Lindzey (Eds.), *The handbook of social psychology* (4th ed., Vol. 2, pp. 193–281). New York: W. H. Freeman.

Bibby, R. (1990). *Mosaic madness: The poverty and potential of life in Canada.* Toronto: Stoddart.

Black, H. K. (1999). A sense of the sacred: Altering or enhancing the self-portrait in older age? *Narrative Inquiry, 9,* 327–345.

Blake, R. R., & Mouton, J. S. (1985). *The managerial grid III* (3rd ed.). Houston, TX: Gulf.

Blieszner, R., & Adams, R. G. (1992). *Adult friendship.* Newbury Park, CA: Sage.

Blumstein, P., & Schwartz, P. (1983). *American couples: Money, work, sex.* New York: Morrow.

Bochner, S. (1994). Cross-cultural differences in the self-concept: A test of Hofstede's individualism/collectivism distinction. *Journal of Cross-Cultural Psychology, 25,* 273–283.

Bok, S. (1978). *Lying: Moral choice in public and private life.* New York: Pantheon.

Bok, S. (1983). *Secrets.* New York: Vintage.

Bongiorno, R., & David, B. (2003). Gender and the categorization of powerful others. *Australian Journal of Psychology, 55,* 34.

Bordia, P., et al. (2003). Management are aliens: Rumors and stress during organizational change. *Group and Organization Management, 35*(3), 601–621.

Bower, B. (2001). Self-illusions come back to bite students. *Science News, 159,* 148.

Brashers, D. E. (2007). A theory of communication and uncertainty management. In B. B. Whaley & W. Samter (Eds.), *Explaining communication: Contemporary theories and exem-*

plars (pp. 201–218). Mahwah, NJ: Lawrence Erlbaum.

Brody, L. R. (1985, June). Gender differences in emotional development: A review of theories and research. *Journal of Personality, 53,* 102–149.

·Brown, A. (2003). Developing a productive, respectful manager–employee relationship. *Canadian HR Reporter, 7,* 10.

Brown, P., & Levinson, S. C. (1987). *Politeness: Some universals of language usage.* Cambridge, UK: Cambridge University Press.

Brownell, J. (2006). *Listening: Attitudes, principles, and skills* (3rd ed.). Boston: Allyn & Bacon.

Brownell, J. (2010). *Listening: Attitudes, principles, and skills* (5th ed.). Boston: Allyn & Bacon.

Bruneau, T. (1985). The time dimension in intercultural communication. In L. A. Samovar & R. E. Porter (Eds.), *Intercultural communication: A reader* (4th ed., pp. 280–289). Belmont, CA: Wadsworth.

Bruneau, T. (1990). Chronemics: The study of time in human interaction. In J. A. DeVito & M. L. Hecht (Eds.), *The nonverbal communication reader* (pp. 301–311). Prospect Heights, IL: Waveland Press.

Bruneau, T. (2009/2010). Chronemics: Time-binding and the construction ofpersonal time. *General Semantics Bulletin, 76,* 82–94.

Bugental, J., & Zelen, S. (1950). Investigations into the "self-concept": I. The W–A–Y technique. *Journal of Personality, 18,* 483–498.

Buller, D. B., LePoire, B. A., Aune, K., & Eloy, S. (1992). Social perceptions as mediators of the effect of speech rate similarity on compliance. *Human Communication Research, 19,* 286–311.

Buller, D. J. (2005). *Adapting minds: Evolutionary psychology and the persistent quest for human nature.* Cambridge, MA: MIT Press.

Bulsing, P. J., Smeets, M. A., Gemeinhardt, C, et al. (2010). Irritancy expectancy alters odor perception: Evidence from olfactory event-related potential research. *Journal of Neurophysiology, 104*(5), 2749–2756.

Bunz, U., & Campbell, S. W. (2004). Politeness accommodation in electronic mail. *Communication Research Reports, 21*, 11–25.

Burgoon, J. K., & Bacue, A. E. (2003). Nonverbal communication skills. In J. O. Greene & B. R. Burleson (Eds.), *Handbook of communication and social interaction skills* (pp. 179–220). Mahwah, NJ: Erlbaum.

Burgoon, J. K., & Hoobler, G. D. (2002). Nonverbal signals. In M. L. Knapp & J. A. Daly (Eds.), *Handbook of interpersonal communication* (3rd ed., pp. 240–299). Thousand Oaks, CA: Sage.

Burgoon, J. K., Berger, C. R., & Waldron, V. R. (2000). Mindfulness and interpersonal communication. *Journal of Social Issues, 56*, 105–127.

Burgoon, J., Guerrero, L., & Floyd, K. (2010). *Nonverbal communication.* Boston: Allyn & Bacon.

Burgstahler, S. (2007). Managing an e-mentoring community to support students with disabilities: A case study. *Distance Education Report 11* (July), 7–15.

Burleson, B. R. (2003). Emotional support skills. In J. O. Greene & B. R. Burleson (Eds.), *Handbook of communication and social interaction skills* (pp. 551–594). Mahwah, NJ: Erlbaum.

Buss, D. M. (2000). *The dangerous passion: Why jealousy is as necessary as love and sex.* New York: Free Press.

Butler, P. E. (1981). *Talking to yourself: Learning the language of self-support.* New York: Harper & Row.

Buunk, B. P., & Dijkstra, P. (2004). Gender differences in rival characteristics that evoke jealousy in response to emotional versus sexual infidelity. *Personal Relationships, 11*(December), 395–408.

Cahn, D. D., & Abigail, R. A. (2007). *Managing conflict through communication* (3rd ed.). Boston: Allyn & Bacon.

Cain, S. (2012). *Quiet: The Power of Introverts in a World That Can't Stop Talking.* NY: Random House.

Canary, D. J., & Hause, K. (1993). Is there any reason to research sex differences in-communication? *Communication Quarterly, 41*, 129–144.

Canary, D. J., Cupach, W. R., & Messman, S. J. (1995). *Relationship conflict: Conflict in parent-child, friendship, and romantic relationships.* Thousand Oaks, CA: Sage.

Cappella, J. N. (1993). The facial feedback hypothesis in human interaction: Review and speculation. *Journal of Language and Social Psychology, 12*, 13–29.

Cappella, J. N., & Schreiber, D. M. (2006). The interaction management function of nonverbal cues. In V. Manusov & M. L. Patterson (Eds.), *The SAGE handbook of nonverbal communication* (pp. 361–379). Thousand Oaks, CA: Sage Publications.

Carey, B. (2005). Have you heard? Gossip turns out to serve a purpose. *The New York Times* (August 16), F1, F6.

Carroll, D. W. (1994). *Psychology of language* (2nd ed.). Pacific Grove, CA: Brooks/Cole.

Chang, H., & Holt, G. R. (1996, Winter). The changing Chinese interpersonal world: Popular themes in interpersonal communication books in modern Taiwan. *Communication Quarterly, 44*, 85–106.

Chang, W. L., & Hsieh-Liang, L. (2010) The impact of colour traits on corporate branding. *African Journal of Business Management, 4*, 3344–55.

Chanowitz, B., & Langer, E. (1981). Premature cognitive commitment. *Journal of Personality and Social Psychology, 41*, 1051–1063.

Chao, G. T., & Moon, H. (2005). The cultural mosaic: A metatheory for understanding the complexity of culture. *Journal of Applied Psychology, 90*(6), 1128–1140.

Cherry, K. (2014a). The cognitive tasks of multi-tasking. Retrieved from http://psychology.about.com./od/cognitivepsychology/a/costs-of-multitasking.htm

Cherry, K. (2014b). What is transformational leadership? Retrieved from http://psychology.about.com./od/leadership/a/leadership/transformational.htm

Cho, S. H. (2007). Effects of motivation and gender on adolescents' self-disclosure in online chatting. *CyberPsychology and Behavior, 10*(3), 339–345.

Chris Hadfield, n.d. *bio.* Retrieved from http://www.biography.com/people/chris-hadfield-21230027#globalstar&awesm=~oGqLD26CfaeyL5

Chung, L. C., & Ting-Toomey, S. (1999). Ethnic identity and relational expectations among Asian Americans. *Communication Research Reports, 16*, 157–166.

Clance, P. (1985). *The impostor phenomenon: Overcoming the fear that haunts your success.* Atlanta: Peachtree Publishers.

Cline, M. G. (1956). The influence of social context on the perception of faces. *Journal of Personality, 2*, 142–185.

Cloud, J. (2008). Are gay relationships different? *Time* (January 28), 78–80.

Coates, J., & Sutton-Spence, R. (2001). Turn-taking patterns in deaf conversation. *Journal of Sociolinguistics, 5* (November), 507–529.

Coats, E. J., & Feldman, R. S. (1996). Gender differences in nonverbal correlates of social status. *Personality and Social Psychology Bulletin, 22*, 1014–1022.

Cohen, J. (2001, January 18). On the Internet, love really is blind. *The New York Times*, pp. G1, G9.

Colley, A., Todd, Z., Bland, M., Holmes, M., Khanom, N., & Pike, H. (2004, September). Style and content in e-mails and letters to male and female friends. *Journal of Language and Social Psychology, 23*, 369–378.

Collins, N. L., & Miller, L. C. (1994). Self-disclosure and liking: A meta-analytic review. *Psychological Bulletin, 116* (November), 457–475.

Cooley, C. H. (1922). *Human nature and the social order* (Rev. ed.). New York: Scribner's.

Cooper, A., & Sportolari, L. (1997). Romance in cyberspace: Understanding online attraction. *Journal of Sex Education and Therapy, 22*, 7–14.

Cummings, J., Butler, B., & Kraut, R. (2002). The quality of online social relationships. *Communications of the ACM, 45*(7), 103–108.

Dalai Lama Center (2008). Exercise your pre-frontal cortex. Adapted from presentations at the 2008 UBC Brain Development and Learning Conference. Retrieved from http://dalailamacenter.org/sites/dalailamacenter.org/files/u28/exercise%20your%20prefrontal%20cortex%20on%20letterhead.pdf

Darling, A. L., & Dannels, D. P. (2003). Practicing engineers talk about the importance of talk: A report on the role of oral communication in the workplace. *Communication Education, 52,* 1–16.

Davis, M. S. (1973). *Intimate relations.* New York: Free Press.

DePaulo, B. M., Lindsay, J. J., Malone, B. E., Muhlenbruck, L., Charlton, K., & Cooper, H. (2003). Cues to deception. *Psychological Bulletin, 129,* 74–118.

Derlega, V. J., Winstead, B. A., Greene, K., Serovich, J., & Elwood, W. N. (2004). Reasons for HIV disclosure/nondisclosure in close relationships: Testing a model of HIV-disclosure decision making. *Journal of Social and Clinical Psychology, 23* (December), 747–767.

DePaulo, B. M. (1992). Nonverbal behavior and self-presentation. *Psychological Bulletin, 111,* 203–212.

Desprez-Bouanchaud, A., Doolaege, J., Ruprecht, L., & Pavlic, B. (1987). Guidelines on gender-neutral language. UNESCO. Retrieved from http://unesdoc.unesco.org/images/0011/001149/114950mo.pdf

Difonzo, N., Bordia, P., & Rosnow, R. L. (1994). Reining in rumors. *Organizational Dynamics, 23,* 47–62.

Dillard, J. P., & Marshall, L. J. (2003). Persuasion as a social skill. In J. O. Greene & B. R. Burleson (Eds.), *Handbook of communication and social interaction skills* (pp. 479–514). Mahwah, NJ: Erlbaum.

Dindia, K., & Allen, M. (1992). Sex differences in self-disclosure: A meta-analysis. *Psychological Bulletin, 112,* 106–124.

Dindia, K., & Canary, D. J. (Eds.) (2006). *Sex differences and similarities in communication* (2nd ed.). Mahwah, NJ: Lawrence Erlbaum.

Dindia, K., & Timmerman, L. (2003). Accomplishing romantic relationships. In J. O. Greene & B. R. Burleson (Eds.), *Handbook of communication and social interaction skills* (pp. 685–722). Mahwah, NJ: Erlbaum.

Doherty, R. W., Orimoto, L., Singelis, T. M., Hatfield, E., & Hebb, J. (1995). Emotional contagion: Gender and occupational differences. *Psychology of Women Quarterly, 19,* 355–371.

Dolgin, K. G., Meyer, L., & Schwartz, J. (1991, September). Effects of gender, target's gender, topic, and self-esteem on disclosure to best and middling friends. *Sex Roles, 25,* 311–329.

Donohue, W. A., & Kolt, R. (1992). *Managing interpersonal conflict.* Thousand Oaks, CA: Sage.

Douglas, W. (1994). The acquaintanceship process: An examination of uncertainty, information seeking, and social attraction during initial conversation. *Communication Research, 21,* 154–176.

Dovidio, J. F., Gaertner, S. E., Kawakami, K., & Hodson, G. (2002). Why can't we just get along? Interpersonal biases and interracial distrust. *Cultural Diversity and Ethnic Minority Psychology, 8,* 88–102.

Dresser, N. (1999). *Multicultural celebrations: Today's rules of etiquette for life's special occasions.* New York: Three Rivers Press.

Dresser, N. (2005). *Multicultural manners: Essential rules of etiquette for the 21st century* (Rev. ed.). New York: Wiley.

Dreyfuss, H. (1971). *Symbol sourcebook.* New York: McGraw-Hill.

Duke, M., & Nowicki, S. (2005). The Emory dyssemia index. In V. Manusov (Ed.), *The sourcebook of nonverbal measures: Going beyond words* (35–46). Mahwah, NJ: Lawrence Erlbaum.

Dunbar, R. I. M. (2004). Gossip in evolutionary perspective. *Review of General Psychology, 8,* 100–110.

Duncan, S. D., Jr. (1972). Some signals and rules for taking speaking turns in conversation. *Journal of Personality and Social Psychology, 23,* 283–292.

Eden, D. (1992, Winter). Leadership and expectations: Pygmalion effects and other self-fulfilling prophecies in organizations. *Leadership Quarterly, 3,* 271–305.

Eder, D., & Enke, J. L. (1991). The structure of gossip: Opportunities and constraints on collective expression among adolescents. *American Sociological Review, 56,* 494–508.

Ehrenhaus, P. (1988). Silence and symbolic expression. *Communication Monographs, 55,* 41–57.

Einhorn, L. (2006). Using e-prime and English minus absolutisms to provide self-empathy. *ETC: A Review of General Semantics, 63,* 180–186.

Einstein, E. (1995). Success or sabotage: Which self-fulfilling prophecy will the stepfamily create? In D. K. Huntley (Ed.), *Understanding stepfamilies: Implications for assessment and treatment.* Alexandria, VA: American Counseling Association.

Elfenbein, H. A., & Ambady, N. (2002). Is there an in-group advantage in emotion recognition? *Psychological Bulletin, 128,* 243–249.

Eliot, T. S. in The Cocktail Party. Faber and Faber.

Ellis, A. (1988). *How to stubbornly refuse to make yourself miserable about anything, yes anything.* Secaucus, NJ: Lyle Stuart.

Ellis, A., & Harper, R. A. (1975). *A new guide to rational living.* Hollywood, CA: Wilshire Books.

Elmes, M. B., & Gemmill, G. (1990). The psychodynamics of mindlessness and dissent in small groups. *Small Group Research, 21,* 28–44.

Epstein, R. (2005). The loose screw awards: Psychology's top 10 misguided ideas. *Psychology Today* (February), 55–62.

Epstein, R. M., & Hundert, E. M. (2002). Defining and assessing professional competence. *JAMA: Journal of the American Medical Association, 287,* 226–235.

Erber, R., & Erber, M. W. (2011). *Intimate relationships: Issues, theories, and research* (2nd ed.). Boston: Allyn and Bacon.

Fallows, D. (2005). How women and men use the Internet. Pew Internet & American Life Project, www.pewinternet.org.

Fesko, S. L. (2001, November). Disclosure of HIV status in the workplace: Considerations and strategies. *Health and Social Work, 26,* 235–244.

Fischer, A. H. (1993). Sex differences in emotionality: Fact or stereotype? *Feminism and Psychology, 3,* 303–318.

Fischer, A. H., & Manstead, A. S. R. (2000). The relation between gender and emotion in different cultures. In A. Fischer (Ed.), *Gender and emotion: Social psychological perspectives* (pp. 71–94). Paris: Cambridge University Press.

Fitzpatrick, M. A., Jandt, F. E., Myrick, F. L., & Edgar, T. (1994). Gay and lesbian couple relationships.

In R. J. Ringer (Ed.), *Queer words, queer images: Communication and the construction of homosexuality* (pp.265–285). New York: New York University Press.

Floyd, J. J. (1985). *Listening: A practical approach.* Glenview, IL: Scott, Foresman.

Floyd, K., & Mikkelson, A. C. (2005). In V. Manusov (Ed.), *The sourcebook of nonverbal measures: Going beyond words* (pp. 47–56). Mahwah, NJ: Lawrence Erlbaum.

Folger, J. P., Poole, M. S., & Stutman, R. K. (2013). *Working through conflict: A communication perspective* (7th ed.). New York: Longman.

Fogel, J., & Nehmad, E. (2009). Internet social network communities: Risk taking, trust, and privacy concerns. *Computers in Human Behavior, 25*(1), 153–160.

Forbes, G. B. (2001). College students with tattoos and piercings: Motives, family experiences, personality factors, and perception by others. *Psychological Reports, 89*, 774–786.

Fourie, M. M., Thomas, K. G., Amodio, D. M., Warton, C. M., & Meintjes. E. M. (2014). Neural correlates of experienced moral emotion: An fMRI investigation of emotion in response to prejudice feedback. *Social Neuroscience, 9*(2), 203–218.

Franklin, C. W., & Mizell, C. A. (1995). Some factors influencing success among African-American men: A preliminary study. *Journal of Men's Studies, 3*, 191–204.

Free the Children. Bond of brothers: Two brothers, one goal: empower youth to change the world. Retrieved from http://www.freethechildren.com/marc-and-craig/bond-of-brothers. Reprinted with permission.

French, J. R. P., Jr., & Raven, B. (1968). The bases of social power. In D. Cartwright & A. Zander (Eds.), *Group dynamics: Research and theory* (3rd ed., pp. 259–269). New York: Harper & Row.

Frentz, T. (1976). A general approach to episodic structure. Paper presented at the Western Speech Association Convention, San Francisco. Cited in Reardon (1987).

Frye, N., & Dornish, M. (2010). When is trust not enough? The role of perceived privacy of communication tools in comfort with self disclosure. *Computers in Human Behavior, 25*(5), 1120–1127.

Fukushima, S. (2000). *Requests and culture: Politeness in British English and Japanese.* New York: Peter Lang.

Furnham, A., & Bochner, S. (1986). *Culture shock: Psychological reactions to unfamiliar environments.* New York: Methuen.

Galea, M. (2012). Express Your Emotions Learning the language of self by Melissa Galea. Alive Publishing Group. Retrieved from http://www.alive.com/articles/view/23385/express_your_emotions.

Galvin, K., Bylund, C. L., & Brommel, B. J. (2004). *Family communication: Cohesion and change* (6th ed.). Boston: Allyn & Bacon.

Galvin, K., Bylund, C., & Brommel, B. J. (2012). *Family communication: Cohesion and change* (8th ed.). New York: Longman.

Gamble, T. K., & Gamble, M. W. (2003). *The gender communication connection.* Boston: Houghton Mifflin.

Geddes, John. (2012, February 27). In conversation: Justin Trudeau. *Maclean's.* Retrieved from http://www.macleans.ca/general/what-would-push-him-to-the-separatist-side-and-why-hes-his-mothers-not-his-fathers-son.

Gelles, R., & Cornell, C. (1985). *Intimate violence in families.* Newbury Park, CA: Sage.

Gendron, R. (2011). The meaning of silence during conflict. *Journal of Conflictology, 2*(1), 1–6.

Georgas, J., et al. (2001). Functional relationships in the nuclear and extended family: A 16-culture study. *International Journal of Psychology, 36*, 289–300.

Gibb, J. (1961). Defensive communication. *Journal of Communication, 11*, 141–148.

Giles, H. (2009). Communication accommodation theory. In L. A. Baxter & D. O. Braithwaite (Eds.), *Engaging theories in interpersonal communication: Multiple perspectives* (pp. 161–173). Los Angeles: Sage.

Giles, H., Mulac, A., Bradac, J. J., & Johnson, P. (1987). Speech accommodation theory: The first decade and beyond. In M. L. McLaughlin (Ed.), *Communication yearbook 10* (pp. 13–48). Thousand Oaks, CA: Sage.

Gladstone, G. L., & Parker, G. B. (2002, June). When you're smiling, does the whole world smile with you? *Australasian Psychiatry, 10*, 144–146.

Goffman, E. (1967). *Interaction ritual: Essays on face-to-face behavior.* New York: Pantheon.

Goffman, E. (1971). *Relations in public: Microstudies of the public order.* New York: HarperCollins.

Goldsmith, D. J. (2007). Brown and Levinson's politeness theory. In B. B. Whaley & W. Samter (Eds.), *Explaining communication: Contemporary theories and exemplars* (pp. 219–236). Mahwah, NJ: Lawrence Erlbaum.

Goleman, D. (1995a). *Emotional intelligence.* New York: Bantam.

Goleman, D. (1995b, February 14). For man and beast, language of love shares many traits. *The New York Times,* pp. C1, C9.

Goleman, D. (2013). *Focus: The hidden driver of excellence.* New York, NY: HarperCollins.

Goode, Erica. (2000, August 8). How culture molds habits of thought. *The New York Times,* pp. F1, F8.

Goodstein, A. (2007). *Totally wired: What teens and tweens are really doing online.* New York: St. Martin's Griffin.

Gordon, A. (2010). Facing up to fatigue. *Psychology Today, 43*, 29.

Gordon, T. (1975). *P.E.T.: Parent effectiveness training.* New York: New American Library.

Gottman, J. M., & Carrere, S. (1994). Why can't men and women get along? Developmental roots and marital inequities. In D. J. Canary and Laura Stafford (Eds.), *Communication and relational maintenance* (pp. 203–229). San Diego, CA: Academic Press.

Gottman, J. M., & Levenson, R. W. (1999). Dysfunctional marital conflict: Women are being unfairly blamed. *Journal of Divorce and Remarriage, 31*, 1–17.

Grace, S. L., & Cramer, K. L. (2003). The elusive nature of self-measurement: The self-construal scale versus the twenty statements test. *Journal of Social Psychology, 143* (October), 649–668.

Graham, J. A., & Argyle, M. (1975). The effects of different patterns of gaze combined with different facial expressions on impression formation. *Journal of Movement Studies, 1,* 178–182.

Graham, J. A., Bitti, P. R., & Argyle, M. (1975). A cross-cultural study of the communication of emotion by facial and gestural cues. *Journal of Human Movement Studies, 1,* 68–77.

Grandey, A. A. (2000). Emotion regulation in the workplace: A new way to conceptualize emotional labor. *Journal of Occupational Health and Psychology, 5,* 95–110.

Greengard, S. (2001). Gossip poisons business. HR can stop it. *Workforce, 80,* 24–28.

Grenny, J. (2005). Talking hi-tech at work. *T+D, 59*(11), 14–14.

Griffin, E., & Sparks, G. G. (1990). Friends forever: A longitudinal exploration of intimacy in same-sex friends and platonic pairs. *Journal of Social and Personal Relationships, 7,* 29–46.

Grosch, H. (1994). Dehumanizing the workplace. *Communications of the ACM, 37*(11), 122–122.

Gudykunst, W. B. (1989). Culture and the development of interpersonal relationships. In J. A. Anderson (Ed.), *Communication yearbook 12* (pp. 315–354). Thousand Oaks, CA: Sage.

Gudykunst, W. B. (1991). *Bridging differences: Effective intergroup communication.* Newbury Park, CA: Sage.

Gudykunst, W. B. (1993). Toward a theory of effective interpersonal and intergroup communication: An anxiety/uncertainty management (AUM) perspective. In R. L. Wiseman (Ed.), *Intercultural communication competence.* Thousand Oaks, CA: Sage.

Gudykunst, W. B. (1994). *Bridging differences: Effective intergroup communication* (2nd ed.). Newbury Park, CA: Sage.

Gudykunst, W. B. (Ed.). (1983). *Intercultural communication theory: Current perspectives.* Newbury Park, CA: Sage.

Gudykunst, W. B., & Kim, Y. Y. (Eds.). (1992). *Readings on communication with strangers: An approach to intercultural communication.* New York: McGraw-Hill.

Guerin, B. (2003). Combating prejudice and racism: New interventions from a fictional analysis of fictional racist language. *Journal of Community and Applied Social Psychology,* 13 (January), 29–45.

Guerrero, L. K., & Andersen, P. A. (1991). The waxing and waning of relational intimacy: Touch as a function of relational stage, gender and touch avoidance. *Journal of Social and Personal Relationships, 8,* 147–165.

Guerrero, L. K., Andersen, P. A., & Afifi, W. A. (2007). *Close encounters: Communication in relationships* (2nd ed.). Thousand Oaks, CA: Sage.

Guerrero, L. K., & Hecht, M. L. (Eds.). (2008). *The nonverbal communication reader: Class and contemporary readings* (3rd ed.). Prospect Heights, IL: Waveland Press.

Guerrero, L. K., Andersen, P. A., Jorgensen, P. F., Spitzberg, B. H., & Eloy, S. V. (1995). Coping with the green-eyed monster: Conceptualizing and measuring communicative response to romantic jealousy. *Western Journal of Communication, 59,* 270–304.

Guerrero, L. K., Jones, S. M., & Boburka, R. R. (2006). Sex differences in emotional communication. In K. Dindia & D. J. Canary (Eds.), *Sex differences and similarities incommunication* (2nd ed., pp. 241–262). Mahwah, NJ: Erlbaum.

Hafen, S. (2004). Organizational gossip: A revolving door of regulation and resistance, *Southern Communication Journal,* 69 (Spring), 223–240.

Hajek, C., & Giles, H. (2003). New directions in intercultural communication competence: The process model. In J. O. Greene & B. R. Burleson (Eds.), *Handbook of communication and social interaction skills* (pp. 935–957). Mahwah, NJ: Erlbaum.

Hall, E. T. (1963). A system for the notation of proxemic behavior. *American Anthropologist, 65,* 1003–1026.

Hall, E. T. (1966). *The hidden dimension.* Garden City, NY: Doubleday.

Hall, E. T. (1983). *The dance of life: The other dimension of time.* New York: Anchor Books/Doubleday.

Hall, E. T., & Hall, M. R. (1987). *Hidden differences: Doing business with the Japanese.* Garden City, NY: Doubleday.

Hall, J. A. (1996, Spring). Touch, status, and gender at professional meetings. *Journal of Nonverbal Behavior, 20,* 23–44.

Hall, P. (2005). Interprofessional teamwork: Professional cultures as barriers. *Journal of Interprofessional Care,* Supplement 1, 188–196.

Hampton, K., Goulet, L. S., Rainie, L., & Purcell, K. (2011). Social networking sites and our lives. Pew Internet & American Life Project (http://www.pewinternet.org/Reports/2011/Technology-and-social-networks/Summary.aspx).

Handy, C. B. (1985). *Understanding organizations* (3rd ed.). Harmondsworth: Penguin Books.

Harris, C. R. (2003). A review of sex differences in sexual jealousy, including self-report data, psychophysiological responses, interpersonal violence, and morbid jealousy, *Personality and Social Psychology Review 7,* 102–128.

Harris, M. (1993). *Culture, people, nature: An introduction to general anthropology* (6th ed.). Boston: Allyn & Bacon.

Harrison, J. R., & Carroll, G. R. (2006). *Culture and demography in organizations.* Princeton, NJ: Princeton University Press.

Hart Research Associates. (2010). Raising the bar: Employers' views on college learning in the wake of the economic downturn: A survey among employers conducted on behalf of the Association of American Colleges and Universities. Washington, DC.

Harvey, J. C., & Katz, C. (1985). *If I'm so successful, why do I feel like a fake: The impostor phenomenon.* New York: St. Martin's Press.

Hatfield, E., & Rapson, R. L. (1996). *Love and sex: Cross-cultural perspectives.* Boston: Allyn & Bacon.

Havlena, W. J., Holbrook, M. B., & Lehmann, D. R. (1989, Summer). Assessing the validity of emotional typologies. *Psychology and Marketing, 6,* 97–112.

Hays, R. B. (1989). The day-to-day functioning of close versus casual friendships. *Journal of Social and Personal Relationships, 6,* 21–37.

Heasley, J. B., Babbitt, C. E., & Burbach, H. J. (1995). Gender differences in college students' perceptions of "fighting words." *Sociological Viewpoints, 11* (Fall), 30–40.

Hecht, M. L., Jackson, R. L., & Ribeau, S. (2003). *African American communication: Exploring identity and culture* (2nd ed.). Mahwah, NJ: Erlbaum.

Heenehan, M. (1997). *Networking*. New York: Random House.

Hess, U., Kappas, A., McHugo, G. J., Lanzetta, J. T., et al. (1992, May). The facilitative effect of facial expression on the self-generation of emotion. *International Journal of Psychophysiology, 12,* 251–265.

Hewitt, J. P. (1998). *The myth of self-esteem: Finding happiness and solving problems in America.* New York: St. Martin's Press.

Hicks, C. (2011) Guiding group work: Activities to maximize student learning from group projects. *Teaching innovation projects, 1*(1). Retrieved from http://www.ryerson.ca/content/dam/it/resources/handouts/group-workconflict.pdf

Hinduja, S., & Patchin, J. W. (2008). *Bullying: Beyond the schoolyard.* Thousand Oaks, CA: Corwin Press/Sage.

Hocker, J. L., & Wilmot, W. W. (2007). *Interpersonal conflict* (2nd ed.). Dubuque, IA: William C. Brown.

Hofstede, G. (1997). *Cultures and organizations: Software of the mind.* New York: McGraw-Hill.

Hoft, N. L. (1995). *International technical communication: How to export information about high technology.* New York: Wiley.

Hogg, M. (2002). *Handbook of social psychology.* London: Sage.

Holmes, J. (1995). *Women, men and politeness.* New York: Longman.

Holmes, J. (2003). Small talk at work: Potential problems for workers with an intellectual disability. *Research on Language and Social Interaction, 36,* 65–84.

Holmes, J., & Marra, M. (2002). Having a laugh at work: How humour contributes to workplace culture. *Journal of Pragmatics, 34,* 1683–1710.

Horsfall, J. (1998). Structural impediments to effective communication. *Australian and New Zealand Journal of Mental Health Nursing, 7,* 74–80.

Hunt, M. O. (2000). Status, religion, and the "belief in a just world": Comparing African Americans, Latinos, and whites. *Social Science Quarterly, 81,* 325–343.

Infante, D. A., & Rancer, A. S. (1996). Argumentativeness and verbal aggressiveness: A review of recent theory and research. In B. R. Burleson (Ed.), *Communication yearbook 19* (pp. 319–351). Thousand Oaks, CA: Sage.

Infante, D. A., & Wigley, C. J. (1986). Verbal aggressiveness: An interpersonal model and measure. *Communication Monographs, 53,* 61–69.

Infante, D. A., Rancer, A. S., & Avtgis, T. A. (2010). *Contemporary communication theory.* Dubuque, IA: Kendall Hunt.

Ingegneri, R. (2008). How should you handle tattoos and body piercing during a job interview. http://ezinearticles?.com/?expert=Rachel_Ingegneri.

Insel, P. M., & Jacobson, L. F. (Eds.) (1975). *What do you expect? An inquiry into self-fulfilling prophecies.* Menlo Park, CA: Cummings.

Irizarry, C. A. (2004). Face and the female professional: A thematic analysis of face-threatening communication in the workplace. *Qualitative Research Reports in Communication, 5,* 15–21.

Irvine, M. (2006). Instant, text messaging takeover. *Calgary Herald.* July 19, 2006, pp. A13.

Jackson, L. A., & Ervin, K. S. (1992, August). Height stereotypes of women and men: The liabilities of shortness for both sexes. *Journal of Social Psychology, 132,* 433–445.

Jambor, E., & Elliott, M. (2005, Winter). Self-esteem and coping strategies among deaf students. *Journal of Deaf Studies and Deaf Education, 10,* 63–81.

Jameel, M. J., Joshi, A. R., & Melinkeri, R. R. (2014). Effects of various physical stress models on serum cortisol level I wistar rats. *Journal of Clinical and Diagnostic Research, 8*(3), 181–183.

James, W. (1884). What is emotion? *Mind, 9,* 188–205.

Jandt, F. E. (2009). *Intercultural communication* (6th ed.). Thousand Oaks, CA: Sage.

Jennings, L. (2000). Trends in the multigenerational workplace. *Futurist, 34*(2), 60–62.

Janus, S. S., & Janus, C. L. (1993). *The Janus report on sexual behavior.* Hoboken, NJ: Wiley.

Jaworski, A. (1993). *The power of silence: Social and pragmatic perspectives.* Newbury Park, CA: Sage.

Johannesen, R. L. (1974, Winter). The functions of silence: A plea for communication research. *Western Speech, 38,* 25–35.

Johnson, C. E. (1987). An introduction to powerful and powerless talk in the classroom. *Communication Education, 36,* 167–172.

Johnson, S. M., & O'Connor, E. (2002). *The gay baby boom: The psychology of gay parenthood.* New York: New York University Press.

Joiner, T. E. (1994). Contagious depression: Existence, specificity to depressed symptoms, and the role of reassurance seeking. *Journal of Personality and Social Psychology, 67,* 287–296.

Joinson, A. N. (2001). Self-disclosure in computer-mediated communication: The role of self-awareness and visual anonymity. *European Journal of Social Psychology, 31,* 177–192.

Jones, C., Berry, L., & Stevens, C. (2007). Synthesized speech intelligibility and persuasion: Speech rate and non-native listeners. *Computer Speech and Language, 21,* 641–651.

Jones, Q., Ravid, G., & Rafaeli, S. (2004). Information overload and the message dynamics of online interaction spaces: A theoretical model and empirical exploration. *Information Systems Research, 15* (June), 194–210.

Jones, S., & Yarbrough, A. E. (1985). A naturalistic study of the meanings of touch. *Communication Monographs, 52,* 19–56.

Judge, T. A., & Cable, D. M. (2004). The effect of physical height on workplace success and income. *Journal of Applied Psychology, 89,* 428–441.

Kagan, J. (2002). *Surprise, uncertainty and mental structures.* Cambridge, MA: Harvard University Press.

Kahane, A. (2007). *Solving tough problems: An open way of talking, listening, and creating new realities.* San Francisco: Berrett-Koehler.

Kapoor, S., Hughes, P. C., Baldwin, J. R., & Blue, J. (2003). The relationship of individualism-collectivism and self-construals to communication styles in India and the United States.

International Journal of Intercultural Relations, 27, 683–700.

Karczmar, A. (2014). Cholinergic behaviors, emotions, and the "self." *Journal of Molecular Neuroscience, 53*(3), 291–97.

Katz, S. (2003). The importance of being beautiful. In J. W. Henslin (Ed.), *Down to earth sociology: Introductory readings* (11th ed., pp. 313–320). New York: Free Press.

Kennedy, C. W., & Camden, C. T. (1988). A new look at interruptions. *Western Journal of Speech Communication, 47*, 45–58.

Kennedy-Moore, E., & Watson, J. C. (1999). *Expressing emotion: Myths, realities, and therapeutic strategies.* New York: Guilford Press.

Keyes, R. (1980). *The height of your life.* New York: Warner.

Kiecolt-Glaser, J. K., Graham, J. E., Malarkey, W. B., et al. (2008). Olfactory influences on mood and autonomic, endocrine, and immune function. *Psychoneuroendocrinology. 33*(3), 328–39.

Kim, Y. Y. (1988). Communication and acculturation. In L. A. Samovar & R. E. Porter (Eds.), *Intercultural communication: A reader* (5th ed., pp. 344–354). Belmont, CA: Wadsworth.

Kindred, J., & Roper, S. L. (2004). Making connections via instant messenger (IM): Student use of IM to maintain personal relationships. *Qualitative Research Reports in Communication, 5*, 48–54.

King, R., & DiMichael, E. (1992). *Voice and diction.* Prospect Heights, IL: Waveland Press.

Kisilevich, S., & Mansmann, F. (2010). Analysis of privacy in online social networks of Runet. *Proceedings of the 3rd International Conference on Security of Information and Networks*, ACM, 46–55.

Kleinke, C. L. (1986). *Meeting and understanding people.* New York: W. H. Freeman.

Klineberg, O., & Hull, W. F. (1979). *At a foreign university: An international study of adaptation and coping.* New York: Praeger.

Kluger, J. (2005, January 9). The funny thing about laughter. *Time,* pp. A25–A29.

Knapp, M. L. (2008). *Lying and deception in human interaction.* Boston: Pearson.

Knapp, M. L., & Hall, J. (1996). *Nonverbal behavior in human interaction.* (3rd ed.). New York: Holt, Rinehart, & Winston.

Knapp, M. L., & Hall, J. (2010). *Nonverbal communication in human interaction* (7th ed.). Belmont, CA: Wadsworth.

Knobloch, L. K., & Solomon, D. H. (1999). Measuring the sources and content of relational uncertainty. *Communication Studies, 50*, 261–278.

Knobloch, S., et al. (2003). Imagery effects on the selective reading of internet newsmagazines. *Communication Research, 30*(1), 3–29.

Koelsch, S., Skouras, S., Fritz, T., Herrera, P., Bonhage, C., Küssner, M. B., & Jacobs, A. M. (2013). The roles of superficial amygdala and auditory cortex in music-evoked fear and joy. *Neuroimage, 81*, 49–60.

Koerner, A. F., & Fitzpatrick, M. A. (2002). You never leave your family in a fight: The impact of family of origin of conflict behavior in romantic relationships. *Communication Studies, 53* (Fall), 234–252.

Koppelman, K. L., with Goodhart, R. L. (2005). *Understanding human differences: Multicultural education for a diverse America.* Boston: Allyn & Bacon.

Koscriski, K. (2007). Facial attractiveness: General patterns of facial preferences. *Anthropological Review, 70,* 45–79.

Kumfor, F., Irish, M., Hodges, J. R., Piguet, O. (2013). Discrete neural correlates for the recognition of emotions: Insights from frontotemporal dementia. *PLoS One, 8*(6). Retrieved from http://www.plosone.org/…info%3Adoi%2F10/1371%Fjournal.pone0067457.

Kurland, N. B., & Pelled, L. H. (2000). Passing the word: Toward a model of gossip and power in the workplace. *Academy of Management Review, 25,* 428–439.

Lachnit, C. (2001). Giving up gossip. *Workforce, 80,* 8.

Lakoff, R. (1975). *Language and women's place.* New York: Harper & Row.

Langer, E. J. (1989). *Mindfulness.* Reading, MA: Addison-Wesley.

Lantz, A. (2001). Meetings in a distributed group of experts: Comparing face-to-face, chat and collaborative virtual environments. *Behaviour and Information Technology, 20,* 111–117.

L'Arche Canada. (2005). More than inclusion. Retrieved from http://www.larche.ca.

Larsen, R. J., Kasimatis, M., & Frey, K. (1992). Facilitating the furrowed brow: An unobtrusive test of the facial feedback hypothesis applied to unpleasant affect. *Cognition and Emotion, 6,* 321–338.

Lauer, C. (2004). Cross with wireless. *Modern Healthcare, 34*(51), 20–20.

Lederer, W. J. (1984). *Creating a good relationship.* New York: Norton.

Lee, H. O., & Boster, F. J. (1992). Collectivism–individualism in perceptions of speech rate: A cross-cultural comparison. *Journal of Cross-Cultural Psychology, 23,* 377–388.

Lee, K. (2000). Information overload threatens employee productivity. *Employee Benefit News* (November 1), 1.

Leech, G. (1983). *Principles of pragmatics.* London: Longman.

Lenhart, A., Madden, M., Macgill, A. R., & Smith, A. (2007). Teens and social media: The use of social media gains a greater foothold in teen life as they embrace the conversational nature of interaction online media. *Pew Internet & American Life Project.* Retrieved from http://www.pewinternet.org.

Lenhart, A., Madden, M., Smith, A., Purcell, K., Zickuhr, K., & Rainie, L. (2011). Teens, kindness and cruelty on social network sites. Retrieved from http://pewinterest.org/Reports/2011/Teens-and-social-media.aspx

Leung, S. A. (2001). Editor's introduction. *Asian Journal of Counseling, 8,* 107–109.

Lever, J. (1995). The 1995 Advocate survey of sexuality and relationships: The women, lesbian sex survey. *The Advocate, 687/688,* 22–30.

LeVine, R., Sato, S., Hashimoto, T., & Verma, J. (1994). Love and marriage in eleven cultures. Unpublished manuscript. California State University,

Fresno. Cited in Hatfield & Rapson (1996).

Lindeman, M., Harakka, T., & Keltikangas-Jarvinen, L. (1997). Age and gender differences in adolescents' reactions to conflict situations: Aggression, prosociality, and withdrawal. *Journal of Youth and Adolescence, 26*, 339–351.

Lloyd, S. R. (2001). *Developing positive assertiveness* (3rd ed.). Menlo Park, CA: Crisp Publications.

Luft, J. (1984). *Group process: An introduction of group dynamics* (3rd ed.). Palo Alto, CA: Mayfield.

Lukens, J. (1978). Ethnocentric speech. *Ethnic Groups, 2*, 35–53.

Lustig, M. W., & Koester, J. (2010). *Intercultural competence: Interpersonal communication across cultures* (6th ed.). Boston: Allyn & Bacon.

Macdonald, J., & Poniatowsjka, B. (2011). Designing the professional development of staff for teaching online: An OU (UK) Case Study. *Distance Education, 32*(1), 119–134.

MacLachlan, J. (1979). What people really think of fast talkers. *Psychology Today, 13*, 113–117.

Madon, S., Guyll, M., & Spoth, R. L. (2004). The self-fulfilling prophecy as an intrafamily dynamic. *Journal of Family Psychology, 18*, 459–469.

Macmillan, P. (2001). *The performance factor: Unlocking the secrets of teamwork*. Nashville: B & H Publishing Group.

Mahaffey, A. L., Bryan, A., & Hutchison, K. E. (2005, March). Using startle eye blink to measure the affective component of antigay bias. *Basic and Applied Social Psychology, 27*, 37–45.

Malandro, L. A., Barker, L., & Barker, D. A. (1989). *Nonverbal communication* (2nd ed.). New York: Random House.

Manzoni, J. F. (2012). Building and nurturing a high-performance-high-integrity corporate culture. InA. Davila, M. J. Epstein, and J. F. Manzoni (Eds.), *Performance measurement and management control: Global issues* (pp. 41–63). Bingley, UK: Emerald.

MarketWired. (2013). Job prospects for students and grads: BMO poll reveals half of businesses plan to hire.

Retrieved from http://www.marketwired.com/press-release/job-prospects-students-grads-bmo-poll-reveals-half-businesses-plan-hire-tsx-bmo-1783675.htm

Marsh, P. (1988). *Eye to eye: How people interact*. Topside, MA: Salem House.

Martin, M. M., & Rubin, R. B. (1994). A new measure of cognitive flexibility. *Psychological Reports, 76*, 623–626.

McBroom, W. H., & Reed, F. W. (1992). Toward a reconceptualization of attitude-behavior consistency. Special Issue. Theoretical advances in social psychology. *Social Psychology Quarterly, 55*, 205–216.

McCann, R. M., & Giles, H. (2006). Communicating with people of different ages in the workplace: Thai and American data. *Human Communication Research, 32*(1), 74–108.

McCroskey, J. C. (1997). *Introduction to rhetorical communication* (7th ed.). Englewood Cliffs, NJ: Prentice-Hall.

McCroskey, J. C., & Richmond, V. P. (1996). *Fundamentals of human communication: An interpersonal perspective*. Prospect Heights, IL: Waveland Press, Inc.

McDonald, E. J., McCabe, K., Yeh, M., Lau, A., Garland, A., & Hough, R. L. (2005). Cultural affiliation and self-esteem as predictors of internalizing symptoms among Mexican American adolescents. *Journal of Clinical Childand Adolescent Psychology, 34*, 163–171.

McGinley, S. (2000). Children and lying. *The University of Arizona College of Agriculture and Life Sciences*. Retrieved from http://www.ag.arizona.edu/pubs/general/resrpt2000/childrenlying.pdf

McLaren, L. (2005, April 16). Fine young cannibals. *The Globe and Mail*.

McNatt, D. B. (2001). Ancient Pygmalion joins contemporary management: A meta-analysis of the result. *Journal of Applied Psychology, 85*, 314–322.

McQuillen, J. (2003). The influence of technology on the initiation of interpersonal relationships. *Education, 123*(3).

Mealy, M., Stephan, W., & Urrutia, C. (2007). The acceptability of lies: A comparison of Ecuadorians and Euro-Americans. *International*

Journal of Intercultural Relations, 31, 689–702.

Mehl, M. R., Vazire, S., Ramirez-Esparza, N., Slatcher, R. B., & Pennebaker, J. W. (2007, July). Are women really more talkative than men? *Science, 6*, 82.

Merchant, K. (2012). How men and women differ: Gender differences in communication styles influence tactics and leadership styles. CMC Senior Theses. Retrieved from http://scholarship.claremont.edu/cmc_theses/513

Merton, R. K. (1957). *Social theory and social structure*. New York: Free Press.

Mesch, G., & Talmud, I. (2006). The quality of online and offline social relationships: The role of multiplexity and duration of social relationships. *Information Society, 22*(3), 137–148.

Messick, R. M., & Cook, K. S. (Eds.). (1983). *Equity theory: Psychological and sociological perspectives*. New York: Praeger.

Metts, S., & Planalp, S. (2002). Emotional communication. In M. L. Knapp & J. A. Daly (Eds.), *Handbook of interpersonal communication* (3rd ed., pp. 339–373). Thousand Oaks, CA: Sage.

Miller, G. R. (1978). The current state of theory and research in interpersonal communication. *Human Communication Research, 4*, 164–178.

Miller, G. R. (1990). Interpersonal communication. In G. L. Dahnke & G. W. Clatterbuck (Eds.), *Human communication: Theory and research* (pp. 91–122). Belmont, CA: Wadsworth.

Miller, L. R. (1997, December). Better ways to think and communicate. *Association Management, 49*, 71–73.

Miller, R. (2003). Blogging for business. *EContent, 26*(10), 30–34.

Miller, S., & Weckert, J. (2000). Privacy, the workplace, and the internet. *Journal of Business Ethics, 28*(3), 255–265.

Mind Tools, n.d. Conflict resolution: Resolving conflict rationally and effectively. Retrieved from http://www.mindtools.com/pages/article/newLDR_81.htm

Moghaddam, F. M., Taylor, D. M., & Wright, S. C. (1993). *Social psychology in cross-cultural perspective*. New York: W. H. Freeman.

Molloy, J. (1977). *The woman's dress for success book*. Chicago: Follett.

Molloy, J. (1981). *Molloy's live for success*. New York: Bantam.

Moon, D. G. (1996). Concepts of "culture": Implications for intercultural communication research. *Communication Quarterly, 44*, 70–84.

Moon, H., & Williams, P. (2000). Managing cross cultural business ethics. *Journal of Business Ethics, 27*, 105–115.

Morgan, R. (2008). A crash course in online gossip. *The New York Times* (March 16), Styles, p. 7.

Morreale, S. P., & Pearson, J. C. (2008). Why communication education is important: The centrality of the discipline in the 21st century. *Communication Education, 57* (April), 224–240.

Mosteller, T. (2008). *Relativism: A guide for the perplexed*. London: Continuum International Publishing Group.

Mottet, T., & Richmond, V. P. (1998). Verbal approach and avoidance items. *Communication Quarterly, 46*, 25–40.

Munro, K. (2002). How to resolve conflict online. Retrieved from http://users.rider.edu/~suler/psycyber/conflict.html

Myers, S. A., & Zhong, M. (2004). Perceived Chinese instructor use of affinity-seeking strategies and Chinese college student motivation. *Journal of Intercultural Communication Research, 33* (September–December), 119–130.

Neher, W. W., & Sandin, P. J. (2007). *Communicating ethically: Character, duties, consequences, and relationships*. Boston: Allyn & Bacon.

Newport, F. (2007, September 28). Black or African American? Gallup News Service. Retrieved from http://www.gallup.com/poll/28816/black-african-american.aspx. Acessed October 2010.

Nguyen, M., Bin, Y. S., & Campbell, A. (2012). Comparing online and offline self-disclosure: A systematic review. *Cyberpsychology, Behavior and Social Networking, 15*(2), 103–11.

Nichols, M. P. (1995). *The lost art of listening: How learning to listen can improve relationships*. New York: Guilford Press.

Nichols, R., & Stevens, L. (1957). *Are you listening?* New York: McGraw-Hill.

Noelle-Neumann, E. (1991). The theory of public opinion: The concept of the spiral of silence. In J. A. Anderson (Ed.), *Communication yearbook 14* (pp. 256–287). Thousand Oaks, CA: Sage.

Noller, P., & Fitzpatrick, M. A. (1993). *Communication in family relationships*. Englewood Cliffs, NJ: Prentice Hall.

Norton, R., & Warnick, B. (1976). Assertiveness as a communication construct. *Human Communication Research, 3*, 62–66.

Oatley, K., & Duncan, E. (1994). The experience of emotions in everyday life. *Cognition and Emotion, 8*, 369–381.

Oberg, K. (1960). Cultural shock: Adjustment to new cultural environments. *Practical Anthropology, 7*, 177–182.

Ostrander, B. (2007). Problems and solutions to corporate blogging: Model corporate blogging guidelines. *Journal of High Technology Law, 7*, 226–248.

Park, M., Hennig-Fast, K., Bao, Y., Carl, P., Pöppel, E., Welker, L., Reiser, M., Meindl, T., & Gutyrchik, E. (2013). Personality traits modulate neural responses to emotions expressed in music. *Brain Research, 1523*, 68–76.

Parker, J. G. (2004, September). Planning and communication crucial to preventing workplace violence. *Safety and Health, 170*, 58–61.

Parks, M. R. (1995). Webs of influence in interpersonal relationships. In C. R. Berger & M. E. Burgoon (Eds.), *Communication and social influence processes* (pp. 155–178). East Lansing: Michigan State University Press.

Parks, M. R., & Floyd, K. (1996). Making friends in cyberspace. *Journal of Communication, 46*, 80–97.

Paul, A. M. (2001). Self-help: Shattering the myths. *Psychology Today, 34*, 60ff.

Pearson, J. C. (1993). *Communication in the family* (2nd ed.). Boston: Allyn & Bacon.

Pearson, J. C., & Spitzberg, B. H. (1990). *Interpersonal communication: Concepts, components, and contexts* (2nd ed.). Dubuque, IA: William C. Brown.

Pearson, J. C., West, R., & Turner, L. H. (1995). *Gender and communication* (3rd ed.). Dubuque, IA: William C. Brown.

Penfield, J. (Ed.). (1987). *Women and language in transition*. Albany, NY: State University of New York Press.

Pennebacker, J. W. (1991). *Opening up: The healing power of confiding in others*. New York: Avon.

Peplau, L. A. (1988). Research on homosexual couples: An overview. In J. DeCecco (Ed.), *Gay relationships* (pp. 33–40). New York: Harrington Park Press.

Pittenger, R. E., Hockett, C. F., & Danehy, J. J. (1960). *The first five minutes*. Ithaca, NY: Paul Martineau.

Plaks, J. E., Grant, H., & Dweck, C. S. (2005). Violations of implicit theories and the sense of prediction and control: Implications for motivated person perception. *Journal of Personality and Social Psychology, 88*, 245–262.

Plutchik, R. (1980). *Emotion: A psycho-evolutionary synthesis*. New York: Harper & Row.

Porter, R. H., & Moore, J. D. (1981). Human kin recognition by olfactory cues. *Physiology and Behavior, 27*, 493–495.

Pruett, K., & Pruett, M. K. (2009). *Partnership parenting: How men and women parent differently—why it helps your kids and can strengthen your marriage*. Cambridge, MA: Da Capo Press.

Psychometrics. (2010). Warring egos, toxic individuals, feeble leadership: A study of conflict in the Canadian workplace. Retrieved from http://www.psychometrics.com/docs/conflictstudy_09.pdf

Raby, M. (2012). Facebook access becoming mandatory part of job, college applications. Retrieved from http://www.slashgear.com/facebook-access-becoming-mandatory-part-of-job-college-applications-06217136

Rancer, A. S., & Avtgis, T. A. (2006). *Argumentative and aggressive communication: Theory, research, and application*. Thousand Oaks, CA: Sage.

Rancer, A. S., Lin, Y., Durbin, J. M., & Faulkner, E. C. (2010). Nonverbal "verbal" aggression: Its forms and its relation to trait verbal aggressiveness. In T. A. Avtgis & A. S. Rancer (Eds.), *Arguments, aggression, and conflict: New directions in theory and research* (pp. 267–284). New York: Routledge/Taylor & Francis.

Rapsa, R., & Cusack, J. (1990). Psychiatric implications of tattoos. *American Family Physician, 41*, 1481–1486.

Raven, R., Centers, C., & Rodrigues, A. (1975). The bases of conjugal power. In R. E. Cromwell & D. H. Olson (Eds.), *Power in families* (pp. 217–234). New York: Halsted Press.

Read, A. W. (2004). Language revision by deletion of absolutisms. *ETC: A Review of General Semantics, 61* (December), 456–462.

Reardon, K. K. (1987). *Where minds meet: Interpersonal communication.* Belmont, CA: Wadsworth.

Rector, M., & Neiva, E. (1996). Communication and personal relationships in Brazil. In W. B. Gudykunst, S. Ting-Toomey, & T. Nishida (Eds.), *Communication in personal relationships across cultures* (pp. 156–173). Thousand Oaks, CA: Sage.

Reed, M. D. (1993, Fall). Sudden death and bereavement outcomes: The impact of resources on grief, symptomatology and detachment. *Suicide and Life-Threatening Behavior, 23,* 204–220.

Reiner, D., & Blanton, K. (1997). *Person to person on the Internet.* Boston: AP Professional.

Reisenzein, R. (1983). The Schachter theory of emotion: Two decades later. *Psychological Bulletin, 94,* 239–264.

Rice, M. (2007). Domestic violence. *National Center for PTSD Fact Sheet.* Retrieved from http://www.ncptsd.va.gov/ncmain/ncdocs/fact_shts/fs_domestic_violence.html

Rich, A. L. (1974). Interracial communication. New York: Harper & Row.

Richmond, V. P., McCroskey, J. C., & Hickson, M. L. (2008). *Nonverbal behavior in interpersonal relations* (6th ed.). Boston: Allyn & Bacon.

Richmond, V., McCroskey, J. C., & Hickson, M. (2012). *Nonverbal behavior in interpersonal relations* (7th ed.). Boston: Allyn & Bacon.

Riggio, R. E., & Feldman, R. S. (Eds.). (2005). *Applications of nonverbal communication.* Mahwah, NJ: Lawrence Erlbaum.

Riggio, R. E. (2009). Are you a transformational leader? Retrieved from http://blogs.psychologytoday.com/blog/cutting-edge-leadership/200903/are-you-transformational-leader

Righton, B. (2006, June 5). Hey, boss, your pants are on fire. *Maclean's,* p. 42.

Valliant-Molina, M., Bahrick, L. E., & Flom, R. (2013). Young infants match facial and vocal emotional expressions of other infants. *Infancy, 18* (Supplement s1), E97–E111.

Robertson, R. G. (2005). Rumours: Constructive or corrosive. *Journal of Medical Ethics, 31,* 540–541.

Robinson, A. (2014, February 14). Beyond male and female, definition of Facebook's new gender options. *Dayton Daily News.* Retrieved from http://www.daytondailynews.com/news/lifestyles/beyond-male-and-female-definition-of-facebooks-new/ndPn3

Rochester, J. (2002). Becoming a professional—Education is only the beginning. IEEE-USA *Today's Engineering Online.* Retrieved from http://www.todaysengineer.org/archives/te_archives/feb02/tel.asp

Rogers, C. (1970). *Carl Rogers on encounter groups.* New York: Harrow Books.

Rogers, C., & Farson, R. (1981). Active listening. In J. DeVito (Ed.), *Communication: Concepts and processes* (3rd ed., pp. 137–147). Upper Saddle River, NJ: Prentice Hall.

Roizen, M. F., & Oz, M. C. (2009). *You, having a baby: An owners' manual to a happy and healthy pregnancy.* New York: Simon & Schuster.

Rokach, A. (1998). The relation of cultural background to the causes of loneliness. *Journal of Social and Clinical Psychology, 17,* 75–88.

Rokach, A., & Brock, H. (1995). The effects of gender, marital status, and the chronicity and immediacy of loneliness. *Journal of Social Behavior and Personality, 19,* 833–848.

Rohlfing, M. E. (1995). "Doesn't anybody stay in one place anymore?" An exploration of the under-studied phenomenon of long-distance relationships. In J. T. Wood & S. Duck (Eds.), *Under-studied relationships: Off the beaten track* (pp. 173–196). Thousand Oaks, CA: Sage.

Roper Starch (1999). How Americans communicate. Retrieved from http://www.natcom.org/research/Roper/how_americans_communicate.htm

Rosen, E. (1998, October). Think like a shrink. *Psychology Today,* pp. 54–59.

Rosengren, A., et al. (1993, October 19). Stressful life events, social support, and mortality in men born in 1933. *British Medical Journal.* Cited in Goleman (1995a).

Rosenthal, R. (2002). Covert communication in classrooms, clinics, courtroom, and cubicles. *American Psychologist, 57,* 839–849.

Rosenthal, R., & Jacobson, L. (1968). *Pygmalion in the classroom.* New York: Holt, Rinehart and Winston.

Rosnow, R. L. (1988). Rumor as communication: A contextualist approach. *Journal of Communication, 38,* 12–28.

Rosnow, R. L., & Fine, G. A. (1976). *Rumor and gossip: The social psychology of hearsay.* New York: Elsevier.

Roth, L., Kaffenberger, T., Herwig, U., & Brühl, A. B. (2014). Brain activation associated with pride and shame. *Neuropsychobiology, 69*(2), 95–106.

Ruben, B. D. (1985). Human communication and cross-cultural effectiveness. In L. A. Samovar & R. E. Porter (Eds.), *Intercultural communication: A reader* (4th ed., pp. 338–346). Belmont, CA: Wadsworth.

Saboonchi, F., Lundh, L. G., & Ost, L. G. (1999). Perfectionism and self-consciousness in social phobia and panic disorder with agoraphobia. *Behaviour Research and Therapy, 37*(9), 799–808.

Safdar, S., Friedlmeier, W., Matsumoto, D., Yoo, S., Kwantes, C., Kakai, H., et al. (2009). Variations of emotional display rules within and across cultures: A comparison between Canada, USA, and Japan. *Canadian Journal of Behavioural Science/Revue canadienne des sciences du comportement, 41*(1), 1–10.

Sanders, J. A., Wiseman, R. L., & Matz, S. I. (1991). Uncertainty reduction in acquaintance relationships in Ghanaand the United States. In S. Ting-Toomey & F. Korzenny (Eds.), *Cross-cultural interpersonal communication* (pp. 79–98). Thousand Oaks, CA: Sage.

Satir, V. (1983). *Conjoint family therapy* (3rd ed.). Palo Alto, CA: Science and Behavior Books.

Savitsky, K., Epley, N., & Gilovich, T. (2001). Do others judge us as harshly as we think? Overestimating the impact of our failures, shortcomings, and mishaps. *Journal of Personality and Social Psychology 81* (July), 44–56.

Schachter, S. (1971). *Emotion, obesity and crime.* New York: Academic Press.

Schaap, C., Buunk, B., & Kerkstra, A. (1988). Marital conflict resolution. In P. Noller & M. A. Fitzpatrick (Eds.), *Perspectives on marital interaction* (pp. 203–244). Philadelphia: Multilingual Matters.

Scheele, D., Wille, A., Kendrick, K. M., Birgit Stoffel-Wagner, B., Becker, B., Gunturkun, O., Maier, W., & Hurlemann, R. (2013). Oxytocin enhances brain reward system responses in men viewing the face of their female partner. *Proceedings of the National Academy of Sciences, 110*(50), 20308–20313.

Scherer, K. R. (1986). Vocal affect expression. *Psychological Bulletin, 99,* 143–165.

Schiffer, B., Pawliczek, C., Muller, B. W., Gizewski, E. R., & Walter, H. (2013). Why don't men understand women? Altered neural networks for reading the language of male and female eyes. *PLoS One, 8*(4), e60278.

Schott, G., & Selwyn, N. (2000). Examining the "male, antisocial" stereotype of high computer users. *Journal of Educational Computing Research, 23,* 291–303.

Scott, C. R., & Rains, S. A. (2005). Anonymous communication in organizations. *Management Communication Quarterly, 19,* 157–197.

Seo, H. S., Roidl, E., Muller, F., et al. (2010). Odors enhance visual attention to congruent objects. *Appetite, 54*(3), 544–49.

Shaw, L. H., & Grant, L. M. (2002). Users divided? Exploring the gender gap in Internet use. *CyberPsychology & Behavior, 5* (December), 517–527.

Sheldon, P. (2013). Examining gender differences in self disclosure on Facebook versus face-to-face. *Journal of Social Media in Society, 2*(1), 89–103.

Sieter, J. S. (2007). Ingratiation and gratuity: The effect of complimenting customers on tipping behavior in restaurants. *Journal of Applied Social Psychology, 37,* 478–485.

Silverman, T. (2001). Expanding community: The Internet and relational theory. *Community, Work and Family, 4,* 231–237.

Singh, S. (2006). Impact of colour on marketing. *Emerald Insight, 44*(6), 783–789.

Singh, N., & Pereira, A. (2005). *The culturally customized web site.* Oxford, UK: Elsevier Butterworth-Heinemann.

Sipior, J., & Ward, B. (1999). The dark side of employee email. *Communications of the ACM, 42*(7), 88–95.

Smart, R. G., Asbridge, M., Mann, R. E., & Adlaf, E. M. (2003). Psychiatric distress among road rage victims and perpetrators. *Canadian Journal of Psychiatry, 48,* 681–688.

Smart, R. G., & Mann, R. E. (2002). Is road rage a serious traffic problem? *Journal of Traffic Medicine, 3,* 183–189.

Smart, R. G., & Mann, R. E. (2005). Deaths and injuries from road rage: Cases in Canadian newspapers. *Canadian Medical Association Journal, 167,* 761–762.

Smith, A. (2011). Why Americans use social media. Pew Research Center Publications. Retrieved from www.pewresearch.org

Smith, M. H. (2003). Body adornment: Know the limits. *Nursing Management, 34,* 22–23.

Smith, R. (2004, April 10). The teaching of communication skills may be misguided. *British Medical Journal, 328,* 1–2.

Snyder, M. (1992). A gender-informed model of couple and family therapy: Relationship enhancement therapy. *Contemporary Family Therapy: An International Journal, 14,* 15–31.

Solomon, G. B. et al. (1996). The self-fulfilling prophecy in college basketball: Implications for effective coaching. *Journal of Applied Sport Psychology, 8,* 44–59.

Sorenson, P. S., Hawkins, K., & Sorenson, R. L. (1995). Gender, psychological type and conflict style preferences. *Management Communication Quarterly, 9,* 115–126.

Spence, C. (2008). Sensing the future. Retrieved from www.aqr.org.uk/inbrief/document.shtml?doc=charles.spence.28-02-2008.fut

Spencer, R. (2014). To disclose or not to disclose? The Chronicle of Evidence-Based Mentoring. Retrieved from http://chronicle.umbmentoring.org/to-disclose-or-not-to-disclose

Spett, M. (2004). Expressing negative emotions: Healthy catharsis or sign of pathology? Retrieved from http://www.nj-act.org/article2.html

Spitzberg, B. H. (1991). Intercultural communication competence. In L. A. Samovar & R. E. Porter (Eds.), *Intercultural communication: A reader* (pp. 353–365). Belmont, CA: Wadsworth.

Spitzberg, B. H., & Cupach, W. R. (1989). *Handbook of interpersonal competence research.* New York: Springer.

Sprecher, S., & Hendrick, S. S. (2004). Self-disclosure in intimate relationships: Associations with individual and relationship characteristics over time. *Journal of Social and Clinical Psychology, 23* (December), 857–877.

Sprecher, S., Treger, S., Wondra, J. D., Hilaire, N., & Walpe, K. (2013). Taking turns: Reciprocal self disclosure promotes liking in initial interactions. *Journal of Experimental Social Psychology, 49*(5), 860–866.

Sriram, K., & Shyam, S. S. (2006). The psychological appeal of personalized content in web portals: Does customization affect attitudes and behaviour? *Journal of Communication, 56,* 110–132.

Statistics Canada. (2001). Profile of marital status, common-law status, families, dwellings and households, for Canada, provinces, territories, census divisions, census subdivisions and dissemination areas, 2001 census. Cat. No. 95F0487XCB2001002. Retrieved from http://www12.statcan.ca/english/census01/products/standard/profiles/ListProducts.cfm?Temporal=2001&APATH=1&RL=3&FREE=0

Steil, L. K., Barker, L. L., & Watson, K. W. (1983). *Effective listening: Key to your success.* Reading, MA: Addison-Wesley.

Stein, S. J., & Book, H. E. (2011). *The EQ edge: Emotional intelligence and your success.* Hoboken, NJ: Wiley.

Steiner, C. (1981). *The other side of power.* New York: Grove.

Stephan, W. G., & Stephan, C. W. (1985). Intergroup anxiety. *Journal of Social Issues, 41,* 157–175.

Stewart, S. (2006). A pilot study of email in an e-mentoring relationship. *Journal of Telemedicine and Telecare 12* (October), 83–85.

Stone N. J. (2001). Designing effective study environments. *Journal of Environmental Psychology, 21*(2), 179–190.

Suominen, T., Kovasin, M., & Ketola, O. (1997). Nursing culture—some viewpoints. *Journal of Advanced Nursing, 25,* 186–190.

Suler, J. (2004). The online disinhibition effect. *CyberPsychology and Behavior, 7,* 321–326.

Sutcliffe, K., Lewton, E., & Rosenthal, M. M. (2004, February). Communication failures: An insidious contributor to medical mishaps. *Academic Medicine, 79,* 186–194.

Swanbrow, D. (2011, May 16). Persuasive speech: The way we, um, talk sways our listeners. University of Michigan, Institute for Social Research, ISR Sampler. Retrieved from ns.umich.edu/new/releases/8404

Tamir, D., & Mitchell, J. (2012). Disclosing information about the self is intrinsically rewarding. *Proceedings of the National Academy of Sciences, 109*(21), 8038–8043.

Tannen, D. (1990). *You just don't understand: Women and men in conversation.* New York: Morrow.

Tannen, D. (1994a). *Gender and discourse.* New York: Oxford University Press.

Tannen, D. (1994b). *Talking from 9 to 5: How women's and men's conversational styles affect who gets heard, who gets credit, and what gets done at work.* New York: Morrow.

Tannen, D. (2006). *You're wearing that? Understanding mothers and daughters in conversation.* New York: Random House.

Tavris, C. (1989). *Anger: The misunderstood emotion* (2nd ed.). New York: Simon & Schuster.

Teven, J. J., Richmond, V. P., & McCroskey, J. C. (1998). Measuring tolerance for disagreement. *Communication Research Reports, 15,* 209–221.

Thiebaud, J. R. (2010). Effects of technology on people: Living F2F conversation and social interaction. *Proceedings of the Media Ecology Association, 11,* 117–127.

Thorne, B., Kramarae, C., & Henley, N. (Eds.). (1983). *Language, gender and society.* Rowley, MA: Newbury House.

Tidwell, L., & Walther, J. (2002). Computer-mediated communication effects on disclosure, impressions, and interpersonal evaluations. *Human Communication Research, 28*(3), 317–348.

Tierney, P., & Farmer, S. M. (2004). The Pygmalion process and employee creativity. *Journal of Management, 30,* 413–432.

Timmerman, L. J. (2002). Comparing the production of power in language on the basis of sex. In M. Allen & R. W. Preiss (Eds.), *Interpersonal communication research: Advances through meta-analysis* (pp. 117–88). Mahwah, NJ: Erlbaum.

Ting-Toomey, S. (1985). Toward a theory of conflict and culture. *International and Intercultural Communication Annual, 9,* 71–86.

Torbiorn, I. (1982). *Living abroad.* New York: Wiley.

Trager, G. L. (1958). Paralanguage: A first approximation. *Studies in Linguistics, 13,* 1–12.

Trager, G. L. (1961). The typology of paralanguage. *Anthropological Linguistics, 3,* 17–21.

Turati, C., Montirosso, R., Brenna, V., Ferrara, V., & Borgatti, R. (2010). A smile enhances 3-month-olds' recognition of an individual face. *Infancy, 16*(3), 306–317.

Turkle, S. (2012, April 21). The flight from conversation. *The New York Times Sunday Review.*

Tyler, J. J., Feldman, R. S., & Reichert, A. (2006). The price of deceptive behavior: Disliking and lying to people who lie to us. *Journal of Experimental Social Psychology, 42,* 69–77.

Vainiomaki, T. (2004). Silence as a cultural sign. *Semiotica, 150,* 347–361.

Van Praagh, J. (2010). I am! I can! I will! Retrieved from http://www.healyourlife.com

Varenik, T. (2010). How tattoos and body piercing affect your career. Retrieved from http://www.resumark.com/blog/tatiana/how-tattoos-and-body-piercing-affect-your-career

Varma, A., Toh, S. M, Pichler, S. (2006). Ingratiation in job applications: Impact on selection decisions. *Journal of Managerial Psychology, 21,* 200–210.

Victor, D. (1992). *International business communication.* New York: HarperCollins.

Vonk, R. (2002). Self-serving interpretations of flattery: Why ingratiation works. *Journal of Personality and Social Psychology, 82,* 515–526.

Waddington, K. (2004). Psst—spread the word—gossiping is good for you. *Practice Nurse, 27,* 7–10.

Wade, C., & Tavris, C. (1998). *Psychology* (5th ed.). New York: Longman.

Waldeck, J., Durante, C., Helmuth, B., & Marcia, B. (2012). Communication in a changing world: Contemporary perspectives on business communication competence. *Journal of Education for Business, 87*(4), 230–240.

Wallis, C. (2006). The multitasking generation. *Time Canada, 167,* 13.

Walsh, M. (2005). Gendered endeavours: Women and the reshaping of business culture. *Women's History Review, 14,* 181–202.

Walster, E., Walster, G. W., & Berscheid, E. (1978). *Equity: Theory and research.* Boston: Allyn & Bacon.

Walther, J. B. (2011). Theories of computer-mediated communication and interpersonal relations. In M. L. Knapp & J. A. Daly (Eds.), *The SAGE handbook of interpersonal communication* (4th ed., pp. 443–480). Los Angeles: Sage.

Watzlawick, P. (1978). *The language of change: Elements of therapeutic communication.* New York: Basic Books.

Weathers, M. D., Frank, E. M., & Spell, L. A. (2002). Differences in the communication of affect: Members of the same race versus members of a different race. *Journal of Black Psychology, 28,* 66–77.

Weber, S. T., & Heuberger, E. (2008). The impact of natural odors on affective states in humans. *Chemical Senses, 33*(5), 441–47.

Wert, S. R., & Salovey, P. (2004). Introduction to the special issue on gossip. *Review of General Psychology, 8,* 76–77.

Wheeless, L. R., & Grotz, J. (1977). The measurement of trust and its relationship to self-disclosure. *Human Communication Research, 3,* 250–257.

Willander, J., & Larsson, M. (2007). Olfaction and emotion: The case of autobiographical memory. *Memory & Cognition, 35*(7), 1659–63.

Wilkins, B. M., & Andersen, P. A. (1991). Gender differences and similarities in management communication: A meta-analysis. *Management Communication Quarterly, 5,* 6–35.

Willson, R., & Branch, R. (2006). *Cognitive behavioural therapy for dummies.* West Sussex, England: Wiley.

Wilson, S. R., & Sabee, C. M. (2003). Explicating communicative competence as a theoretical term. In J. O. Greene & B. R. Burleson (Eds.), *Handbook of communication and social interaction skills* (pp. 3–50). Mahwah, NJ: Erlbaum.

Wilson, V. J., McCormack, B. G., & Ives, G. (2005). Understanding the workplace culture of a special care nursery. *Journal of Advanced Nursing, 50*(1), 27–38.

Winquist, L. A., Mohr, D., & Kenny, David A. (1998, September). The female positivity effect in the perception of others. *Journal of Research in Personality, 32,* 370–388.

Wood, J. T. (1994). *Gendered lives: Communication, gender, and culture.* Belmont, CA: Wadsworth.

Workopolis (2013). Job prospects for students and grads. Retrieved from http://www.workopolis.com/content/advice/article/half-of-canadian-businesses-say-they-plan-to-hire-students-recent-grads

Wrench, J. S., McCroskey, J. C., & Richmond, V. P. (2008). *Human communication in everyday life: Explanations and applications.* Boston: Allyn & Bacon.

Wright, P. H. (1978). Toward a theory of friendship based on a conception of self. *Human Communication Research, 4,* 196–207.

Wright, P. H. (1984). Self-referent motivation and the intrinsic quality of friendship. *Journal of Social and Personal Relationships, 1,* 115–130.

Wu, J., & Lu, H. (2010). Cultural and gender differences in self-disclosure on social networking sites. In J. Petley (Ed.), *Media and public shaming.* New York: I. B. Tauris.

Wyshograd, D. (2014). An interview with Diane Wyshogrod. Retrieved from http://www.hidingplacesthebook.com/about/interview-with-diane-wyshogrod. Reprinted with permission from Dr. Dina Wyshogrod.

Yamaguchi, S. (2004). Nursing culture of an operating theatre in Italy. *Nursing and Heath Sciences, 6,* 261–269.

Yau-fai Ho, D., Chan, S. F., Peng, S., & Ng, A. K. (2001). The dialogical self: Converging East–West constructions. *Culture and Psychology, 7,* 393–408.

Young, K. S., Griffin-Shelley, E., Cooper, A., O'Mara, J., & Buchanan, J. (2000). Online infidelity: A new dimension in couple relationships with implications for evaluation and treatment. *Sexual Addiction and Compulsivity, 7,* 59–74.

Yuki, M., Maddux, W. W., Masuda, T. (2007). Are the windows to the soul the same in the East and West? Cultural differences in using the eyes and mouth as cues to recognize emotions in Japan and the United States. *Journal of Experimental Social Psychology, 43,* 303–311.

Yum, Y. O., and Hara, K. (2005). Computer-mediated relationship development: A cross cultural comparison. *Journal of Computer-Mediated Communication, 11*(1), 133–152.

Yun, H. (1976). The Korean personality and treatment considerations. *Social Casework, 57,* 173–178.

Zakay, D. (2012). Psychological time and time perspectives and its impact on conflict resolution: The Israeli Palestinian case. International Association for Conflict Management IACM 25th annual conference. Retrieved from SSRN Social Science Research Network, http://ssm.com/abstract=2092862

Zhao, C., Hinds, P., & Gao, G. (2012). How and to whom people share: The role of culture in self-disclosure in online communities. *Proceedings of the ACM 2012 Conference on Computer Supported Cooperative Work, 67–76.*

Zunin, L. M., & Zunin, N. B. (1991). *Contact: The first four minutes.* Los Angeles: Nash.

INDEX

Note: Italicized letters *f* and *t* following page numbers indicate figures and tables, respectively; italicized page numbers indicate glossary terms.